AN IOWA FARM BOY ON DETOUR

The Story of Henry B. Tippie

By Margaret O. Kirk

Published by:
Henry B. Tippie
Tippie Services, Inc.
3420 Executive Center Drive
Austin, TX 78731

Printed in the United States of America by:
Bang Printing
3323 Oak Street
Brainerd, MN 56401

ISBN: 978-0-692-77574-5
1. Biography. 2. Business

Author: Margaret O. Kirk
Copyeditor: Alexa Selph
Proofreader: Bob Land

Book and jacket design by Jill Dible
jilldibledesign.com

Photo of Henry B. Tippie on dust jacket by:
Impact Photo/Joe Photo
309 Andover Lane SE
Cedar Rapids, IA 52403

Dedicated to

Patricia B. Tippie

"How fortunate for me that you came
to Rehoboth Beach, Delaware."

—HENRY B. TIPPIE

CONTENTS

PART FIVE: 1971–1996 *The Iowa Farm Boy Moves to Texas*

PART SIX: 1996–2015 *A Return to Rollins*

PART SEVEN: 1953–2015
Giving Back: "Repayment for Benefits Received"

FOREWORD

This book is written primarily for my children and grandchildren. My partner and wife, Patricia, has long encouraged me to set forth the facts of my background and environment, most of which my grandchildren have very little knowledge of and, to a lesser extent, neither do our children. This book is not written for sale in a bookstore or for any other outlet. It is being distributed to those who assisted in the writing thereof. For a book of this size, it certainly doesn't indicate each and every detail of my life over the past 89-plus years. However, I feel it covers the high spots and gives a good sense of my life's journey from the very beginning.

A lot of things have taken place for my generation. Among these are the following:

- The advent of radio and its golden days
- The development of television, followed by cable
- Travel by railroad when steam engines were still in style, followed by diesel engines
- The development of commercial aviation travel
- The shift in agriculture from the family farm to today's large operations, along with the agricultural industry change from horses to big farm equipment
- The elimination of the one-room schoolhouse and the development of neighborhood schools and then to large consolidated schools
- The 1930s Depression, WWII, Korea, Vietnam, Desert Storm, Operation Iraqi Freedom, and some other minor episodes along the way
- The boom and bust of the stock markets
- Numerous presidents, starting with Herbert Hoover
- The end of Prohibition
- The ongoing rise in government regulation
- A more partisan political atmosphere
- The advent of Social Security
- The changing work ethic
- The decline of integrity, credibility, and honesty
- The growing dependency upon government assistance
- The continuing demand for more services provided by local and state governments

- Our increasingly litigious society
- The breakdown in the public education system
- The decline of morality
- The demise of small communities
- The development of the high-tech age and the capacity for instant communication
- Cyberspace and cybersecurity
- Robots and drones

This list could go on and on, but I think it sets forth the picture.

A multitude of changes take place during each generation's span. This has been the historical picture, and I think it will continue in this manner. It is hard for one to believe what transpires over a long period of time. I have never been one to spend much time contemplating what the future may hold. When I look back to my very early days, growing up on an Iowa farm in the early 1930s, there is no way I could have ever contemplated all the changes that came into being as time went on.

In fact, new words were even created to go into the dictionary in order to accommodate some of the new developments as time went by. I think, generally speaking, a lot of the changes over the years have been good, but not necessarily all good.

I want to express my thanks to all who assisted in the development of this book project and who are listed elsewhere. There are cases where interviews were conducted, but may not be referenced in the book due to repetition with other interviews. These interviews are appreciated just as much.

I further want to thank the two writers who made this project happen. In 2003, writer May K. Cobb wrote the original book about my life called *Just the Facts*, which covered the first 76 years of my life. Thirteen years later, author Margaret O. Kirk has rewritten that first book, conducted additional research and interviews to enhance the original manuscript and cover events over the past 13 years, and developed important new chapters to tell the story of my life through 2015. This second book, *An Iowa Farm Boy on Detour: The Story of Henry B. Tippie*, was published in 2016, between my 89th and 90th birthdays.

Who knows what the future will hold. We'll find out.

—Henry B. Tippie, June 2016

Interior of the Henry B. Tippie Annex.

INTRODUCTION

In the southwest corner of Benton County, Iowa, in an area of the country known as America's heartland, there sits a rural town called Belle Plaine, a peaceful, picturesque community nestled in a pocket of small family farms, rolling fields for cows and corn, and seemingly endless stretches of grassy plains.

Founded in 1862, Belle Plaine has been known throughout its history for some surprisingly quirky but quintessentially small-town Iowa distinctions: throughout each day and long into every night, the ubiquitous sights and sounds of freight trains have defined this town, passing through Belle Plaine's bustling railroad depot since 1863; it's the home of an artesian well named Jumbo that spewed water uncontrollably onto the town's streets in 1886, baffling engineers from across the nation for over 14 months until it was finally capped by a local family; and it's a stop along the historic Lincoln Highway, America's first transcontinental roadway for automobiles, first established in 1913.

But these legacy touchstones, captured in panoramic murals painted on brick buildings in Belle Plaine's historic district, would give way to a new defining moment on August 25, 2012. On this special day, Belle Plaine welcomed into town an unprecedented gathering of distinguished guests: the governor of Iowa; the University of Iowa president; the head football coach of the University of Iowa Hawkeyes; the University of Iowa provost; the University of Iowa Foundation president; the dean of the University of Iowa Tippie College of Business; a University of Iowa regent; the president of Allegheny College; the vice presidents of Coe College and Kirkwood Community College; business executives and family members from one of the country's leading service companies, Rollins, Inc.; dozens of local citizens and members of the Class of 1944 from Belle Plaine High School; and last but not least, the mayor and former mayor of Belle Plaine, along with assorted Benton County executives. Each individual was in town for one reason: to pay tribute to a Belle Plaine native named Henry B. Tippie and to celebrate the story of his life.

Inside a new two-story building at the corner of 12th Street and 9th Avenue, just a block from the former Lincoln Highway and even closer to the railroad tracks, Henry and his wife, Patricia, welcomed each and every guest to the opening of the Henry B. Tippie Annex. This beautiful, architecturally designed addition to the Belle Plaine Area Museum contains a profound archival collection of photographs, memorabilia, documents, recordings, and narratives that together tell the story of Henry's life, starting from the day he was born near Belle Plaine in 1927.

"All of you know that I spent the first 17 years of my life on a farm east of Belle Plaine," Henry, then 85 years old, told his guests after they assembled in the plush, 160-seat auditorium on the second floor. "Although I physically left this area for the most part over 68 years ago, spiritually I am not sure I ever left, as hardly a day goes by that I don't think about some incident when I lived in this area. It was a very interesting time frame. And I like to think whatever character I may have wound up with started right here, as a farm boy from Iowa.

"I started at a very early age keeping just about everything, as I felt I might never have anything else," he explained, acknowledging the vast collection of items that now lined every wall of the auditorium and filled every exhibit area on the main floor. "It is only fitting that this memorabilia comes back to Belle Plaine, as this is where I started from. I have always considered that I am just a small-town farm boy who has survived swimming with the sharks for a very long time. I think I can summarize a lot by saying this Annex is a partial repayment for benefits received by an Iowa farm boy."

As recordings of Henry's favorite Big Band music played in the background, hundreds of guests soon began to walk through the meticulously arranged historical displays on the first floor. They stopped to look, took time to read, and attempted to absorb a veritable lifetime of information in order to understand how a poor farm boy grew up to become the accomplished World War II veteran, college graduate, successful businessman, husband and father of three, entrepreneur, Texas rancher, and widely lauded educational philanthropist who stood among them on this hot August day. On the one hand, the story of Henry B. Tippie is a classic American success story: a determined young man with nothing to lose leaves his family's dairy farm and finds a better life. But after walking through the Tippie Annex, it becomes very clear that Henry's story is about more than his own journey. Substitute another name for Henry B. Tippie in the majority of historical displays, and this becomes the story of an entire generation that struggled to make something out of lives that originally promised absolutely nothing. Think of any number of veterans who, like Henry, went to college on the G.I. Bill, and Henry's heartfelt appreciation for an education he could never otherwise afford becomes their appreciation, too. Consider the countless number of individuals who risked everything as business entrepreneurs, and Henry's story becomes a universal tale that illustrates how taking risks sometimes leads to enormous success.

What makes Henry's story uniquely his own, however, is the extraordinary degree of success he has experienced, and the depth of what he calls "repayment for benefits received" to his hometown and the university that took a chance on him and became his ticket to a better life. Through a lifetime of educational and civic philanthropy, this former Plainesman has never forgotten where he came from and the people who helped him when he had nothing. Which is why so many people from Henry's hometown and native state gathered in Belle Plaine in August 2012 to celebrate the person who has become one of the town's most defining and revered touchstones, a man whose life story is now as firmly entrenched in Belle Plaine's history as a bustling railroad depot, a well called Jumbo, and a historical highway.

The story of Henry B. Tippie "is a reflection of how America grew up. People from all over the country can see themselves in his story," said his son, Henry II. "But it is also a unique, one-of-a-kind story. And that's what makes it remarkable."

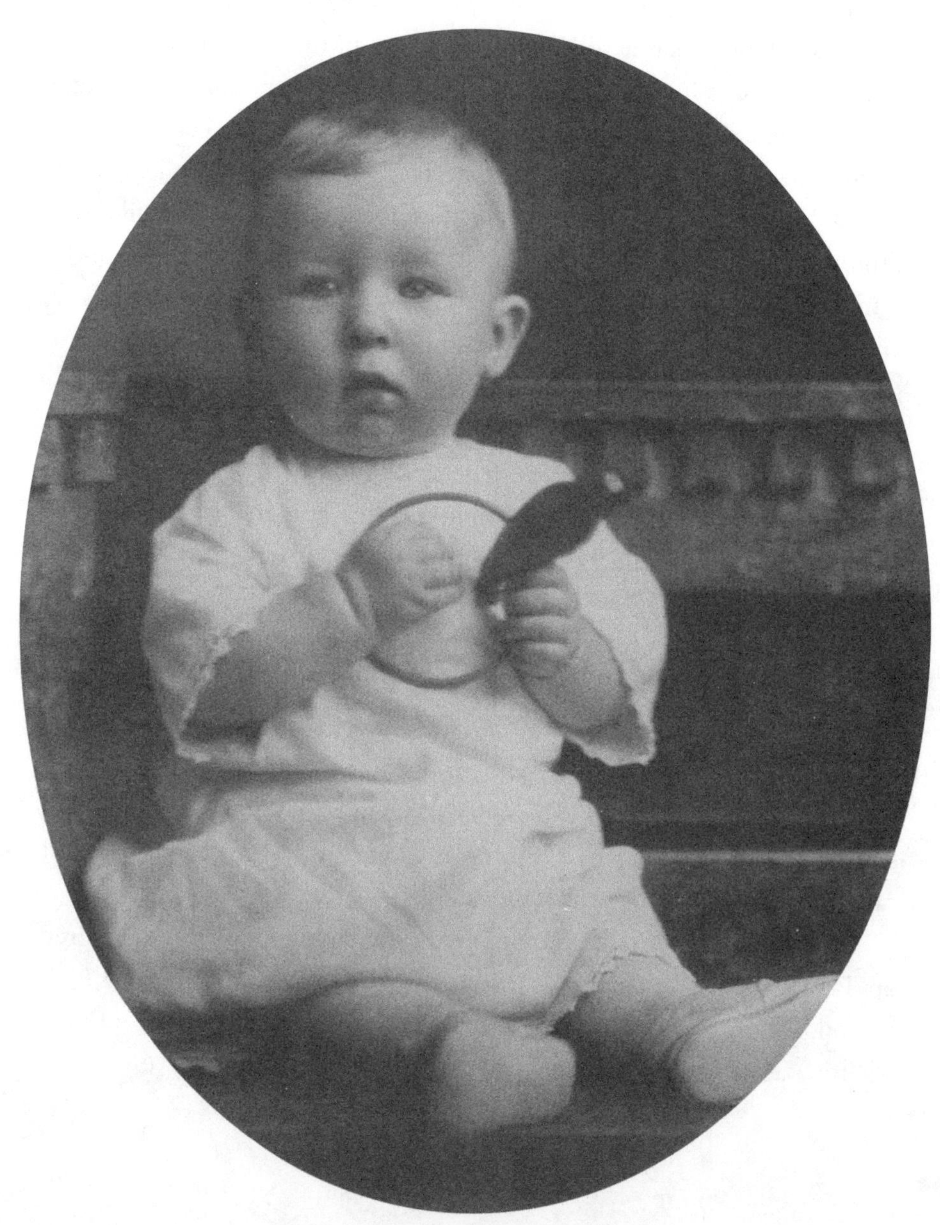

Henry B. Tippie, six months old, summer of 1927.

CHAPTER ONE

THE IOWA FARM BOY AND HIS FAMILY

ON WEDNESDAY, JANUARY 5, 1927, in a tiny farmhouse just a mile east of Belle Plaine, Iowa, a young couple named Robert and Amelia Tippie welcomed their first child, a beautiful baby boy with round cheeks, blue eyes, and slender but pouty pursed lips. The proud parents named their son Henry Bokholt Tippie, and he would forever be known as Henry B. Tippie.

Henry was born on the family's dairy farm, a 46-acre farm that overlooked a stretch of the famous Lincoln Highway and a seemingly endless ribbon of railroad tracks just beyond. In so many ways, the property reflected the poverty and hardships the young couple faced as they started both a family and a dairy business. The original Tippie farmhouse, shaded by a copse of trees and facing the main road, was a primitive structure with no insulation, no running water, no indoor plumbing, and no electricity. The family used an outdoor privy as a bathroom and depended on a kitchen sink fed by water from a nearby cistern for washing and cleaning. Flickering kerosene lanterns brought light into the house at night, and a woodstove heated the house in the winter when the cold Iowa temperatures routinely dipped below freezing and stayed there for weeks on end. A large range, fired by coal or wood, depending on what was available, stood opposite the stove in another corner of the room, not far from a big round table with a few chairs. Henry's crib and, later, his little steel bed, sat in the corner of the only bedroom, which was basically a room with an iron bed and a dresser that hooked onto the main house. A small set of stairs led to an attic, but the only thing up there was a mattress, rarely used. Outside, storm doors led to the basement, a musty but cool room with a dirt floor; Amelia stored her canned goods here, lining up Mason jars one after the other on shelves against the walls. With no other means of refrigeration, the family also stored food in the ground, digging holes just deep enough below the frost line to hold carrots, potatoes, and other vegetables as long as they lasted. The property included a timber-made, gambrel barn and milk house that stood parallel to the road west of the house, with a horse barn and a chicken house farther in the back and up a slight hill.

The land behind the house was as hardscrabble as the lives that depended on it. These 46 acres were, for the most part, hilly and unproductive. At the time Henry was born, a field consisting of only 10 acres had been cleared for raising crops—mostly corn or hay for the cows to eat. The other acreage gave way to land used primarily for pasture, and it was rough terrain, its fields pocked with stumps from trees that had already been cut for lumber. Buckeye Creek cut through the very northeastern corner of the property, its banks lined with willow trees that dipped gracefully into its flowing water. The shrill, lonely sound of the train whistle became the signature call of this farming and railroad community, echoing across Bob and Amelia's farm whenever a train approached. By the time Henry was born, as many as 50 trains from the Chicago & North Western Railway passed in front of his house each day, on their way in and out of Belle Plaine.

Henry would later tell people that he "came from nothing." But he never said those words with regret or despair. "Our money was very tight, but I didn't know I was poor," he said. "There's that quote, 'You don't miss what you never had.' And everyone around me was about the same way. I look back on those days, and I never thought of it as hard times. I didn't know any different."

Beyond the house and fields he called home, Henry grew up surrounded by the gentle, green hills of his native Iowa, endless acres of corn and oat fields, meadows, and pastures on the outskirts of Belle Plaine. The makeup of Belle Plaine's population was predominantly white—railroad men and farmers of mixed heritage who first came to the area in the

Belle Plaine, Iowa, 1928.

early 1800s. For the most part, Belle Plaine was a close-knit community of hardworking immigrants—Belgian, German, English, Bohemian, and Swedish alike who shared in the common thread of poverty.

Trains first arrived in Belle Plaine around 1863, traveling on newly laid tracks all the way from Chicago and Omaha, its rail and boxcars loaded with fruits, vegetables, coal, livestock, and occasionally a 60-piece ragtime band and a circus troupe. According to local historians, the Belle Plaine depot and railway station, complete with a 30-stall roundhouse, was constructed in the heart of the town in 1895, at the corner of Seventh Avenue and Eleventh Street. As a crucial refueling depot and a drop-off point for mail, baggage, passengers, and train crews, the railroad brought people and products to this once isolated area of the prairie, and increased business opportunities for Belle Plaine's citizens. The town's brickyard business thrived as the trains shipped its products throughout the Midwest. And in the late 19th and early 20th centuries, men and women from as far away as Germany and Czechoslovakia came to Belle Plaine to find work and to raise their families. By 1920, Belle Plaine counted nearly 3,500 citizens.

HENRY'S ANCESTORS MAKE THEIR WAY TO BELLE PLAINE

Henry's paternal ancestor, Johannes Tippie, sailed from Rheinland-Pfalz, Germany, to Philadelphia on the *Princess Augusta* on September 16, 1736. He and his wife, Susanna, lived in New Jersey, and their son Uriah was born on July 16, 1759, in Monmouth, East Jersey (now New Jersey). Uriah served as a volunteer in the Revolutionary War with General George Washington, and family historians often report that he was in the boat with General Washington when he made the famous crossing of the Delaware River. Uriah Tippie lived in Pennsylvania after the war and later moved to what was then the western frontier: rural Ohio. Descendants of Uriah Tippie then emigrated from Ohio to Iowa and Belle Plaine. According to Tippie family members, all of the Tippies, no matter how distant, can trace their roots to Uriah Tippie in southeast Ohio, including Henry's paternal grandfather, John A. Tippie. Each family no doubt moved to the Iowa prairie in search of the American Dream, determined to own land and a home. As a headline from a mid-1800s newspaper read: *Wanted—thirty-seven thousand, five hundred farmers! Let the news be scattered. Let the homehunting immigrant be informed that a free home awaits him in Iowa.*

John Tippie and his brothers were among those who moved to the Belle Plaine area from southern Ohio, soon acquiring land and operating a host of individual farms that were scattered in a row on the southeast side of Belle Plaine. John and his first wife had one son named Ernest. After his first wife died in a tragic house fire, John married a woman named Emma Doubek, of Bohemian and Czechoslovakian descent. John's son Ernest died from tuberculosis in his early 20s after serving in World War I, but John and Emma had two children who survived: a daughter named Naomi and a son named Robert W. Tippie.

Born October 27, 1900, Robert W. "Bob" Tippie grew up near Belle Plaine in a family that had farmed for generations. Like a lot of young boys from farming communities during his day, Bob attended a one-room school known as the Buckeye School, situated on a strip of farmland between the main road and the railroad tracks, about two miles east of Belle Plaine on the way to Luzerne. Bob's formal education ended in the ninth grade, so that he could work year-round on his family's farm. But despite his lack of education, Bob was an avid reader of books.

Though a traditional farm family, the Tippies often took part in the local Belle Plaine social scene. The *Belle Plaine Union*, in the "Personals" sections so popular in rural newspapers, often reported family activities, such as this one from November 1910: *Mrs. J. A. Tippie and daughter, Naomi, were Belle Plaine callers Friday.* And there was this report, from February 1911, when Bob was 11 years old:

> *The ladies of the Buckeye Valley Social Club entertained their husbands at the home of Mr. and Mrs. J. A. Tippie. A programme was arranged and opened by Mrs. J. Miner with several musical selections then a reading by Mrs. J. A. Tippie and following that a tree guessing contest to which the prize was awarded to Miss Cora Dodd. While the ladies were preparing supper Mr. W. A. Wehrman and Mrs. J. Miner entertained with some musical selections. After supper the guests departed all having had a good time.*

As a young man, Bob was lean and handsome, with deep-set eyes and a slender smile. He had a bit of a temper and could be moody, and he had a quiet pride and stubbornness that, in Henry's words, could make him "very bullheaded." He was practical and a very hard worker, devoted to his farm and his dairy clients. He loved working on his own, and he could fix or build anything, often developing creative solutions for different farming situations. For instance, he once designed and built a portable building on skids that he could move around for either the hogs or the sheep, depending on where they needed to graze on the farm. And one winter, frustrated that he couldn't use his expensive tractor in the extremely cold weather or at night, Bob went into town, bought some lumber, and built what many consider the first tractor "cab" they had ever seen, complete with headlights for nighttime plowing. His friends initially laughed at him, but they soon appreciated that Bob was ahead of his time.

To celebrate his 21st birthday, Bob's parents gave him a special gift: A trip to California. But the adventure did not spark an interest in the outside world, and Bob continued to live in or near Belle Plaine his entire life. From all accounts, he was relatively content. He neither dreamed of a life away from the farm nor envisioned a life beyond Belle Plaine.

But when Bob Tippie met Amelia Bokholt, he met the woman who would dream enough for both of them. Because Amelia, everyone soon realized, always longed for a life away from the farm for her family.

AMELIA BOKHOLT TIPPIE

The granddaughter of German immigrants, Amelia Bokholt was born on a farm about six miles north of Belle Plaine on July 10, 1898. Her parents, Henry and Dora Bokholt, traced their families to German ancestors. Though Dora's husband was born in Iowa, his parents had emigrated from Germany in the late 1800s. In fact, family histories show that three Bokholt brothers immigrated at different times, coming through Ellis Island at a time when no one spoke their native German during their entrance interviews and no one could discern how to correctly spell their names; consequently, the same last name for all three brothers was spelled differently in the United States, according to members of the Bokholt extended family. Amelia's mother, Dora Pingel Bokholt, was also German, with parents who immigrated to America and settled in Iowa just before Dora was born.

Amelia grew up on the family farm between the small towns of Keystone and Belle Plaine, working alongside her two brothers named John and Louie. They would always be a close-knit family, one that reflected the Old World traditions of the family's German heritage. They were a stoic, rather humorless lot who valued thriftiness, hard work, and industriousness, and rarely gave out compliments or showed emotion. The three Bokholt children went to a country school called Kane County #8, which was very similar to the one-room Buckeye School that the Tippies attended. And like Bob, Amelia's education was limited; she only finished the eighth grade, though Henry remembers his mother as "a very smart lady. She could figure more things in her head."

To all around her, Amelia was quiet and somewhat reserved, characteristics that sometimes belied her staunch independence and her perseverance, two qualities that became the governing forces in her life. She was a pretty, petite, self-possessed lady who never smoked and rarely drank. She enjoyed cooking, and her homemade apple dumplings were always family favorites. In a family photo from the early 1920s, Amelia wears her brown hair pulled away from her face, with a necklace around her neck. The entire family—Henry, Dora, John, Louie, and Amelia—are wearing their Sunday best: a dark Victorian high-neck blouse with buttons and a matching long skirt for Dora; a high-waisted dress with quarter-length sleeves, an overskirt and black heels for Amelia; three-piece suits, starched white shirts, and ties for the three men, with a dangling pocket watch for Henry. As they look straight into the camera lens, their expressions range from stern to just a hint of a smile.

What the vintage sepia photograph doesn't show, however, is that Amelia was a dreamer. Raised on a farm all her life, she saw the back-breaking work of farming as a burden and resolved that the cycle of hard labor would end with her if she ever had a family. She dreamed of having children who went to school and got an advanced education, breaking the cycle of growing up on a farm, working your whole life, and still being poor. Amelia dreamed of a world that was bigger and better than her family farm and envisioned opportunities beyond the boundaries of Belle Plaine. And she didn't give up on those dreams when she met and fell in love with a farmer everyone called Bob.

BOB AND AMELIA TIPPIE

One evening, probably in late 1922 or early 1923, though no one recalls for sure, Amelia Bokholt met Bob Tippie at a dance in Turner Hall in Keystone. Located just 11 miles north of Belle Plaine, Turner Hall had been a regular source of entertainment for the young adults in this rural section of Iowa since its opening in 1892. With its large wooden dance floor and a stage big enough for both local and visiting bands, young adults drove or walked from miles around to get to Turner Hall, where they listened and danced as musicians played the ragtime tunes so popular during and after the First World War. After their first meeting, it didn't take long for Bob and Amelia to realize they had a lot in common. Both families claimed German ancestors, and both families had always been farmers. They grew up in rural Iowa and both had limited educations. Family members on both sides would later describe them as two stubborn and independent individuals who never learned the art of compromise with each other. There was no question, however, that this young couple valued and knew how to work. And it didn't matter to Bob that Amelia was two years older. He was smitten.

Their wedding took place at the home of the bride on a Wednesday evening, June 6, 1923. Amelia wore a beautiful gown of lace over white satin, slipped her feet into a delicate pair of white satin wedding pumps, and carried a shower bouquet of rosebuds and valley lilies. Bob wore a new three-piece suit with a white shirt and tie, with a generous boutonniere of valley lilies, too. They both looked uncharacteristically glamorous and happy as they posed for their wedding portrait, both even daring to smile. After the ceremony, Amelia's mother served a three-course dinner for the small gathering of relatives and family. The next day, the *Belle Plaine Union* newspaper announced the marriage with a front-page story, under a headline that must have made the independent young bride chuckle: *Young Farmer Wins A Bride: Amelia Bokholt Became Wife of Robert Tippie Wednesday Evening. Couple Will Live On Tippie Farm.* The brief news clip reported every detail of the summer wedding at the "country home of Mr. and Mrs. Henry Bokholt," with this description of the bride and groom:

> *The bride is a charming young lady whose winning personality has won her a wide circle of friends. The groom is the son of Mr. and Mrs. J. A. Tippie and the past two years has been farming the home place. He is an exemplary young man, energetic and of sound business judgment and has made a success of his chosen evocation. These young people, among the very best of the community, have a wide circle of friends who will join in wishing them all happiness and prosperity. They will make their home on the Tippie farm.*

With their strong family backgrounds in farming, it is not surprising that Amelia and Bob began their married life on a farm. By all accounts they were happy at first, working hard to establish their own dairy farm on land that overlooked what was then known as Tippie's Corner, right at the T-junction of Lincoln Highway with Luzerne Road. Though money was tight at home, Amelia proved to be as resourceful inside the home as Bob was around the farm. She had her own sewing machine, and she often made the items she wanted but couldn't afford for their house—curtains, and beautiful crocheted rugs. She sewed most of her own clothes, too, including a skirt she made from burlap seed sacks and then dunked in red dye in a pot on top of her stove. And like most young couples, they were anxious to start a family. In 1926, nearly three years after they were

Robert and Amelia Tippie on their wedding day.

married, Bob and Amelia lost an infant son, a personal tragedy that they rarely talked about. But the sadness they felt was lifted within a year when a healthy baby boy they named Henry was born in January 1927, just five days into the New Year.

A NEW BABY BOY, FARMING, AND TOUGH ECONOMIC TIMES

In the early years, as the two adults grew their business, Henry was never far from his parents' side. Before Henry could walk, Bob and Amelia would take him out into the barn, where they milked the cows and placed him inside a horse collar to keep him safe. "A horse collar is probably 10 inches high and it has a big empty place inside," recalled Henry. "They put me in there so they would know where I was. I understand from Mom that one of the people in the area didn't think it was a very nice thing to do." But keeping track of a growing toddler proved difficult. Bob and Amelia often told the story of the time when Henry, almost three years old and wearing a farm kid's typical pair of bib overalls, wandered off while they were milking the cows.

"They could not find me," said Henry. "And this became quite a major situation and apparently they got some neighbors involved. They didn't know what happened to me." The parents were especially worried because the property had two old wells, both located behind the house and down at the bottom of the hill. One well was a working water well and still used by the family. The other well was old and abandoned, its original platform long rotted and filled with holes, its deep well filled with old fence wire haphazardly thrown into it over the years. In a panic, someone looked down the old well. And there was Henry, dangling in the dark hole of the well, hanging precariously by a piece of wire that had snagged his bib overalls after he climbed in and fell.

"According to my mother, I had fallen in the well some way, and the wire had caught the back of my bib overalls, and there I hung. And that's how they found me," said Henry. "They say there was always water in the bottom of that well. That's about all my mother ever told me about that, and I do not remember the incident but she told me several times."

The joy of their son's first few years was forever mingled with the economic downturns of a Depression era that would ultimately grip every state and every family throughout the country. The financial hardships brought on by a depressed economy hit Iowa early and often, first seeping into the state's rural central communities not long after Henry was born, when a string of banks closed from Tama to Marengo to Belle Plaine. On February 21, 1927, Belle Plaine and all the surrounding communities were rocked by the news that the First National Bank in Belle Plaine, the largest bank in Benton County, failed to open its doors for business that Monday morning. The bank's board of directors issued a statement that it decided not to open "in order to protect the bank and its depositors."

The announcement was obviously front-page news in the local papers. **"FIRST NATIONAL CLOSES DOOR"** read the bold banner headline in that week's *Belle Plaine Union*. The story reported that banking officials blamed the closing on heavy withdrawals over the past few months, and especially on the heels of the closing of the First National Bank in Marengo a week earlier. Within days, the community responded with mixed reactions. Within two days, heavy withdrawals caused the nearby Farmers Savings Bank of Hartwick to close its doors, too. The American Legion Auxiliary canceled a home talent play, and some high school activities were curtailed. But the *Belle Plaine Union* reported that otherwise "business was going on as usual Tuesday morning as though nothing had happened. Some of the business houses, particularly those dealing in poultry and cream, were rather handicapped due to their funds being tied up but by Tuesday they had made arrangement to carry on their business as usual."

The harsh reality of banks collapsing and farmers losing everything continued for years, worsening an already fragile economic climate in rural Iowa. During the later years of the Great Depression, on a day in 1933 when yet another bank closed in Belle Plaine, the Tippies would forever recall the moment Bob came home from town and burst into the house, sobbing and nearly inconsolable. "We're ruined! We don't have any money! We'll lose everything!" Bob cried to Amelia as a young Henry sat nearby. Amelia sat somewhat stoically at the table, listening as her husband described what had happened at the bank that morning. Considering what his wife had just heard, Bob probably thought she seemed remarkably calm. And in a scene that the family would describe over and over in the years to come, Amelia then turned and began to speak to Bob. "Well," she said, "I have something to tell you that I didn't want to tell you." It turned out that Amelia had faithfully collected money from her milk customers for the previous month, a process that generally took two days at the end of every month. But, she now admitted, "when I finished, it was so late, the banks were closed. I never put the money in the bank. And I have it all here, in the house."

To Bob's astonishment and utter relief, Amelia quickly retrieved the cash box from its hiding place. And in a matter of minutes, the bleakest day in the young history of Tippie's Dairy turned into one of its finest. Thanks entirely to Amelia's procrastination, the dairy was saved from total loss. The story of Amelia's cash box, tucked safely away at home the day the Belle Plaine banks failed, has been passed along like a family jewel by members of the Tippie family ever since.

GROWING UP ALONE

For almost five years, Henry was the Tippies' only child, which meant that he spent his formative years with adults who were consumed by exhausting, never-ending farm work. The family's entire focus never drifted far from the confines of the farm, because the dairy business required attention every single day of the week. "We worked all the time. We had to milk those cows out there seven days a week, twice a day," Henry explained.

Tippie's Dairy barn and an early advertisement.

To be honest, Henry's family seemed more overwhelmed than most. The constant worry about survival, and the heavy burden of life on the farm, cast a brooding pall over the Tippie household that was at times impossible to escape. The two parents took care of Henry's basic needs—they kept him fed and reasonably safe after the well incident—

but they didn't seem to grasp the concept of nurturing a small child. The family rarely if ever hugged or expressed affection for one another. The family did not celebrate birthdays, and Henry never remembers having a birthday celebration of any kind. When Henry once described a favorite sandbox toy from his childhood, it was almost sad, hearing him recall the metal cement mixer given to him by a hired hand. And for five years, Henry had no one to play with. There were no first cousins around; Henry's uncles on his mother's side, Louie and John Bokholt, remained bachelors and lived in Belle Plaine all their lives, and his father's sister and Henry's aunt, Naomi Tippie Jopling, married and lived in Des Moines, but she never had children. Henry remembers that the nearest child lived three miles away, and he readily admits that he didn't have any playmates or friends until he went to school. From sheer exhaustion and loneliness, it's no wonder Henry often went to bed when the sun went down.

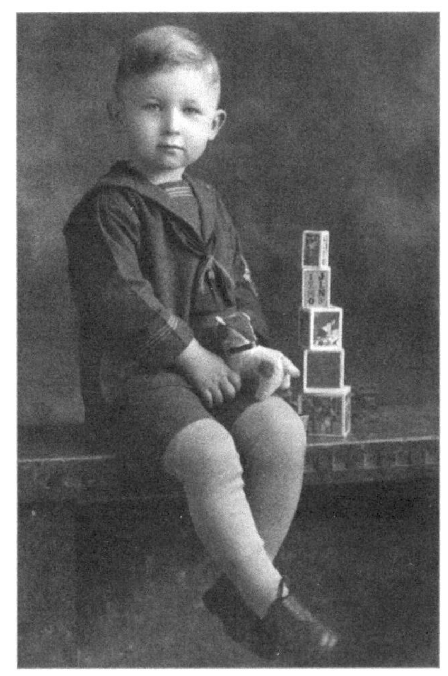

Henry as a toddler.

Henry's acute loneliness either contributed to, or was complicated by, his seeming inability to talk. Concerned, Bob and Amelia took their son to a doctor, who assured them that their nearly four-year-old Henry was healthy. The family tried everything to get Henry to speak; his uncles used to sit him on the fence so they could meet him at eye level and try to coax words out of him. When he finally spoke, Henry's parents claimed his first word was a curse word, a not-so-pleasant reminder of the adult world he lived in.

"I grew up pretty much alone," Henry once said. "I didn't live close to anybody and so I'm basically a loner. In those years, people worked all the time. So I really didn't have any playmates and really had nobody I associated with. I always felt like I grew up by myself."

Though Henry enjoyed the attention he got from his parents and other adults, being the only child had distinct disadvantages. Occasionally, when Henry went on overnight fishing trips with Bob, the young boy was included in the campfire talk and yarn-spinning that produced stories no child should necessarily ever hear; according to Henry, his father sometimes warned Henry not to mention what he heard to his mother. And in what many considered another nod to the fact that Henry grew up too fast, Bob, a smoker, taught Henry to proficiently roll cigarettes for him; his childlike fingers were the perfect size to fashion a cigarette out of rolling papers and Prince Albert tobacco. Henry, as a result, never smoked a day in his life.

And because the adults thought it was funny and didn't do anything to prevent it, Henry actually got drunk on hard cider when he was only four and a half years old, a fairly traumatic memory for Henry that began during an afternoon visit to his Grandpa Tippie's house. Though Henry has little memory of his grandfathers, one of the things he remembers most vividly about his Grandpa Tippie was his apple cider and his cider press. "He had a cider press, and he also had a smokehouse, and would smoke hams, bacon, things like that. In any event, Grandpa Tippie always made some cider, and I remember going with my dad one time down there and Grandpa Tippie gave him a bottle of cider. I had a taste of it and I liked it. I would say it tasted wonderful. We got home and I got into that cider and frankly I got drunk. I couldn't stand up, I was falling down, and I know my mom and dad thought this was hilarious because I'd had too much cider," said Henry, shaking his head years later about a childhood situation he knew was inexcusable. "I was throwing up, stumbling around a coal-burning stove. It was something. I've never forgot that."

With no friends, siblings, or cousins to hang out with, Henry survived by soaking up the rhythms of farm life. It's odd, really, but the whole concept of the farm became something of a surrogate friend to Henry. Even as a young boy, he liked the land. He liked the hard work a farm required. And he discovered on the farm that he liked animals, a feeling of kinship that lasted his whole life. Pictures of Henry as a young boy show him grinning broadly as he pets a dog named Mike or cuddles a barn cat, and his affection for farm animals extended to every creature on the farm, including mules, pigs, and cows. The first two mules he can remember—Punch and Joe, two very big but gentle mules—launched Henry's lifelong affection for farm animals of any kind. "Animals are much smarter than people give them credit for," Henry always said.

And as soon as Amelia would let him, Henry became his father's sidekick, his buddy. "He hardly ever went anyplace without taking me when I was a real young kid," Henry remembered. If Bob went fishing, Henry was by his side, working with his father to craft homemade fishing poles out of the willows that grew along Buckeye Creek, quick to gather grasshoppers or earthworms for bait. When Bob delivered milk on his milk route, Henry rode in the truck with him, quickly learning every street in Belle Plaine by heart at a very young age. "And if he went to pick up milk, like if we needed extra milk from the neighbors, I rode in the truck," Henry said. "I didn't get out of the truck a lot of times, but I rode in the truck so I think from that standpoint, I think I would say that I was probably important to him."

Henry on Grandpa Tippie's porch steps with pets Tom (cat) and Brownie (dachshund).

Back at the farm, Henry followed Bob everywhere. He helped feed the animals and tagged along when Bob plowed the fields with a 10-20 McCormick Deering tractor, purchased in the early 1920s. Some of Henry's earliest memories involve riding on that tractor with Bob, standing somewhat safely on a platform near his father, perfectly content to watch as he plowed the earth.

With a keen memory that he has maintained his entire life, Henry still remembers watching his father break new ground for the first time on their farm. He was about five years old, and the family needed more land to use for growing crops. Long before stump grinders and bulldozers or any large mechanical assistance existed, clearing land was brutal, manual work, especially if the land was covered in tree stumps. To clear the land, farmers like Bob typically blasted the stumps out of the ground with dynamite, no permits required. You'd just drill a hole in the stump, pack it with dynamite, light the fuse—and run. Or as Henry said, "When you're gonna blow the thing, you just get away." Afterward, Henry remembers watching his father use Punch and Joe to pull the remainder of the stumps out of the ground, calling on Henry to help maneuver the stump fragments into a pile that they later burned. Bob could then begin the arduous task of turning the earth, row by row, primarily with a hand plow pulled by the team of mules. "He had this plow hooked up to the mules, and I can see it right now, the reins of the mules tied together," said Henry. "Dad put the reins behind his shoulders. That way, it would give him his arms, out here, to hold the plow. And that's what you call 'breaking the sod.'"

A NEW HOME, TWO NEW BROTHERS, AND A HARSH REALITY

Henry's grandfathers passed away in the early 1930s—first Grandpa Bokholt in 1931, and then Grandpa Tippie in 1933. When Grandpa Bokholt passed away, he left Amelia some money, and she decided to use it to build a new, modern house to replace the decidedly primitive one the family lived in. By now, Henry was no longer an only child: his brother Ernest was born in 1931, and the old house, with its one bedroom, had become crowded. Henry has a vivid memory of baby Ernest. "I can remember being outside and looking to the kitchen window and Ruth Van Scoyc—she was a neighbor lady—had just finished giving my brother a bath in the washtub in the kitchen and held him up by the window," he said. "And I can remember looking through the window and seeing her hold him up. You know, he was just a few days old and I have never forgotten it. That's my first remembrance of my brother Ernest."

The family's new two-story house with a full basement was actually built in the exact same spot as the original home place overlooking Lincoln Highway, after the first house was moved to another location. At the time, Henry thought the new house was huge! The first floor contained Bob and Amelia's bedroom with an adjoining toilet and sink, a modern kitchen, a dining room, a living room, and an enclosed porch. Henry and

The Tippie homestead, which replaced the primitive farmhouse around 1931.

Ernie each had their own room upstairs, with a full bathroom. Unlike the old house, this one had running water and electricity. In addition, Bob had a basement designed and built specifically for the operation of the dairy. After the family collected milk from the cows, they hauled it to the basement to be processed and bottled and cooled until delivery.

The Tippie family soon welcomed its third son: a baby boy named Robert John, born on October 28, 1935. The once spacious, three-bedroom home was quite full again. On hot summer nights, when the air was suffocatingly still indoors, the family often pulled mattresses out to the front yard and slept outside under the oak trees—a country boy's rite of passage and a memory that Henry still delighted in sharing decades later.

With their expanded family, Bob and Amelia worked harder than ever to make a living. The family rarely if ever traveled far from the farm. Henry can only remember a single vacation with his family while growing up. "They got my uncles to take care of the milk business and the milk route for about two or three days. And we had the pickup truck. Mom and Dad and I think my youngest brother, who would have been a baby then, rode in the front of the truck, and Ernie and I sat in the back. We took a drive through Missouri, Arkansas, and the Ozarks that got us down as far as Mountain Home, Arkansas—I always remember that's as far as we got. Drove down through Missouri until he got down to Arkansas,

The Tippie brothers (left to right): Henry, Ernest, and Robert John.

turned around and came back. That's the only time when I grew up that the family as a unit ever had any time together. And that spanned maybe five days, with the weekend tangled up in there, and that's it." Henry once wrote about his family's lone vacation for an English assignment: *We saw many things such as railroad tunnels, steep cliffs, caves, etc. The people that live down there are very different than they are here. They live mostly by hunting and fishing. They raise very little crops as it is hilly and heavily forested. The people talk with a southern accent. . . .*

With the exception of this southern road trip, the only "outside world" Henry ever got to see as a child was the view from his front yard. With the Tippies' house perched on an incline, Henry witnessed the comings and the goings of train after train, and he remembers watching steam engines, loaded down with coal, get stuck as they tried to climb the incline into town. The area across the road in front of his house was known as the "Cut," because if a train got stuck, the railroad workers would have to cut the train in half, pull it to town and come back for the rest later, a scene that Henry watched many times while growing up.

Without fail, the situations that unfolded at the "Cut" allowed Henry to witness just how desperate people could be when they were poor and had no money for food or fuel. Peeking through the curtains on the enclosed front porch, Henry often watched as people parked their cars up the road from his house but within walking distance of the train tracks. "They would come and park their vehicle up the road so it could not be seen, and then they would go and hide in the weeds," Henry recalled. "And they would wait for one of these trains that predominantly pull coal to get stuck. They would wait until they'd have to break the train, and they would then climb up in those coal cars and throw some of the coal out of the car, into the weeds. And after the train pulled out they would take their sacks and fill them up with coal and put them in their vehicle and go back into town. I watched that time after time. And we knew, of course, living in a small community, who the different people doing this were, but we didn't report them. It was interesting to watch this."

Because the Tippies lived right on the Lincoln Highway, it was not unusual for transient and jobless people traveling along the road to come knocking on their door in search of food. If she could spare something from her already bare-bones kitchen, Amelia offered a sandwich for the traveler. At one point, the Tippies began to experience a regular stream of people, more than usual, all stopping by the house and asking for a meal. They eventually found out why: Someone had painted an "X" on their milk house, which could be seen from the highway. The "X" was a code to stop by, an indicator that this home could spare some food.

But the image that had the most profound effect on Henry, the one that reinforced for him that the future is never certain, occurred one morning in the early 1930s, around 6:30 a.m. as he and his dad delivered dairy products on their routine milk route in Belle Plaine. Riding in the truck, they turned down a street like they always did. Only this morning, in the early slice of dawn, Henry saw two children sitting on the sidewalk curb. He recognized the young boy as a student, maybe a year ahead of him. The family had been kicked out of their house in the middle of the night, along with a few belongings and pieces of furniture. "This was at the height of the Depression," Henry one day realized. "They didn't have anything. That has always stuck with me, and I can pin that moment down so exact. That's how bad things got. We had 25 percent unemployment, there were no jobs, and no money. It was a very tough environment."

Henry never saw that family again. But his memory of a family sitting on the curb with nothing ensured that Henry would never take possessions, money, or a job for granted. As an adult, he took the role of provider for his family more seriously than others around him, making sure that he lived on far less than he earned, and never quite trusting that everything wouldn't one day disappear.

But as a young child, caught in the throes of an economic depression he couldn't possibly understand, Henry's immediate response to a family that had lost everything was to begin to save anything he could get his hands on. And just like that, Henry became a collector. Nothing, it seemed, was too small or too big for him to hoard away: receipt stubs from his milk route; tickets from a train ride; all of his schoolbooks and farming notebooks; matchbooks from gas stations along the Lincoln Highway; his father's Horatio Alger books; his own Big Little Book series; a metal red and white Butter-Nut coffee container, wrapped with masking tape that sealed in Henry's extensive marble collection; a red-framed Chinese checkers game board manufactured in 1938 by L. G. Ballard MFG Co. in Topeka, Kansas; a collection of toy tractors and a Sinclair Oil Company dinosaur stamp book; Tippie's Dairy calendars and business cards; pencils; report cards; a 1933 Northwestern Mailbox Company Clown-n-up pinball machine; his grandmother's spinning wheel; and his mother's cash box that helped save the family business during the Depression. "I figured when you don't have anything, if you get something, you might want to hold on to it. Because you never know if you will get another one," Henry said.

And, he once admitted, the haunting memory of that one family—sitting on the sidewalk after losing their home and everything they had—never left him. "When you're young," he said, all but closing his eyes in thought, "you don't forget images. I think the younger you are sometimes, images stand out in your mind your entire life."

CHAPTER TWO

RECORDING EVERY PENNY: YOUNG HENRY AT WORK

WITH MILK FROM 25 DAIRY cows, Tippie's Dairy supplied almost half of Belle Plaine's milk. Which means that Bob Tippie, while driving around town in a black 1931 Ford pickup with "Tippie Dairy" painted on the sides, hand-delivered dozens of bottles of milk and cream every week to homes and businesses throughout Belle Plaine. In 1933 this included the Black-Bird Grill, Bert's Sandwich Shop, the J & H Sandwich Shop, the Commercial Café, and the well-known Lincoln Café at the corner of Lincoln Highway and Ninth Avenue.

A Tippie's Dairy calendar.

The community of Belle Plaine deeply valued the local milkman named Tippie, the high-quality milk his farm produced, and the service he gave his customers in this small town, where citizens depended on each other not only to fulfill their daily needs but on occasion to make the extra effort. And by all accounts, Bob and Amelia always did that at

Tippie's Dairy. During hard times, they continued to deliver milk even when a customer couldn't pay. If a cow dried up and they ran short of milk, they purchased more from nearby farms in order to make full deliveries on time. They provided yearly calendars to their customers and helped furnish milk and cream to support special town events like the yearly Belle Plaine Union Cooking School. And at least once, when a severe snowstorm swept through town, the owners of the Lincoln Café phoned Tippie Dairy at the local exchange known as "164-Black" and begged Bob to bring them some milk. Bob promptly filled two pails of milk, covered each securely, took one in each hand and made the mile-long journey into town, walking along the railroad tracks to avoid the icy roads. And then he turned around and walked back home.

According to the local newspaper advertisements for Tippie's Dairy, Bob and Amelia used "exacting care" to ensure the purity of the Grade A milk and cream they sold. For the Tippies, this meant that they milked only from the highest quality of cows, all tested and found to be free from tuberculosis. After milking, they cooled the milk to just below 50 degrees before they bottled it, a chore made somewhat easier in the new dairy work area below the new house. "Every bottle is filled under strictly sanitary conditions," the Tippies promised in the era before pasteurization. "And we make all milk deliveries during the early hour of the morning to ensure your getting fresh milk and to have the milk to you in time for breakfast use. We welcome you to inspect our dairy any time."

To keep these promises, the Tippies worked from before dawn until dusk, seven days a week, trying to stay one step ahead of poverty while meeting the constant demands of running a dairy farm. And from the time his parents placed an infant Henry inside a horse collar to keep him safe while they worked, Henry was involved in the family's retail dairy, learning every facet of the operation and its daily routines.

Each morning, the Tippies got out of bed before dawn. Amelia cooked a big farmer's breakfast of scrambled eggs and pancakes, sometimes preparing the pancake batter the night before so her only chore at that early hour was to cook. After eating, the entire family headed to the barn. In the spring, summertime, and fall, it was Henry's job to bring the cows in from the pasture to be milked (in the winter, of course, they often stayed in the barn). "They knew the routine," Henry said. "The one thing about the milk cows, they know it's time to come, they are already waiting to be milked. You open the gate and they go right into the barn and a milk cow knows where its location is in the barn."

The milking started in the barn shortly after four o'clock in the morning. Henry cannot even remember a time when he didn't know how to milk cows—and he recalled creating a bit of mischief around this tedious chore. "We had one real old cow, real tame, so I can picture milking that cow today—a big, white cow with a few black spots. And when nobody was looking, sometimes I'd try and squirt the cat—we always had a pan of milk out there for the cat—and then sometimes I'd try to squirt my initials up on the wall of the barn. That's when nobody was looking."

The Tippies kept a hand separator to remove cream from some of the milk, said Henry, and occasionally made cartons of butter from the cream and sold both products alongside bottles of milk. "When I got older, I had a lot of experience running the hand separator."

Traditionally, Amelia bottled the milk while Bob and Henry got ready to head into town, leaving every morning, five days a week at six o'clock sharp to make their rounds in the family's 1931 black Ford pickup. With the Ford's two headlamps lighting an otherwise dark and empty road, they headed west on Lincoln Highway toward Belle Plaine, riding in a truck with no air conditioning in the summer and no heat in the winter, unless you count what Henry called a "manifold heater" that allowed some heat from the engine to enter the cab through a hole in the floor. As the sun began to rise, the Tippies made their way along their familiar routes, delivering

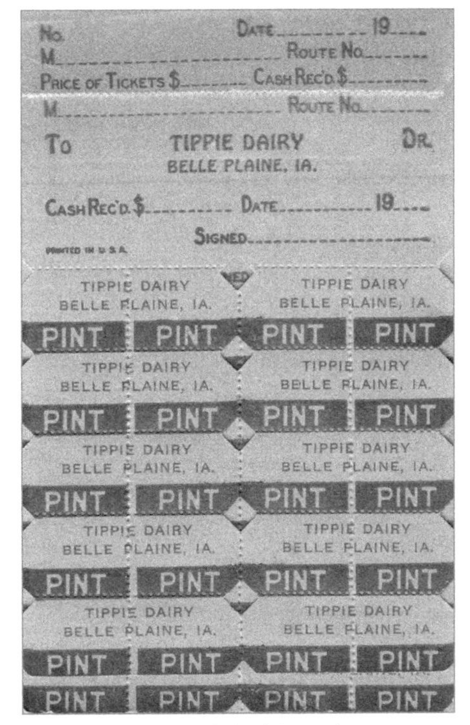
No. DATE ________ 19___
M. ________ ROUTE NO. ______
PRICE OF TICKETS $______ CASH REC'D. $________
M. ________ ROUTE NO. ______
To TIPPIE DAIRY DR.
BELLE PLAINE, IA.
CASH REC'D. $________ DATE ________ 19___
SIGNED ________________
PRINTED IN U.S.A.
TIPPIE DAIRY BELLE PLAINE, IA. TIPPIE DAIRY BELLE PLAINE, IA.
PINT PINT PINT PINT
TIPPIE DAIRY BELLE PLAINE, IA. TIPPIE DAIRY BELLE PLAINE, IA.
PINT PINT PINT PINT
TIPPIE DAIRY BELLE PLAINE, IA. TIPPIE DAIRY BELLE PLAINE, IA.
PINT PINT PINT PINT
TIPPIE DAIRY BELLE PLAINE, IA. TIPPIE DAIRY BELLE PLAINE, IA.
PINT PINT PINT PINT
TIPPIE DAIRY BELLE PLAINE, IA. TIPPIE DAIRY BELLE PLAINE, IA.
PINT PINT PINT PINT
PINT PINT PINT PINT

A Tippie's Dairy ticket stub.

milk. "As soon as I was old enough, part of my job was to carry the milk to some of the houses in town," Henry says. Milk from Tippie's Dairy sold for five to 10 cents for a half-pint, a pint, or a quart. The family recorded every delivery and sale in little red ticket books. "Everybody had a different deal," says Henry. "Some of the houses you didn't go to every day, you only went a couple of times a week. It all depended on the house."

Customers paid for their milk and cream in one of two ways: they left money in the empty milk bottles that Henry picked up on the steps when he dropped off the full bottles; or some customers paid Amelia during her monthly collection rounds. Because of the hard times, collecting payment was often difficult. As Henry remembered: "On occasion, my mom would relate to me that people did not come to the door, or they were not at home, or they didn't have any money. Bear in mind that this is in the early 1930s, and things were very, very difficult, and a lot of people were unemployed, and jobs were hard to come by." Bob and Henry made sure that even the customers who couldn't afford to pay some weeks still received their milk orders.

On December 27, 1928, just before Henry turned two, Bob had published a prominent announcement in the local paper:

Tippie's Dairy

We have established a milk route for the convenience of the people of Belle Plaine.

You can't beat our milk but you can whip our Cream

We produce our own milk

TIPPIE DAIRY
ROBERT TIPPIE, Prop
Phone 10-08 or 15-08

With this 1928 advertisement, Bob and Amelia introduced a marketing slogan that Tippie's Dairy would use for years: *You can't beat our milk but you can whip our cream.* Before long, the slogan appeared consistently in newspaper advertisements and on the Tippie's Dairy Calendars, often alongside pictures of deliciously plump babies drinking milk from their bottles. As time went on, Bob and Amelia often added product information that was designed to reassure (or convince) customers that their dairy was among the best: "Pure, Fresh Milk and Cream," one business card read. "From Tuberculin-tested herds."

Bob and Amelia often used newspaper advertisements to boast about their products or recruit new customers, and they frequently gave a nod to national events in their marketing efforts. For instance, when child actress Shirley Temple was the number-one box office star in 1935, Tippie's Dairy used a picture of a darling Shirley Temple look-alike, a little girl with ringlet curls and a large ribbon hair bow, alongside this ad copy: *MILK Puts the Sparkle In Her Eyes! Ruddy checks, bright eyes, sturdy bodies tell the story of a diet rich in milk. As a drink and on foods—Pure! Wholesome!* In 1936, Tippie's Dairy used another advertisement: *Nations depending heavily upon dairy products for their diet have better Health. Drink more milk—especially Tippie Dairy Milk. Try that on your son.*

By now, Henry was nine years old, going to school during the school year but still helping out on the farm whenever he wasn't in class. From his experience on his family's milk routes, Henry would forever recall—in photographic detail—the streets and the locations of homes and businesses throughout Belle Plaine. As his friend Betty Kent once said, "I think Henry remembered it because as a boy he delivered milk for his father to all these places in town."

Riding through Belle Plaine, Henry couldn't help but hear stories about the history of his hometown. He quickly memorized the tale of the Jumbo Well and the account of the Great Fire of 1894, often glancing at the handsome brick and stone buildings on Main Street constructed to replace the ones destroyed in 1894 when a catastrophic fire wiped out five solid blocks of downtown before firemen from four different towns finally brought the flames under control. And he heard over and over about the importance of transportation and railroads to Belle Plaine, trains that brought people, jobs, and opportunities to a little town that always celebrated the rail system and its spot along America's first transcontinental highway.

As Bob's helper, Henry soon appreciated how businesses in small towns operated. And he learned some decidedly unorthodox history lessons about the Great Depression, banking, and Prohibition on his milk routes through the town. Recalled Henry,

> Prohibition was still in existence, and I well remember this because this is a small community. And there was a certain amount of bootlegging taking place. We delivered milk to a neighborhood grocer on the west side of town, and I always remember one morning going there, as I always tagged along. I never stayed in the truck when we did anything with a commercial establishment. I always tagged along even though there wasn't much for me to do. Anyway, this fellow was telling my dad about a raid they had had during the night and they didn't find anything. And I remember this fellow saying, "Bob, I wanna show you where I had it hid." So we went outside this neighborhood grocery store—all the neighborhood grocery stores were in people's houses and generally they enclosed their porches and that made up the grocery portion of the house. In any event, we walked outside on the south side of the house and the siding was shiplap. So he had a few of those boards that weren't nailed down and here, between the two by fours, were all these bottles of whiskey. Another time, I remember we delivered to a grocery store on Main Street and so they told Dad that they'd had a raid the night before and nobody found anything, and so again he said, "Bob, let me show you where we had it." And in those days they used to get meat brought in in these wicker-type baskets. And so they had one of these wicker baskets there and it had a false bottom, so they showed us how they took the bottom out and here's all these half-pints.

Trusted by everyone in town, Bob and Henry got to see both sides of the raids during Prohibition. In addition to seeing shopkeepers' secret stashes, Henry also saw the liquor that was recovered in some of the raids. "I remember the police chief taking us over to the jailhouse and showing us the stuff that they had picked up during the night, during some kind of a raid," said Henry. "In our kind of situation, we were just seeing things that were going on."

LIVING OFF THE LAND

Though the dairy business did afford some peace of mind and the stability of a monthly income, it didn't actually bring in enough money for the Tippies to live on. Like so many other farmers in that era, the Tippies were never far from the threat of losing everything. So after the dairy needs were taken care of, the Tippies spent the rest of their time trying to find and grow enough food for the family and make some extra cash. Said Henry, "We lived off the land. When you lived off the land, I think you could always eat. It wasn't always fancy. But I've always said that things could go all to heck in a handbasket but I know how to survive. I can raise a garden, I can live off the land. That would be nothing new for me if it came to that. Over the course of my young life, we ate everything. I didn't think anything unusual about it. Nowadays people might look at it differently. But look, you don't miss what you didn't have."

With his fishing pole, Henry caught bullheads and chubs in Buckeye Creek that Amelia then cleaned and cooked for meals. Taking the family's .22 single-shot rifle, Henry hunted for squirrels and rabbits. "I wasn't a particularly good shot but I would certainly get my share of them and Mom would fix those up for us to eat." Henry also laid trap lines for possum, raccoons, and groundhogs, which Amelia cooked in soups and stews. "In my real younger days," Henry remembered, "when it got down to Thanksgiving and Christmastime, we didn't go into town and buy a turkey or something like that. Dad would go down to the Iowa River, around the Dayton area, and maybe get a goose or a duck. And if he didn't, we always had chickens to fall back on."

Amelia raised chickens and butchered them herself. Ernest, Henry's younger brother, never forgot that scene: "My mother would butcher the chicken on Saturday that we would eat on Sunday. She would take a cleaver and chop off the head of the chicken. She did this on a piece of tree trunk by the chicken house. The chicken would jump around headless until all

Henry hunting with his father Robert (left), and uncle John Tippie (right).

of the blood drained away. She would then pick the feathers and then dip it in boiling water to get the pinfeathers out. In the wintertime they would also butcher hogs. You would kill the hog and pull the hog up on the limb of a tree, and you'd have hot scalding water in a big vat to put the hog in. You'd have to get the intestines cleaned out to be used for sausage."

Family meals were simple—the big country breakfast, a noontime meal called dinner, and a light evening meal called supper. "I had never heard of the word 'lunch,'" Henry once reminisced. "Then, it was breakfast, dinner, supper. In the farm country in those days you had what you called supper, it was very, very light. It could be fried potatoes with bacon or scrambled eggs or crackers with milk. You wouldn't be eating any steak, not at night. If you had fried chicken it would be at noontime."

After taking enough eggs and chickens for her family, Amelia used the surplus eggs each week to barter for staples in town, typically on Saturdays. Carrying her wooden case of eggs to the local Cash-and-Carry, Amelia carefully shopped for the essentials, trading the eggs for flour, sugar, and canned goods. "It wasn't just us that did this, it was a lot of people," Henry recalls of the bartering tradition. In fact, local businesses like the Belle Plaine Produce Co. encouraged farmers not only to barter but to bring their eggs into town to sell. "Fancy full fresh eggs are commanding extreme prices," noted one newspaper advertisement. "Held or chilled eggs do not. Keep your eggs at an even temperature, as near forty degrees as possible, and market often and we will pay you fancy prices for them."

Henry loved the family's Saturday evening shopping trips to Belle Plaine, a welcome break from life on the farm. The Tippies typically arrived in town about five o'clock and stayed all evening. People filled the streets, and all of the stores on Main Street stayed open until 9 p.m. In Henry's day, the downtown streetscape was home to hardware and general stores; a wealth of furniture and dress shops for hats, shoes, and clothes; doctors, attorneys, blacksmiths, and lumber offices; and pubs, a creamery, hotels, and auto agencies. The adults shopped and visited, while the children and teenagers headed out to watch a movie at the King Theater, a grand single-screen movie theater that members of the Mansfield family opened on 12th Street in 1930. "The movie would usually be a double feature—a western of the day and a comedy—and it was always packed," said Ernie. The Tippie brothers, along with their friends, watched Olympic swimming champion Johnny Weissmuller star as the vine-swinging Tarzan, the Ape Man; laughed at the slapstick comedy of the Three Stooges; and didn't dare miss native Iowan actor John Wayne in his breakout role as the Ringo Kid in *Stagecoach* in 1939. "Our parents used to give us fifteen cents to go to the movie," Ernie remembered. "Ten cents for the movie and five cents for popcorn."

A FIRE, A MISSING CHILD, AND THE END OF THE DAIRY BUSINESS

Both Henry and Ernie must have thought they were in some surreal and tragic movie of sorts on May 22, 1936, when a series of unfortunate events converged on Tippie's Dairy. When Henry returned home from school, the large one-story wooden barn, filled with feed for cows and miscellaneous farm equipment just that morning, was nothing but ashes. Struggling to comprehend what had happened, Henry knew that the cows were safe out in the fields, but where were the rest of the animals? He looked around for his pets and quickly discovered that his favorite pet mules, Punch and Joe, had been so badly burned and were in such agony that they had been shot and killed. "They were dead, and I can still see them lying there, over the hill," said Henry, recalling a scene he would rather forget.

As the firemen worked to prevent the fire from spreading to the house and the other buildings, Amelia and Bob made a chilling discovery: five-year-old Ernie was missing. In a scene eerily reminiscent of the time Henry fell down the well, no one could find Ernie. Was he in the barn? Had anyone seen him? Did anyone hear him cry out from inside the barn? "Ernie! Ernie!" The forlorn and panicky cries of two parents, firemen, and neighbors who had by now come to help were soon heard as search parties quickly organized to look for the missing boy. Just as the adults began to disperse, Uncle Carlos suddenly arrived on the scene. Hearing that Ernie was missing, Carlos suddenly blurted out, "Wait! I believe I saw him! Heading toward my place! Just a little while ago." The adults rushed to Carlos's property and gas station, about a quarter mile away. "And sure enough," the local newspaper reported in a front-page story about the blaze, "there the lad was found," under the bench in Carlos's gas station. "And soon he was restored to the arms of his mother, and a sigh of relief went up from the entire crowd."

No one ever knew what caused the barn fire. Henry always maintained that a cinder, sparked by a passing train, must have floated in the air and drifted across the road from the railroad tracks, settling on the barn and starting the fire. The entire wooden structure burned so fast that the fire was apparently out of control even before the firemen could respond to Bob's call for help. But a strong, southerly wind that day apparently carried the flames away from the Tippies' home and other farm buildings, a decidedly lucky break that aided the firemen's efforts to protect what was left of the farm and save Tippie's Dairy from complete ruin. In a public "We Thank You" note published in the newspaper the next week, Bob and Amelia stated how grateful they were for everyone's help in fighting the fire and finding their middle son: "We wish to express our appreciation and extend our thanks to the City Firemen for their prompt response and efficient help at the fire at our home last Friday, and also wish to thank the neighbors or others for their loyal assistance at that time."

The Tippie Dairy recovered from the fire over the summer, and by September the Tippies had resumed their newspaper advertisements in the *Belle Plaine Union*: "Milk Customers! We can accept a few more. Wonderful Tippie Dairy Milk from an inspected herd of fine cows."

But Tippie's Dairy was never really the same. In less than two short years, the dairy would be gone, for a number of reasons. First, the Tippies had always sold Grade A milk—which is not pasteurized. When pasteurization laws went into effect, it was no longer possible for Bob to keep the dairy open; given the small size of the family dairy, Bob could not afford to make the switch to a pasteurization process. "So, number one, there was the issue of pasteurization," Ernie recalled. "Number two, the farmers were starting to use milking machines. And my dad never got to the point where he felt that that was something he wanted. And we couldn't get any larger because all of the milk processing was done in the basement of the house."

As Henry recalled, the family didn't shut the dairy business down completely at first. Though the family did stop the dairy's retail business and cut back the herd a bit in 1937, Bob and Henry maintained the dairy's wholesale business until the spring of 1938, continuing to sell milk to stores and restaurants. But even that, Henry admitted, was soon over. "The dairy business is a tough business," he said. "And it was no longer feasible to stay in the business."

A GARDEN AND AN ACCOUNTING SYSTEM

With the dairy officially closed, the Tippie family was without a steady monthly income for the first time since Henry was born. It was a daunting reality. For a few years, Bob hired himself out to neighbors for $2 a day; when Henry could join him, he worked by Bob's side for $1 a day.

And that summer, 11-year-old Henry—who no longer had to help milk cows twice a day and deliver milk on weekends—decided that he had time to try to earn some money and help out the family by planting some vegetables in the garden spot behind the house. He used an old garden plow to work the soil, and pretty soon he was growing peas, corn, beets, lettuce, cucumbers, radishes, beans, onions, potatoes, melons, and tomatoes. The memory of that first garden made him laugh. "Sometimes," he said, "I would have my brother Ernest hooked up like a horse to that plow. He was my horse; he pulled that garden plow, even though it was a push-type deal."

Robert John, Henry, and Ernest (left to right) did chores on the family farm.

Ernie didn't seem to care. Henry paid him "wages" of up to 25 cents a month to help him out. And Ernie watched with a bit of awe as Henry turned around and sold the produce to his mother to use in cooking meals or canning. "Henry was always an entrepreneur," said Ernie.

Henry took his gardening very seriously. He tracked every seed he planted and every penny he spent to grow this food. As Ernie immediately recognized, the garden was Henry's first business endeavor. Henry created meticulous records of all earnings and expenses associated with the garden, recording everything in pencil in spiral and pocket notebooks. His parents were his best customers, and he kept a handwritten record of who bought what, how much, and when. For instance, on May 27, Henry sold a bunch of early spring radishes to "R. Tippie" for six cents; two months later, by the end of July, his garden was producing enough potatoes, onions, turnips, peas, lettuce, kale, beets, cucumbers and corn for Henry to record $1.24 in monthly sales to "R. Tippie" (including his biggest one-day sale on July 22 of 25 cents' worth of potatoes, compared to two cents' worth of onions sold on July 2). At the end of the growing season, on a separate page in his notebook, Henry added up all of his garden receipts and recorded a "Grand Total Garden Money" of $8.31. He then deducted $1.68 in expenses for a net profit of $6.63.

By the time 11-year-old Henry returned to school in the fall of 1938, his mother had a cellar filled with canned food grown in her son's garden, and Henry had created his very first accounting system. Did anyone ever show Henry how to keep such meticulous records? Did he watch his parents settle the books at the kitchen table, and then decide to try to keep his own records? "No," Henry insisted. "And I never took any bookkeeping in high school either. I just did this stuff on my own."

		total
Peas	3, 5, 5	13¢
Corn	6, 7, 5, 6, 7, 7, 7, 20, 5	70¢
beat	25, 1	26¢
lettuce	1, 4, 1, 1, 2	9¢
cucumber	1, 5, 8, 4, 4, 2, 3, 7, 10, 8, 10, 7, 7, 7, 1, 1	97¢
radish	6, 2, 5, 10, 5, 5, 1, 1, 1	36¢
turnip	1, 5	6¢
onion	10, 3, 2, 5, 40	60¢
potatoe	5, 15, 25, 25, 70, $2.50	$3.90
Kale	1, 1	2¢

In notebooks, Henry recorded earnings from his garden.

Perhaps Henry was already thinking about profit-expense ratios and analysis as early as in the sixth grade, judging from a poem he composed in 1938 called "Proud Winter":

Proud Winter

Proud Winter in his robes of white
Goes about in the chilly night.

He hires Jackie Frost,
Without any cost,

To paint the windows
With forests and meadows.

Henry B. Tippie

THRESHING, TOILING, TRYING TO MAKE A LIVING

By 1940 Bob had decided on another plan to support his family. It involved 140 acres of land about three miles from the former dairy farm, land that Bob had inherited from his father a few years prior to the sale of the dairy. It was hilly land, hard to farm, and part of it was covered in tree stumps—"not choice land," Henry always said. Because the land came with a mortgage that had to be paid on time, Bob had originally rented the land out to other families in order to cover the costs. But without the dairy's income, Bob finally decided that he and Henry should farm the land themselves and make some money. "I can always remember my dad saying that if you ever got to where you were making $5,000 a year, that was a lot of money," said Henry. "That was big money."

In pursuit of that goal, Henry's dad purchased an expensive John Deere 1940 model B tractor. "Now, we did not have the money to buy the tractor, but Dad decided we needed it for this farm and he borrowed the money from Uncle John," said Henry. "The tractor cost $1,000 and he got it brand new. You could plow corn with it and it came with rubber tires. It was kind of like my tractor to some extent because when that tractor got delivered, I was big enough to run it. And I lived on that tractor all the time. You name it, I did it. I ran that John Deere tractor like I owned it."

Together, Bob and Henry toiled those 140 acres, working harder than Henry had ever worked in his life. "From 1940 on," Henry said, "we spent our time on what I call farming." Because Bob bought the tractor on borrowed money, they both felt even more pressure to put it to good use. Bob grew anxious as winter approached, and he knew he couldn't be outside on the new machine. That's when Bob went into town, bought some lumber, and built the innovative tractor cab on his new machine, complete with headlights that allowed him to work long days and into the night. "He was about 30 or 40 years ahead of his time," said Ernie, "because his idea was that in the spring, he could also run that tractor in the day and Henry and I could run it at night. And all of the rest of the farmers were making fun of him because he was working at night in the field. But they wouldn't think of laughing now; they all do it."

As a teenager, Henry was a fairly good size for his age. Before he even got his driver's license, he was running both the John Deere tractor as well as other equipment at his neighbors' farms during the era of the threshing ring—a ritual of rural America that involved neighbors coming together to rent a threshing machine to separate grain from the stalk. Henry was no stranger to threshing time. For years he had worked on various neighbors' farms during the complex threshing operations, at first

Robert W. Tippie on his farm, leaning against the John Deere tractor with the cab he built himself.

merely opening and shutting gates between pastures and nearby oat fields or leading a horse on the hay rope. And as he got older, Henry joined in some of the harder work, cutting and binding oats into bundles and stacking them into shocks. The threshing crews then collected the bundles, using hayracks pulled by teams of horses to bring them back to the grain separator being run by the large, heavy steam engine or tractor. Powered by burning coal or wood, the steam engine used water to provide the steam energy to separate the straw from the oats. Members of the threshing ring took the machine to each of their individual farms and worked at each farm until all of the threshing was completed.

Bob didn't have enough cropland on his farm to require a threshing machine. But given Henry's penchant for running farm equipment, neighbors were quick to hire the father-and-son team to help during threshing operations. "We did not have a lot of equipment, so we traded our manual labor," said Henry, who was only 13 when he first ran a tractor for the threshing ring operated by Curt Raue of Luzerne. Curt owned a threshing machine, and "he did custom work like shelling corn," Henry explained. The first tractor Henry drove for Curt—a 15-30 McCormick Deering on steel—was a cumbersome piece of equipment, and Henry developed a reputation for his mechanical skills. Recalled Henry, "The second or third year, Raue got a big Case tractor on rubber. And I got to where I thought I was pretty good. I could pull the separator to the yard or barn as good as anybody. I was pretty proud of myself. And I have to say that I think a lot of people thought I was pretty good at running equipment because sometimes the neighbors would get me or my dad to trade work; and I always wound up, in many cases, running the tractors and buck rakes on the hay they might have." Henry also remembers running a tractor for another neighbor named George Radeke. Henry would run the tractor as George ran the binder and Bob shocked the oats.

For a time, Henry and Bob worked side by side as a team, just as they once did with the milk route. But threshing for neighbors and grinding out a living on land that had never been farmed before was grueling work—never predictable, never secure, and never very successful. And when he looked back, Henry realized that the sale of the dairy represented more than a change in how the family made a

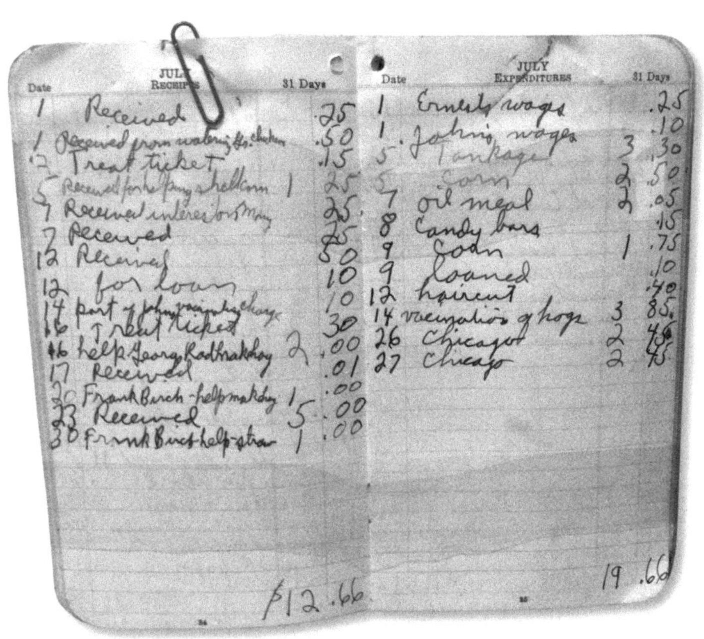

Date	JULY RECEIPTS	31 Days
1	Received	.25
1	Received from watering the chicken	.50
2	Treat ticket	.15
5	Received for helping shell corn	1.25
7	Received interest for May	.25
7	Received	.25
12	Received	.50
12	for loan	.10
14	part of [illegible] charge	.10
16	Treat ticket	.30
16	help George [illegible]	2.00
17	Received	.01
20	Frank Birch - help making hay	1.00
23	Received	5.00
30	Frank Birch help straw	1.00
		$12.66

Date	JULY EXPENDITURES	31 Days
1	Ernest's wages	.25
1	John's wages	.10
5	Tankage	3.30
5	Corn	2.50
7	oil meal	2.05
8	Candy bars	.15
9	Loan	1.75
9	Loaned	.10
12	haircut	.40
14	vaccination of hogs	3.85
26	Chicago	2.46
27	Chicago	2.45
		19.66

Early accounting books document Henry's earnings and expenses.

living. It also precipitated an unfortunate turning point for Henry's family, the beginning of what Henry always called "the family division." It started when Bob borrowed money from Uncle John to buy the tractor; that one monetary exchange somehow created an opening for John, who now thought he had the right to tell the Tippies how to run their lives. The fact that he didn't particularly like Bob, whom he never considered quite good enough for his sister, complicated an increasingly tense situation.

"You have to understand that Old World tradition, that when the father dies, the oldest son takes over the family and runs it." Ernie said, describing the situation in the Bokholt family after Amelia's father died. "And my Uncle John thought that it was his responsibility and his right to run the family. But my mother would never concede the fact that he was running the show."

The simmering disagreements between brother and husband created considerable tension at home. Sick of her brother's interference but unable to stop it, Amelia often lashed out at Bob for taking the loan in the first place. Bob, in turn, lashed out at Amelia for letting her brother think he could run all over his family. And in Henry's mind, Uncle John, being a bachelor, simply couldn't understand why Bob did not have the money for the tractor. After all, Henry said, "Uncle John lived with his mother all his life, and never spent anything. And that's a big difference. My dad and my mother, they had three kids and there were a lot of expenses."

As the oldest son in his family, Henry was particularly aware of the toll that the family division began to take on his parents' marriage. "My dad and my mom could get into terrible arguments," he said, recalling the time his dad threw his mother's shoes out the window, in the middle of winter. And though Henry often felt like he took his mother's side, he was a child in the middle of two adults, trying to get both parents to calm down while recognizing that they both had tempers. "She could get hot like him," he observed. Henry really couldn't tolerate when his mother would confide in him that her marriage was in trouble, and then ask for her son's advice. "She'd say, 'Maybe I ought to leave. What do you think?' And I'm thinking, 'I'm 14 years old!' But you know, she was just looking for someone to talk to."

As much as his parents had in common, everyone knew that Amelia and Bob had one seemingly insurmountable difference: Amelia dreamed of getting away from the farm, while Bob could not imagine another kind of life.

"I think his world—I wouldn't call it small—but I think it was much more confined," Henry would one day conclude. "He was basically always in farming and in the dairy business." Ernie agreed, saying, "He didn't have any vision, he just sort of existed from day to day. To Dad, if you were born and raised on a farm, it always looked like your future was to do the same thing, to stay in farming."

GROWING LIVESTOCK, TRACKING PENNIES

As Henry got older, he wasn't content to just grow a garden. Around the age of 14, to help make ends meet for his family and to put some money in his own pocket, Henry started to raise livestock—generally a sheep, a few lambs, and some hogs. He had been around the animals his entire life, so he already knew the basics when he decided to raise these animals, which included a few O.I.C. Swine, or Ohio Improved Chester hogs. They were shipped one at a time in a crate, and Henry and his dad would pick up the hogs at the freight depot.

Henry taking care of his livestock on the Tippie farm.

Like his many gardening ventures, Henry kept a detailed log of his livestock-raising enterprise, making notes about his purchases in a journal provided by the O.I.C. Swine Breeder's Association:

Name—Rosemary
Sex—Sow
Farrowed 4/24/41
Number in litter—11
Raised—boars = 5
sows=3.

In a separate spiral notebook, on a page Henry labeled "Hog Record and Remarks," Henry kept track of how much he paid for his animals and who bought, sold, and traded with him. The fickle, unpredictable side of farming and raising animals clearly comes through in these brief but detailed records.

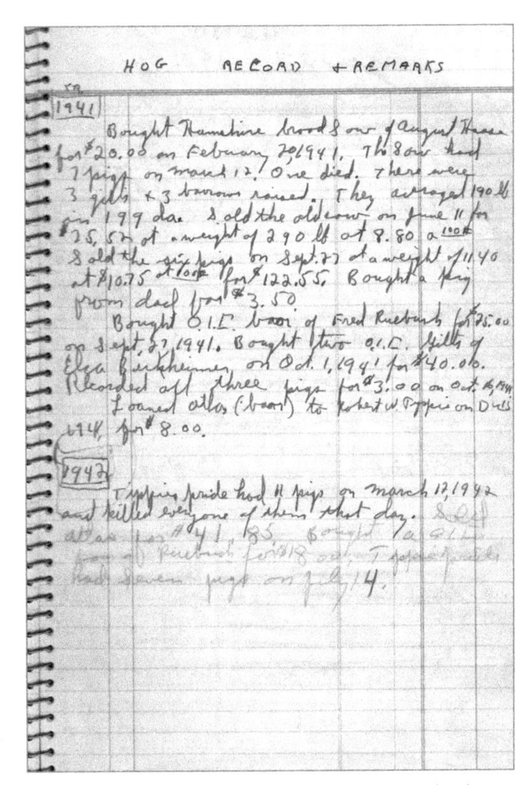

HOG RECORD + REMARKS

1941

Bought Hampshire brood sow of August [illegible] for $20.00 on February 7, 1941. The sow had 7 pigs on March 12. One died. There were 3 gilts + 3 barrows raised. They averaged 190 lb in 199 days. Sold the old sow on June 11 for $25.52 at a weight of 290 lb at 8.80 a 100#. Sold the six pigs on Sept. 27 at a weight of 1140 at $10.75 a 100# for $122.55. Bought a pig from dad for $3.50.

Bought O.I.C. boar of Fred Ruebush for $25.00 on Sept. 27, 1941. Bought two O.I.C. gilts of Elsa [illegible] on Oct. 1, 1941 for $40.00. Recorded all three pigs for $3.00 on Oct. [illegible], 1941.

Loaned Atlas (boar) to Robert W. Tippie on Dec. [illegible] 1941, for $8.00.

1942

Tippie's Pride had 11 pigs on March 17, 1942 and killed everyone of them that day. Sold Atlas for $41.85. Bought a O.I.C. [illegible] of Ruebush for $18.00. Tippie's Pride had seven pigs on July 14.

Henry's early accounting records for raising animals.

By raising hogs and other animals, Henry was able to help out when finances were especially fragile. "On occasion," he remembered, "something would need to be done and a couple of times I would have to go and sell a hog or a sheep to get $20 because Mom needed the money. And so she would say, 'We'll pay it back,' and they always did. But they just needed the money. And that was never a problem with me."

Henry kept what little money he had in an envelope taped to the back of his dresser. And as more money crossed his hands, Henry's system of accounting expanded. Starting on his 14th birthday, Henry kept a meticulous account of every money exchange in a "Farmer's Pocket Ledger." No expense, for work or pleasure, went unrecorded: *Oil meal $2.05; corn $2.50; pail $.30; candy bars $.15; haircut $.40; vaccinations of hogs $3.85; pencils $.05; Ernest's wages $.25; John's wages $.10. Money for Band Tickets $1.05; Music Contest $1.60.* Similarly, the record of Henry's receipts reveal the extent of jobs the 14-year-old did for money: *Trapping gophers $.05; watering chickens $.50; Helping shell corn $1.25; Help make hay $2.* And each month, Henry recorded the money his parents and sometimes his brothers paid him back for various loans: *Received from loans $5.00; Received from Ernest $.01; Received interest on money $.25; For loan $.10; Part of John's vaccination charge $.10.*

And in addition to his daily summaries, Henry created a separate sheet to reflect his assets and liabilities for each year: "January 1, 1942, Inventory: 'Real Estate' = Granary, $11.50; Self-feeder, $1.50; What others owe me—Robert W Tippie, $38.00; and so forth."

From his 14th birthday until the day he graduated from high school, Henry kept a daily record of every penny he earned, spent, or loaned to others. Taken together, these journals paint a fairly bleak picture for a young man growing up poor near Belle Plaine. But they also show how determination, stubbornness, and a desire to work could help keep that poverty at bay, giving a kid a chance to occasionally buy a candy bar, get a haircut, earn a few extra dollars raising hogs, loan his struggling parents $20, and still save enough money to buy a car when he turned 16.

It's interesting to try to imagine what drove this teenager named Henry to sit down at the end of every day—he never missed a single day—and accurately account for his money while dealing squarely with the economic reality of how little he had. Did this activity give Henry a sense of control and order to the bleakness that defined his life? Was it an escape from his parents' constant and escalating bickering? Was it possible that he actually enjoyed his crude bookkeeping tasks, that he relished sitting down and creating columns of numbers on page after page of notebook paper, delighting in the black-and-white information those numbers shouted back at him? The answer to each of these questions is probably yes. Because after all, Henry knew long before he recorded his numbers that the columns weren't going to add up to be *great*, but at least they represented something *real*. "Just the facts," he always said. "Just give me the facts."

But what no one could possibly imagine in the 1940s was that Henry—with his journals and his columns of numbers and his obsessive desire to keep track of every penny—had started to lay the groundwork for what would one day be an unbelievably successful life. Clearly predisposed to finding numbers and financial figures fascinating, Henry actually had a remarkable gift and a burgeoning business talent. And one day, this lonely farm boy's quirky habits and unique talents would translate into the very skills he needed to be a successful entrepreneur, one who just happened to start out growing vegetables and raising hogs on a farm in Iowa.

The Buckeye School.

CHAPTER THREE

EDUCATION

ONE MORNING IN SEPTEMBER 1932, when Henry was five and a half years old, he finished his morning dairy chores and milk route, waited patiently as his mother handed him his lunch pail and checked to make sure he had on clean overalls, and then proceeded to walk about a mile east from the farm on the road toward Luzerne. He eventually turned right off the main road onto a dirt lane that led to a white clapboard building with a stubby bell tower, standing right in the middle of a field between the road and the railroad tracks.

"Welcome to Buckeye School, Henry," a teacher named Esther Palmer would've said to her new first-grade student. And so began Henry's formal education, in the exact same one-room country schoolhouse that his father attended when he was a boy, over 25 years earlier. Henry soon found the initials that Bob Tippie once carved on the woodshed behind the school, which still provided education in grades 1 through 8 for children who lived in the country.

An average of 20 students, ranging from 6 to 13 years old, entered the rectangular building every day through a door on the north side of the schoolhouse. A partial wall between the door and the main room helped shelter the students and teacher from the blasts of Iowa's cold winter air, and gave them room to hang their coats and hats. The classroom occupied the rest of the room. Students sat together by grade level in five or six parallel rows of wooden desks; the younger students sat toward the left side of the room, with the older ones sitting at the far right. There were only one or two students in some grades, but Henry's class had five. A recitation bench stood at the far end, just in front of the teacher's desk. A small library with books and shelves occupied the southeast corner of the room, and a picture of George Washington hung on the wall.

Buckeye School had no electricity or plumbing, and natural sunlight from the windows provided the only lighting in the room. There were two outdoor privies—one for boys and one for girls. Since there was no well at the school, students carried a bucket filled with water to school every day from a quarter mile away, supporting the weight of the full bucket by sliding a stick under the handle of the water pail. Each student always brought a cup to drink water from the pail, which sat in the northeastern corner of the room. During the cold winter months, a thin layer of ice formed on the top of the water because the pail sat in a far corner, away from the warmth of the big black stove positioned in the middle of the room to heat the school. There was a sparse playground outside, and the woodshed sat right behind the school building. Every year farmers throughout the area would pitch in to fill it with wood. As Henry recalled, "When the farmers cut any wood in the wintertime, and most farmers did, they would always bring some of the wood over to the schoolhouse and throw it into the woodshed. If anybody shelled corn, they would maybe bring some corncobs and throw those in there, too. As a consequence there wasn't too much coal, because coal had to be bought. So most of the time the stove was run on the cobs to get it going and then wood."

Buckeye was typical of the numerous one-room schools that existed in the Iowa countryside for the express purpose of educating the state's rural population. These schools flourished in the late 1800s until they started to decline after World War II, amid concerns from Iowa's Department of Public Instruction that these one-room rural schools were somehow lacking. But Henry and many others who attended these schools held strongly to the view that their education in these little rooms far surpassed that of town schools, and they stayed loyal to the schools and their educational foundations their entire lives.

Henry and his parents had actually visited the Buckeye School the previous spring. Since Henry wasn't used to being around children his own age, Bob and Amelia, showing an uncharacteristically protective and insightful concern for their oldest son, thought it would be a good idea for him to visit Buckeye and see what it was like. "They took me down there and left me a half a day or all day to get acquainted with the school," remembers Henry. "I didn't really have anyone I associated with—I was just kind of by myself—so one of the reasons they took me down there was to at least get me exposed to being with other kids my age. I don't remember that being any big deal other than that's what took place."

By all accounts, Henry did just fine when he started first grade. Wearing his long-sleeved white shirt and clean bib overalls, his light brown hair carefully parted and combed to the right, Henry looked exactly like the other nine boys in the school when he posed for a picture during his first year, standing in the first row with the other boys under the big oak tree near the school. Though other students thought of Henry as their friend, he didn't necessarily try to have a "best" friend and remained something of a quiet, content loner. It helped that Mrs. Palmer, the only teacher at the school, was forever one of Henry's favorite teachers. Married to a local machinist named Ralph Palmer, Esther Palmer had no children of her own. But this tall, elegant teacher expertly oversaw a classroom of students ranging from ages 5 to 13.

Henry (front row, third from left) and other Buckeye School students.

"She was a really good teacher," says Henry, who stayed in contact with Mrs. Palmer for as long as she lived. "She had a great interest in each student. I always felt that all of the students enjoyed going to school with Mrs. Palmer as their teacher. She always called me her 'little man.' Where she came up with that, I don't know. But I was her 'little man.'"

Henry's school day started around 8 a.m., a start signaled when Mrs. Palmer reached for the long, sturdy rope to ring the school bell and raised the flag on the flagpole in the yard. Once inside, each student stood and recited the Pledge of Allegiance. Though country schools had more leeway in devising their day's schedule than town schools, teachers were required to cover certain subjects and record each student's attendance and progress. In a large ledger, Mrs. Palmer kept a detailed account of her school's daily proceedings:

Forenoon:

Opening Exercises
Music, Stories, Current Events
Numbers
Arithmetic
Spelling

Recess

Penmanship
Reading
Language

Lunch (every student brought a lunch)

Afternoon:

Phonics, Geography
History or Civics
Reading
Physical Training

Recess

Reading
Hygiene

Because Mrs. Palmer taught all grades simultaneously, different grade levels would take turns at the front of the room on the recitation bench, reciting their lessons for the day. The other students in the room were supposed to be involved with their own studies during recitation, and Henry claims that he didn't pay any attention to the other students. But even though Henry wasn't consciously listening to the older classmates recite the lessons he had yet to learn, he might have picked up on some of the information. At Buckeye, some of the students were so advanced that they were allowed to take two grades at once, a situation that Henry said was not uncommon.

There was no homework in those days. Farm kids like Henry were expected to do much-needed chores in the evening. When school was dismissed around 3:15 in the afternoon, the students left their schoolbooks—reading, spelling, music, and numbers books like the orange-colored *Ideal Speller* and the lime-green *Essentials of English*, which cost a dime or twenty-five cents each—in the classroom overnight, which helped make the walk to and from school a little easier. Generally, all of the students who attended Buckeye walked to school, though Henry remembers one boy who used to arrive occasionally by horseback and would simply tie his horse to the fencepost during the school day.

At least once a year, the county superintendent would drop in for a visit, an occasion Henry never forgot: "She came from the county seat of Vinton, and we always knew when she was going to come. We always got ready, and we knew that it was a very important day. She had a great big car, I remember. And she would come and visit with the teacher and look everything over." Henry's former classmate, Gladys Werner, also remembered these visits. "She was an old maid and she would come in very quiet and we never heard her open the door," said Gladys. "And you'd sit down and look around and there she was."

LEARNING TO READ, EXPLORING THE WORLD

Starting his education in the little country school, Henry remembers the moment he put all the words together and grasped the process of reading. For a child who spent much of his time alone, his newfound skill must have been like finding a longed-for friend. He started with a series of reading textbooks like *The New Path to Reading*, books One, Two and Three, with their whimsical, light-blue covers depicting happy children playing games with animals. Henry quickly expanded his reading at home, collecting the popular 1930s *Billy Whiskers* children's book series by Frances Trego Montgomery about a "frolicsome, adventuresome" goat that the author promised "will make all the boys and girls chuckle." No doubt, the series combined Henry's love of animals with reading, and he happily followed Billy Whiskers as a stowaway, on a treasure hunt, and at the circus. As he grew older, Henry read his father's collection of Horatio Alger stories, absorbing the messages of determination, hard work, honesty, and the promise of the American Dream in these popular turn-of-the-century novels. If anything, the solitude of farm life, his lack of close friends, and his ability to dream about life beyond his immediate surroundings helped to make young Henry a fan of reading. "I didn't have a lot of friendships so I indulged myself, at least in my early years, in reading," Henry said. He eventually subscribed to some of the boys' magazines that were in vogue, outdoor publications like *Open Road for Boys* and *American Boy*, and later *Sporting News*, when he became fascinated with baseball.

"I would read these cover to cover," Henry recalls. "I have always been a great reader, and I think back then I was a fairly good student. Because it seemed to me like we were far ahead in country school. I was kind of quiet and the type of student who would like to be in the back row and hope nobody called on me."

Em Neibes, an early schoolmate who was two grades ahead of Henry at Buckeye, confirmed that Henry "was pretty quiet. Early on he was a real good kid. He never got into trouble. He was ambitious and worked hard, so I always felt good about Henry. I knew Henry well because his father used to buy milk from my father on our farm when they would run out."

A quick glance at Henry's report cards in grades 1 through 3 reveals that he was a very dedicated young student, continuously earning grades in the mid- to high 90s that were considered "excellent" and "good" according to the grading scale. And in the margins of his second-grade report card, Mrs. Palmer wrote that Henry "does very good work in every subject."

Henry does recall having trouble mastering the ornate style of penmanship called the Palmer Method that teachers taught to students in his day. "I have some correspondence that my Grandpa Tippie wrote to his eventual bride-to-be, my grandmother, and his handwriting is beautiful, just absolutely beautiful," said Henry. "But I never did learn to write very well, so my handwriting is poor. But other than that I think I was a fairly good student."

Buckeye was open from September through May, no matter the weather, and that included Iowa's brutal winters, when temperatures would sometimes drop to 10 to 20 degrees below zero and the snow fell for days on end. "That school ran every day," Henry says. "I have seen the

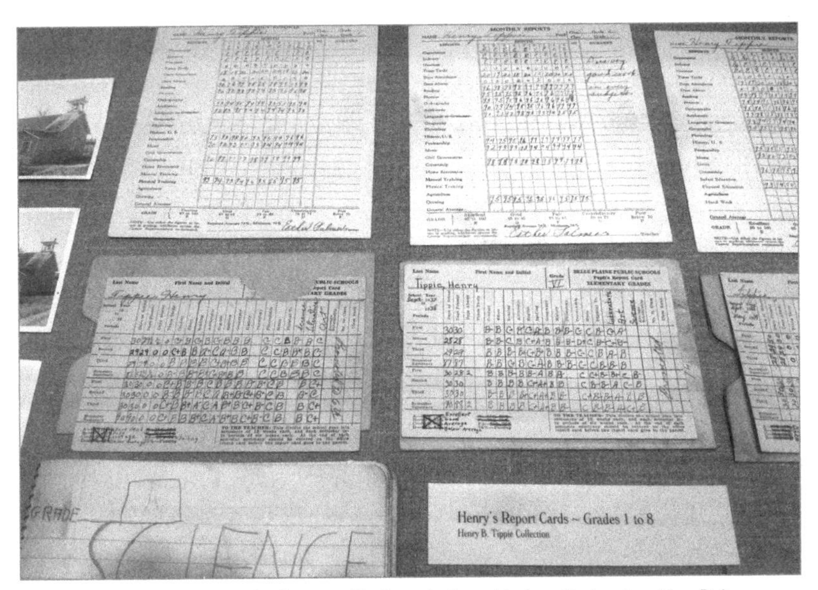

Henry's early report cards show excellent marks from his favorite teacher, Mrs. Palmer.

weather so bad that the roads are totally shut down, and there's no traffic, but country school was open because most people walked." Trudging to school through the snow, wearing a big sheep-lined coat and four-buckle boots, Henry remembers stopping at his great uncle Carlos's house, about a quarter of a mile on the way to Buckeye, just to try to warm up. On the long walk to school, "The snow was just falling off of me all over the place. You couldn't see 200 feet maybe. And nobody thought anything about this. We just walked." When Henry finally reached the school, the stove in the little classroom provided warmth for those sitting around it, but the wooden walls had no insulation and the cold would creep in. The students not lucky enough to sit by the hot stove wore their heavy coats throughout the school day.

In every season, Henry and his fellow classmates enjoyed recess, consisting of a half-hour break outdoors in the mornings and afternoons to make sure everyone got some fresh air. Since Buckeye was a small school, there were never enough students to form teams and play sports with other schools. But Henry recalled that Mrs. Palmer got involved during recess to make sure there was fair play among all the children. In the spring Mrs. Palmer would sometimes take the students on a half-day picnic, where the boys would stage their annual wrestling matches. But more often than not, the students relied on their natural surroundings and imagination for play. Henry recalls that he "fell in the mud a couple of times and got all muddy. Another time I fell and got a great big bump on my head. There were some trees on the west side of the schoolhouse with some limbs that had fallen, and I can remember running around with one of these limbs in the shape of a triangle, and I thought I had a vehicle or airplane or something. I was running around making the sound and guiding it." The schoolyard could also provide its own surprises. During one recess, Henry was the first pupil out the door, and he ran out and sat on the ground in front of the woodshed. The other students soon followed but they froze, midstride, as they approached Henry: a bull snake, about five feet long, sat coiled up right at Henry's back. "I was pretty traumatized," said Henry, when he became aware of what was going on. "And then of course they got me away from the snake and a boy killed it, cut his tail off, and put it in his lunch pail."

Henry's long walks to and from school had their own share of surprises—some better than others. One morning before school, Henry wandered away from his traditional route with his friend Em Neibes to check Em's trap lines. Em had established the lines to catch game for food, but on this particular day, the boys found a skunk in the trap line. Em immediately backed away, but not Henry. "I was not fast enough or smart enough," Henry said, "to stay away from the skunk. So you want to talk about somebody getting all smelled up!" As soon as Henry arrived at the country school, covered in the nasty skunk odor, Mrs. Palmer sent him home. "And when I got home, Mom was angry. I had to change clothes, and about the only way you could get the smell off your clothes was to dig a hole in the ground and bury them for a while. Of course I lost half a morning with all this taking place."

MORE THAN A SCHOOL

For the rural community between Belle Plaine and Luzerne, Buckeye was more than a school. It was the cornerstone of their community, a central meeting and polling place. Gladys Werner, a lifelong friend of Henry's who also attended Buckeye, always had a crystal-clear memory of the election box, "a huge gray box, and every election they would open it up and the kids would get to vote, just for fun." Around Christmas, everybody from the school district would gather at Buckeye for a holiday get-together, recalled Henry. People brought kerosene lanterns to hang on hooks along the wall to light the room, and someone created a makeshift stage with some sheets to create a stage curtain for the annual Christmas program performed by the students. "And after the program was over, it was kind of a community affair," said Henry. "The neighbors brought sandwiches and the students got hard candies and Santa Claus always came to visit the kids. He would come in the door unexpectedly, doing the 'ho-ho-ho,' wearing a suit and so forth. I found out later, much later, that my dad was a Santa Claus one year because I found the Santa Claus suit buried in the house under some things. So I suspected that he was a Santa Claus. I think that's a good guess."

Even when the adults and students weren't gathered at the school, the extended Buckeye community provided a valuable social network for farming families with children. A group of these families called the "Friendly Neighbors" got together frequently to discuss politics, the school district, farming woes, and anything else deemed newsworthy in the community. Recalled Henry,

> This takes place back in the early school days in the fall, but mainly the wintertime. And neighbors would gather up at someone's home, and what they all discussed, I'm not sure because the kids, of course, were outside, or if it was bad weather we'd play upstairs if there was an upstairs. So I well remember several places around there, and there'd be several kids gathered up and we'd play hide-and-seek under the moonlight. Everybody brought food so there'd be sandwiches to eat and cookies and coffee or juice or milk, and then everybody went home. Of course, some of the people would bring lanterns because, for the most part, nobody had any electricity as far as I can recall.

Throughout Henry's childhood, there was a continuous debate over whether one-room country schools like Buckeye should be closed and the students consolidated at the various town schools. The rural population felt strongly that the country school was vital to their community, and they opposed consolidation. Recalled Ernie, "The farmers didn't want to consolidate. They felt it was going to be too expensive and that maybe they would lose part of their identity. Country schools were far more affordable than town schools. The increase in school tax that consolidation would bring was another cost that most farmers couldn't bear."

HENRY LEAVES BUCKEYE

The Buckeye School remained open for students until 1955. And though Henry said he never wanted to leave Buckeye, the Tippie family moved Henry to the town school in Belle Plaine in the fall of 1935 to start the fourth grade. According to both Henry and Ernie, their parents left Buckeye because they had "a disagreement over a change in teachers" when Henry was ready to enter the fourth grade, and their stubborn pride prevented them from sending Henry back. And because the family's daily dairy route already took Henry into town every morning, it seemed to make sense for the children to attend school there.

But there were other factors at play. Amelia never denied that she dreamed of a better life for her sons, one that didn't include the constant demands of farming and the arduous conditions of country living. In her mind, a better life with better opportunities started with a good education, and she was convinced that her sons would get a better education in town. Because the Tippies lived outside the Belle Plaine town limits, the family had to actually pay to send their sons to school in town, a cost that the Tippies couldn't easily afford but somehow managed. Ernie remembered his mother working extra jobs to find the additional cash for schooling, recalling that "she detassled corn to make enough money to send us to town school."

Amelia and Bob's financial sacrifice for their sons' education was obviously considerable. And in addition to the added cost of schooling, the switch to town school required additional money to cover the cost of new clothes. Amelia insisted that her boys not go to town school dressed like farmers. "Her scruples," Ernie said, "were that she didn't allow any of her children to go to school in Levi's. We always had to wear corduroys, and we would go to Cedar Rapids every year a month before school started and buy some new cords. She didn't believe in going to school dressed like a farmer or somebody who worked for day wages. You had to be dressed up."

Henry wasn't particularly happy with his parents' decision—academically or socially. He always argued that he got a superior education at Buckeye under Mrs. Palmer, and he maintained that his fourth-grade education in town school seemed like a mere repeat of third grade at

The Tippie brothers dressed in their Sunday best for church, and traded their everyday overalls for better clothes when they switched to town school.

Buckeye. Too, changing schools increased Henry's sense of being alone. "There was a larger group of students" at the town school, he recalled, "most of whom I did not know."

Due to a shortage of classrooms when he started in town, Henry's fourth-grade class actually met in the two-story brick Belle Plaine High School building, located a few blocks from downtown Belle Plaine in a residential section on the north side of town. The school was only about a block from where Henry's Grandmother Bokholt lived. Each morning, after completing their dairy route, Bob dropped Henry off at Grandma Bokholt's red clapboard house, where she lived with Henry's Uncle John and Uncle Louie. Henry then walked to school, but returned to the house every day around noon to eat lunch with his relatives, enjoying tasty, filling German food like wieners, mashed potatoes, and rice pudding with raisins. While eating, his relatives always spoke their native German. "Maybe they wanted to say things in front of me that they didn't want me to understand," he reasoned. Henry often stayed at the house after school until Bob picked him up, occasionally spending the night if he had a school activity. But sometimes, particularly on a Friday ahead of a long weekend, Henry walked home alone.

In the fall of 1936, when Ernie was five years old, Ernie's parents sent him to town school, too, and he started first grade at Belle Plaine Elementary. That same year, Henry moved to Whittier Middle School for fifth and sixth grades. Here, it appears that Henry began to find his social footing. In an essay written when he was 13 years old, Henry reminisced about his time at Whittier, recalling that "many happy times were spent there. We would play ball, marbles, and coast on our sleds in the wintertime." But overall, Henry remembers his elementary and middle school years at town school as pretty unremarkable. "Fifth and sixth grade—I don't remember anything particular or spectacular either," he said. And in fact, Henry's report cards from his two years at Whittier show a dramatic change from the straight-A student he had been at Buckeye, reflecting a student who was perhaps beginning to lose interest in school or one who no longer wanted to perform for a favorite teacher. His fifth-year grades ranged from As to Cs, with a C-plus in conduct and a B for effort; he did his best work in math, geography, spelling, and history (a mix of As and

Bs) but struggled in English and music (all Cs). His sixth-grade report card told a similar story: Henry ended the school year with two C-pluses, nine Bs or B-minuses, one A-minus, and one A-plus in Spelling. A telltale English assignment in sixth grade revealed that Henry, ever nostalgic for his old one-room schoolhouse, still deeply missed Buckeye. Consider this poem Henry wrote, called "Country School":

When school is out,
And we say goodbye
To the old schoolhouse,
I linger along my homeward way,
And wonder if the old schoolhouse
Is saying goodbye to me.

JUNIOR HIGH AND HIGH SCHOOL

For Henry, seventh and eighth grades were considered junior high, and these classes were held back at Belle Plaine High School, where Henry remained through the 12th grade. His junior high school years were particularly difficult for Henry, as his family struggled to transition from dairy farming to farming their own land from 1938 to 1940. Every spare moment, Henry worked with his father on the farm, struggling to clear land and plant crops on the family's farmland while growing hogs on the side and sometimes earning extra money thrashing grain for others.

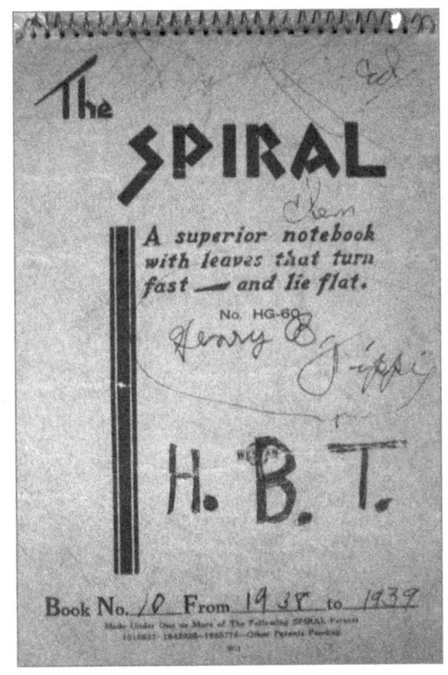

Henry's spiral notebook from 7th grade.

By the time he entered high school in the fall of 1940, Henry's classmates described him as a quiet, serious teenager. He was the student who sheepishly sat in the back of the classroom, hoping not to be noticed, praying the teacher wouldn't call on him, and adopting the unassuming, muted quality of an outsider looking in. As Henry conceded, "I wasn't running any popularity contests." Gladys, a former Buckeye classmate who also attended town school, remained close friends with Henry but had to admit he was as quiet as ever. "You didn't even know he was around. Even in high school," she said. "He was very nice and very considerate. It just seems like his nose was always in a book." Some took Henry's quietness as a sign of his maturity. "He always seemed to be thinking," said Betty Kent, a former classmate and longtime friend. "Do you ever notice when you talk to him, he is thinking? You can just tell that he is."

Reserved as he may have been, Henry was not the student who buried his head in books and studied constantly for tests. Quite the opposite. Henry struggled through high school, never aspiring to be named on the honor rolls or recognized for academic achievement. As Ernie once said, "Henry went to school to get out of school." Henry described his high school career as "unspectacular" and recalls specific likes and dislikes when it came to curriculum choices. He took business mathematics and thought it was a simple course. He hated geometry, "and I never took 'Future

Belle Plaine High School.

Farmers' or anything like that because I didn't think that a guy living on a farm needed it and thought it was too highbrow for me." Henry did not take any bookkeeping courses, even though they were offered. He didn't care too much for science and, least of all, literature. "I didn't like literature, even though I was a great reader. You know, too much of that stuff gets into interpretation. I read words for what they are, and not for some other type of meaning. That's not my cup of tea. You know, I realize a lot of this is great literature that people wrote hundreds of years ago, but I am a more practical thinker." Henry did spend a lot of time in the school's library, arguing that at one time "my name was probably on more of those checkout cards than anybody else." Henry once discovered a book about engineering and, for a short time, considered working in that field. "I read all kinds of engineering books, and it looked interesting and I would drift off on this or that. I certainly never thought about getting into what I eventually got into. In high school, I just didn't have a clue."

When it came to grades, "Let's just say it was a mixed bag," Henry recalled. "I liked some of the courses and others I did not. You know, I could have a semester where I might have an A in one course and an F or D in something else. I mean, I am all over the lot. I would get called in on occasion to the principal's office and the conversation would go something like, 'Well, you can do better, you have the ability to do better,' and this and that. And so I might strain for a good two or three weeks, and then I'm back to where I was. I think at times I was a good student, but other times, I was a failed student. And I didn't have a lot of guidance at home, either."

A quick glance at Henry's report cards confirms his memories. Henry ended his sophomore year of high school with a C in American history; a D-plus in literature; a B-plus in typing; a B in basic math (which he switched to after getting a D-minus the previous semester in advanced algebra). For a while, it looked like "the longer I was in school, the lower the grades got," Henry once said, with a slight grin crossing his face. But by his senior year, he managed to earn all B-pluses, Bs, and B-minuses in subjects ranging from physics to sociology to commercial law, though he got a C in economics.

As a student, Henry could also be downright mischievous, especially if he didn't respect the teacher. "We did have physics my senior year, and I thought that course was a total disaster. I used to cause problems in there. When I came in the room, if there was going to be an experiment or something, I would put a penny in the electrical slots so when the teacher turned it on, it would blow out, or if there was a gas jet, it may have been accidentally turned at a low level. I never did get caught."

Throughout high school, Henry wanted to do as little as possible academically and enjoy himself as much as possible in order to still graduate. "My feeling used to be, 'Well, if I could just get through high school, I couldn't care less,'" said Henry. "At that time, I guess my whole life was agriculture. A life of farming was becoming a more certain future. But I have to say to start with, I was uncertain where I was going."

And there was definitely a part of Henry that felt—correctly or incorrectly—that the odds of accomplishing anything in high school were stacked against him. When Henry started his freshman year at Belle Plaine High School, there were about 100 students in his class; by the time he graduated, there were only about 53. "Some of them disappeared into the military service, others moved away for plant jobs, and of course others just plain dropped out," Henry explained. And though virtually everyone in Belle Plaine shared the same economic fate, there was still an "upper class" in Henry's high school, and he wasn't in it. "Let's put it this way," Henry explained. "Every class has some people that are more popular than others, and in every class there are certainly some that have more economic affluence than others."

Brother Ernie put it less diplomatically. "The town people were the in-crowd, so to speak, and that's the reason that Henry indicates that he wasn't accepted. Being from the farm, he wasn't a part of that crowd. When I was in high school, it was the same way. You were somebody else, you were an outcast. A lot of farm kids were."

Asked to recall his high school days, Henry's memories provided a clear picture of what being a social outcast looked like in a rural community in the early 1940s:

> I don't think it's intentional, I think it's just the way it happens. For instance, when you're a freshman and sophomore, they would always invite a certain group each year to perform or help out for

junior-senior banquet. I never did get asked. Then they'd have these various clubs, and I was never invited to any of those, with the exception of the Hobby Club, but it was a small club. Then they would have some of these other things for young people, like young people's groups that are not necessarily connected with the high school, and I have a perfect record of never being invited to any. Totally zero. They would have country club functions sometimes for young people and I have a perfect record of never being invited to those, either. In fact, I think I have only been to the country club in Belle Plaine twice in my entire life.

Ernie believed that Henry's rejection by the high school in-crowd was like a spur under the proverbial saddle for his brother. "Oh, I think that has probably driven him more than anything else." Ernie said. "The fact that back in those days, when we lived on the farm, he didn't feel like he was accepted by the people in town and he had to prove himself."

Over time, Henry figured out a way to put his high school experience into perspective. "In retrospect, I think they did me a favor," he said. "You can look at these things in a lot of ways. You can look at them in terms of letting them get you down, or you can go the other way and say, 'I'm going to see how much I can do without ya!' And I think I wound up in the latter camp."

Henry also argued that his high school experience did him another favor. Taking the pain he experienced as a teenager, Henry vowed to never look down on others because of their financial standing, and to never allow himself to feel superior because he might have more money in his pocket than the next person. "One thing I got out of that experience," Henry said, "is to try to be nice to everybody. Because you don't ever know about what the future may hold."

Henry in full band uniform with his clarinet.

CHAPTER FOUR

A YOUNG BOY GROWS UP

GROWING UP IN BELLE PLAINE, there were many defining moments in Henry's life: the day his mom saved the farm because she hadn't gone to the bank; the morning he survived falling down a dark well; afternoons spent riding with his dad on a tractor, and the day he first drove one by himself; the day he started school at Buckeye; and the afternoon the barn burned to the ground.

But perhaps nothing compared to the evening of June 22, 1938, when Henry heard a radio broadcast for the first time in his life. And it wasn't just any broadcast—it was a historic radio moment, when an estimated 70 million people around the country, believed to the largest radio audience in history, listened as American heavyweight champion Joe Louis and German boxer Max Schmeling battled for the 1938 heavyweight championship.

The Tippies didn't even own a radio, so Henry and his dad walked down the hill to Uncle Carlos's Wayfarer's Cottage Camp in order to listen to the broadcast at Uncle Carlos's home. The camp, spread out along three acres of land at the intersection of Luzerne Road and Lincoln Highway, consisted of nine single and two double cottages, tucked in behind a gas station that faced the highway. From 1924 to 1942, Carlos and his wife Leona Tippie built the cottages and the gas station for the vacationers, campers, and salesmen who traveled along the historic highway. Henry was excited when he found out they had purchased a radio, and delighted when they invited Henry and his dad to listen to the fight.

From the moment they walked into Uncle Carlos's house that night, Henry's life was transformed. "I was dumbfounded," Henry vividly recalled about that evening in June 1938. "And I could always remember everything about that night."

Arthur Donovan was the referee. NBC radio announcer Clem McCarthy called the blow-by-blow action. As Henry leaned in and listened intently, Louis went on the attack from the opening bell. . . . Schmeling met Louis in the center of the ring and then quickly retreated after feeling the power of the champion. . . . Barely two minutes into the fight, Announcer Clem McCarthy was nearly breathless, describing the unbelievable scene in front of him. . . . *Schmeling is down. Schmeling is down. The count is four. It's . . . and he's up. And Louis right and left to the head. A left to the jaw. A right to the head. Arthur Donovan is watching carefully. Louis measures him. Right to the body. A left hook to the jaw. And Schmeling is down. The count is five. Five, six, seven, eight—the men are in the ring! The fight is over! On a technical knockout! Max Schmeling is beaten in one round. The first time that a world heavyweight championship is ever seen ends in one round, in less than a round!*

The fight billed as the "Fight of the Century" was over in two minutes and four seconds. "I was mesmerized," said Henry. "These names come to me like yesterday. I really thought this was something."

The Tippie family soon purchased its own radio—an Atwater Kent broadcast receiver, made in Philadelphia, Pennsylvania, with a $30 price tag when new. The mahogany brown, cathedral-style wooden radio sat upright on a table, featuring delicate fretwork in three places on the front grille, three wooden dials to control volume and tuning, and a nickel-plated chassis. The radio instantly became a welcome presence in Henry's home, and it would be difficult to overstate how important this electronic device would be to Henry. For the first time in his life, Henry's world began to expand, exposing the soon-to-be teenager to experiences and resources previously thought to be unreachable from the Iowa prairie. Henry routinely huddled close to the radio to make sure he heard every sound that came out. Without a doubt, the radio put him in contact with two new worlds that would become lifelong passions: baseball and music.

As a young boy, the quiet and unassuming Henry nonetheless developed a competitive spirit. It played out when he engaged in shooting marbles or playing Chinese checkers with friends, or even when he went sledding down his favorite hill in town, 11th Avenue, a long street with a steep incline that was usually blocked off by the city in the winter. Henry learned early on that if you dumped a few pails of water down the center of the hill, the snow would ice over and "your sled would go faster." In fact, the kids from Henry's fourth-grade town school class would sled down the hill so fast that the city officials became afraid they would run straight into Lincoln Highway, which intersected at the bottom of 11th Avenue. "So they put cinders down there at the bottom of the street to stop us from running onto the highway."

But when it came to a team sport like baseball, Henry's competitive edge reached a new level. "I guess you could say that I was kind of a fanatic," he said. Henry routinely clipped the sports section out of the newspaper when he stayed over at his Grandma Bokholt's house and read the *Cedar Rapids Gazette*. He pasted the articles in a scrapbook, noting that "it was something to keep me occupied." His favorite teams were the Chicago Cubs, the New York Giants, and the Detroit Tigers. When the radio entered his life, Henry quickly tuned in to live broadcasts of the games with his favorite teams. "You could get WGN live from Chicago. And I probably heard more on Sunday than any other time." One of the highlights of his youth—and the only time he left Iowa while growing up, other than his family's vacation to Arkansas—was when he took the train to Chicago with his Uncle John in the summer of 1941 to watch his first-ever professional baseball game with two of his favorite teams, the Giants and the Cubs. Henry was 14 years old, and the trip took place on Saturday, July 26, and Sunday, July 27. Henry's meticulous records of receipts and expenditures in his "Farmer's Pocket Ledger" for July 1941 show that he paid $2.45 for his train ticket to Chicago on July 26, and $2.45 for a ticket back home the next day. It appears that Uncle John picked up the tab for the hotel, or his nephew would have surely recorded the cost. Just thinking about the trip makes Henry smile.

"We were gone maybe two days. We went to Wrigley Field to see the New York Giants play the Chicago Cubs. We stayed at the Atlantic Hotel. I think it had a restaurant there called the Three Deuces. And we went out to the Arlington Racetrack. We rode the train, and I don't think I had ever been on a train before. We left at like three or four in the morning from the Belle Plaine Station and the train ticket was about $2.50 and the hotel about $3. I still have the program from the baseball game at home." Part of a three-game home series for the Cubs, the Cubs lost to the Giants 5-2 on Friday, but Henry and Uncle John and 6,942 other baseball fans sat in the stands at Wrigley Field on Saturday and watched the Cubs beat the Giants 5-3. The Sunday game went to the Cubs, too, by a score of 9-2.

In addition to fueling Henry's penchant for keeping statistics, baseball helped introduce Henry to his first real friend: Richard "Flea" Wright. Flea was a year ahead of Henry in school, and they were polar opposites when it came to personalities: Henry was reserved and introverted, while Flea was outgoing, described by mutual friends as "a character" who cared enough about academic grades to later be named salutatorian of his class. "We knew each other," Henry says, "because his dad and my Uncle John were good friends, and when I was a young kid we would

The BPHS baseball team, with Henry in the middle of the back row.

go down to Cedar Rapids on a Saturday night and see baseball games. Flea's dad was an auto salesman, and we would ride the 30 miles to Cedar Rapids in a car with them."

Henry, striking a batter's pose.

In high school, Henry no longer just watched and listened to the games. He joined the Belle Plaine High School baseball team and played his first ever team sport. Though he didn't get to play during his freshman year, the baseball team chose Henry to be their team manager, and he would field, throw, and bat with the team during practice. For the next three straight years, from his sophomore year until he graduated, Henry secured a position on the team, playing on a field his own father helped build with his 1940 John Deere tractor. Bob Tippie, it turns out, never begrudged the time his son took away from the farm to be on the team; instead, he was proud of him, and watched his son play every chance he got.

"I was a fairly good hitter," Henry says, who batted left and threw right. "I generally batted the first three spots, but I would say that my arm would be a weak arm. As a consequence, I generally played right field or second base." Henry always wore his Carl Hubbell Championship Model Fielder's Glove, a tribute to one of Henry's all-time favorite pitchers, who played for the New York Giants from 1928 to 1943. Fellow teammate and friend Mike Bevins remembered Henry as a player who "was a hustler."

"Just like you'd expect Henry to be, he didn't make many bad moves," said Mike. "He thought everything through, and then it got to be mechanical and he kept the chatter up. He was into the game."

The Belle Plaine team won the sectional baseball tournament in 1943, defeating Keystone by a score of 16-4. Henry "got three hits in four times at bat," the newspaper account of the game reported, and Henry and his teammates posed for a picture after the winning game.

True to his record-keeping habits, Henry documented every game he played, recording the number of innings, his times-at-bat, and his batting average. He saved every baseball record book he kept, and he also refused to throw out his favorite baseball cleats and his beloved fielder's glove (along with the orange and blue box the glove came in). Henry won a varsity letter and an Athlete Council Certificate every year for the three straight years in high school that he was on the team. And until he graduated, he proudly wore the purple "B-P" varsity letters his mother stitched in place on the left side of his golden yellow wool letter sweater, the one with the brown leather elbow patches.

BIG BAND MUSIC AND HENRY

If Henry loved anything more than baseball, it was music—an unexpected gift delivered to him, much like baseball, through the advent of radio. Courtesy of his family's Atwater Kent console, in the latter half of the 1930s Henry began listening to AM radio during the golden age of jazz and blues, the so-called Swing Era when Big Bands like Benny Goodman, Artie Shaw, Tommy Dorsey, and Glenn Miller reigned and radio was king. From his house, Henry listened to performances called "live remotes"—Big Band musical performances that were broadcast live from orchestra halls, dance halls, and recording studios all over the country. The magical sounds of these orchestras—rich with the velvety tones of saxophones, trumpets, trombones, clarinets, and the toe-tapping beats of the rhythm sections—thoroughly enchanted Henry. The Big Band sound "experimented with a more orchestral range of colors," a reviewer once wrote, "and for many students of American music, 'big band' swing represents a pinnacle of American musical form, combining harmonic sophistication, improvisational brilliance, and danceable accessibility." Henry certainly agreed.

"The bands would be playing in Chicago, like the Glenn Miller Band or Tommy Dorsey, and of course it was tremendous to hear those shows," he recalled. And Henry never tired of sitting by the radio, waiting for the signature sound of the Big Band introduction: "And now live! From the Hollywood Palladium on Sunset Boulevard in Hollywood, California! Tommy Dorsey and his Orchestra with band vocalist Frank Sinatra!"

Henry soon developed an ear for a wide range of Big Band tunes recorded in the '30s and '40s, songs with both instrumentals and vocals like "Moonlight Serenade," "Juke Box Saturday Night," "Along the Santa Fe Trail," "Pennsylvania 6-5000," and "(I've Got a Gal in) Kalamazoo." And as he listened over and over to the melancholy "It's a Blue World," a song by Chet Forrest and Bob Wright, which was nominated in 1940 for an Academy Award for Best Original Song, Henry soon knew the lyrics by heart:

It's a blue world / Without you / It's a through world / For me
The days and nights / That once were filled / With heaven
With you away / How empty they have grown
It's a blue world / From now on / It's a through world / For me
The sea, the sky / My heart and I / Are all an indigo hue
Without you / It's a blue, blue / World

"It's an era," Henry concluded, "that we will never return to."

INSPIRED BY RADIO, HENRY JOINS A BAND

The radio also provided Henry and his family with other sources of entertainment. They listened regularly to shows like *Jack Armstrong the All-American Boy*, he said. "On Sundays it would be the *Green Hornet*, and Sammy Kaye and his *Sunday Serenade*. You'd have Bing Crosby, Phil Harris, and Rudy Vallee. I'll never forget that the Rudy Vallee show came on Saturday afternoons because it always came on about the time we were getting ready to go to town for Saturday night."

There's no doubt that Henry's radio time inspired him to take his musical interests one step further. In the sixth grade, about a year after he started listening to music on the radio, then 11-year-old Henry joined the school band and decided to learn to play the clarinet. Uncle John bought the instrument for him, and the school provided the band uniform and a blue and gold cape. He took his lessons seriously, and he practiced regularly from his lesson books. And though Henry later insisted, "I don't think I was any great clarinet player," the budding young clarinetist continued to play at school from the seventh through the tenth grades, and served as president of the band in the tenth grade. Though Henry recalls that his dad "didn't care one way or the other" about him playing in the band, his mom was proud of Henry and encouraged him to pursue his musical talents.

Despite Henry's opinion of his own abilities, there's no doubt he was talented. In the spring of 1942, while he was still in the tenth grade, Henry was a part of the clarinet quartet that won the State Music championship at the Oskaloosa High School, the first time since 1938 that anyone from Belle Plaine had won a state championship. The quartet included Henry, Jack Haloupek, Alan Fisher, and Charles McLennan. Though winning the state championship entitled the four students to proceed to the national competition, Henry's quartet did not get to go; the championships were called off in 1942, due to the start of America's involvement in World War II. And after Henry's sophomore year, he abruptly quit the band. The man who had been Henry's band director since the sixth grade left Belle Plaine to enlist in the Navy, and apparently Henry was one of many who didn't get along with the new director. "He got into a flap, so to speak, with some of the people in the band, and as a consequence, some of the band members quit, including me."

FRIENDS, AT LAST

Without a doubt, Henry's participation in the high school band and the baseball team gave him something he had never really experienced before: a group of friends. They were a relatively small but nonetheless loyal group, with a core of two or three boys and the same number of girls. And oddly enough, considering Henry's feeling of being universally ostracized by the town kids, his new group of friends came from both sides of the railroad tracks, a mix of town and country kids; for example, Flea Wright's family ran the local car dealership in town, while Henry's parents ran a dairy farm. The town-country division Henry felt so acutely when he first started going to school in town no longer seemed to matter. And using the exact same words that Henry once used to describe himself, Betty Kent said that they got along because "we all came from nothing."

Henry's new posse of friends later teased him that "his claim to fame in high school was the fact that he was the only one who had a car," said Mike Bevins. And because his family had farm equipment that required gasoline, Henry also had gas stamps, which were rationed at the time. Thanks to the combination of his dad's 1937 Chevrolet, access to a tank of gas, and extensive knowledge of Big Band music and local dance halls, Henry's social life was suddenly golden.

With Flea Wright as his main sidekick, Henry made the rounds to all the surrounding towns on weekend nights. No longer content to listen to music on the radio and armed with his newly acquired driver's license, Henry sought out every live musical performance he could find within driving distance. Henry and Flea, sometimes accompanied by other teens, sought out dance pavilions in regional Iowa towns to hear the Big Bands, dance the jitterbug and the fox-trot, and toss back a few beers or a soda while listening to "Serenade in Blue," "I Know Why," "Moonlight Cocktail," "At Last," and "The Nearness of You." Some of Henry's favorite destinations included Danceland in Cedar Rapids, where an outstanding dance floor above the Red Crown Bowling Alleys was just a 30-minute drive away; Turner Hall in Keystone, where Henry's parents first met; Blazek's near Chelsea, an outdoor pavilion just a few miles west of Belle Plaine; the Legion Hall at Blairstown, just east of Belle Plaine; and Fireman's Park south of Belle Plaine. Occasionally, the dancehalls had theme nights, and it rarely cost over 35 cents to get in and dance all night.

"His car never cooled off," joked Mike Bevins.

Henry admits as much. "I have always loved that music, the Big Band era," Henry says. "And these places, like Blazek's Dance Pavilion at nearby Chelsea, weren't necessarily bringing in the name bands, but they were bringing in regional bands that were very good. You could hear a twelve- to fourteen-piece orchestra that would play just wonderful music, and they would draw big crowds on Saturday nights. You could buy beer and hamburgers—and this wasn't an expensive situation. We would always have a few beers. I looked older than my age so I never had any problems even in Belle Plaine. I could get a beer anyplace even though I was in high school. It all depended on who you were, and I can't remember anyone not selling me a beer."

Granted, borrowing the family car had its drawbacks. The car was certainly nobody's dream-of-an-automobile: it was not in good shape, and Bob Tippie frequently used the backseat to haul pigs or sheep to sales, a chore that left dirt and the smell of animals all over the Chevrolet. But it was the only set of wheels in Henry's crowd, and no one dared complain. Plus, Henry admits, "I was no angel. I think as I got older, as a teenager I could really get Dad mad." He remembers one particularly heated run-in with his father, after borrowing his car to take to a Saturday dance in Keystone. "So on the way home—I guess I was about a mile and a half away—I had a blowout. This was late at night and there were two or three carloads of people with us, so I took a ride with one of my friends and left the car in the field. Well, on Sunday mornings, Dad had a habit of going into town and getting the newspaper, and of course, on this Sunday there's no automobile. 'Where is the automobile?' he asked. And I had to tell him, 'Well, it's over in the pasture.' He just skyrocketed over the fact that the car was in the field. He sure was hot, and Mom had to work hard to cool him down."

During his senior year of high school, Henry took a job at Funk Brothers, a hybrid seed corn operation that was one of the biggest employers in Belle Plaine at the time. Excluding baseball season, he worked after school from four in the afternoon until midnight, five days a week. His new job definitely cut into the time Henry could devote to his dad's farm, but he was pretty desperate to earn some money. Pretty soon Henry had saved enough to buy his own car, a Model A Ford that he purchased for $105. It wasn't much to look at, but it ran.

"The main reason I bought it was that it had excellent tires, and tires were being rationed at that time," remembers Henry about the war years and the restrictions on the whole country. "I had a certain amount of fun with it, at the expense of my dad's gasoline barrel on the farm, because this was during the time of gas rations."

Described by everyone as both a gentleman and very handsome during his junior and senior years, Henry never dated anyone special during high school. He followed the football and basketball teams in the fall and winter months, carefully recording the scores on the school's blue athletic schedule, but he never went to the games with a date. Too, he went stag to both his junior and senior banquets and proms, and saved the student-autographed programs from both events, which always took place between 6:30 p.m. and midnight inside the high school auditorium. By all accounts, Henry and Flea enjoyed meeting girls from neighboring towns when they went to the dances, but Henry definitely preferred to keep his private life private when he returned to Belle Plaine. Between his music, baseball, cars, and dancing road trips on the weekends, no one worried about Henry's social life. "He had a good time in high school," Mike concluded. "He was all boy!"

GRADUATION, JOINING THE AIR FORCE, LEAVING THE FARM

There was another topic that Henry kept to himself during the first semester of his senior year of high school. Namely, what to do after graduation? The dilemma occupied his thoughts more than he cared to admit. He recalls sitting on the hilltop near his house, perched atop the cistern, and daydreaming about his future:

> A lot of times, late in the day or near sunset, I would go up there and sit on the cistern and dream. I would daydream about where I was headed, but when you're a teenager you never think in terms of being 30 or 50 years old, that's so far away, I couldn't even imagine it. I don't ever remember thinking about going to college to be honest about it. I was just thinking, "If I could ever get out of high school . . .", and I would think about my goal to one day have 160 acres. I also dreamed about maybe seeing some places in my lifetime, maybe I would like to go to the city? And I would think, "What is beyond the farm?"

Henry's tendency to daydream, which the whole family knew about, often made his father angry. Ernie recalled the moment one night after supper, when "Henry got up from the supper table and walked out in the barnyard, and was just walking around a little bit and daydreaming." Bob Tippie muttered under his breath and lashed out at his son as he watched him from the kitchen window. "My dad got up and got a glass of water and looked out the window and saw Henry walking," said Ernie. "And his comment was, 'That kid will never amount to nothing because he's always daydreaming.' And I will never forget this."

But Henry's mother was a different story. Amelia Bokholt Tippie wanted each of her sons to daydream, to envision a life for themselves beyond the farm. "Get off the farm," she repeatedly told her sons. "There's a better life." And just as she had worked to provide them with an education in town that was more advanced than the one-room schoolhouse down the road, she clung to her dream of a future beyond the farm for each of her sons.

"Henry and I have talked about it several times, that our mother, bless her soul, decided that she wanted her children to have a better opportunity at life than she had," Ernie said. "Because she was born and raised on a farm and there were tough times. I don't think she was happy with her station in life. I think she felt that things hadn't gone her way. She didn't feel like she was in the social structure that, well, you have to understand, in those days farmers were considered to be hicks. She had a vision that she wanted her kids to have the opportunity that she never had and that involved education. She wanted us to graduate from high school, because she never had a chance to go. Our mother was trying to push us and lead us into better things in life."

For a long time, Henry didn't really understand or care about his mother's dreams for him to have a different, better life. Even when it came to education, Ernie pointed out, "It was meaningless to Henry at the time. He just went to school to have fun and to get out." Henry admits as much. "I had no vision," he says.

And truthfully, Henry never allowed his daydreaming on the cistern to take him very far. The odds of getting off the farm, it seemed, were bleak. For starters, he had no money to even think about paying for college or moving away from Belle Plaine. And second, while Henry was on the path to graduate from high school and fulfill at least one of his mother's dreams, his education was still limited. He was ill-prepared for any career or vocation except farming. The farm was all he knew, and as he got older and more adept at running the equipment, life on the farm began to appeal to him more and more. At one point, if he dared to dream of anything, he dreamed of one day being the biggest farmer in Benton County and having the nicest-looking farm.

"I have to say that generally I liked a lot of things on the farm," Henry admitted. "I thought it was great to be making hay and plowing corn. I mean, I could sit on that tractor for weeks and months, early in the morning until sundown. Running the tractor and doing this and doing that, I didn't think anything about it. I really liked it. I never got that out of my blood. And I felt I was pretty good at running the equipment."

Granted, there were grueling aspects of farming that didn't appeal to Henry. Among his least favorite tasks? "If I remember right, we had a 10-acre cornfield and we put in hybrid corn. And then you had to detassle the corn several different times to make sure there weren't any tassels coming out, and that's how they'd grow hybrid corn. I didn't like that because a lot of times you would be very wet, just soaking wet, walking down those rows and pulling the tassels out. I'm thinking I may have gotten paid $10 a month to do that. I guess the other thing I wasn't enthralled with is that I never did like to clean the manure out of the chicken house. That is very dusty. It gets in your lungs and your nose and it is not an easy task. So that was not something I desired."

But with Henry, the joys and challenges of being on thc farm always outweighed the negatives. "When you're on the farm, you had to use your mind a little bit to be innovative," he recalls. "Also you learned a lot of things. You didn't just run the equipment; there was a whole lot of other things you had to do. You had to take care of the animals, milk the cows and vaccinate the pigs, slaughter the chickens, castrate the pigs. You had to be a carpenter or you had to be able to repair things and figure things out and estimate different things, and I think that's good. It's also out in the open air, and I think that the open air is healthy. And, yeah, you get dirty and you get sweaty but that's no bad thing. And you're out there with the livestock and animals so I think there's a whole lot of things that I like about agriculture and the country."

As the farm became the place that Henry could not imagine leaving, Amelia continued to imagine it for him. "My mother used to always tell me that I needed to get off the farm. She said that she always felt that they made a mistake staying on the farm, that they should have gone away. And she said this to me more than once, 'You need to get off the farm.'"

On February 15, 1944, just over a month after he turned 17 years old and still a high school senior, Henry took a dramatic step to do just that. During a trip to Des Moines to take a final test and join the military before he was drafted, Henry enlisted in the Army Air Force in the U.S. Army. He was placed on the reserve list for future calls. His enlistment identification card stated his occupation as "student" and noted that this blue-eyed, brown-haired, 5-foot 10-inches-tall 17-year-old had agreed to serve "during war plus 6 mos." Because he was under 18, Henry's parents had to sign papers and give permission for their son to enlist. Amelia Tippie signed the military papers immediately, focusing on the fact that enlisting in the service was perhaps her oldest son's only certain path off the farm. But Bob Tippie initially refused to sign. He thought Henry was too young. And he couldn't help but worry about the dangers his son faced being in the military for a country at war, and he immediately recognized the loss the family farm would experience without Henry. It took several days for Bob to come around and sign the papers. But when he did, Henry was ecstatic.

"I couldn't wait to get into the service. In fact, it's fair to say that once I made up my mind, I couldn't get there fast enough," Henry remembered. "That was the attitude that existed, and it wasn't just me. You know, it was 'the world's out there and you really don't know much about it and you're ready to take it on.' The atmosphere at the time was, 'I need to get into the service.' There was a lot of patriotism, and it was a whole different atmosphere that has never existed since. And once I decided it was the right thing to do, I was ready. I didn't spend a lot of time looking back or rethinking or wondering if I had made the right decision."

The rest of Henry's senior year played out in something of a predictable and, by now, comfortable pattern. He continued to drive his buddies around to hear Big Band performances on the weekends, after working around the farm and helping out at the seed company. He faithfully followed the basketball team and even attended the sectional basketball tournament in Tama with a few friends only two weeks after he enlisted. He suited up for baseball in the spring, excited about playing his last year of

IDENTIFICATION CARD—ENLISTED RESERVE CORPS

This is to Certify, That HENRY B. TIPPIE (Name) PVT. (Grade) (Section)

Serial No. 17,117,465 Home address Belle Plaine (City), Ia. (State)

was ~~transferred to~~ / enlisted in *grade shown in Air-Force

Enlisted Reserve Corps of the Army of the United States, on the 15th day of February, one thousand nine hundred and forty-four, for the period of dur war plus 6 mos year. When ~~transferred~~ / enlisted *he was 17 years of age, and by occupation a student. He has blue eyes, brown hair, medium complexion, and is 5 feet 10 inches in height.

Dates of immunization: Smallpox 7-21-44 Typhoid 8-4-44

X Other X X X Blood type

X

Given at Headquarters Des Moines, Iowa, this 15th day of February, one thousand nine hundred and forty-four.

* Cross out words not applicable.

FOR THE COMMANDING OFFICER MARVIN V. LITTLETON, 2nd Lt., AUS (Giver)

W. D., A. G. O. Form No. 166—March 11, 1943 16-28066-1

Henry's identification card when he enlisted in the military in February 1944.

high school baseball; always a hustler and a team leader, Henry was quietly fuming when the returning champions of 1943 failed to advance in the playoffs his senior year, a situation he blamed on teammates who stayed out too late on prom night the evening before the big game.

In the weeks leading up to the May graduation ceremony, Henry joined the other 52 seniors in his class for some senior rituals: they ordered name cards ("Henry B. Tippie" in cursive) and invitations for both Baccalaureate and Graduation ceremonies. They didn't study at all, and who could blame them? But they did dress up and pose for their all-important senior-year portraits. Henry wore his dark pin-striped gabardine suit with pleated pants and wide jacket lapels, his striped necktie perfectly positioned against his crisp white shirt, and a white handkerchief folded in his left suit pocket. He was a dashing yet serious young man, allowing just a hint of a smile as he stared straight into the camera.

On Wednesday evening, May 17, 1944, the 53 students in the Belle Plaine High School Class of 1944 gathered in the high school auditorium for the last time. In front of a large crowd of family and friends, the

Henry B. Tippie, high school senior portrait.

program opened with an impressive senior class processional to the beat of a dignified march performed by the high school band. Dressed in their caps and gowns of golden and purple school colors, the seniors remained standing while Reverend O. W. Crosby gave the invocation, and then settled in their seats before the Girls Glee Club sang two numbers. Dr. J. P. Ryan, professor of speech at Grinnell College in Des Moines, gave the evening's address, entitled, "In War, Our Rights; In Peace, Our Duties." The subject must have been particularly significant and perhaps daunting to Henry, who would report for active duty just two weeks from this night.

But if the professor's words or the thought of reporting for duty made the 17-year-old anxious, Henry didn't show it. Like the young man captured in his senior portrait, Henry B. Tippie looked straight ahead when he accepted his high school graduation diploma, exuding a quiet calm that belied the significance of this moment. Diploma in hand, Henry became the first person in the history of the Tippie and Bokholt families to earn a high school degree. And he was the first of three sons in Amelia and Bob Tippie's family to fulfill a mother's dream that her children would be educated.

In many ways, nothing less was expected from Henry, or from any of the 53 seniors in the Class of '44. The majority of the class may have been born in the same year that Charles Lindbergh flew solo across the Atlantic Ocean and Babe Ruth hit a record 60 home runs, but this class would never be defined by the feel-good news that trickled out during their youth. Rather, this was a class shaped by the struggles of their families and their town to survive the Great Depression. This was a class where every member knew what it was like to wonder whether they or someone close to them had enough to eat; to recall family stories about what happened the day the banks failed and grown men cried; to witness the unimaginable sight of a fellow classmate sitting on a sidewalk curb in darkness after losing a home and everything in it. Future generations would use expressions like "hardscrabble" and "hard knocks" and "pulled up by their boot straps" to describe those shaped by misfortune—students like Henry, Mike, Betty, and Gladys, who grew up in the Depression era and had to wrestle mightily just to move their lives forward.

From their front-row seats into these difficult times and their own challenging futures, the Belle Plaine High School Class of 1944 crafted a class motto that managed to capture the struggles and dreams of their generation better than anyone else possibly could:

Take the stairs; the elevator is not working.

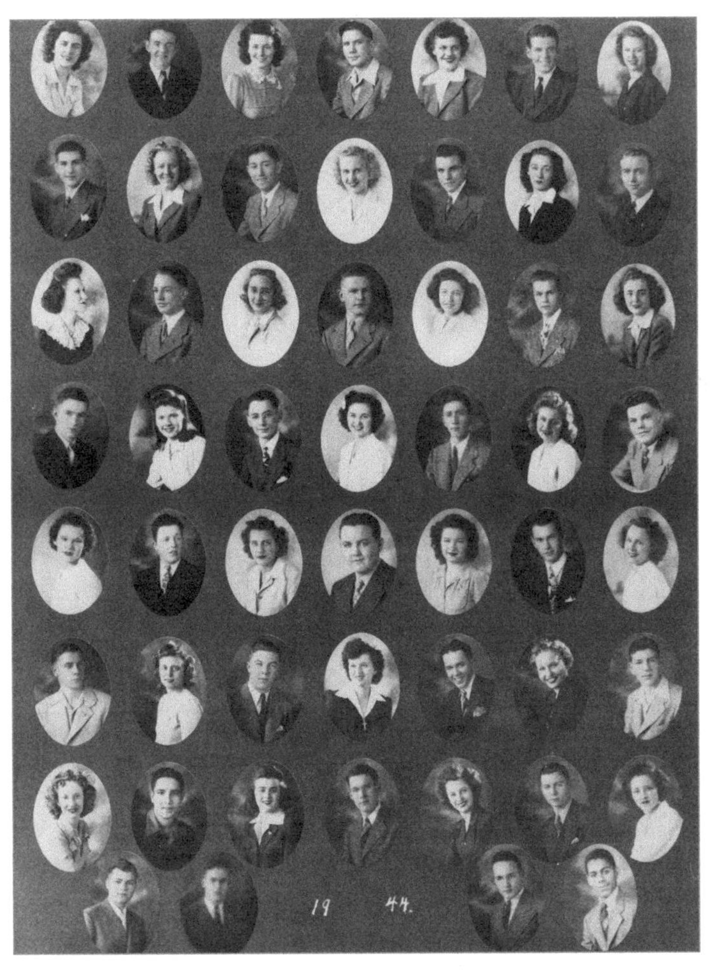

Belle Plaine High School, Class of 1944; Henry is pictured in the next to the last row, second from the right.

Henry B. Tippie in his Air Force uniform.

CHAPTER FIVE

WORLD WAR II JOURNEY: HENRY JOINS THE MILITARY

EIGHTEEN DAYS AFTER HE GRADUATED from high school, 17-year-old Henry said good-bye to his parents and his two younger brothers, hopped on a train bound for Des Moines, and reported to Camp Dodge on the outskirts of the Iowa capital. It was June 5, 1944. Camp Dodge, a processing center for incoming servicemen from across the Midwest, was a well-known, multiacre compound filled with stretches of low one-story barracks that stood side by side among office buildings, equipment facilities, dining halls, and training grounds. Henry soon traded in his civilian clothes for an everyday khaki uniform and an "OD," or Olive Drab Class A Dress Uniform, and instantly had to adjust to a life of regimented routines. The remarkable timing of Henry's arrival was something he remembered the rest of his life.

"The first morning we were there, June 6, was D-Day," he recalled. At four o'clock in the morning, the sound of the staff sergeant's voice woke everyone: "Get out of bed! We just invaded Europe!" Recalled Henry, "They had announcements coming over the squawk boxes in the barracks all day. There was a recorded message about soldiers, sailors, and airmen. The message played over and over about the D-Day invasion, and I will never forget that."

Henry remained at Camp Dodge for only two or three days. Then he and about 200 other Air Corps enlistees under 18 years of age boarded a troop train and headed to Cedar Rapids and Coe College, a small liberal arts college about 30 miles from Belle Plaine. Founded in 1851 and operating under the name "Coe" since 1881, the campus was known for excellence and intellectual rigor. The military program at Coe during World War II—called the "Aviation Cadet Training for the Army Air Forces"—was specifically designed for young new recruits like Henry, offering them an introduction to college coursework as well as military training. And when the cadets finally arrived in Cedar Rapids around midnight, patriotic citizens, caught up in the war effort and the recent events surrounding D-Day, lined the streets to cheer as Henry and his fellow cadets marched up 13th Street and entered Coe's campus.

For the next eight months, Henry studied on a college campus, but he wasn't a college student. With cadets divided up into five sections, the military program was distinctly separate from the college program: the cadets attended school every day from 8 a.m. to 4 p.m. during the week and from 8 a.m. to 11 a.m. on Saturday; Henry sat in compulsory study hall every night but Saturday, and the only free time he had was from Saturday afternoon to Sunday evening before study hall. Henry lived in the collegiate indoor track gymnasium, where two long rows of lockers and bunks lined up on opposite sides of the cavernous space that housed the 200 cadets. On individual clothes racks, each cadet lined up his clothes in a specific sequence—overcoat, dress uniform, school uniform, etc. If the clothes didn't hang in the proper order, if the shoes were not placed under the bed properly, or if a locker was in disarray, a cadet would earn a "Gig" that required him to report to the fields on Saturday afternoons during a cadet's free time and engage in "march tours" up and down the field. To his credit, the organized and methodical Henry never had a so-called Gig for the way he maintained his wardrobe. But he did get several Gigs for sneaking off the campus and going across the street to see a movie.

At Coe, Henry immediately became aware of the shortcomings of his small-town education and felt "out of my league" when it came to course work and educational skills. "We had a lot of people there who had ROTC training in high school, they came out of the cities with a different background, and I think we had one or two people who had a quarter of a year in college," he said. "And of course, I didn't have anything like that. During the first part of what took place at Coe as far as classes and education, I didn't feel I could handle that, and I couldn't. I didn't have any business doing that." For instance, the college training courses at Coe started with chemistry, which Henry had never studied at Belle Plaine High School. "I floundered in chemistry. In our high school, no chemistry was offered. So at Coe, I'm out of my league and the instructor really felt sorry for me. It was a struggle."

Henry was not alone. Stanley "Stan" Hladik, a fellow 17-year-old recruit from the rural town of Traer in Tama County, Iowa, was in the same section of cadets as Henry, and recalls that he faced "major challenges" in math and science courses, too. He recalled that after lights-out and taps, he and another friend would sneak out of their beds and head for the bathroom (the only place with lights on), and work together through the course assignments they didn't understand. "I can concur with Henry that it was academically challenging. And everything was different. You were trying to accept and acknowledge your surroundings as they were, but you were scared to death of the sergeants. But you couldn't express anything one way or the other."

For the first time in his life, Henry was exposed to a wide variety of people with backgrounds from both rural and urban populations. With their wider exposure to education, culture, politics, and current events, Henry admitted that he often didn't know what they were talking about. "It was an entirely different world," he said. Plus, Henry had to live alongside a large number of people in a gymnasium filled with bunk beds, something not exactly second nature to a young man who grew up describing himself as a loner.

"Coe College opened his eyes quite a bit," said Ernie. "Fellow students were from various areas in the United States, and that gave Henry some contact and something to think about a little bit."

Despite his misgivings about his performance, Henry impressed his superior officers, and they selected him to be a leader of his section. Henry was petrified and didn't think he was qualified for such a position, particularly after hearing that the leaders of some of the other sections already had ROTC training and much more education. Henry protested and the officers relented, but they immediately pitched Henry another idea that he couldn't refuse: They appointed him band director of the newly formed 30-member band.

"I had done some band leading in high school and I think that's probably how they arrived at the decision to make me leader," said Henry. "And I have to say, I kind of enjoyed that."

Henry remained the band director during his entire stint at Coe, a position that came with some perks. "Being band director meant I was a cadet officer," said Henry, "and I was what you called a first lieutenant." But trying to conduct this band of 30 was not always an easy proposition. The band members were all as young as Henry, they loved to embarrass each other and goof around, and they weren't always easy to control. In fact, Henry was routinely hassled by a musician who played a brass musical instrument called the euphonium as loud as he could, whenever he wanted, even when the musical score didn't call for it. He was, in short, a conductor's nightmare.

But on a Thursday night in December 1944, when the band performed for a war bond rally at the Paramount Theater in downtown Cedar Rapids two weeks before Christmas, Henry's Coe College military band members put their antics aside and behaved like professional musicians. Henry was thrilled. The preholiday, festive evening was a standing-room-only, sold-out performance, and Henry even took a bow after the closing number while the audience continued to applaud. But the best part—and unbeknownst to Henry until after the performance—was that the person in the audience clapping and cheering the loudest was his own mother! After hearing about the forthcoming performance, Amelia took a bus from Belle Plaine to Cedar Rapids to see Henry conduct and to surprise him. The mother-and-son reunion was dutifully reported in the Belle Plaine newspaper the next week on December 21: *Mrs. Robert Tippie spent Thursday in Cedar Rapids where she attended the bond rally program at the Paramount Theatre in which her son, Henry Tippie, took part.*

When Henry enlisted in the military in 1944, he joined a group of young men later described by renowned television journalist Tom Brokaw as "young daredevils who were fascinated by the new frontiers of flight who volunteered for pilot training." And though the demand for new pilots was high when Henry signed up, that was not the case within a year of his enlistment. By the time most of the young military cadets had turned 18, the flight schools that had once so eagerly recruited them no longer needed additional pilots. Too, the war in the air had shifted, the number of casualties had diminished, and the war on the European and the Pacific fronts was coming to a close.

But the military still needed enlisted men, and Henry stayed in the program at Coe College until March 3, 1945. After a brief visit home, he then shuttled around the rest of the year between a number of different stateside bases: Jefferson Barracks, near St. Louis; Keesler Field, in Biloxi, Mississippi; Scott Field in the St. Louis area; and Truax Field at Madison, Wisconsin. To the delight of his parents and younger brothers, Henry briefly returned home to Belle Plaine in November 1945, stopping in for a high school reunion for students and alumni in the gymnasium after the homecoming football game against Vinton. He was happy just to listen to some jukebox music, play a little Ping-Pong at the far end of the gym, and catch up with Class of '44 classmates like Betty Eichmeyer, Don Van Scoyc, Private Jack Dunlap, Joye Higgins, Hilbert J. Lorenz, Harley Malcolm, Steve Malcolm, and Wilma Benda (they all signed the guest register book at the main entrance, and the newspaper published their names the next week). Henry told everyone that he was headed to Riverside, California, in December, which meant he was probably going to be deployed to somewhere in the South Pacific. "But all I knew at the time was that I was headed west," he said. "They don't tell you anything about where you're headed other than you're going to be in the Pacific someplace."

When Henry arrived in California, he saw very few familiar faces from Coe College. "The group I started out with in Cedar Rapids is, at this point, spread out all over the place. I think there were only three or four people still together." In fact, only one of his fellow cadets from Coe followed the same path in the military as Henry: James O'Brien, from Independence, Iowa, who shared the same January birthday month as Henry (their serial numbers were different by only five or six digits). "He was a close friend," said Henry, "and he and I went together every place."

Henry's brief stay in California and the looming Pacific journey would be an eye-opening experience for this Iowa farm boy. Before leaving the Riverside/Los Angeles area, which proved to be his last stop before shipping out, Henry and his fellow enlisted men hit the town. Predictably, Henry took his love for Big Band music and sought out the world-famous venues that were home to the live remote broadcasts he had listened to since he was a boy. It was simply amazing, Henry thought, for him to see the Hollywood Palladium and the fabled Cocoanut Grove in the Ambassador Hotel in L.A., and he never forgot the experience:

> I remember we walked up to that hotel, a bunch of 18-year-old kids with no money. We were too scared to be in the place and that was just our station in life at that point. So we went over to where CBS had those 15-minute radio shows. And people in the service got a free ticket to get in. So we did that. Then we would go to some bar room, and in those days they had nickelodeons, where you put a dime in the machine and it plays a record and there is some live voice from some central place, and people would try to carry on conversations. It was crazy. If you can imagine, having half-a-dozen Gls from all walks of life, with what goes on. The night before they were set to ship out, the GIs had a party in Riverside. People weren't certain when they were going to get back, so it was quite a party.

Their boozy revelry behind them, Henry and his fellow GIs started out early the next morning on the U.S.S. *Howell M. Lykes*, a converted freighter headed to the island of Guam. This U.S. island territory in the Western Pacific was captured by the Japanese in 1941, just hours after the attack on Pearl Harbor, and occupied for two and a half years before U.S. troops recaptured the island on July 21, 1944. Known for its tropical beaches, ancient latte stones, and villages of indigenous people called Chamorros, Guam was an important U.S. military outpost in the final months of World War II. But if the Pacific Ocean freighter voyage was any indication, Henry's time in Guam was going to be very difficult.

"We were in a terrible storm for several days and stuck in the bowels of the ship," Henry recalls. "That thing would roll up on one side and come down and roll the other way. It was terrible. People all over the place were sick, and if you ever got to eat and got down to the mess hall, it would only be like a can of soup or an apple or something. And with the smell coming out of the place, you just didn't care to eat anyway. It was just unbelievable. It was almost like pigs have a better existence than what they put us into. One fellow was so bad that they had to feed him intravenously."

After three weeks on the freighter, Henry was relieved to finally set foot on Guam's shores in December 1945. The U.S. flag with its 48 stars, flying over the base of the 20th Air Force, was a welcome sight for these ocean-weary servicemen, who quickly settled into open-air barracks and tried to adapt to the humid tropical climate and the sight of palm trees. Some unexpected news greeted Henry almost immediately. Though the South Pacific was about as far away from Belle Plaine, Iowa, as you could get, there was already word from home for Henry. Amelia had written to her oldest son while he was based in Riverside, California, but her three letters to him had been returned, unopened, due to an incorrect address. Worried, Amelia had contacted the Red Cross, who tracked Henry down in Guam. Never big on letter writing and not particularly prone to being homesick, Henry decided it was nonetheless time to be in touch, and he finally wrote back to his family.

Henry appreciated little about the island's beauty and tropical habitat during the first few weeks after he arrived. He was very sick. Unfortunately, he acquired a horrific tropical skin disease that caused gaping fissures to open the outer layers of his skin. Known by servicemen as "jungle crud," the infection confined Henry for days to his cot, his body smeared head to foot with penicillin ointment as he tried to stay cool and dry in the humid weather. At the height of his misery, Henry could barely stand to have a sheet draped over him, and if he looked down at his open skin, "you could see muscle" in the open skin. Slowly, his wounds healed, and Henry could finally put his auspicious introduction to Guam behind him.

Henry's first assignment in Guam took him to Air Surgeon headquarters. He started out as a medical technician, giving shots and dispensing medicine under a doctor's supervision. And in this environment, Henry began a fast-paced military career climb in an unexpected direction: medical administration. "At that time there was a tremendous turnover," he explained. "And in order to get this position I had to get the background, so I worked with our captain as a medical administrative

Henry in front of the Air Surgeon Quonset, 20th Air Force Headquarters, Guam.

specialist. When I started out at Coe College, the emphasis was on an engineering-type activity. I don't have the foggiest idea how that had anything to do with me eventually being in the medical field."

In just 12 months, Henry became the highest-ranking enlisted person in the Air Surgeon Office. His advancement was so rapid that he earned a commendation from the 20th Air Force's commanding general. "I got promoted every four weeks until I got up to staff sergeant. And as time evolved, I replaced a major and a master sergeant. I became a sergeant major."

Although Japan surrendered in August 1945, fugitive Japanese soldiers were still known to be hiding in Guam's jungles in 1946, an open secret that got drilled into all of the servicemen stationed there. Henry knew to be careful. "If you went anywhere at nighttime, you went with a group, and you went like a bat out of hell and didn't stop for nothing," he recalled.

But aside from avoiding enemy soldiers and working his way up the ranks, Henry found very little else to do in Guam. Naturally, he saved much of his pay, noting that "when you get on these small islands, there isn't anything there. The only thing to spend your money on would be beer, and some of that wasn't very good beer. Or you could buy whiskey for a dollar and a half a bottle. So there wasn't a lot of need for money unless you got in the card-playing business, and there was a lot of card playing over there."

Toward the final months of 1946, Henry and two of his buddies were asked to reenlist and stay on for another year to serve with the Air Force in Tokyo. If they agreed, they would instantly become second lieutenants.

But they all said no. The war was over, and they didn't want a career in the military. Each young man decided it was time to return to the United States. And Henry knew that by the end of 1946, he would have successfully fulfilled the agreement he signed as a 17-year-old to serve "during war plus 6 mos." Years later, looking back on that high school senior who enlisted, Henry realized with equal parts astonishment and admiration, that "I was just a kid, a 17-year-old kid. I went overseas when I was 18 years old and my 19th birthday was over there." From that moment on, he discovered that he could no longer relate to typical 17- or 18-year-olds. "Because I was about that age when I was in the service," he reasoned. "I think we grew up faster or matured quicker."

Henry would always be extremely grateful for his military experience. He recognized that the military opened the world to him, introducing him to people from all walks of life with families whose professional careers ranged from farming to medicine to engineering to law and bookkeeping. As Henry once described it, "Was everything good? No. But for somebody coming from the farm who had never been any place, I mean talk about somebody seeing the world out there! I met a lot of people the same age as I was. And I listened to what they were thinking about doing for the future. Most of them talked about going to college. So I was exposed to a whole lot of things that, without being in the service, would have never happened."

In short, Henry was no longer daydreaming on the cistern about "what was beyond the farm." Henry had *seen* it. He had *lived* it. And the military ultimately did more than just show Henry what was out there; the military held out the promise that a life beyond the farm was within Henry's grasp. It was an astonishing notion, really, for a kid "who came from nothing." By serving in World War II, Henry was now eligible to take advantage of a unique program that would cover all expenses if he chose to go to college. The Servicemen's Readjustment Act—commonly called "the G.I. Bill"—was signed on June 22, 1944, just days after Henry reported for military duty. Among the law's provisions was financial aid for veterans seeking higher education. The transforming effect of such a piece of legislation cannot be overstated: farm kids like Henry, blocked from the professional world by their limited economic status, now had a chance for a college education, something Henry had never dared to dream about.

On his return ocean voyage back to the States from Guam in late 1946, Henry had a lot to think about. Thankfully, the return trip was far better than his turbulent voyage to the island nearly a year ago; the ocean was glasslike smooth, and the three weeks on the ship passed without a single unpleasant incident. When the ship reached Honolulu, the military immediately issued 24-hour passes to Henry and his fellow Air Force servicemen, and Henry readily admits that they enjoyed every minute of their Hawaiian layover. Actually, says Henry, "I remember very little about that. I know we loaded up in a taxicab and went to see the Royal Hawaiian Hotel, and where else we went I don't know, but I'm guessing that we hit several bars." From Honolulu, the servicemen soon sailed to Oakland, California, and the military gave them another round of 24-hour passes. Henry and his buddies headed straight to San Francisco, where Henry remembers, "We caught a good evening there and went to a really fancy place to eat."

Henry was discharged the following day in November 1946 (effective December 31, 1946, the official end of World War II), at Camp Beale in Marysville, California. He arranged for the Air Force to ship his duffle bag, full of his military gear, back to Iowa. And then he began the long journey home by way of the Chicago & North Western Railroad on a train with standing room only. After a few days of traveling into the heart of the Midwest, Henry finally arrived around four o'clock in the morning at the familiar Belle Plaine Depot. He walked just up the street to the Herring Hotel on Lincoln Highway, known since 1922 as the "Swellest Little Hotel in Iowa." The sun wasn't even up yet as he entered the hotel and asked if he could use the telephone to call home. Within no time, Henry's father and youngest brother were on their way to town to pick up Sergeant Major Henry B. Tippie, home from the war. Unbeknownst to Henry's family, their oldest son would not stay on the farm for very long. Henry had already made up his mind: He wanted to go to college on the G.I. Bill.

"The G.I. Bill was probably the greatest thing to ever come out of that war," Henry later concluded. "And while war is certainly not good, the

G.I. Bill made a lot of educational opportunities available for many, many people who might not have otherwise had an opportunity to go to college, and that has, in many cases, benefited themselves *and* this country. It was a really major item in my life, a crossroads. The service was my ticket to a different future. And it became my ticket off the farm."

Henry back in Iowa, late 1946.

Henry graduated from the University of Iowa in only 24 months.

CHAPTER SIX

THE UNIVERSITY OF IOWA AND A CAREER PATH

INSPIRED BY THE PROMISE OF the G.I. Bill and emboldened by the prospect of going to college, Henry started off 1947 by taking steps to plan for his future and decide what it would look like. After all, if he wasn't going to return to farming, what *was* he going to do? What did he want to study in college?

To find some answers, Henry took a road trip in January that allowed him to visit his friends from the 20th Air Force and see what they were doing after being discharged. In Illinois, he reconnected with a service buddy who was going to be a dentist. In Minnesota, another friend announced he was going to be an engineer. Back in Belle Plaine, Henry's closest friend in the service, James O'Brien from Independence, Iowa, came to visit the Tippies and revealed that he had his sights set on becoming a veterinarian. As someone who had loved and taken care of animals his whole life, Henry found the idea appealing and initially thought he might do the same. Together, Henry and James made a trip to Ames, Iowa, to tour Iowa State—the only college in the state with a vet school. After meeting with university representatives and hearing about the program, Henry soon realized that he wouldn't be pursuing that career path. To be admitted into the program, each student had to be sponsored by a veterinarian, and the only veterinarian in Belle Plaine was already slated to sponsor his future son-in-law.

Henry quickly moved on. Having grown up during the Depression and still able to recall the area's 25 percent unemployment rate during those years, Henry turned his sights to a profession that could sustain him financially through tough times. "I don't know where I picked this up along the line, but back then I guess I was probably looking at, 'Well, what happens to all these jobs if there's a recession?' And I had heard that if there was a recession or a depression, that maybe you could still get a job keeping books."

Henry's embrace of bookkeeping and accounting reflected more than his quest for employment security. It tapped into the very fabric of his childhood experiences and passions, when he dutifully kept track of every financial transaction he ever made. With a clear goal to become an accountant, Henry applied to the University of Iowa; his high school grades were so low that he was admitted on probation. He didn't apply anywhere else, but he didn't worry about the possibility that he might not get in. Like anybody who enlisted during World War II and wanted to go to college, Henry was granted admission regardless of his less-than-stellar high school academic record or his financial background, thanks entirely to one of the tenets of the G.I. Bill: any institution that accepted funds from the government had to allow a veteran to enroll. The bulk of Henry's expenses would be covered, too.

With the college admissions paperwork taken care of and his next few years planned out, Henry decided to get out of Belle Plaine during the summer of '47. After his friend James O'Brien was tragically killed in an accident while working on a line crew, Henry was determined to make every day count. He soon took on a series of jobs that at first seemed promising, but eventually delivered mixed results.

In Cedar Rapids, Henry lived in a boardinghouse that cost $13 a week while he took a job on a night shift, running a punch machine at an engineering company; but Henry, who had no idea what he was doing and no one to explain it to him, quit and never even asked for his pay. From there Henry went to work at a meatpacking plant, where he experienced his first brush with what he calls "the Union situation." He recalled one man in particular who would stop a job midstream if the break horn sounded, and Henry felt pressured to join the union, to the point where he was wary of an "accident" on the job if he did not. After nearly two months, Henry left the

THE STATE UNIVERSITY OF IOWA

NOTICE OF ACCEPTANCE OF APPLICATION
ACADEMIC YEAR - NEW APPLICANTS

Name of Applicant ....Henry B. Tippie........

Address of Applicant .... (Street) Belle Plaine, (City) Iowa (State)

Your application for living quarters in a University Student Residence is hereby accepted and you have been assigned quarters as follows: Single .... Suite .... Double .... Multiple X... in ....

South Quadrangle #217........ at the rate of $.......112.50....... for the year.

Signed this .....18th.. day of ...June........ 1947..

THE STATE UNIVERSITY OF IOWA

By .... Office of Student Affairs

THE STATE UNIVERSITY OF IOWA
IOWA CITY

OFFICE OF STUDENT AFFAIRS

August 20, 1947

Mr. Henry B. Tippie
Belle Plaine, Iowa

Dear Mr. Tippie:

I am in receipt of your letter dated August 19. All rooms are completely furnished, including pillow and one blanket. Bed linens are furnished and laundered. You will need to bring all personal articles such as wash-cloths, towels, etc.

You have been assigned Room 217 in South Quadrangle for the academic year 1947-48. This is a large room and accommodates four men.

If I can be of any further assistance, do not hesitate to write me.

Sincerely yours

Imelda C. Murphy

(Mrs.) Imelda C. Murphy
Manager
Dormitory Assignment Office

Two letters related to Henry's room assignment and furnishings, University of Iowa.

meatpacking job and hired himself out to a farmer north of Cedar Rapids for about $100 a month. That ended, however, when the farmer berated him unfairly one day and Henry simply told the man that he had had enough. Henry moved back to Belle Plaine, staying with his folks in his former second-floor bedroom and earning $35 a week for college while working at Froning Grain and Lumber in nearby Luzerne.

Henry at the University of Iowa, dressed in leftover WWII clothing.

Henry's father didn't quite know what to make of his oldest son's decision to go to college. His mother, however, helped Henry get all of his clothes and belongings ready, telling him more than once that she was proud of him. And Henry, in his quiet way, used the comfort of those last few days at home to carefully think through exactly how he intended to go about this business of college. Before he left, Henry had a plan. Because he was older than most college freshmen, he had a lot of life experience behind him. He saw college as a stepping-stone on the road to a better place, and Henry wasn't going to waste any time getting there.

With a sense of purpose not known to most newly admitted college freshmen, Henry moved to Iowa City and entered the University of Iowa in the fall of 1947. Veterans-turned-college students were everywhere, as young men like Henry strolled through campus wearing their leftover World War II khaki clothing, which was popular attire for students at the time. Henry, in fact, wore his khaki jacket and a white shirt and tie when he sat for his first student ID photo, marked with his Student Identification Number, which Henry never forgot: Student No. 30748. The swell of veterans on campus meant that classrooms were sometimes packed to three times their normal capacity. The 1947 *Hawkeye Yearbook,* which celebrated the 100th anniversary of the university, described the challenges associated with meeting the needs of these new students:

> *Veterans, who fought on every front to bring the war to a triumphant conclusion, have returned—not to the homes and firesides of which they dreamed under distant skies but to trainers, Quonset huts and metal barracks, to crowded classrooms and to youthful instructors. Yet it is this or nothing. Harassed faculties and administrators would do more if they could.*

Men are not lacking; but materials are. In the presence of all these temporarily insolvable difficulties, the urge to attend universities and colleges has never been greater. Stimulated by the provisions of the G.I. Bill of Rights, veterans crowd the campuses. Today, the university has fifty per cent more students than it ever had before.

Despite the presence of hundreds of veterans like him on campus, Henry kept to himself as he walked through the long corridors of University Hall to attend classes, crossed the Union footbridge that spanned the muddy Iowa River near campus, and strolled into the South Quadrangle, a brick dormitory structure where Henry lived with three other freshmen in Room 217. Henry later claimed he wasn't trying to be rude or distant; he simply preferred not to waste his time on things or people that could distract him. He routinely chose early morning classes so he could study during the afternoons, holed up with his books, his Underwood typewriter, and his desktop radio in his college dorm room. More than anything, Henry adopted this schedule to get his work done before the evening chaos of living with three younger roommates. He was never asked, nor did he seek, to join a single college organization. He seldom dabbled in any collegiate extracurricular activities other than going to an occasional Hawkeye football or basketball game. Without a hint of regret or embarrassment, Henry describes himself as a "total unknown" on campus.

Henry's first University of Iowa college ID card with his student number.

What Henry liked and appreciated most about the college atmosphere was that "it was very disciplined in my day. People went to college because they wanted to, and they looked at it as a privilege. And it didn't cost anything and I don't

Henry dressed for classes.

think that anyone left with any debt. You lived in a room in a dormitory, and the dormitories had waiting lists to get in, you ate your meals in a cafeteria. We had curfews in the dorms at night, even on weekends. And it was highly respectful. Most of the classes I was in, they started on time. Nearly everyone dressed up. I can't think of anytime that I went to class that you didn't have on a shirt and maybe a jacket, and the girls wore dresses. There was no one in slacks."

The G.I. Bill provided single veterans like Henry with tuition, books, supplies, and $65 a month in spending money. Henry stretched this cash allotment as much as he could, bringing back his farm-day accounting methods to record his expenses down to the last penny. Every day after studying, Henry took out a notebook and dutifully recorded his daily expenditures during his entire college experience, organized by each calendar year. At the start of his second semester, during the month of January 1948, Henry's records show that he spent an average of just $1.50 every day to eat. He spent 25 cents on razor blades and 31 cents for cold pills on his birthday on January 5, and treated himself to a new (no doubt warm) hat for $8.67 on January 8. His most expensive item for the month was the $56.25 Henry paid on January 12 for his dorm room on the South Quadrangle for the second semester, "and that included maid service," he recalled. And "I have written down here, 'heel plates, 10 cents.' If you put heel plates on your shoes, you could save your heels."

Henry existed entirely on the allowance from the G.I. Bill and the occasional $5 from his Uncle John. He rarely had money to spend on a date. "Did I have any close friends in my graduating class? The answer is no and the reason is, I was just kind of passing through. I was just a face in the crowd. My social life was highly limited," he admits. The only place where Henry ever seemed to relax was Joe's, a bar about two blocks from the main campus on Iowa Avenue that attracted veterans and independent students. "That's where a lot of us would be on a weekend night, and the place would be jam-packed and the smoke in the place—you could cut it with a knife. Draft beer was a dime, and that's where we congregated, the veterans and the independent students. I would be an independent, I didn't belong to any fraternity and never was asked to join one, but I wouldn't have joined anyway. So I would go down to Joe's and have a few beers and spend fifty cents. My outlay was minimal."

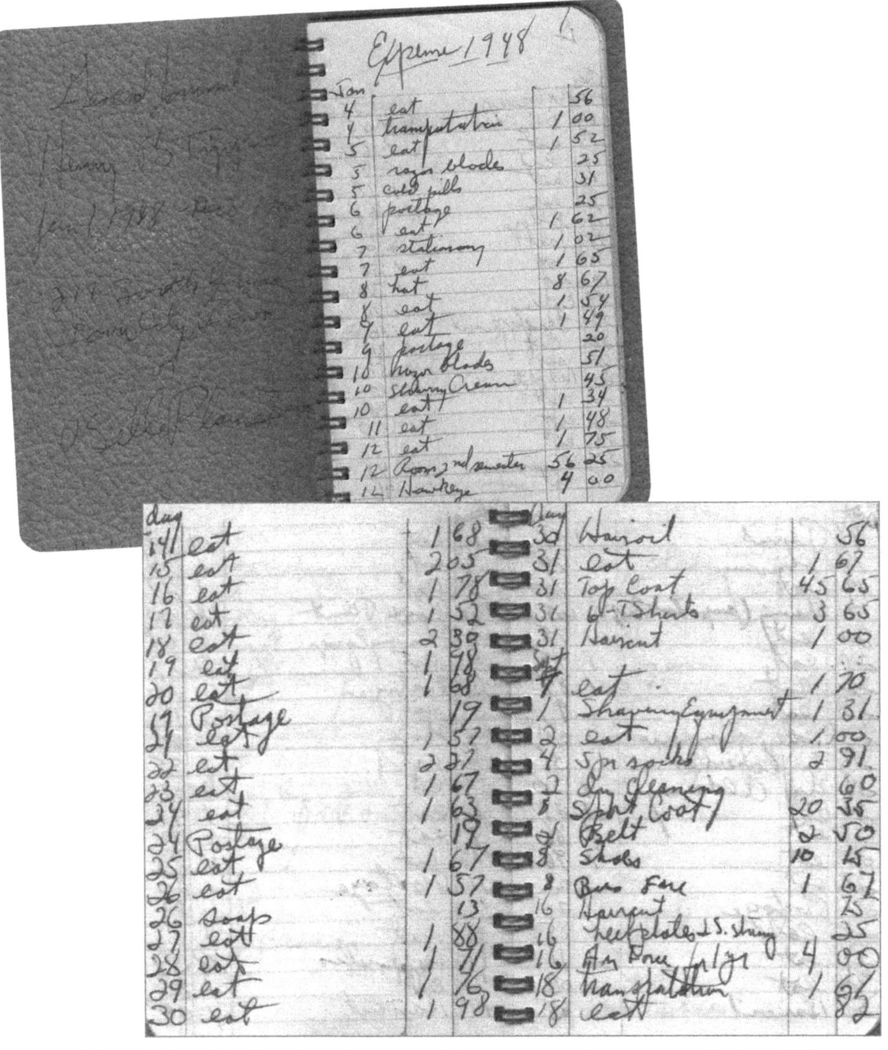

At the end of each day in college, Henry recorded his expenses. Here are examples from 1948.

Because he had no car, Henry rarely went home, even for the holidays, when he routinely stayed in the dorm to catch up on his studies. He studied straight through the year, staying on campus during the summer to take a full load of courses in summer school. Henry recalls being a part of a "vicious hearts game" that took place one summer in the dorm room, but he can't really recall any other distractions.

And that's how Henry went through college. "That was my program," he said. "I was there for a purpose, and my purpose was to get the hours in and graduate and do the best I could. I was not down there for a good time. My idea when I went to Iowa City was that I wanted to get out of there at the earliest possible moment, because I am already about to be twenty-one years old. I also made my mind up on the front end that I wanted to major in accounting, and that meant that you had to get into the College of Commerce. You had to have certain prerequisites in liberal arts to apply, and that doesn't happen until you're in your third year. That's how I started out, and I was ultimately accepted."

In the classroom, Henry was a fair student, with grades ranging from As to Cs and one D. Henry admits that "nothing about me" stood out. "I can quote you chapter and verse, every teacher or instructor I had there and in many cases the head of the department. But did they know me? The answer is no." He took what he considered to be some very good courses with some very good instructors, "others I should label average." Henry attended the classes almost ghostlike, preferring in his customary manner not to be noticed. He was too busy keeping to himself, slogging his way through college courses backed only by his limited high school education and a handful of courses in the military. He remembers enjoying political science, western civilization, and his accounting courses. "The accounting field was radically different at that time," he recalled. "There was no exposure to investments or the stock market. I don't think the trading volume was even a million shares a day then."

The one class Henry struggled with the most was Constitutional Law—a class based entirely in theory. "I thought it would be pretty easy. I had already done well in Business Law, and I thought the two would be similar. But I got the surprise of my life. When you read a sentence in there—you know I read things for what they *are*, for what the words *say*—and when I got into that course, the meaning was not what the words are, it was all interpretation. And midway through the course, I'm failing. And I'm thinking, 'My God, if I don't pass this course, I don't graduate. I will be one hour short.' So I went to see the professor, who happened to be the head of the department, and I did everything I could to remain in the course. And I got a D. I was so happy to get the D. And I did get a couple of As in other courses at the same time."

During his two intensive years in college, Henry missed only one class due to a bad cold and flu. He lived for two straight years on campus, never wavering from his focused vision to graduate and get to work. And while this may have been counter to the experiences of many other college undergraduates, it was not at all unusual for college freshmen who had already served in the military. As historian and author Stephen Ambrose once said during a radio interview,

> Millions of GIs, who never, never dreamed that they might be able to go to college suddenly had the opportunity, and these guys went, and they became—there isn't a teacher in this country who isn't aware of this—the best students we've ever had. God, they worked so hard, and they—all of them—came back to America feeling I just wasted the best years of my life. I know how to man a machine gun; I know how to fire a mortar, but I can't make a living out of this. And now they had college opened up to them, and these guys went on to take 21 hours a semester, 24 hours a semester, and they worked. They just wanted to get that education.

In many ways, Henry approached college the same way he approached the military: he took what it had to offer and slowly pieced together a string of disparate experiences that would help him become the first member of his family to get a college education, find a way out of poverty, and pursue a career that wasn't farming. Faced with a series of sometimes grim and usually challenging circumstances throughout his life, Henry consistently chose to work with what he had and move forward. He never complained or tossed up his hands in despair.

Which is exactly why Henry was able to graduate with a bachelor of science degree from the University of Iowa at the end of the summer of 1949 in a record-breaking 24 months—a feat made all the more astounding considering his lackluster high school record and his admission "on probation" to the university. When he later reflected on his experience at the university, Henry realized that the attributes he valued most—integrity, purpose, hard work, and sheer determination—were all characteristics that he practiced during his two years on a college campus in Iowa City. As he noted,

> You know, I think you make things pretty well what you want to make out of them, irrespective of the situation. You could go there and either take advantage of the course, or you could go there and just get through it. So there's two different avenues. And I think that's kinda in life, too. I've always felt that we all come into this world, and to a large extent, your destination of course is ultimately gonna be the cemetery. But what I'm getting at is in between the time you come into the world and until you get to that point, you're going to have a lot to say about what happens. You know, you can decide to coast, just kind of get by. Or you can develop knowledge, expand your horizons, and then when opportunities show themselves, lots of times you're in a position to take advantage of the opportunity.
>
> People talk about, well, isn't he lucky? And I'm thinking to myself, most of the luck is created. There is something to be said about being at the right place at the right time, but you can be at the right place at the right time and still it will pass you by because you don't have any preparation to take advantage of what may be there. And I think all of this gets back to the college business a little bit. I have always felt that the best thing that a person can do is expand your knowledge. When I was in college, I was a total unknown. And when I got out of there, I had a foundation, a foundation that would prepare me for things ahead. I am the recipient of somebody giving me a chance.

CHAPTER SEVEN

THE NUMBERS MAN GOES TO WORK

AFTER HENRY GRADUATED FROM THE University of Iowa in August 1949, the opportunities and advantages he dreamed a college education would offer did not immediately materialize. In a painful déjà vu harking back to the Depression era he lived through as a child, Henry had to face the fact that the country was in the midst of an economic downturn commonly referred to as the Recession of 1949. It began in November 1948, shortly after President Truman set his "Fair Deal" economic reforms in motion, and it would last until roughly October 1949. The timing could not have been worse for Henry. Armed with his new accounting degree after finishing all of his courses during summer school, Henry discovered that any major accounting firms looking to hire had already visited the Iowa campus earlier that year to recruit the June accounting graduates. There were no recruiters in sight when he graduated in August. And without a job, Henry was keenly aware that he was missing out on more than just a paycheck. With every passing week that he remained unemployed, Henry realized that he was slipping further behind with his plan to pass the CPA test, become an accountant, and start his professional career. "You could not take that test until you had at least one year's experience working for a CPA firm, so that was on my radar screen," said Henry. "Now, how do I get there?"

With no contacts and no job leads, Henry reluctantly moved back to Belle Plaine to live with his family. He was pretty devastated. He was now the first in his family to graduate from both a high school and a university, he had finished in only two years, and he had never asked his family for a dime. He had dared to leave the farm, see the world, and earn his accounting degree—but what did he have to show for it? "What's the good of college if you don't have a job?" Henry asked himself, over and over.

Too, Henry felt the disappointment of his father, who had always had a difficult time seeing the point of college. Both Henry and Ernie agreed that the only time their father believed that Henry's college education had value was when Bob and Amelia sold the farm in January 1948, just as Henry started his second college semester. From the business courses he had already completed, Henry figured out that his father could realize a tremendous savings after selling the farm and all the equipment, a sale that took place on January 31 during a heavily advertised "Complete Closing Out Farm Sale." Beginning at 1 p.m. that day, auctioneer Oscar Myers sold everything from Bob's 1940 John Deere Model B tractor and his 240-gallon oil tank to 60 bales of second-growth clover and a child's iron bed, no doubt the same one Henry slept in as a child. "SOLD," Myers shouted all afternoon, as the gavel signaled another cash exchange for what remained of Tippie's Dairy Farm and some miscellaneous household furniture that would not be moved into their new home at 810 Seventh Street in Belle Plaine.

"Henry realized that my dad could come up with tremendous savings from the farm sale because he had never taken depreciation on any of his equipment," said Ernie. "The people that had always done his taxes before just knew that two and two makes four; they really didn't know those kinds of things about depreciation laws. And I think that's the only time my dad really appreciated that there was something out there that Henry was learning that was worthwhile."

Henry was never certain that his father took his financial advice—and he was too proud to ask him a year after the fact. In August 1949, when he returned home and moved in with his family, he discovered that his family members were fairly settled into their postfarm lives. Amelia now worked for a nearby florist shop, and Bob had started his own electrician's business and worked part-time as a police officer. Ernie, 18, who initially balked at leaving the farm and threatened to live with neighbors so he could keep farming, had eventually moved into town, graduated from high school, and joined the U.S. Air Force. John was 14, just starting high school, and he loved science and engineering. The basement in the new home, and probably the garage out back, contained many of the old farm and household items that Henry had insisted on saving—lots of tools and farm benches, a feeding trough or two, his mother's cash box from the dairy farm, and several boxes filled with old receipts, calendars, school report cards, and Henry's high school memorabilia. Still, the 22-year-old Henry felt oddly out of place. He had no money, and the only thing on his mind was getting out again as fast as possible. He stoically buckled down and looked for work, mailing out over 200 résumés and letters to accounting firms throughout the Midwest. He received a few replies, but no job offers or requests for interviews came through the mail slot at the Tippie house on Seventh Street.

Bob saw that his son was getting nowhere just writing letters to the accounting firms. So in a rare moment that showed how deeply he recognized, and perhaps empathized with, his son's predicament, Bob arranged for Henry to get an overnight ride to Chicago in order to pound the pavement and conduct some face-to-face, one-on-one interviews. While the ride was free, it was far from glamorous. Turns out, Bob knew the man who ran the livestock yard in Belle Plaine, and Henry's ride to Chicago was on a hog transfer truck, the kind that left the local livestock yards in Belle Plaine every night around 10 p.m. and arrived at the packing yards of Chicago about five o'clock the next morning.

Recalled Henry, "I rode with a double-deck load of hogs, riding in the August heat with no air conditioning. It could get very hot, and you ride all night in the truck. The driver let me off in Chicago at South Cicero, which at that time was a very rough area, and he told me that I could get the streetcar to West Madison Avenue and then switch streetcars—or I could walk toward downtown. I knew I wanted to get to the Chicago Northwestern Depot, which was near the financial district where all the major accounting firms were headquartered. "

Henry was dressed like a bum—wearing his old army field jacket and carrying a beat-up cardboard suitcase that held his only business suit and tie. He smelled, well, like he had just been riding all night in a truck hauling hogs. And as he navigated his way through Chicago, he recalls that he stepped over more than one drunken body and homeless person. "Nobody bothered me. And the reason nobody bothered me is they probably figured that I'm one of them." Once inside the Depot, Henry went straight to the men's public restroom, where he washed up and changed clothes. He soon stepped out in his fresh suit, full of anticipation yet weary from the long night, carrying a map and a phone book that he used to locate the major accounting firms he wanted to visit.

As Henry entered each office in the financial district, he was greeted with the sight of eager, smiling faces plastered on a dozen young men just like him, waiting in the lobbies and looking for work. The competition was intense, and Henry walked away after a long day with no leads and no offers. Tired from the trip and a day of job hunting, Henry found the Atlantic Hotel, where he had previously stayed with his Uncle John during his boyhood adventure to see a Chicago Cubs baseball game. The hotel Henry remembered through a child's eyes was now dramatically deteriorated and dangerous, but Henry stayed there because it was all he could afford. Part of the door lock was missing, so Henry took a chair and propped it against the door as he tried to sleep. And for two days, Henry searched the financial district of Chicago, looking doggedly and systematically for work. He then took what little money he had left and caught the Greyhound bus home. He was exhausted, and he still didn't have a job.

Without a doubt, this was a low point in Henry's young life. But this 22-year-old soon learned something about himself that he never forgot. "I'm probably at my best when things are toughest," he realized. "When things get tough, I feel the need to organize and straighten things out. I'm strong on planning, wherever I'm going."

Henry's job search soon took him to Des Moines, just a few hours from Belle Plaine. Though he wanted to get farther away from his hometown, Henry's aunt Naomi Jopling lived in Des Moines with her husband, and they offered Henry a place to stay while he continued to look for a job. Once settled, Henry systematically pored through the Des Moines Yellow Pages, looking up each firm alphabetically. Henry quickly noted that unlike the firms in Chicago, there were no major accounting firms in Des

Moines in 1949, only regional and local ones. They were pretty small, but Henry didn't care, and his diligence paid off. He soon scheduled several interviews with accounting firms that were looking to hire.

One interview—for a position with one of the area's larger firms with a stellar reputation—went extremely well, Henry thought, and he quickly surmised that the partner sitting across the table was very interested in him. They even discussed a starting salary of $225 a month, which Henry thought right away was a solid living wage. But the partner said he had to wait a few days to make a final decision because he needed to talk to a second partner who happened to be out of town. "I'll be in touch," the partner said, and Henry shook his hand and left.

Checking through his list, Henry proceeded to his next interview at the accounting firm of James C. Addison and Company. Immediately, Henry and the partner clicked. The partner told Henry that the company had an opening for a junior accountant, and the starting salary would be $175 a month or $2,100 a year. Before Henry had time to wonder if he was going to get an offer, the partner told Henry, "We need your answer immediately." In a decidedly unceremonious moment, Henry finally had a job offer. "It was the first job offer I ever had from anybody. *Anybody*!" he remembered, smiling. "And the partner didn't want a deal where I'm trying to find out the best place to go and say yes, and then two or three days later get a better job someplace else. He wanted the answer right then."

As desperate as Henry was for a job, he didn't accept the offer immediately. Instead, he excused himself and went out to the lobby to think it over for a while. "When he told me the pay, I'm sitting there thinking, 'I don't know if I can live on this. It's $50 less every month than the other job might offer.' So I'm sitting out there thinking, 'What am I gonna do?' I've got this possibility over here and maybe that will be $225 a month, and it's with a very good organization that has an excellent reputation. And here's this small firm over here at only $175 a month, but that's a bird in the hand, not a bird in the bush." And the other factor that Henry had to consider was the CPA test. "I could not take the CPA test until I had one year's experience. And I'm thinking, if I could get under way here and start this job in October, that maybe I could survive for a year at least. And then I could take the test."

Henry returned to the partner's office and accepted the position with James C. Addison and Company. "I told him, 'It's gonna be tough on this salary, but I want to get the experience.'" Two months after graduating from the University of Iowa, and after a grueling two months' job search, Henry started his job on October 1, 1949, as a low-paid junior accountant. "I guess 'flunky' would be a better word for it," Henry said of the position. "You do what everybody tells you to do. And you're going to have to put up with anything because otherwise, you got no job, you got no experience."

Though he earned $175 a month, Henry's take-home pay after taxes was a mere $135 a month. Financially, he faced a dire situation. "With that little money, you get into, well, how are you gonna survive?" Henry knew he had to keep his expenses to a minimum, so he rented a single room for a dollar a day at the downtown YMCA, a distinctive, six-story, square brick building at 524 Fourth Street in Des Moines that featured ironwork in the stairway, marble stairs, and tall arching windows at the double-door granite entrance. In stark contrast, Henry's sparsely furnished room had only a bed, a sink, a desk, and a place to hang some clothes; the shower and toilet

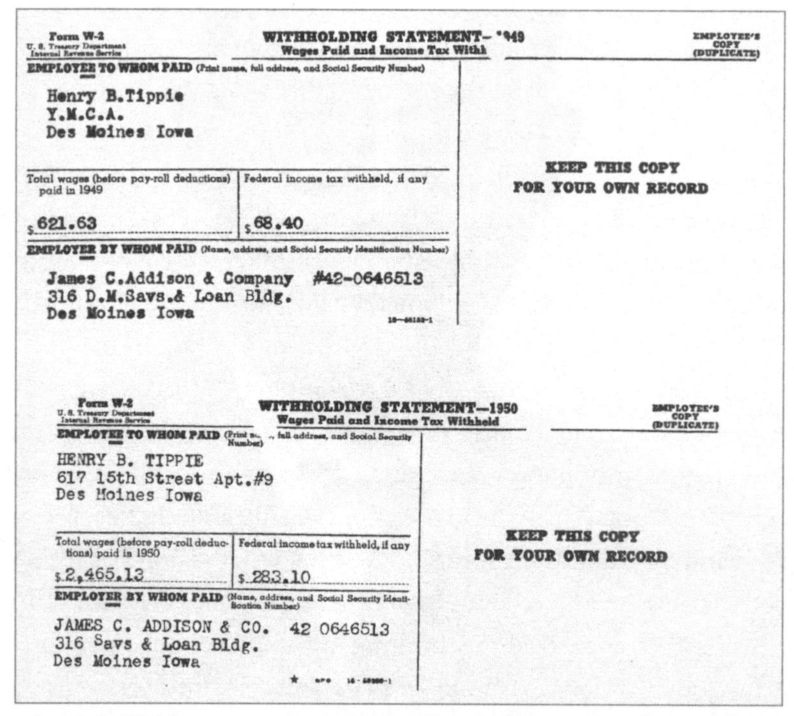

Form W-2
U. S. Treasury Department
Internal Revenue Service

WITHHOLDING STATEMENT—1949
Wages Paid and Income Tax Withh

EMPLOYEE'S COPY (DUPLICATE)

EMPLOYEE TO WHOM PAID (Print name, full address, and Social Security Number)

Henry B.Tippie
Y.M.C.A.
Des Moines Iowa

Total wages (before pay-roll deductions) paid in 1949	Federal income tax withheld, if any
$621.63	$68.40

EMPLOYER BY WHOM PAID (Name, address, and Social Security Identification Number)

James C.Addison & Company #42-0646513
316 D.M.Savs.& Loan Bldg.
Des Moines Iowa

KEEP THIS COPY
FOR YOUR OWN RECORD

Form W-2
U. S. Treasury Department
Internal Revenue Service

WITHHOLDING STATEMENT—1950
Wages Paid and Income Tax Withheld

EMPLOYEE'S COPY (DUPLICATE)

EMPLOYEE TO WHOM PAID (Print name, full address, and Social Security Number)

HENRY B. TIPPIE
617 15th Street Apt.#9
Des Moines Iowa

Total wages (before pay-roll deductions) paid in 1950	Federal income tax withheld, if any
$2,465.13	$283.10

EMPLOYER BY WHOM PAID (Name, address, and Social Security Identification Number)

JAMES C. ADDISON & CO. 42 0646513
316 Savs & Loan Bldg.
Des Moines Iowa

KEEP THIS COPY
FOR YOUR OWN RECORD

Henry's first W-2 forms as an accountant, when his goal in life was to earn $15,000 a year.

were down the hall. "I was on the top floor on the east side of the building, and in the wintertime there would be ice on the window. But they did clean the room for you a couple of times a week," he said. For meals, Henry always ate inexpensively at Bishop's Cafeteria, located midway between work and the YMCA. But after a few weeks, Henry decided that paying $7 a week for a room was too much. So he teamed up with a roommate and split the cost of a double, slightly larger room at the Y that cost Henry $3.75 a week, a savings of $3.25 a week. The lower rent gave Henry some financial breathing space. And Henry took comfort in the fact that everyone was in the same boat; the YMCA was full of struggling young men, just starting out.

Henry lived at the YMCA in downtown Des Moines.

"I think there were some pretty nice people in there," he said. "And the YWCA was three blocks away, and it would be comparable, and the girls in there would have secretarial-type positions. These were desirable places to live because in those days, everything was downtown. They would have music over at the YWCA on Saturday nights and maybe have some cookies and you didn't have to spend any money."

Henry soon discovered that there was no training program for junior accountants at Addison, and the firm was extremely disorganized. As Henry remembered it, he could sink or swim. "Sometimes I'd be sent out of town with another fellow who would just drop me off with a client someplace and say, 'I'll be back in two or three days.' I mean, you were totally lost, so that's how that guy worked." Armed with the client's previous year's tax papers, Henry learned to navigate his way through a job to the best of his ability. "You had to learn to be self-sufficient. You had to learn to figure things out. The other advantage to working in this firm is that we did everything. We not only did tax returns, we did audit work, so it was a complete deal. You're kind of like a jack-of-all-trades in these small firms. And I got diversification in terms of who we worked with—from automobile dealerships to canning operations."

Bill Shambaugh, a lifelong friend of Henry's who worked at the firm during the same time, once described the work environment at Addison with his customary dry wit. "It wasn't extremely painful, really," Bill said. "One of the problems was pay, starting at the grand sum of $175 a month. I really accomplished something when I got to $200. And Jim Addison, the boss, insisted that all the men working there wear hats. And that didn't bother me because I wore one anyway, but he fired this fellow who came from Ames, Iowa, who told the rest of the office, 'Nobody tells me to wear a hat, I'll do as I please.' During tax season, Jim would always make his 'circuit,' as he called it. He had these friends who had businesses, and he would go around and collect their tax information for the federal return, and then bring the file back and then give it to whoever needed something to do. We always shuddered."

Paul Caswell, another accountant who worked at the firm and became close friends with Henry, didn't paint a glowing picture of the company either. "James C. Addison was a curmudgeon, if there ever was such a word. He was a big Scotchman and he smoked cigars and had a hat that was always mashed," said Caswell. "And we weren't paid too well. It was a dollar an hour, and at the time I worked six days a week and we didn't get time and a half. We got the 'b-low' plan, where the more you worked the less you got per hour."

In a pattern that served Henry well his entire life, he decided to make the best of an unremarkable situation. Though the higher-paying job offer at the larger firm did eventually come through, Henry thought it would be unethical to leave the position he had just accepted, so he turned it down. And Henry never looked back at what could or should have been. "I just keep moving on down the road," he soon began to say, a mantra that he would repeat his entire life.

As a junior accountant in Des Moines, Henry soon put his situation into perspective. "I did not look at this firm as a disadvantage; in the long term, I think it was an advantage." First and foremost, he completed the required year of experience he needed in order to take the CPA exam. Second, he was exposed to a wide variety of clients and cases, which turned out to be a plus. Without any mentoring or training, Henry learned to think fast on his feet while developing a deep well of different work experiences. This type of work environment, though chaotic, was actually good for Henry. Because he worked straight through college, he had had no summer jobs or internships in the accounting field, and his eyes were opened by the diverse situations he encountered at Addison. Third, Henry often got assigned to jobs that were out of town, which exposed him to numerous situations and people that helped "further my education"—another soon-to-be favorite Tippie catchphrase—in how to get along with people and understand human nature. "You would go out of town with different people to do the grunt work, I mean the most mundane type tasks," Henry said. He recalled one particular trip: "The fellow that I was sent to work with had a loud voice. And we'd go out on the job and he would love to get out in the center of the floor and talk to me. You could hear him in the next county. And he would describe the most basic, mundane type deal in the most elaborate detail, as to what you were supposed to do. It would sound like you were somebody that absolutely never even had an accounting course. And sometimes I would want to fall down between the cracks in the floor, but I just sat there calmly and listened."

And last but not least, Henry actually looked forward to taking jobs outside Des Moines. Why? Because the firm covered all expenses during the road trips, including meals, so Henry started to save a little money. He opened a savings account. And by diligently sticking to his plan to save, Henry managed to scrape a few dollars off the top of each paycheck to put away each month.

The discipline required to start saving was not something he saw mirrored at his workplace. There was a lot of downtime at the small firm, and a lot of that time was wasted (Bill and Paul remembered shooting paper clips across the street at pigeons). But that wasn't true of Henry. His colleagues described Henry as being very serious about work, even then. "Oh yes, he was always focused," said Paul. "Actually, he was very quiet, he didn't joke like the rest of us." Added Bill, "I kind of looked up to these fellows with military backgrounds and coming through the G.I. Bill with accounting degrees, and I thought, they are coming on board much more qualified than either Paul or myself. And you look at Henry. He used his time to do a lot of reading, probably the *Wall Street Journal*."

Indeed, Henry used the slow time in the office wisely. When there was absolutely no work to be done, he tucked himself into the office's library and studied tax pamphlets and case summaries. "I was trying to broaden my horizons a little bit," said Henry. "The firm hired one more young fellow after me, and I watched as he goofed off. He would go to the movies in the afternoon and invite me along, which I declined. He would just disappear." His coworker's behavior was anathema to Henry. "I feel anytime you're on someone's payroll, you owe that operation your best. If you decided to go on to another job later, you need to leave through the front door, not the back door. Some people go out the back door and they leave a bad memory. And at a later date that comes back to haunt them. Always go out the front door."

In May 1950, seven months after starting his job, Henry had saved enough to buy a car. But instead of buying a used Model T for $150 like he did in high school, Henry ordered a brand-new 1950 Chevrolet, a "Fleetline De Luxe 2-Door Sedan," from the Malcolm Brothers in Belle Plaine, delivered on May 8, 1950, for the grand sum of $1,859.29, which included the luxury tax and insurance. Henry's new Chevrolet was "loaded," as car dealers liked to say, with a push-button radio, air conditioning, heater, a defroster, and whitewall tires.

Henry loved the relative freedom the new car brought to his life, even though he continued to describe his social life in Des Moines as "nonexistent." Since Paul and Bill were married with children, they went home to their families at the end of the workday while bachelor Henry went back to the YMCA. There, Henry's main friend was an Addison colleague and a former summer school roommate at the University of Iowa named Bob Rienders. Together, Rienders and Henry studied for the upcoming CPA test. Henry knew it was going to be challenging, especially for him: in college, he was told to drop the CPA course because "I didn't have advanced accounting and some other prerequisites. But that didn't stop me from buying the book, so I studied the book." The test material came easily to Rienders, but Henry "had to study like the dickens," said Bill. "Because they both came from Iowa City and were both single and lived at the Y, we thought of those two as a team."

The two-man study sessions and Henry's tenacious attitude eventually paid off. Henry took his Certified Public Accountant exam in November 1950, passing all of the sections except for Theory—a subject he had struggled with in college, too. Henry was eligible to take that portion of the test again, and he went ahead and scheduled the repeat exam for the next May. With the bulk of the test behind him, Henry decided that a year living in the YMCA was enough, and he found an apartment in a three-story house on the fringe of downtown Des Moines. He shared it with Ed Jobe, then a student at the American Institute of Business who was also living at the YMCA and, like Henry, was ready to move out.

Though Henry felt the neighborhood around the new apartment was less than desirable, it was still a step up from living in a boxlike room at the Y. Splitting the $55 monthly rent, the two young men moved into a rather large area that was actually the front of a whole floor in a house that had been divided in half by the tenant who already lived there; a woman lived in the back part of the space that included the kitchen, and Henry and Ed lived in the front section. A door with a lock separated the two spaces, and that lock turned out to be pretty important. Henry enjoyed describing the situation, which he and Ed would laugh about for years to come, long after they were successful businessmen. "We found out that this other tenant was in her mid-50s and we were in our 20s, and we also found out that she was a lady of the evening," Henry recalled. "On Friday and Saturday nights, the cigar smoke would curl up under her door; she had visitors. We rarely ever saw her. But we did find out."

After working as a junior accountant for 18 months at Addison and Company, Henry decided it was time to move on. Henry saw no room for advancement at the firm, and even though his salary had been upped to $200 a month, Henry concluded that "I was going nowhere at this place." At the end of January 1951, he gave his boss 30 days' notice and left in late February in search of new opportunities. Because he had so few belongings, Henry liked to say that it took him less than 30 minutes to pack up everything in his Chevrolet and hit the road. He first headed west to Colorado, but a job-scouting stop in Denver produced no discernible leads. On the way back to the Midwest, Henry stopped over in Omaha, Nebraska, for an interview with the largest accounting firm in the city—Congdon, O'Hara & Becker. The firm just happened to be one of the 200 places that Henry wrote to in August 1949, when he was fresh out of college and looking for his first job.

This time, Henry secured an interview with the partners at Congdon, O'Hara & Becker, inside the company's headquarters in the Woodmen of the World (W.O.W.) Building on Farnam Street. By all accounts it went very well. Henry thought the suggested $325 monthly salary was outstanding, and he was impressed by the firm's sense of organization and its dedicated, specialized departments. And even though he wasn't offered a job immediately, Henry left the interview feeling good about the possibility of landing a job. Said Henry, "It was organized. They had their own tax section, they had a review section, they had some major clientele. And I would have more status there than just a junior accountant. I'd say it was promising."

Henry's confidence was rewarded. Just a few days later, when Henry was in Belle Plaine visiting his family, a letter arrived for Henry at his parents' Seventh Street address. It was dated March 15, 1951, and carefully typed on Congdon, O'Hara & Becker letterhead:

> Dear Mr. Tippie:
> This is to advise that we have decided to accept you as an employee at the agreed starting salary of $325 per month.
> It will be satisfactory to us for you to come to work immediately if you desire. However, if you wish to take next week off and come to work on Monday, March 26, this will also be satisfactory.
>
> Very truly yours,
> Congdon, O'Hara & Becker

Henry was really happy as he read this letter. His instinct to leave a job "where I was going nowhere" had actually paid off, and his starting monthly salary of $325 impressed everyone—especially the new employee himself. "I'm thinking, 'I'm in the big time now; this is big, big money' because I was making $200 a month in Des Moines," said Henry, who added the letter to his growing collection of career artifacts.

Henry's parents appreciated their son's success, and his youngest brother, John, clearly benefited from it. Remembered Ernie, "John might want a fishing pole or a baseball glove and he would beg my folks to buy it. And they just honestly would say, 'We can't afford it.' But Henry would come along because he was an entrepreneur, and would take him off to the side and say, 'Next time we go to town, I'll get that for you.'"

Henry thrived at his new job in Omaha. He lived in a room in a private house, just one block from the end of the electric streetcar line in what was then known as a "streetcar suburb." It's no wonder that this young accountant from Iowa, who grew up watching and hearing trains pass his house all day long, would decide to park his Chevrolet during the week and take the streetcar downtown to work. Walking up Farnam Street every morning, he marveled at the architecture of the building where he worked—a 19-story, Italian Renaissance skyscraper with exterior ornamentation in pink granite and terra-cotta, a motor-operated revolving front door, and a lobby with grand 30-foot ceilings and polished floors that caught the tap of Henry's footsteps each day. Six elevators carried employees like Henry to the upper floors and into the Congdon, O'Hara & Becker office suites. Here, Henry's career in numbers, foreshadowed in the accounting books he kept as a child and all through college, came together in a professional atmosphere that perfectly matched Henry's disciplined, meticulous nature. Said Henry, "I performed duties as an auditor on varying types of businesses, and I also prepared

Henry B. Tippie, the young accountant, Omaha, Nebraska.

tax returns on a federal and local level. I obtained a considerable background of experiences about financial operations for businesses."

And for the first time in years, Henry looked forward to his time away from the office. Henry could finally afford the social life that living in a city like Omaha offered, so he hit the town and started to enjoy his beloved Big Band music once again. "To me it was an outstanding place for a person of my age to live," Henry recalled. "Everything was downtown. They had nightclubs, and stuff was inexpensive. I had a great time. And I had a good job, I enjoyed the firm I worked at, just nice people."

Henry had been employed at the firm for just three months when he heard that the company was looking to hire more people. He immediately thought of Paul Caswell and Bob Rienders, his friends back in Des Moines at James C. Addison, and he arranged for them to be interviewed by his new company. As Paul recalls, "Henry's the reason we came to Omaha. He called me up one day and said, 'Why don't you come over here? I'll set it up to get you an appointment.'" With Henry's introduction and stellar recommendations, both Paul and Bob soon had new jobs and moved to Omaha with their families.

Ruth Caswell, Paul's wife, recalled going out as a couple to catch some live music with Henry, and she remembered, too, what it was like when Henry took a date along. "He was always dressed nice and he was always a gentleman and did the proper thing," she said. And Henry "was not a cheap date, either, he was a good date." Right after the Caswells first arrived in Omaha, Paul went out of town for six weeks to work for his new firm on an assignment in Longview, Texas. Henry and Bob regularly visited Ruth to "check on me," she recalled, and the sight of both old friends was comforting. Paul noted that Henry and Bob would check on Ruth, "but they wouldn't come inside because they knew the neighbors would talk. They were two purists, both of them."

Of all of Henry's Omaha experiences, it could be argued that the most valuable one was riding the streetcar. Riding home on the streetcar every night, Henry had plenty of time to read the *Omaha World Herald Newspaper*, and he discovered that he was particularly interested in the financial section. As Henry became familiar with the rhythm of the streetcar—with regular stops spaced predictably at short intervals throughout neighborhoods and small business districts—he sat alone on his route home and devoured newspaper stories about business, finance, and investing. He became familiar with the stock tables and the workings of the stock market. And Henry soon came to a conclusion, something that no college course or professor ever taught him but something that this 24-year-old realized on his own:

> I decided that the only way a person could ever have much chance to accumulate any worth, any assets, was through investments, excluding, of course, anything from inheritance, the latter of which I didn't see on the radar screen. It seemed to me that the best approach would be to invest in securities. And my whole life I've always felt that you develop worth with investments. I do not feel that you develop worth with a paycheck. Paychecks wind up being taxed. And what happens with a paycheck? Standards of living flow with the paycheck. People get more cars, bigger houses, they may get a second house, take more expensive-type vacations. This is what happens with a paycheck. How do you do something about that? I started right off the bat with saying, "I'm setting aside a certain amount for investments." I did it in a very disciplined manner, on a monthly basis. And I think that's the only way you'll ever save anything. If a person thinks that they are going to periodically save some money, it doesn't happen. You have to discipline yourself and set that money aside if you think you can afford to. You can certainly, if your paycheck increases. And if you get dividends or bonuses or anything like that, I used to look at those as, "That's just extra money that I don't need, I can get along without it." Does all this take place overnight? The answer is no. It's a long, drawn-out process, takes a lot of time. But I come back to this: if you have a program, if you have a plan and the discipline, that's the only way it's going to work.

Several months after starting his job in Omaha, and several months into studying the newspaper and analyzing the business and financial pages while riding the streetcar, Henry knew it was time to invest the $1,000 he had in savings, money he had gradually saved since buying his car in 1950.

So how did Henry do it? "One noon hour I walked into Lamson Brothers, which at the time was a well-known Midwest investment house. I had made up my mind to spread my money over three different securities—namely a few shares of General Motors, U.S. Steel, and a sugar company. The timing, of course, could not have been better, inasmuch as the stocks were quite cheap and paid excellent dividends. I further felt at the time that both GM and U.S. Steel were rock-solid companies, and should they ever fail, the whole U.S. would be in very serious trouble. That was true, certainly in those days. This was my first investment, and since that time I have never ceased to have involvement with securities."

What about dividends and reinvesting? "I set up a separate savings account for all dividends, and as I got enough dividends, coupled with any other amounts that I felt like I could invest, I would add to my holdings. Or as time went on, I could look at other securities, which I felt were a good buy. My initial purchases were in the size of 5 to 25 shares—that's all I could afford. Over the years of course I was able to finally be looking at purchasing at least 50 shares. Then I finally got into the 100 shares, what is known as the round lot. And of a more later vintage, in the thousands."

Who did Henry turn to for advice? "I had no discussion with anybody else relative to advice. My approach was to buy and hold, contrasted to trading and trying to outsmart which direction the market may go in. Fortunately as the years went by, this proved to be a very good approach, and one that I have basically not deviated from except for the occasional flyer. And as time went on, I found that flyers were not a very good venture."

Of course, the question always is, did Henry ever have a failure? "The answer is yes, but fortunately, not very many. I further feel that if anybody ever tells you they've never had a failure, you can pretty well dismiss the rest of their comments. Failures become a learning experience as to what not to repeat."

Henry's reflection on failure came partially from personal experience. He had passed three sections of the CPA exam in November 1950, but he had failed the Theory portion of the exam, something he had to pass to become a certified public accountant. In May 1951, Henry traveled from Omaha back to Des Moines to once more tackle the Theory portion of the CPA exam. This time he passed. On July 21, 1951, Henry B. Tippie officially became a Certified Public Accountant, Certificate No. 276, granted by the State of Iowa Board of Accountancy and recorded on a diploma-like document that Henry proudly displayed for the rest of his life. Henry could now legally and officially practice public accounting. With a headline that no doubt caught the attention of members of the Belle Plaine High School Class of '44, the *Belle Plaine Union* published an article about Henry's accomplishment on August 1, 1951: *Henry B. Tippie a Certified Public Accountant—Was One of Fifteen Iowans Who Took Examinations in May.* "He was one of the three who ranked highest," the paper reported. "There are more than 40,000 certified public accountants in the nation. Public accounting is America's fastest growing profession, showing an increase of 800 percent since 1920." Now an official CPA, Henry soon joined the American Institute of Accountants (known then as the AIA, but later changed to the American Institute of Certified Public Accountants), and paid $7 for a yearly subscription to the organization's professional magazine, *The Journal of Accountancy.* Like the kid who once pored over baseball magazines, Henry religiously read every article in the journal, cover to cover.

For several months, Henry's work routine remained the same, and he continued as an accountant with Congdon, O'Hara & Becker. But in the fall of 1951, several things happened that changed Henry's career. The firm merged with a so-called Big Eight accounting firm of Peat, Marwick, and Mitchell. Around the same time as the merger, a client of Henry's at Congdon, O'Hara & Becker, who happened to be located in the same building, offered Henry a highly paid position within the company; the client wanted Henry to be the company's treasurer, with a salary of $175 a week, roughly doubling Henry's pay. Recognizing that this was a tremendous opportunity, Henry jumped at the chance, but the opportunity was short-lived. After five months as treasurer of the company, the death of one of the corporation's co-owners precipitated the operation's liquidation. By the spring of 1952, Henry was again out of work, but there was a silver lining to his brief experience as treasurer: he could now see himself as growing with an enterprise, rather than limiting himself to an accountant's position. "Once I got out," Henry realized, "I had no interest in going back."

In a matter of weeks, Henry returned to Des Moines and accepted a position as the controller of a small manufacturing company with two plants but a relatively uncertain future. Henry had some doubts about the position, but he wanted to test his theory that he could do more for a company than just be its accountant. He had to admit, however, that it was difficult to leave Omaha, and not just because he loved the city. By now, Henry was engaged to be married. His fiancée was a lovely, very attractive young woman from Omaha who worked in an accounts payable department of a local company. Henry knew and liked her family, and he left Omaha thinking that everything was set: the engaged couple had scheduled the wedding and mailed out the invitations, and Henry had lined up his former high school buddy Flea Wright to be the best man.

Without any warning, Henry got the deeply upsetting news by telegram in Des Moines: "The wedding will not take place." Recalled Henry, "I can still picture the guy at the Western Union, bringing me the telegram. He was kind of crippled, and he must have been about 70 years old and I can see him walking up there, very sad, bringing me this. And I'm reading this and I can't believe it. I never said a word to a person. I just read it two or three times and put it in my pocket." As soon as he could, Henry drove to Omaha to confront his fiancée and "find out what the hell was going on. But it was pretty obvious that it wasn't going to take place. And the message kind of came through to me that I wasn't good enough, and I wasn't going anyplace, and I'm just kind of floundering around. And she was a very attractive young lady, she was a nice person. I cannot say anything bad about her. But I think her parents got in the way of it. They took her on a vacation and when they got back, that's when the telegram took place."

The news shocked Henry's friends, too. Bill Shambaugh, who was still living in Des Moines, remembers the day Henry came over to the house and shared the news. "It was a sad Sunday afternoon that we spent with Henry, when he told us the situation, about how he was horrified to receive a cancellation notice via telegraph," said Bill. "It was a sad afternoon and we didn't hardly know what to talk about, and Henry didn't either. So we commiserated anyway. "

Paul and Ruth Caswell were just as stunned as Bill. "Paul was supposed to be an usher in the wedding, and then out of the blue, we got this formal thing in the mail that said, 'The wedding will not take place,'" said Ruth. "Henry was devastated at that time."

Though Henry would later look back and declare that the canceled wedding was "probably one of the best things that ever happened to me," he was angry. He was hurt. He was embarrassed. The only immediate takeaway that Henry could see from this debacle is that he survived. Said Henry, "Something like that would be so devastating to some people and I'm not sure they would ever recover. But I did. And so again, I come back to all these disappointments, rejections, frustrations in life, and I've always looked at them in terms of a learning experience. Something to build on. It's an education, if nothing else. And you take all these deals and you build on them for the future."

Henry continued to work in Des Moines, but "kept my eyes and ears open" for new opportunities. Still stung by what had happened to him, he reluctantly decided to skip his younger brother's wedding in Belle Plaine in September, when Airman First Class Ernest A. Tippie married Margaret Catherine Hazen, also a Belle Plaine native. Henry's youngest brother, John, now a 17-year-old high school senior who planned to attend the University of Iowa to study engineering one day, stepped in and served as best man in Henry's place.

And though Henry would be the first to insist he is not a philosopher, he continued to allow himself time to ponder some important questions after being rejected by someone he loved and someone he thought loved him—questions rooted in adult experiences that he now recognized as disappointing and painful but beyond his control. Slowly, Henry embraced some answers that would help shape his approach to life and work:

> For instance, how do you handle rejection? Well, do you let that get you down or do you pick yourself up and say, "I just learned something"? And a lot of people don't ever learn anything. And I think some of your greatest learning comes from failure. I have always felt that the good Lord is up there and I don't know what his plan is, but you go through a lot of testing. But I still think each

> individual has a lot to do with the road out here that you're on. You know, if you go down the wrong road, then you try to get back on the main road. I figured I just went off on the side road here with this marriage business, and I needed to get back on the main road and keep moving.

Henry knew that he was the only person who could determine his future. He decided he wanted a new road, and in December 1952, Henry ran a one-paragraph ad in the professional accounting publication he subscribed to, *The Journal of Accountancy.* Henry's simple and direct posting landed on page 770 and let the accounting world know his services and skills were now available:

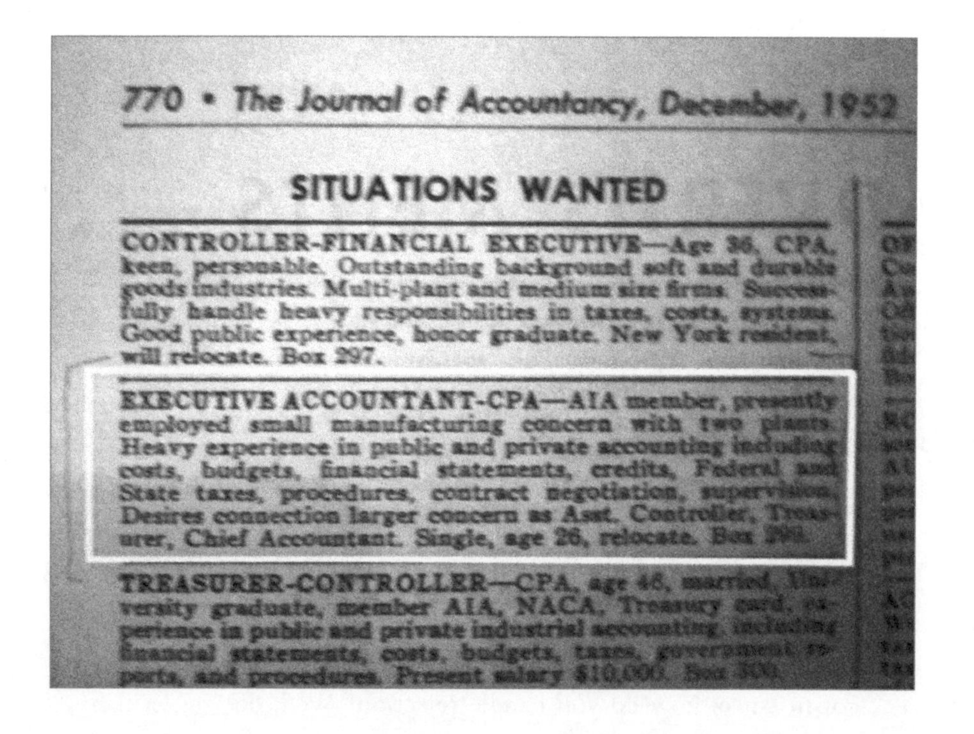

770 • The Journal of Accountancy, December, 1952

SITUATIONS WANTED

CONTROLLER-FINANCIAL EXECUTIVE—Age 36, CPA, keen, personable. Outstanding background soft and durable goods industries. Multi-plant and medium size firms. Successfully handle heavy responsibilities in taxes, costs, systems. Good public experience, honor graduate. New York resident, will relocate. Box 297.

EXECUTIVE ACCOUNTANT-CPA—AIA member, presently employed small manufacturing concern with two plants. Heavy experience in public and private accounting including costs, budgets, financial statements, credits, Federal and State taxes, procedures, contract negotiation, supervision. Desires connection larger concern as Asst. Controller, Treasurer, Chief Accountant. Single, age 26, relocate. Box [illegible]

TREASURER-CONTROLLER—CPA, age 46, married, University graduate, member AIA, NACA. Treasury [illegible], experience in public and private industrial accounting, including financial statements, costs, budgets, taxes, government reports, and procedures. Present salary $10,000. Box [illegible]

CHAPTER EIGHT

HENRY FINDS HIS WAY TO REHOBOTH BEACH

INSIDE HIS SECOND-FLOOR OFFICE in Rehoboth Beach, Delaware, O. Wayne Rollins picked up the December 1952 copy of *The Journal of Accountancy* and turned immediately to the "Situations Wanted" section on page 770. Wayne wanted to hire a new controller for the company, which was an unusual mix of radio stations and automobile dealerships in Delaware, Maryland, and Virginia. Wayne and his brother, John W. Rollins, first started the business in 1948, and it was growing.

Wayne and John would be the first to admit that they were so busy building their business that they were terrible bookkeepers. They didn't even balance their checkbooks, and they weren't exactly sure how much money they had in the bank. And over time, their controller of several years had developed into more of a business nuisance than an asset. According to Wayne, "He was the type of fella who always had to get extensions for the IRS, and he never did anything on time in his life." And he had a habit that nearly drove Wayne to distraction: He couldn't find his way anywhere. "If I was going to send him to Norfolk, Virginia, where we had an automobile dealership, or to Radford, Virginia, where we had a radio station, you'd have to make his reservations for him. And he was never prepared. He took his dirty clothes with him, and the first thing he had to do was to get them laundered when he got there. And you had to handle his hotel reservations and everything. You had to handle all that." By mutual consent, the controller left the Rollins' business in the fall of 1952, and the brothers started looking for a replacement.

When December rolled around, the brothers were still searching for the right person, and time was running out. Recently elected lieutenant governor of Delaware, John was scheduled to take office in January, and they wanted the new controller in place before then. Wayne figured he had nothing to lose by thumbing through the accounting journal. As he glanced through the "Situations Wanted" column, the first three listings on page 770 caught Wayne's eye, especially the second one. *Good credentials, solid experience, single, only 26 years old, would relocate.* Wayne thought the person sounded ambitious without being arrogant, and he didn't boast of an "outstanding background" or being a "university graduate" like the other two listings. Wayne didn't want any attitude. And he was looking to hire their next controller based on a set of unusual criteria.

"The next damn fella I get," Wayne Rollins said, "he has got to be able to follow directions. I'm not going to tell him anything. If he doesn't ask, 'How do you get to Rehoboth?' or 'Can you meet me in Washington?' that will be the test. And he'll be hired."

100 MILES FROM ANYPLACE

Henry got five replies to his advertisement in the accounting journal. He ignored the three from government agencies, because he knew he didn't want to work for the government. The fourth reply, from a division of General Motors in Muncie, Indiana, piqued his interest, but after some initial correspondence, Henry got a notice that it wasn't going to be pursued. The fifth and final reply was from Rollins, a very small operation on the East Coast, located in Rehoboth Beach, Delaware, "a place I never heard of," said Henry.

Rehoboth Beach, as Henry discovered, was "100 miles from anyplace." He had to get out a map and, he joked, a flashlight to find where it was located. This sleepy little village on the Delaware shoreline, about two hours from Washington, D.C., primarily came to life during the summers, when vacationers flocked to its sunny beaches. At one point in its history, Rehoboth Beach was referred to as the "nation's summer capital." In 1952 it was also the headquarters for the Rollins brothers' expanding business, and they desperately needed a controller, a position they had been trying to fill for months when Henry's ad appeared.

Wayne and John responded to Henry's ad with a letter. Henry learned that the Rollins brothers had a handful of radio stations and auto agencies, and that John had just begun his foray into the auto-lease business, a very new field. "It sounded to me in the letter that it might be an interesting situation," said Henry, who later realized that a few of the facts in the letter had been somewhat inflated. But Henry was intrigued and replied that he was willing to travel east for an interview.

Wayne next sent Henry a telegram, detailing the date, time, and place of their first meeting: Saturday, January 24, 1953; 11 a.m., second floor, Rollins, Moore Building, Rehoboth Beach, Delaware. "I told Henry where the place was and what time the interview was, and then it was up to him to get there," said Wayne. "And it was a difficult thing to get to Rehoboth Beach at that time."

NO DIRECTIONS NECESSARY

After three and a half years in the accounting field, Henry had learned not to bother a client with unnecessary questions. So he didn't. Though Henry had never traveled east of Chicago, he quickly realized that he could fly from Des Moines to Washington, D.C.—but he wasn't at all sure of the route to Delaware after that. In 1953 there was really no way to rent a car. So Henry thought his best bet was to take a Greyhound bus. He visited the bus depot in Des Moines, explained the situation, and discovered there was one bus every day that left D.C. for Rehoboth Beach, departing at 6:30 a.m. and arriving shortly after 10 o'clock.

On January 23, wearing a heavy, double-breasted winter coat with a thick lining and a fur collar, Henry left Iowa in the middle of a January blizzard. He arrived safely in Washington that evening, spent the night with a friend from Belle Plaine, and was up and out the next day in time to board the 6:30 a.m. bus for Rehoboth Beach. By the time the Greyhound reached this seaside town over three hours later, Henry was the only person left on the bus. It truly was at the end of the line. And in the wintertime, Rehoboth Beach also turned into a ghost town, a phantom image of its bustling summer season. Henry quickly located the Moore Building that housed the Rollins headquarters, which was only about a block away from the bus depot and closer than he expected. With just under an hour before the interview, he stopped in for a quick bite to eat and a cup of coffee at one of the only restaurants open in the entire town. The outdoor temperature was moderate in this beach town, and Henry definitely looked out of place in his winter coat. "As I was leaving the restaurant, a lady near the cash register tapped me on the shoulder and said, 'Sir, you're not from around here, are you?'" Henry loved to recall. "And I said, 'No, ma'am, I am not.' And she said, 'I didn't think so.' So this was my entrance to Rehoboth Beach."

Henry's interview with the Rollins brothers took place within their spartan second-floor office space in the Moore Building. Henry was on time. He introduced himself to John first, and after a while, he also sat down with Wayne. Henry could tell from the way they talked that the brothers were from the South, and Henry soon discovered they had grown up on a farm in Georgia, which this Iowa farm boy saw as an advantage for him.

"The Rollins brothers came from a small, rural area, and I always felt that this assisted in compatibility—people coming from similar areas," said Henry. "I think that's a lot different from people coming out of the city. I think growing up on a farm is more difficult to relate to. And in our case I think that we all related well because of our background."

Indeed, the three men shared the same rough-and-tumble childhood experiences, growing up in the shadow of the Depression era. All three were educated at some point in one-room country schools; all three were raised for a while in homes without heat or electricity; and all three had sharp, defining memories of the backbreaking work of farming.

The three men had some distinct differences, however, and these were immediately apparent. For starters, Wayne was 14 years older than the 26-year-old Henry, and John was about 10 years older. Both Wayne and John graduated from high school, but only Henry had a college degree.

Both Wayne and John were married with children, and Henry was single. And though all three men embraced an all-consuming work ethic rarely matched by those around them, they came at it differently. Wayne and John were guided by a strict set of work ethics and homespun maxims that they absorbed while growing up, surrounded by hardworking elders. Their grandmother's wisdom forever echoed in Wayne's words: "She told me, and I believed her, that if you are average and the other person is average, and he works eight hours and you work twelve, you are 50 percent better than he is." Though Henry always remembered his mother's advice to "get off the farm," it simply wasn't in his family's midwestern, understated, and modest nature to offer advice or try to dispense wisdom from one generation to the next. Without a lot of family support or professional mentorship to date, Henry had to develop his business and life maxims on his own. It dawned on him, sitting in that second-floor office in Rehoboth Beach, that he could probably learn how to do that from the Rollins brothers.

HOW ROLLINS, INC., BEGAN

Born near the town of Ringgold in the north Georgia mountains, Wayne and John Rollins grew up on the family farm. After graduating from high school, they worked as farmers, laborers, engineers, and eventually entrepreneurs, as both married and started their families. By 1948 John had started an automobile dealership business in Delaware and would eventually establish his own empire of public companies in trucking, leasing, and environmental services based in Wilmington, Delaware. By 1948, Wayne had worked not only as a farmer but as a laborer and as a supervisor in a textile mill and a powder plant making dynamite before he and John teamed up to start their own bottled spring mineral water business in Catoosa Springs, Georgia. Lifting the heavy bottles of water, however, damaged Wayne's back. While recuperating from two ruptured disks, Wayne studied the possibility of getting into the radio business, a business venture he zeroed in on after reading a newspaper article about an acquaintance who owned a radio station and made enough money to purchase a sizeable tract of expensive land.

When Wayne proposed the idea of a broadcasting company to John during a telephone call in 1947, he pointed out that John already spent nearly $200 a month on radio advertising for his automobile dealerships in Lewes, Delaware; Princess Anne, Maryland; and Radford, Virginia. Wayne argued that John's own advertising budget would be a good revenue base for their new radio venture. The brothers quickly agreed that it was an idea worth pursuing.

While John concentrated on building the automobile and leasing business, Wayne immersed himself in developing the broadcasting business. He took responsibility for market research and reportedly visited 28 radio stations over a two-year period. When choosing a market for a new radio station, he found that a key objective was to find an area where the FCC would grant a license, and that license would be expanded. He ultimately decided to pursue building radio stations in Radford, Virginia, and Georgetown, Delaware, close to two of John's car dealerships and in communities that Wayne had determined were likely prospects for a radio station and the advertising dollars that it would generate.

Early on, the Rollins brothers combined two businesses: radio stations and automobile dealerships.

On February 24, 1948, the two brothers officially launched Rollins Broadcasting, Inc. They each contributed $12,500 to the new venture, incorporated in Delaware, set up the office in Rehoboth Beach, and quickly filed applications with the Federal Communications Commission for radio licenses in Radford and Georgetown, a process that could take six months to two years to complete. After the FCC approved the station in Radford, John contributed another $12,500 to help build the new station, a contribution Wayne later matched in order to "stay even as far as the cash was concerned."

Wayne and John Rollins inside one of the first radio stations owned by Rollins Broadcasting.

Just over two years after incorporating, Rollins began broadcasting on May 5, 1950, at WRAD-1340 AM, a 250-watt station in Radford, Virginia. Less than three years later, by the time Wayne and John invited Henry to interview for the vacant controller's job in January 1953, they had added three more radio stations: in Fayetteville, North Carolina; Georgetown, Delaware; and Norfolk, Virginia.

As Henry listened to the men describe their businesses and their plans to expand in the future, it was obvious to him that the two brothers complemented each other. Wayne was the more reserved, studied brother who, as Henry would one day find out, used his considerable business instincts and knowledge to meticulously analyze every deal before jumping in. John was gregarious, an idea-a-minute man who provided the bravura and the energy that made business deals seem worth the risk. "John really did want to buy everything, and he never did think about what it cost or anything like that," Wayne once said of his younger brother. "I'd regularly ask him, 'Where are you going to get the money?' and he'd say, 'That kind of thinking will just ruin my deal.'"

Henry was confident that he could bring a much-needed balance to the two brothers, that he was the person who offered the black-and-white, "just the facts" financial background and analytical skills that they needed. And while he admired the force of the brothers' ambition and the sheer will of their very different personalities, Henry now realized that the letter he received in Iowa detailing the company was a little inflated. John had only a few automobile dealerships, not a large conglomerate; though they had incorporated in February 1948, the brothers had not officially started the broadcast operation until May 1950; and John's quest to build an auto-leasing operation was still more of a concept than a reality. But Henry was intrigued. In his head, he began to envision that he could stay with the company for a few years, gain experience in two areas he knew relatively little about (broadcasting and auto dealerships), and then head back to the Midwest.

Henry B. Tippie in Rehoboth Beach, Delaware.

Granted, Wayne and John had already decided to hire Henry, based on the fact that he was the first guy who didn't ask for directions to Rehoboth Beach. But they didn't offer him the job on the spot. Wayne had one more unusual question before the interview was over: Would Henry take a $5-a-week reduction in pay from his current salary to come and work for Rollins? Wayne's thinking, which he later explained to Henry, was this: "I've always thought that I had to have a person who wanted to come to work with me, who really wanted to come in and saw an opportunity. If the person was just changing jobs, that wouldn't be the person I wanted. The way I tested that was dangerous and very unusual. I offered them less money than they were making. They had to really want to take it."

Henry later admitted that "I did not particularly like this, but I thought, 'Well, I'll give it a whirl.'" Henry countered that, yes, he would accept the pay cut, but he wanted Wayne to agree to consider him for higher pay once he got the job and he performed well. Wayne agreed.

Said Henry, "Wayne was certainly a super negotiator, as history shows. Also, his word was certainly more valuable than probably all the papers that you could have. What you do in business, of course, is build a reputation of integrity and character. Wayne certainly did that. And I might add that I later picked up the money with a payroll change. It was the best $5 investment I have ever made in my life."

The interview ended on a good note. After John and Wayne realized that Henry planned to spend the night in Rehoboth (there was only one bus a day back to Washington, so he didn't have any choice), they invited him to dinner with their wives at the Rehoboth Country Club. "It wasn't what you normally think of as a 'country club,'" recalled Henry. "It was just the only place to eat that was open into the evening." Henry figured that Wayne and his wife, Grace, along with John and his first wife, Kitty, "were looking me over further," and they all shared a few more stories about their backgrounds and work experiences. John casually asked Henry what salary he hoped to make in the future. Henry responded that he wanted to make $15,000 a year—a figure he landed on after doing tax returns for successful people, and he thought $10,000 to $15,000 was a very good living.

When the man who didn't have to ask for directions stepped back on the Greyhound bus bound for Washington the next morning, Wayne and John already knew that Henry had the job. And on January 26, 1953, at 9:22 a.m., Henry knew it, too, when he signed for a Western Union telegram from O. Wayne Rollins:

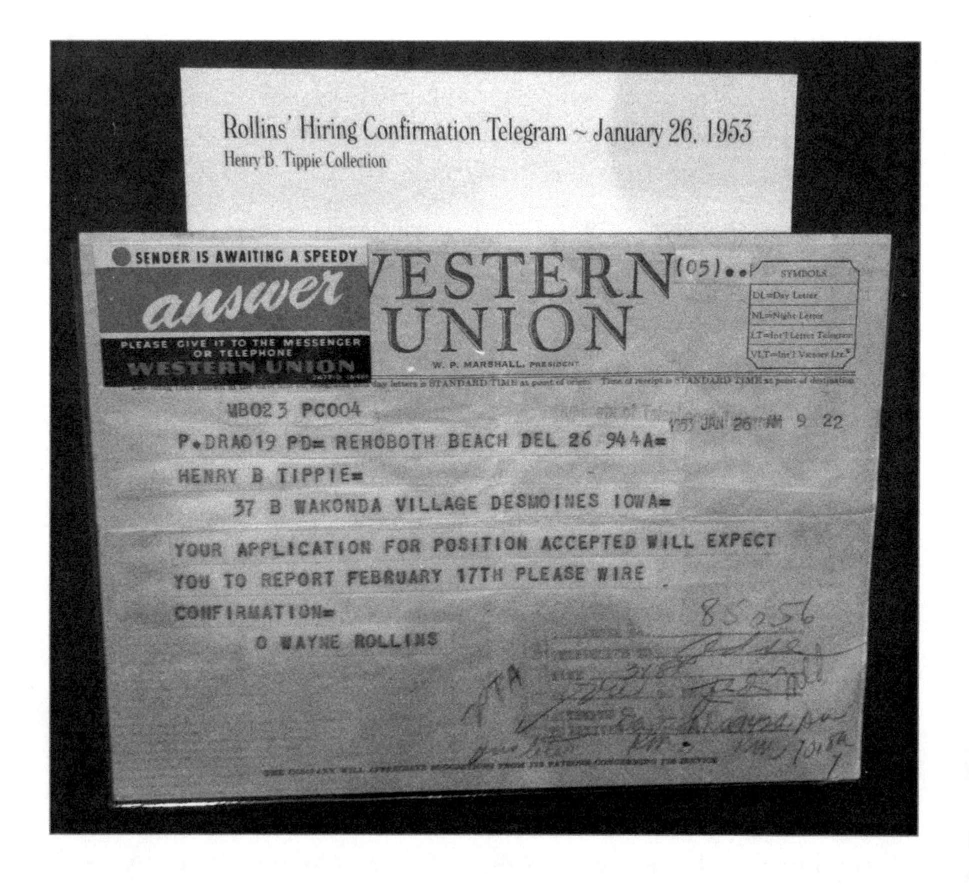
Rollins' Hiring Confirmation Telegram ~ January 26, 1953
Henry B. Tippie Collection

SENDER IS AWAITING A SPEEDY answer PLEASE GIVE IT TO THE MESSENGER OR TELEPHONE WESTERN UNION

WESTERN UNION
W. P. MARSHALL, PRESIDENT

SYMBOLS
DL=Day Letter
NL=Night Letter
LT=Int'l Letter Telegram
VLT=Int'l Victory Ltr.

WB023 PC004
1953 JAN 26 AM 9 22
P.DRA019 PD= REHOBOTH BEACH DEL 26 944A=
HENRY B TIPPIE=
37 B WAKONDA VILLAGE DESMOINES IOWA=
YOUR APPLICATION FOR POSITION ACCEPTED WILL EXPECT YOU TO REPORT FEBRUARY 17TH PLEASE WIRE CONFIRMATION=
O WAYNE ROLLINS

CHAPTER NINE

THE DREAMER, THE OPERATOR, AND DR. NO

IMPROBABLE AS IT SEEMS, HENRY showed up late for his first day of work at Rollins, due to weather conditions beyond his control. After giving notice and closing out his last day of work in Des Moines on February 13, 1953, Henry packed his car and headed east on Valentine's Day. He was making great progress until he hit a snowstorm in the mountains of West Virginia, and the two-day drive suddenly turned into a nearly three-day adventure. Henry finally made it to the second floor of the Moore Building around noon on Tuesday, February 17, the date he agreed to start. He was exhausted from the 1,125-mile trip, and his slightly rumpled appearance gave secretary Dorothy Harrison pause when he pushed through the front door. "A typical farm boy," was Dorothy's first impression of Henry. "He needed some polishing, and Mr. Rollins saw that he got it. But I liked him from the very first, and he kept Mr. Rollins on an even keel as far as finances were concerned."

Henry's first task as new controller was to file tax returns for the previous year. This meticulous, record-keeping, data-driven CPA quickly realized that parts of the company's financial affairs were in complete chaos. Long focused on building their businesses, the Rollins brothers had all but lost track of how much money was going out and coming in. Only the radio operation was making money, and that was "only a few dollars," Henry estimated after reviewing the books for the four radio stations in

Georgetown, Delaware; Radford and Norfolk, Virginia; and Fayetteville, North Carolina. Luckily for Henry, each station had its own bookkeeper, so Henry was able to get the tax returns filed without too much hassle.

Henry next turned to the company's very insignificant electronics operation, which he immediately described as "a semi-disaster and another loser," located in an old church building in Lewes, Delaware; Henry filled out the forms for 1952 and soon convinced the brothers to close this operation. And last but not least, Henry asked John to see the books for the leasing operations.

"There aren't any," John replied.

"What do you mean, there aren't any?" Henry shot back.

"Well, we just don't have any. But here's our checkbook," John said.

Henry looked at the checkbook—about two or three inches thick—and he was dumbfounded. And to make matters worse, the checkbook had never been reconciled. "They had a little money," said Henry, "but they didn't know how much." While the new controller didn't dare say so out loud, it's fair to say that 14-year-old Henry kept better record books for his hog business and his vegetable garden in Belle Plaine than the 40- and 34-year-old Rollins brothers maintained for their businesses in Delaware. "It was just all fun and games," Henry said, shaking his head, about the company's nonexistent accounting system.

So the man who routinely tracked every penny he ever spent went to work. Rollins' automobile dealerships and auto-leasing operations were separate companies, "all of which were losing money," Henry determined. Without any record or business transaction books, Henry knew the first thing he had to do was reconcile the checkbook. With all the numbers finally added up, Henry discovered that John Rollins had $20,000 in the bank for the auto-leasing business that no one knew about. "Nobody knew it existed!" said Henry, a situation he attributed to "checks being written, voided, rewritten in different amounts, improper add-backs and rewrites on the check stubs."

The so-called found money was fantastic news to Wayne and John. And for Henry, finding the money paved the way for some creative accounting steps that would help the company establish a more solid financial footing. Said Henry, "In order to get some opening balances in 1953 to go forward, I did what you call a 'net worth balance sheet,' which I had learned to do while working on some tax cases in Omaha. In other words, I established the opening balances for items like cash, accounts receivable, vehicles, depreciation, liabilities that were owed on the vehicles, etc. And of course the differential between assets and liabilities became what the opening net worth was."

Henry's next task was to locate all of the automobiles that were on lease, and this turned out to be no easy task due, again, to sloppy bookkeeping and tracking. Henry tracked the last car down to the Rollins Motor Dealership in Newport News, Virginia, where it sat, lost in the body shop.

BAPTISM BY FIRE LEADS TO TRUST

Henry's baptism by fire into the Rollins brothers' companies, and the positive results he immediately produced, helped Henry quickly earn the brothers' trust. And the organization's haphazard system of accounting, coupled with the brothers' tendency to launch a business idea and figure out the details later, didn't bother Henry; instead, he saw it as an opportunity, and quickly realized he had landed in an organization that offered him the chance to grow and make a contribution. Did Wayne and John need Henry B. Tippie? "They needed *somebody*," Henry once said, characteristically modest. "And they told me at a later date that the number-one criterion they had to hire someone was to hire the first person who did not ask how to get to Rehoboth. I happened to be that person. They needed somebody and they wound up with me, let's put it that way."

John Rollins

Henry B. Tippie

Wayne Rollins

Beyond simply being "the first guy who didn't ask for directions," Henry proved to be something of a kindred spirit for the Rollins brothers. His purposefulness, his work ethic, and his integrity mirrored their own business principles. Coming from similar backgrounds, the Rollins brothers and Henry held a common conviction: Your word is your bond. And from the beginning, Henry was not just another employee who did what he was told; Henry brought value to the company, spoke his mind, and quickly set out to establish organizational structure and business methods that the Rollins brothers didn't even know were missing.

For the first time since the two brothers had paired up in 1948, their team was complete, with each of the three men playing a distinct role that no one dared to challenge:

John W. Rollins Sr. was the Dreamer, the team's idea man, a salesman, and a gambler who wasn't afraid of taking risks. One of his most far-reaching dreams was getting into the auto-lease industry when it was still in its infancy. "I have never met anybody who would have near the personality of John W. Rollins," Henry claimed. "He was in a class by himself. He was very optimistic. If it was raining bucketfuls, John could see the sunshine on the horizon."

O. Wayne Rollins was the Operator. A brilliant entrepreneur who could take an idea and forecast its path to success way into the future, Wayne focused on operations and the communications side of the business. Like John, he, too, was a man of action, but his approach was more conservative. Endowed with a razor-sharp mind and memory, Wayne was a natural, serious leader who inspired confidence in his employees and brought out their strengths by challenging them to do more. "Just sandwich it in," was one of his favorite sayings.

Henry B. Tippie was Dr. No, the financial watchdog of the company with a relentless focus on the bottom line that neither Wayne nor John necessarily had the time or the inclination to safeguard. Henry's guiding principle turned out to be very simple: "'If this were my money, what would I do?' That's a different way of operating than if you think in terms of managing someone else's money." Henry quickly developed the reputation for saying no to an idea if it was not financially sound, and then helping the Rollins brothers develop strategies that would make the idea not only work but make money, too. According to Wilton Looney, a close associate and friend of Wayne's from Atlanta, "Probably the best thing that ever happened to both John and Wayne was when Henry came along and asked for a job."

All three were plainspoken, eschewing complicated words to explain an idea. Each one could make the most complicated business transaction sound simple. Granted, John could be intimidating, a strong personality with a voice to match. Wayne, too, was a strong personality, but he rarely raised his voice and he let his keen memory for details dominate conversations. Henry, who did not hesitate to express his opinion, was often blunt but quiet, content sometimes to let his columns of numbers do the talking.

Henry's impact was immediate. From the time he found the missing $20,000 and transformed bookkeeping chaos into order, the Rollins

The Dreamer, Dr. No, and the Operator: John W. Rollins, Henry B. Tippie, and O. Wayne Rollins.

brothers knew they had someone who would always have their back. They trusted Henry, and they never once doubted his integrity and his honesty. "Henry's been instrumental ever since he came over on that bus to see my dad in Rehoboth in the Moore Building," John Rollins Jr., John's oldest son, once said. "He's been instrumental in their lives and in the success that they and their families have been able to accomplish. There's no question about integrity, honesty, straight-shooting—there's just no BS ever. You get a straight shot, whether you like it or not. The three of them always operated as a team. My dad was a salesman, my uncle Wayne was an operator, and Henry has the world's greatest financial mind. They could do *anything*."

DR. NO GOES TO WORK

After Henry joined the company, their remote Delaware location and lack of extra funds created a lean, no-frills operation. "We did just about everything ourselves," Henry said, "and a lot of this was unplowed ground for everybody. We didn't have the luxury of attorneys, access to law firms, accounting firms, etc. If we were buying something, for the most part, we either drew it up ourselves the best we could using other situations as a guideline, or perhaps the seller had some kind of document and we would take that and redo it. In other cases, we operated with just a letter of agreement, etc. Very rarely did we ever employ any lawyers. You have to bear in mind that when you are 100 miles away from any big town and have to rely on mail service and so forth, plus probably overriding all that, we didn't have any money, and dollars were extremely precious, so we tried to make do with the best we had."

With lenders particularly tight and the company virtually unknown when Henry joined the company, Henry often resorted to what can only be called "creative financing"—moving money between John's automobile and leasing business and Wayne's broadcasting concerns—to keep the broadcasting company moving forward. In 1953, for instance, on the eve of buying radio station WNJR in Newark, New Jersey, the bank in Lewes, Delaware, suddenly reneged on an earlier promise to loan the company $40,000 to cover the down payment. According to Henry,

> At that time, we had about three or four automotive agencies, none of them, of course, flush with any money whatsoever. In those days, you had until the 15th of the following month to pay your payroll taxes for the preceding month to the government. And in order to have the payroll tax money available, we had separate payroll accounts. Each payday, we would deposit not only the amount needed for the payroll but also the payroll taxes in the accounts for each one of the auto agencies. We're now looking at the first of November, with this settlement on the radio station and no advance notice whatsoever that the bank would not lend us the money. What we did was strip all the payroll tax money out of each account. I don't remember what that added up to, but we were still a bit short. So we then increased our sold-out-of-trust position a little bit, which was not unusual for automobile dealers in those days, which is where you sell the car and you've got the money but you haven't paid off the floor plan for that car. So we merely increased that a little bit and took that along with the payroll tax funds to come up with the $40,000 so that the transactions could be closed to acquire radio station WNJR.

From 1950 to 1964, Rollins built or purchased 10 radio stations and three television stations in locations all over the country. Broadcasting proved to be Wayne's area of expertise, and he routinely bought stations that were not doing well and then set out to improve them through marketing, lean management, and engineering upgrades. Wayne worked his magic by building and then relying on a core broadcasting executive team that included Fitzgerald "Mac" McDaniel, an engineer who designed the stations' formats; G. Russell Chambers, a brilliant engineer who regularly increased each station's power capacity and target audience, pulling in more revenue; and H. Tim Crow, a radio station operations manager who would later become the company's first public relations executive.

"Way back at the very beginning, there wasn't any money, and that's hard for people to believe today," said Henry. "We concentrated on buying with a little bit of money down and a lot payable over the future. And another thing, most of what we started out with was somebody else's failures, because we didn't pay much money that way."

For example, when Rollins purchased the WRAP radio station in Norfolk about three months before Henry arrived, the brothers were able to buy the property at a substantial discount due to its debts and losses. Purchased for $90,000 in October 1952, Wayne liked to say that the deal cost nothing, particularly after Henry, who came on board three months later, figured out that the cost of the station was nearly equal to its tax savings, due to the $200,000 in losses carried by the station. And another one of Henry's accounting methods, which involved viewing eventual gains as a capital gain as opposed to ordinary income, would eventually be tested in court. Said Henry,

> That transaction consisted of buying the stock of WRAP for a small amount of money, with John and Wayne individually buying the notes outstanding by the station to the sellers at a huge discount. I think the total notes outstanding at the station were in excess of $200,000. To the best of my recollection I think these notes were acquired for between $50,000 and $75,000. This meant that as the notes got paid off at face value, the Rollins brothers realized a gain of the difference between the purchase price of the notes and the face value. This was handled as a capital gain item as contrasted to ordinary income. As you know, the capital gain tax rate is substantially lower than the ordinary income tax rate. Ultimately, when we had a tax examination with the two Rollins brothers, this became an issue regarding how to handle the gain. This wound up in Philadelphia at the Appellate tax level, with a very favorable tax settlement from our standpoint. Rollins Broadcasting acquired the stock of WRAP on a time-payment plan. The other part of the equation was that the WRAP-acquired corporate entity had a substantial tax loss, which we were able to take advantage of as earnings began to accrue in the entity. The bottom line was that the tax savings by utilization of the loss carry-forwards in effect recovered most, if not all, of the stock purchase price, whereas the two Rollins brothers benefited individually by the purchase of the notes and resultant payoff at face value.

At Rollins, Henry discovered that he actually "enjoyed straightening out organizations." Which certainly worked in his favor as he juggled both the broadcasting side and the automobile leasing part of the company. Though the auto business's motto was "Troubles Cease When You Lease from Rollins," Henry would have probably argued the opposite in 1953.

ROLLINS FLEET LEASING, INC.

In 1953 John's auto-leasing company was one of the first of its kind, an idea that would eventually spread across the country after starting in Delaware with 160 vehicles (after Henry located all of them). Though John and Wayne co-owned the Lincoln-Mercury dealership in Roanoke, Virginia, and while John was equal owner with Wayne in the early days of the broadcasting side of the company, John was the sole proprietor of John W. Rollins and Associates, the company that controlled the auto-leasing business. In the beginning, it was a fledgling operation at best. Though John had secured a half-a-million-dollar line of credit from Farmers' Bank in Delaware, Henry soon realized that "John kept running over the limit by $50,000 or $60,000." The company always needed more funds. Henry remembered going to New York with John, visiting multiple banks and lending institutions, and getting nowhere.

"We were very, very hard-pressed for money," said Henry. "We didn't *have* any money. We always got the salaries paid, but when it came to paying the bills, that became a real problem. And if we owed somebody $5,000, maybe I'd send them $1,000—at least they got something. And the phones are almost ringing off the wall."

Faced with the cold, hard numbers day in and day out, Henry sensed potential disaster. John, never losing the bounce in his step, could only blindly see potential. "They were some wildly disparate personalities," said Jeff Rollins, John Sr.'s son. "Mr. Tippie would never have a dime of debt in his life if he didn't have to. He's so conservative. And Dad was the kind of guy, you know, Mr. Tippie used to say he never met a line of credit he didn't like. And Dad used to say that Henry was so cheap he wouldn't give a nickel to see a piss ant eat a bale of hay."

John knew that his leasing idea would fail unless he sold big companies on the idea and then had the resources to back that up. To expand, John and Henry figured they needed another line of credit for half a million dollars. In early 1954, John and Henry had the good fortune to schedule a meeting with Dick Wilson, the second vice president of State Mutual Life Insurance in Worcester, Massachusetts. Dick Wilson listened carefully as John and Henry put on their best pitch. John described what the auto-leasing business was all about, followed by Henry, who went through all the mechanics of how it operated. John's concept, after all, represented an entirely different approach to the traditional leasing operation. "We did maintenance fleet leasing as contrasted to finance fleet leasing," said Henry. "In other words, we provided the maintenance and tires, and I explained that's how this would work."

Dick Wilson absorbed what they had to say, letting them finish before he told them that there were two problems: first, State Mutual didn't lend any money to individuals, only to corporate entities; and second, the half a million dollars that John and Henry asked for was below their lending minimum. State Mutual's lines of credit started at one million dollars.

"We didn't bat an eyelash," Henry recalled. "We told him right there, 'We don't think we have a problem here. Number one, we'll need the million-dollar line in due course, because of the way we're growing and expanding. And the second thing is, there's no problem with being a corporation. We'll incorporate at once.'" The three men shook hands, and Rollins Leasing had a million-dollar line of credit.

To meet the requirements of the new loan, John wrote a check for $1,000 (the minimum to incorporate), and the two set up the new corporation called Rollins Fleet Leasing, Inc.; John was president, and Henry was vice president and treasurer. There was no celebrating, however, because Henry and John soon realized yet another hurdle: there wasn't enough in the bank to cover the $1,000 check that John had written to incorporate. If there was ever a moment of tension and an extended, heated verbal exchange between an accountant and his boss, this was it! Henry quietly advised a no-panic approach. With fingers crossed, the State Mutual loan came through before the incorporation check cleared, and the new business used the loan to cover the cost of incorporating. Looking back on their precarious financial situation, Henry later admitted that they probably set some kind of financial ratio record—daring to take a nonexistent $1,000 in capital and securing a million-dollar line of credit. "But that's the way it went down," said Henry. "It's hard for people to believe that today, but I know that from being on the scene."

THE LANE-WELLS CONTRACT: THE BIGGEST ACCOUNT EVER

In addition to covering the incorporation check, the State Mutual loan provided the funds for Rollins Fleet Leasing to service its first national client, which, in something of another backward, risky business gamble, John and Henry had secured *before* they had the money to expand. In yet another "hard for people to believe" scenario, Henry recounts a story that happened prior to their meeting with Dick Wilson. When they were still scrounging for a line of credit, John and Henry ran an ad in a magazine called *Dunn's Review and Modern Industry*. "We had a coupon ad in there about the virtues of automobile leasing," Henry says. "And you could put your name, address, and company on the coupon and we would get it back in the mail." One of the replies they received was from Lane-Wells, an oil field services company in Los Angeles, California. John decided that they needed to meet the company representatives in person, so he and Henry headed out west. When they arrived in L.A., John set them up in a cottage at the posh Ambassador Hotel and rented a Cadillac convertible. "So you would have thought that we were well heeled, when in fact, things were quite difficult," said Henry. "John Sr. always believed in going first-class."

The next morning, the two men entered the Lane-Wells building, a three-story, terraced structure with a tower in the center, to meet with the purchasing agent who had filled out the coupon. Though they had a nice visit with him, he told them on the spot that he liked their program, but they would still have to meet with the senior vice president for a final decision. Said Henry, "We came back the next day and we went over everything again with him. And he indicated that he liked what we had to say and had been thinking about getting in the leasing business with their vehicle fleet and getting their money freed up."

The more they heard, the more Henry and John liked the idea of making this deal. They could, no doubt, anticipate that it was going to be the cornerstone of their leasing business. The Lane-Wells company fleet consisted of 300 automobiles and 200 pickup trucks, almost two times the size of Rollins' total fleet. "To make a long story short," Henry says, "we signed a fleet leasing agreement with them and we put everything on non-maintenance rates, figuring that if we got anything back it wasn't going to be worth much. But the facts are, they took care of their equipment immaculately. They kept it cleaned and washed. We needed to start getting those vehicles in, but we had no money to pay for the vehicles at all."

Once again, John and Henry held their breaths and signed the deal, knowing the vehicles would be delivered over a span of months. "And by the time that we needed to be under way with the fleet of vehicles for them, our State Mutual deal became effective and we had money for operating," he said. "The very first account in the new corporate entity was the Lane-Wells deal. And I've always said that the Lane-Wells account—which turned out to be the biggest account ever signed in terms of number of vehicles in the history of Rollins Leasing Corp.—is what made that company become a survivor and a success. We did extremely well. I don't think we ever had another account that had 500 vehicles that I'm aware of."

EXPANDED RESPONSIBILITIES

Although he still largely operated as the accountant, Henry gradually broadened the scope of his responsibilities as the auto-leasing endeavor started to take off. Soon, Henry was in charge of small acquisitions. "If somebody had 200 or 300 units, it might be an automobile dealer, they might be located all over the place," he explained, "but all you really bought were the vehicles and the leases. And you could have a closing and bring that company home in your briefcase. That's about how simple it was. You would notify the lessees that they were now your lessees and no longer the seller's lessees."

With the momentum of success gaining around the auto-leasing business and the growth of Wayne's broadcast empire, it became increasingly clear that John, Wayne, and Henry needed to narrow their focus solely to those enterprises. Slowly, they shed everything else, including John's automobile dealerships. By the time the company moved from Rehoboth to Wilmington on Labor Day of 1956, they had sold all of the automobile dealerships except the Ford agency in Wilmington.

When he joined the Rollins Company in 1953, Henry originally planned to stay a few years, get some experience, and then head back to the Midwest. But after just two and a half years in Delaware, Henry knew he wasn't leaving anytime soon. He now appreciated the depth of the brothers' ambitions and abilities. He understood the rhythms of the fiercely loyal, but very different, Rollins men, and was now able to grasp as well as anyone the distinctions between the Dreamer and the Operator. He had even grown accustomed to their daily phone habits, which resulted in calls several times a day but never a hint of a "hello" or a "good-bye" before or after their brief exchanges. John's wife once commented that the habit was rude. John fired back, "What the hell do you mean, I'm rude? He does the same thing to me. He just tells me what he's thinking about."

Together, the three men worked famously long hours every day, five and a half days a week, which included the first half of each Saturday. And just as Henry had gotten used to the two very different styles of his bosses, the Rollins brothers had grown accustomed to Henry's unpretentious, sometimes abrupt, manner.

"One of the things Henry was strong in was his position," said Wayne. "It never did bother him about hurting people's feelings or anything that way. He was just strong in his position. And the other thing, he always had his job done. He was efficient. One of the things he was strong in was tax planning, and as a controller, he controlled the expenses and so forth. He was strong at that."

John Sr. agreed. "Henry's one of the most brilliant guys, where he gets in and he looks and he digs. He has the greatest follow-up systems in businesses. It can drive you absolutely crazy, but he has a plan for the plan and he doesn't procrastinate. He also can operate a dollar better than anyone. And whenever he told us anything, we believed him. And that's one of the things that's been very responsible for my success. When Wayne told me something, I never doubted it. When Tippie told me something, I never had a doubt. The way we worked, we never had any questions. We always operated on the basis that all of us were sincere."

MUSIC, SOCIALIZING, AND FAMILY

Outside of work, the 28-year-old Henry mostly kept to himself. Once again, his love for Big Band music took him on a search for musical venues in the area, and he soon discovered a club called the Paddock in Ocean City, about a 20-minute drive from Rehoboth. "You could be there in a heartbeat," said Henry, "And they always had these combos or quintets that played all the really good music." Occasionally, Henry took a date to dance and listen to music, but he didn't really date anyone seriously during his first 18 months in Delaware.

Henry socialized with the Rollins brothers and their families on several occasions—he once joined Wayne and Grace in Lewes, Delaware, for square dancing, and John invited him over occasionally for Thanksgiving dinner or a beach weekend with his family at their home right on the Delaware Bay. But Henry maintained that his relationship with the Rollins brothers was business, not social. After all, Wayne and Grace were busy raising their younger son, Gary, when Henry arrived in Rehoboth ("He was in knee pants," Henry remembers about Gary), and their older son, Randall, was in the Coast Guard, stationed at nearby Bethany Beach. John and Kitty had four children, and John's double-duty in politics and business meant his free time for socializing with a young bachelor was nonexistent. "In terms of what I would call social, I don't really think it was a social-type friendship," said Henry.

But when work is your life, Henry discovered that your coworkers eventually become like family. As Jeff Rollins once noted, when asked about his father's relationship with Henry, "It was as social as it could get for two guys who grew up in the Depression. If you asked the two of them if they were best friends, did they go on vacation together? No. Did you ever have the wife and kids together? Rarely. But was there one ounce of doubt in your mind that the two of them have the utmost admiration and caring and love for each other? No doubt in your mind. Not one doubt."

During his second summer in Delaware, Henry asked his parents to visit him and happily paid for their flights from Iowa. They stayed for about two weeks and had a great time, Henry recalled. But when he bought them tickets for the following year in 1955, they sent word that they were not going to be able to make it. Henry soon found out that Bob and Amelia's marriage, decidedly fragile at times during their 32 years together, had deteriorated dramatically. Henry remembers his father calling with the news, "Your mother is going to divorce me." Henry soon made a trip to Belle Plaine to see if there was anything he could do. Henry knew that his parents had always had a complicated relationship, and he would never forget their harsh fights. But he thought that selling the farm and moving into Belle Plaine would make life simpler for them. Apparently, it hadn't worked out that way.

With Ernest married and Henry's youngest brother John now out of the house, Bob continued to work two jobs: he ran an electrical supply shop during the day, and in the evening he was a night patrolman for Belle Plaine. Henry quickly surmised that his Uncle John, who didn't like his father, had convinced Amelia that Bob was being unfaithful during the hours he worked as a cop. Henry thought it was all fabrication, and others in town agreed. But when gossip spread through the small town and Uncle John was constantly present to cast doubt, the situation went from bad to worse. Before Henry could stop it, Amelia's brother drove her to the county seat in Vinton to file the divorce papers. Henry attempted to broker a compromise between his parents before the divorce was finalized, and his father made a lot of effort, including quitting his job as a policeman. But Amelia was determined. "To make a long story short, she went ahead with the divorce," said Henry, realizing that the outcome he had feared most from the long-simmering family division had now taken place. "I think Uncle John pushed it."

When his parents divorced in 1955, Henry wasn't looking to enter into a relationship. Though his brother Ernest and his wife, Margaret, had a happy marriage, Henry was deeply troubled by his parents' divorce. And he couldn't forget that his only experience with being in love had ended painfully, with a telegram of rejection in Des Moines.

But Henry's luck in love, and his bleak outlook on marriage, would change in the summer of 1955, as the vacation crowd and the seasonal rush of temporary summer employees returned to this little resort town by the ocean. And it began the day Henry sat down for a late lunch at the Plantation Restaurant in Rehoboth and ordered a glass of tomato juice.

Patricia Sue Bush as a college coed.

CHAPTER TEN

DR. NO MEETS MRS. RIGHT: PATRICIA SUE BUSH

WALKING DOWN REHOBOTH AVENUE, Patricia Sue Bush spotted a "Help Wanted" sign in the window of the Plantation Restaurant, a small, inexpensive family restaurant that served American and Italian food not far from the beach. She peeked inside. The waitresses wore crisp, all-white uniforms with kerchief-style aprons and white open-toed sandals, and the people sitting around the tables and tucked into booths looked friendly and respectful. Patricia thought carefully for a minute, and then she walked into the restaurant to apply for the waitress job. And in that moment, this petite, 20-year-old college student from northwestern Pennsylvania, who had come to Rehoboth Beach during the summer of 1955 looking for a job and perhaps a little adventure in the "nation's summer capital," knew she was about to do something she shouldn't do: She was going to lie.

"I told them I had waited tables before," said Patricia, a knowing smile crossing her face as she recalled the story. "And they knew I lied as soon as they saw me carry a cup of coffee. All the other girls there could carry all these plates up and down their arms, but I didn't know how to do that. But they said I could stay for a week and see how it worked out. I worked hard, so they kept me."

And though Patricia didn't know it yet, the small lie she told to get a summer waitressing job would absolutely change her life.

When their daughter was born on March 17, 1935, in the small railroad town of New Castle, Pennsylvania, Harvey and Eila Bush named her Patricia, in honor of St. Patrick's Day. With two older brothers, she was forever the family's baby girl, and the whole family loved to spoil the youngster with the curly brown hair and sparkling eyes. Her parents operated an old-fashioned neighborhood grocery store, where the entire family worked at one time or another helping out. As a girl, Patricia would "take the pamphlets and hang them on the door for the specials for the weekends." Her family was warm and loving: "We had lots of hugs and things like that." They were not affluent by any means, and the emergence of large supermarkets would one day put their family's grocery store out of business. But the Bush family made enough money to send Patricia to college about an hour away from home at Allegheny College, a small liberal arts school in Meadville. Patricia studied accounting and took secretarial courses. And in the summer between her junior and senior years, she found herself on a bus to Rehoboth Beach, after friends from college sent word that they had a job for her and a place to live.

When she arrived, Patricia realized immediately that she couldn't take the job her friends had lined up for her: it was a night-shift position in a place that was open 24 hours a day, and Patricia "knew my parents wouldn't want me working evening shifts." But she desperately wanted to stay in Rehoboth. She loved living in the little apartment over the garage with her friends, and she couldn't think of anything she'd rather do that summer than head to the beach every day and enjoy the sun. So when that "Help Wanted" sign appeared in the window that day, Patricia jumped at the chance to get a job and stay in Rehoboth.

The waitressing job at the Plantation Restaurant turned out to be the perfect summer job. The owners didn't serve breakfast, so Patricia could stay up late the night before and then head to the beach every morning to "work on my tan" before coming to work. She started promptly at 11 a.m. and she worked steadily until 9 or 10 at night, serving lunch, dinner, coffee, and desserts. She got the hang of waitressing pretty fast. As it turned out, the Plantation was a very popular restaurant, and the hungry vacationers frequently formed lines outside under the awning as they stood waiting for a table.

Henry B. Tippie was one of the restaurant's most loyal customers. With his office just down the street, he once said that he was "paying to eat there twelve months a year and I knew the menu by heart." He always ordered applesauce and liked tomato juice with his lunch, which was typically a meat entrée with vegetables. "I was not a soup person, and I was not too much into the sandwich business," he noted. The owners knew Henry so well that they told him to feel free to skip the lines—"to pay no attention and to just come on up to the front." And in the summer of 1955, Henry was well known to more than just the Plantation Restaurant crowd. The local newspaper had named this handsome, 28-year-old Rollins accountant, with his signature horn-rimmed glasses, short haircut, and easygoing smile, one of the "Three Most Available Bachelors" in Rehoboth Beach. Just two years after Henry came to town, it appeared that the secretary's observation that all Henry needed was "some polishing" had come true.

The Plantation Restaurant, where Henry and Patricia first met.

But Patricia certainly didn't think so—judging from the story they both told about the first time Patricia met Henry at the Plantation Restaurant:

> *Henry:* I came in one day and I wound up at one of the tables assigned to her, and I had a newspaper with me. I knew the menu by heart, and of course she had no experience as a waitress. And so she comes over to get my order and I just bark out my order—*boom, boom, boom, boom.* And she's inexperienced, and so she asked me if I "would repeat my order, sir." And I put the newspaper down, and I very carefully detailed my order again. And that was that. She told the ownership of the restaurant that she didn't want to wait on me again; somebody else could wait on me in the future, because I had apparently barked out my order, right and left.

Patricia: He didn't look up from the newspaper. And I didn't get his order. So I said, "Sir, all I got was your tomato juice," and he put the newspaper down and very slowly told me everything he wanted. And I went back in the kitchen and told everybody that I never wanted to wait on that man again. So whenever he came in and he was in my station, some other girl took him.

But these two young people, who had such an inauspicious introduction, were destined to meet at the restaurant again soon.

Henry: I came in there at a later date, and there was almost nobody there. It was mid-afternoon when everybody cleared out and they only kept one waitress. I show up, I had apparently been tied up at work or something, and Patricia was the only person there, so she had to wait on me. And so I didn't have a newspaper with me and, according to her, I was quite nice. And I inquired about her background, about where she went to school, and you know, about her. And according to her, I was much more friendly.
Patricia: He came in one day, and I was the only one there. And he was nicer then. He asked me what I was majoring in—I was majoring in accounting and minoring in secretarial—and said he would help me if he could and he gave me his business card. So I wrote home and told my mother that maybe I had some help after I graduated, that this man had given me his business card.

After weeks of dancing around each other, the two finally knew each other's names. And that day, Henry B. Tippie left a young waitress named Patricia Sue Bush more than his business card. He left her a silver dollar as a tip. Patricia gasped when she saw it, quickly tucking it away in a safe place, wondering: Does he like me?

Henry eventually decided to ask Patricia out for a date.

Henry, finishing his evening meal at the restaurant: What time do you get off work?

> *Patricia, trying to be discreet, because she actually had another date already lined up:* Well, come back to the restaurant when we close, around nine o'clock.

In what can only be described as young love melodrama, it turns out that there was a guy called "Larry" who used to come around to the restaurant and flirt with the waitresses; he always said he would come back later and take them out, but he never did. So Patricia immediately thought that Henry "was just another Larry, you know." But when Henry *did* show up, right on time, Patricia decided that she should take a chance and go out with him and ditch the other guy. Wasting no time, Patricia asked Henry to take her home first, and while Henry waited outside, she ran up to her apartment, showered and changed, and breathlessly begged her roommates to "polish my shoes and get me outta here before my other date comes!" Telling the story years later, Patricia still seems surprised with the boldness of her plan. "We were pulling away from the curb, when the other guy pulled up!"

With the evening's melodrama safely behind them, Patricia and Henry's first date was nothing short of magical. He drove to his favorite club, the Paddock in Ocean City, where the young couple were soon dancing to the sounds of Henry's favorite Big Band music. They talked for hours and danced until the music stopped, and they didn't get back to Rehoboth until around 2 a.m. Patricia was so giddy, she couldn't sleep.

> *Patricia:* I was pretty excited that night. I don't know why, I mean, he was just nice.
> *Henry:* She was a nice person. She wasn't somebody that had a false atmosphere about her. And she didn't come from an affluent background. Did I think anything was going to develop out of that to start with? I don't think so. I think she got more interested earlier than maybe I did.

Patricia, in fact, waited up all night to tell her girlfriends some important news the very next morning: "I think I met the man I want to marry!"

COURTING PATRICIA

For the rest of the summer, Patricia and Henry saw each other almost every night, routinely staying out until two in the morning. They went dancing in Ocean City. They enjoyed parties on the weekends with her roommates. They played cards. "I thought he was spending too much money," recalled Patricia, "so I asked him if we could play cards one night, and I think maybe that impressed him because he was used to girls who wanted him to spend money on them." They also didn't mind babysitting for the couple who owned the garage apartment Patricia lived in. "We didn't have a TV and they did," she said, "so we loved babysitting because we got to watch their TV." At one point, Henry asked to meet Patricia at the beach on Sunday, and Patricia told him she would, but only after she went to church. Henry, who had long given up practicing his Methodist upbringing, innocently asked Patricia if she was Catholic. "No," she replied, slightly amused. "I'm Presbyterian. Other people go to church besides Catholics. "

Within no time, Patricia wrote to her mother with some news: "Remember that man who gave me his business card? Well, I'm dating him!" And because Patricia had made Henry sound like a "business executive, I think maybe she thought this guy was about 50 years old or something," Patricia remembered. "She was concerned. So she sent my brother down here to see what was going on. He saw the offices they were in, and he wasn't very impressed, but it didn't matter. *I* was impressed."

When the summer ended, Patricia went back to college and Henry stayed in Rehoboth, working for the Rollins brothers. Ever the romantic, Patricia practically ditched her studies and spent hours every night writing Henry love letters, mailing them all to "Mr. Henry B. Tippie, 57 Sussex St., Apt. #6, Rehoboth Beach, Delaware." By now, she had a favorite endearment for Henry: She called him "Tip."

> *Patricia, smiling:* I knew I was in love when I went back to school, but Tip never told me. And I think he had to think about it. And it was probably hard for him to trust me. I think he really had to think about it. All I did was write him letters, sometimes three hours a night.

> *Henry, smiling, too:* There was a correspondence that developed, but you don't ever know where all that's headed. But she was a good letter writer. I have all the letters. She majored in economics and accounting, and I don't understand her accounting but that's another story.

Henry wrote to Patricia, too, especially when he traveled with John Rollins for work related to the growing leasing business. On October 2, 1955, he wrote a quick postcard from the Ambassador Hotel in Los Angeles, where he had just seen a show with Tony Martin, the popular American actor and singer who starred in *The Tony Martin Show*, a 15-minute variety program that aired on NBC from 1954 to 1956 prior to the evening newscast. The postcard read: "The Tony Martin show was really wonderful. Weather is beautiful here. 'Tip'" And he mailed it to "Miss Patricia Bush, 177 Walker Hall, Allegheny College, Meadville, Penn."

In January, right after Christmas and before Patricia returned to Allegheny to finish her last semester, Henry took Patricia to New York City to the iconic Rainbow Room in the RCA Building, an elegant, formal supper club with a revolving dance floor and the first restaurant ever located in a skyscraper. Like their first date, it was magical. There were cocktails, a delicious four-course dinner, and music and dancing, not to mention incredible views of the twinkling New York City skyline. Under the spell of this romantic setting, the ever-practical Henry decided for once to lead with his heart. He had only known Patricia a little over six months, and he didn't yet have an engagement ring, but when he looked across the table

Letters written by Henry and Patricia while dating, and the silver dollar that Henry gave Patricia as a tip.

at Patricia, he couldn't imagine being without her. In this moment, without any doubts, Henry proposed to Patricia.

> *Henry:* With all these letters taking place, I would say it was getting pretty serious, so we had a discussion about getting married.
> *Patricia:* I was so surprised! I really wasn't expecting it. I was still working on him!

Before they left the Rainbow Room that night, it was official: Patricia and Henry were engaged. Patricia returned to college in a daze, happier than she had ever been in her life. On March 4, 1956, Henry came to New Castle on what turned out to be Patricia's mother's birthday and gave his fiancée a beautiful engagement ring. They decided to get married that summer, just after Patricia graduated.

The Rollins brothers were thrilled for Henry, and Patricia always remembered fondly that Grace, Wayne's wife, thought she was perfect for Henry. But with a wedding just three months away, there were a few issues to resolve and plans to make.

"When Tip asked me to get married, he told me that his parents were divorced and asked how I felt about it," said Patricia, who did not meet Henry's parents until the wedding. "I said that I didn't think it was going to affect us, and then we talked about divorce in general. We felt that too many young people think, 'If this doesn't work out, I can always get a divorce.' But he and I didn't feel that way. So that was a part of his life, probably a sad part, but I didn't think it would affect us."

Patricia's parents had a few reservations about Henry because he was eight years older than their daughter. But they put their doubts aside and wrote letters to their future son-in-law. "My father wrote that he knew I was very much in love with Henry, and that he hoped Henry would treat me well," said Patricia, who would stumble upon the letter nearly 60 years later. "Tip saved the letter all these years. He astounds me."

Henry saved all of the letters that Patricia wrote to him, too. And though Patricia's habit of writing love letters to Henry played a delightful role in their love story, her declarations of love nearly cost her a college degree from Allegheny College. "All I did was write him letters," she recalled, with a slight roll of her eyes. "And I didn't work on my senior comp. So when I turned it in, the professor said it was no good, and that I would not be able to graduate. So I went to him and I told him that I was getting married in two weeks. And I promised him that if he would let me graduate, I would never use my degree! So he let me graduate."

Two weeks after a very grateful and relieved Patricia walked across the stage with her college diploma, she and Henry walked down the aisle. The scrambling college coed, so anxious that she wouldn't graduate, had

Mr. and Mrs. Henry B. Tippie, June 27, 1956.

waited so long to book the ceremony that there were no summer weekends available in June for a church wedding. So Henry and Patricia got married in the First United Presbyterian Church in New Castle on a Wednesday afternoon, June 27, 1956.

Henry didn't care what day they got married—he was just so happy, and he looked relaxed and handsome in a dark suit with a single white carnation in his lapel. And Patricia looked absolutely beautiful. Wearing a gorgeous satin gown with a cap-sleeve bodice made out of lace that matched her opera-length lace gloves, she took everyone's breath away when she walked down the aisle carrying a bouquet of orchids and mixed white flowers. Patricia's entire family was there, and almost all of Henry's family came for the ceremony, too. Ernest and Margaret drove from Iowa with Amelia, and Bob rode out with Flea Wright, who was Henry's best man. Only Henry's youngest brother, John, couldn't make it. "It was a very nice wedding." Henry says. "But I think that it was probably a wedding that her parents could not afford, but she did not know that at the time."

After the ceremony, Patricia had tears in her eyes when she presented Henry with a wedding gift—a simple case used for packing ties and putting them into a suitcase when traveling. "She was upset that she didn't have anything more for me, but I didn't expect anything," said Henry. "And coming from my background, I didn't even know that you did that—give wedding presents to each other. You don't miss what you don't know, I guess."

The newlyweds' honeymoon consisted of a leisurely drive from New Castle to Rehoboth Beach, with a stop in the Pocono Mountains. Four days after they got married, Henry and Patricia moved into Henry's bachelor apartment in Rehoboth. Patricia didn't particularly like its sparse furnishings, but she knew it was only temporary, and besides, she enjoyed going to the beach and her new home was only a few blocks from the ocean.

On Monday, after just one day in their first home, Henry left on a business trip, carrying his ties in the case Patricia gave him as a wedding present.

CHAPTER ELEVEN

ROLLINS EXPANDS AND MOVES TO WILMINGTON

OVER LABOR DAY WEEKEND OF 1956, just a few months after Henry and Patricia were married, the Rollins companies moved their headquarters from Rehoboth Beach to Wilmington, Delaware. The broadcasting operations moved to 414 French Street, and the leasing operation moved to a building at 14th and Union Streets. The reasons were pretty simple. The Rollins enterprises were now clearly divided between the diverse businesses of broadcasting and fleet leasing, and both operations had begun to expand: Wayne had recently acquired WAMS, a radio station in Wilmington located in the French Street building, and regional offices for John's leasing companies were springing up all over the country. It was becoming increasingly difficult to find qualified personnel who were willing to move to a seasonal town like Rehoboth. "A good part of the year you're off in no place," Henry explained, "and a lot of wives would not want to be there. They would want to be in a place that's more active." Plus, the Philadelphia International Airport was closer to Wilmington, making it easier for company executives to fly on commercial airlines.

And no one would deny that the company moved its headquarters to Wilmington in part to be closer to stronger financial institutions in New York that could help finance future growth. After purchasing its first television station in Plattsburgh, New York, in 1956, Rollins Broadcasting began to attract attention from financial analysts and credit rating services, even while still a private company. With revenues of $1.097 million in 1956, climbing to $1.661 million in 1957, and jumping an impressive 41 percent to $2.338 million in fiscal year 1958, the company received the highest credit rating from Dun & Bradstreet, Inc., which issued the following report about Rollins Broadcasting on December 20, 1957:

> Revenues and Earnings expanding rapidly, reflecting the acquisition of additional radio stations, coupled with the vigorous sales tactics employed by management. The retention of earnings and the revaluation of fixed assets have resulted in substantial growth to tangible net worth ($2.1 million). Activities soundly financed through the combination of retained earnings, outside financial support and prompt collection of receivables.

Around the time of the Dun & Bradstreet report, Henry saw an article in *Fortune* magazine that featured Lehman Brothers, a prominent Wall Street investment firm that liked to work with special and new-growth businesses. Henry showed the article to Wayne, suggesting that maybe his broadcast operation would be a good business to go public. After discussing the article, Rollins executives agreed that taking their company public could be an excellent idea, for several reasons. In addition to providing an important source of financing for the company, the employees would benefit far more from owning stock in a publicly held company than in a private one; Henry explained that the company could attract better people into the company if there was a way to make the stock available, such as through stock option plans. And with the growth of Wayne's and John's wealth, Henry knew that it was time to think about the advantages of publicly traded stock for estate-planning purposes.

With the brothers' approval, Henry wrote to Lehman, pointing out Rollins' growth over the past few years. As a result, representatives from the firm came to Wilmington in early 1958 to review Rollins Broadcasting. Though the executives were impressed, "They indicated they thought we were premature, and needed to wait maybe another year or so and then talk about it again," said Henry.

With the topic tabled for the time being, Henry refocused his attention on Rollins Fleet Leasing. Since 1954, when John and Henry first incorporated the leasing company, Henry had served as the company's vice president and treasurer. But neither Henry nor John was in charge of the day-to-day operations of the company. With John's four-year term as Delaware's lieutenant governor extending into January 1957, John had hired executives with backgrounds in governmental positions to run the company. Their business skills had failed to impress Henry. "These guys did not do a good job," he said. "They failed miserably, and I complained for a long time about them."

True to Henry's character to speak the truth, no matter who got caught in the crossfire, he soon discovered a problem that involved Wayne's older son, Randall. Though he had been out of the Coast Guard for a few years, Randall had struggled somewhat professionally. He had lost a lot of money with an dishonest partner in Lewes, Delaware, when he got involved in a used car lot and a gas station with pinball machines; Henry helped Randall secure a bank loan and get his debts straightened out, and a relieved Randall; his wife, Peggy; and their young family moved to Wilmington when the company relocated. Randall now worked for the Rollins Leasing Division and was in charge of handling the disposal of cars that came off lease agreements. To Henry's chagrin, he discovered that Randall was operating a company on the side called Miracle Motors that would take the cars coming in from the leasing operation, resell them, and make a profit.

Behind Randall's back, the operations manager squealed to Henry about the situation: "Look, he's over here, doing this and that, taking these cars and making money. The money really should be going to the company."

"Well, we can't have this," Henry said. "This isn't right."

So Henry fired Randall, the boss's son—though he always preferred to say he "let Randall go. I felt bad about it, but I thought, 'This is the way it's got to be.' I called his dad and uncle, and explained what happened. They never once questioned that decision. I know it upset Randall badly. I certainly was not at the top of his list."

Years later both Randall and Henry discussed the entire situation and, with the value of hindsight, finally realized exactly what had happened.

The operations manager, it turned out, was orchestrating the entire scenario, pitting Randall and Henry against each other for what he hoped would be his own professional gain. "The operations manager, the same one who had dimed Randall out, had actually been telling Randall what do to, step by step," Henry eventually understood. "Now this was the same guy who was telling me the exact opposite, that Randall was calling the shots. So it turns out, the operations manager was playing both of us against each other. He thought that I would be fired for firing Randall, and that he would get my job. That's what would have happened at most other businesses, but not with the Rollins brothers. They stood behind me and never questioned my decision. And in retrospect, I think it probably did both of us a favor. I realized how loyal Wayne and John could be, and Randall got more engaged with his dad in the broadcast company and later the outdoor advertising operation."

ACCOUNTANTS CAN BE MANAGERS, TOO: HENRY RUNS ROLLINS LEASING

As Randall began what would one day be a remarkable career with Rollins Broadcasting, Henry turned his attention once more to the leasing operation. Henry constantly complained about how much money the leasing business spent on unnecessary offices and expenses. "To make a long story short, the company was doing poorly, not doing well; money was being wasted. Offices had been set up in New York City, Chicago, Dallas, Los Angeles, and I'm thinking maybe Atlanta. I think some of this was ill conceived. In addition, we had gone off into the daily rental of automobiles at the Los Angeles airport, and also at the Miami airport. And vehicles are being purchased, and I don't know about them. And then we get into whether or not we have the money to pay for them, and cars are bought to be on lease and they don't have any leases, and so forth. And the interest rates on some of this stuff was not good."

Henry had never bought into the stereotype that "accountants can't run things." But he did acknowledge that an accountant who wants to be in management "has to look at other things besides dollars and cents." And three years after moving to Wilmington, when the need for manage-

Henry B. Tippie at the helm of Rollins Fleet Leasing in Wilmington, Delaware.

rial change was starkly evident at the leasing operation, Henry seized the opportunity to showcase his managerial prowess by positioning himself as head of Rollins Fleet Leasing. The timing of the move, which took place in 1959, surprised everyone, including Henry.

As Henry recalled, "The fellow that's in charge of Rollins Fleet Leasing had an office next to me. And one Friday afternoon at noontime, he just never returned. He didn't even come in to clear out his stuff. I think he went out—I don't know what all took place between he and John Sr.—but the bottom line is, the fellow never came back. I cleaned off the desk, and at this point there is nobody else there to really watch after the operation. So before anybody could really get under way to get somebody, I would have to say that I probably assumed command of the place because we needed to have somebody in charge of it. And I had a plan that I had put together very quickly about how to get this company turned around. I presented that plan, and it was accepted. Before they could get anyone else hired, I'm making money."

Under Henry's watchful eye, the company closed all of its regional offices except the one in Los Angeles. "I got rid of them," he said. "In addition to that, we got rid of maybe a third of the business that the company had that was unprofitable, and immediately, the company is profitable. And we never looked back. I think at that point I began to get the recognition that I could run something. The greatest way to get attention is to take something that's losing money and start making money. I shut down offices we didn't need, consolidated, got rid of unprofitable business, and bingo, I'm on my way. After that, there was never any question about getting someone else to run the auto leasing. And there's no doubt in my mind, I proved to *myself* that I could take a failing business and turn it around."

ROLLINS BROADCASTING BECOMES A PUBLIC COMPANY

With Henry taking charge of the leasing business, John Rollins devoted more time to his love for politics and, in 1960, began a campaign for governor of Delaware (he won the Republican nomination in September, but lost in the general election two months later). At Rollins Broadcasting, Wayne soon faced a business problem that forced him to revisit taking the company public. In the spring of 1960, Wayne lost the chance to buy WSFA-TV in Montgomery, Alabama, in part because Wayne refused to personally endorse a bank's loan to help finance the deal, arguing that the company's financial strength was enough to back the loan. The banker noted that it would be different if "Rollins were a public company." Wayne needed no more convincing. It was time to try once more to take Rollins Broadcasting public.

By the end of fiscal year 1960, just 10 years after it opened its first radio station, Rollins Broadcasting reported $3.8 million in revenues, 156 employees, seven AM radio stations (the limit imposed by the Multiple Ownership Rule of the FCC), and three television stations, with national radio sales offices in New York and Chicago. After another meeting with Lehman Brothers, Henry prepared the prospectus and the proper documents. "As that moved along, I was very much involved in working all this out. You get involved with prospectus preparations with the Securities and Exchange Commission and getting everything cleared." When Henry and Wayne traveled to New York to meet for a second time with Frank Manheim and Gordon Calder at Lehman Brothers, Wayne surprised the seasoned Wall Street investors *and* Henry when he announced that he intended to grow the current $4 million business to $100 million in sales. But Henry always thought that Wayne gave the perfect response to explain his assertion.

"I think we've got the knowledge now," Wayne told Frank Manheim in response to Manheim's question about how he planned to grow the business by that much. "We know how to run television stations to make money. We know how to run radio stations profitably. We know how to program a radio station to minorities where it is profitable. I think our margins show we know how to make a profit."

Though Lehman Brothers as a rule refused to take companies public if they had less than $25 million in revenue, the company decided to make an exception for Rollins Broadcasting. Henry, then vice president of the corporation, always felt that taking the company public contributed significantly to Rollins' success, calling it a "major milestone in the evolvement of Wayne and what was then Rollins Broadcasting, Inc."

On September 13, 1960, Rollins Broadcasting went public with an over-the-counter offering of 110,000 shares of common stock at $8 a share. Henry purchased the first 1,500 shares of common stock offered that day, and he still has the first 15 stock certificates ever issued: C1, C2, C3 . . . C15, all representing 100 shares each. And as an officer of the company, Henry also got a stock option out of the deal. By the end of the day, 90 percent of the stock was owned by members of the Rollins family and company executives, so even though Rollins Broadcasting was now a publicly owned company, "We didn't have a vast array of outside shareholders," said Henry. In fact, according to Henry, Wayne disregarded Wall Street advice to reduce his personal holdings and become a minority stockholder in his own company. Going forward, the Rollins family would always maintain a majority ownership, creating what Henry called a "controlled public company."

Though the Rollins stock came out at $8 a share, the market promptly went into somewhat of a sell-off, and over the next 90 days, the stock dipped below $6 a share. "That was our introduction to the securities business," said Henry. "I decided that was a good time to buy some stock, so I sold some of my stock I had in other companies and turned around and bought stock in Rollins, which I still have. I figured it could have some future possibilities."

The Rollins Broadcasting stock moved over to the American Stock Exchange the following February 14, 1961. On Wall Street in New York City, Henry joined O. Wayne Rollins, John W. Rollins Sr., long-term Rollins employee and corporate secretary Madalyn Copley, and then stock exchange president Edward McCormick to witness the listing for the first time. The five later posed for a photograph, all gingerly holding the ticker tape that represented the historical moment the first "ROL" crossed the exchange board. Standing next to Wayne, Henry smiled as he held the tape in his left hand. On his mind, no doubt, was more than just that remarkable moment. Wayne, after all, had promised to grow the company to $100 million in sales, and Henry was steadily on a path to see that Rollins Broadcasting would one day trade on the New York Stock Exchange (NYSE). And though no one on the floor of the American

(Left to right) John W. Rollins, Madalyn Copley, Edward McCormick, O. Wayne Rollins, and Henry B. Tippie celebrate Rollins Broadcasting's listing on the American Stock Exchange, February 14, 1961.

(Left to right) Madalyn Copley, Henry B. Tippie, Jarvis L. Slade, and O. Wayne Rollins at the first annual shareholders' meeting for Rollins Broadcasting, August 1961.

Stock Exchange that day in 1961 could have predicted it, Henry's future connections with the NYSE would far surpass his ties to just one company. This farm boy from Iowa, whose father once said he daydreamed so much he would never amount to anything, would one day be associated with nine companies listed on the NYSE.

ROLLINS BROADCASTING, OUTDOOR ADVERTISING, AND A LOAN NOT SIGNED

True to Wayne's prediction, Rollins Broadcasting not only continued to grow, it branched out into a completely new direction—outdoor advertising.

A company within a company, the Outdoor Advertising Division started as a part of Rollins Broadcasting in 1961—making a somewhat dramatic entrance through the acquisition of a family-owned Texas business named Tribble Outdoor in San Antonio, Texas, on August 1, 1961, in the middle of a Category 5 Texas hurricane named Carla. The move signaled Rollins' intent to diversify its communications operations, branching out into a complementary business that would attract national advertisers. From day one, Randall Rollins was in charge of the operation, which proved to be one of Rollins' most successful and sustained businesses. After opening another branch in Laredo, Texas, Rollins Outdoor expanded into Wilmington, Delaware, in 1962. A year later, in November 1963, Rollins acquired its first international business when it purchased an outdoor advertising business headquartered in Mexico City and a subsidiary of Philadelphia's General Outdoor Advertising, Inc. (G.O.A.), one of the largest outdoor advertising companies in the country. In March 1964 Rollins Outdoor Advertising acquired the rest of General Outdoor Advertising for $5.8 million, including locations in Philadelphia; Washington, D.C.; Camden, New Jersey; and Salisbury, Maryland. The acquisition added 37 advertising markets. As a result, Rollins Outdoor Advertising became the fourth-largest outdoor advertising company in the country, after only three years under Rollins' watch.

The creative financing technique that Rollins used in 1964 to make the second G.O.A. acquisition was, according to Henry, of "extreme importance and sometimes gets overlooked." Here's why, said Henry:

> When Rollins went public in 1960, we were encouraged by the investment bankers to open a New York banking relationship, and we did that. We didn't ask to borrow anything, but we did keep some money on deposit, to build a base to help make acquisitions and so forth. In the early part of 1964, Wayne had worked out the acquisition of the General Outdoor Advertising operations in Philadelphia and the Delmarva Peninsula area. When the outdoor operation became available, we needed to borrow some money in order to put up the money needed for the down payment, with the balance, of course, being financed by the sellers. So Wayne talked to the people at the New York bank, and they said that would be no problem whatsoever.

When the paperwork to purchase G.O.A. arrived from the New York bank, Henry recalled, "they had so many restrictions in them," including a provision that prohibited the company from making future acquisitions over a certain size. Henry and Wayne knew that Rollins should not sign the bank loan with so many restrictions in place, but they were between a rock and a hard place: the company already had a commitment to the outdoor advertising acquisition and needed roughly $300,000 to $400,000 to close the deal. Working closely with Henry, Wayne had an idea: Why not borrow money from Rollins' leasing business to help finance the G.O.A. transaction, much like the company did in 1953 to help purchase WNJR? Said Henry,

> At that time, we had accumulated about $600,000 to $700,000 of cash in the Leasing Company. Wayne talked to me about whether we could lend that money for a short period of time over to Rollins Broadcasting and go ahead and make the acquisition and not get tangled up in this loan agreement with all its onerous provisions. We had done a similar transaction in 1953, when I first joined the company. And so that's what we did. We felt once we got the acquisition made, that we could probably go to one of the Wilmington banks and work out some kind of loan and get the money back into the Leasing Company. That, of course, is what took place.

Henry always appreciated the fact that the company could make the G.O.A. deal work on its own terms, and he frequently commented on Wayne's wisdom in figuring out how the deal should be financed. But the full impact of the company's decision to avoid signing restrictive loan agreements would not become completely evident until several months later, when Rollins decided to pursue the acquisition of a pest control company named Orkin, a history-making purchase for Rollins that was already in the pipeline in the spring of 1964. As it turns out, the Orkin acquisition would have violated the New York bank's requirement that Rollins avoid "acquisitions over a certain size." If the company had signed those loan agreement papers, Henry later recognized, "the Orkin acquisition would have been impossible."

"And *that,*" Henry always marveled, "would have resulted in an entirely different future."

Henry and Patricia on an early fishing vacation (above) and
in formal attire for an evening out (below).

CHAPTER TWELVE

A FIRST HOME, A GROWING FAMILY

DURING THEIR FIRST SUMMER TOGETHER, Henry and Patricia soon found themselves traveling north to Wilmington to look for a new home. Since the Rollins Company planned to move its headquarters to the city in September 1956, the young couple needed their own place and quickly decided to buy their first home. They zeroed in on Liftwood Estates, a newly developing subdivision on the outskirts of Wilmington, and Henry soon determined that buying the two-story, three-bedroom model home would be a good value because he figured it was well built. Still, he hesitated. "I wanted the house really badly, and he thought it was more than we needed," said Patricia. "But John Rollins talked him into it, and we lived there for 11 years."

For Patricia, their home in Delaware would always represent "my favorite neighborhood. It was the friendliest neighborhood we ever lived in. But maybe that's because we were all young and struggling, and all the women got together and played with their children every day. And if we wanted to have a party, we would call and say, 'We're going to get together so bring something.' So you would grab something, some cheeses and crackers, nobody could really throw a party."

The Tippies' first home remained largely unfurnished during the first few years of their marriage. The young couple didn't believe in buying furnishings "on time," and when they did save enough, they wanted to buy furniture that would last. In the beginning they had only a bedroom set and a kitchen table. When John Sr. first heard that Patricia didn't have a television set, he bought one and sent it to her. He couldn't imagine Patricia without a television, especially when he and Henry were away so often, trying to build up the leasing company. Patricia, though appreciative, didn't really care. Her favorite thing to do, when Henry traveled, was to sit in the crook of her bedroom window and read or write letters, content in the cool night air.

Henry would later brag about his wife's unassuming nature: "She went without furniture, along with many other items, in our first house for a long time when we started out." And in those lean first years, Henry and Patricia established a pattern of earning and spending that they embraced their entire lives: They always lived without spending all that they earned.

"Patricia and I had budgets for years and years, month by month, showing how much cash is coming in and how much cash is going out. And as our income went up, Patricia and I did not change our lifestyle," said Henry proudly. "So whatever gains we had, and they were certainly substantial, we just kept them and intended to live like we always lived, just like the gains didn't exist. I've watched others out there, frittering theirs away."

Another thing that Henry insisted upon was that Patricia needed her own bank account, even though she didn't have a job outside the home. For the era, it was a very progressive notion, particularly for a young husband in the 1950s when men and women were not yet considered equals in the home or the workplace. But Henry, ever the numbers man, looked at it strictly as a smart financial arrangement—not as a social commentary. "I think a lot of problems get involved with joint bank accounts. So right off the bat, I established Patricia's own personal bank account. I think initially I deposited $200 a month in her account. And she knew that she had responsibilities, to pay certain things out of that account, and then I had to do the house payment out of my account. And we also figured out how much we were going to spend for clothes, for vacations, and so forth. I feel strongly that that's the way you do it. And I know Patricia feels the same way. That's how we started out, and we watched our money very carefully."

REFLECTIONS ON FAMILIES, BOTH OLD AND NEW

Henry and Patricia were reminded of just how important marriage could be in the early winter of 1956, when Henry's Grandma Bokholt passed away and they returned to Belle Plaine for the funeral. Henry hadn't seen his divorced parents since he and Patricia got married that summer, and he was deeply disturbed by the situation he encountered when he paid a visit to his father.

"At that point my dad was living in the Iowa Hotel, not a very good place. So Ernest and John and I went to see him after the funeral. And I think he had probably been drinking the night before because he was kind of glassy-eyed. And when we got to the room he was sort of loud like, 'What are you doing here?' A few other things were said that indicated he was angry, so we just turned around and left. And I didn't see him again for the next several years. The whole thing was upsetting. "

Ernie, too, remembers that painful run-in with his father. "I don't think our dad ever forgave Henry or me. He thought we had taken Mother's side of the issue," he recalled. "So I don't think he ever forgave us for that. In fact, I'm positive he never did because he told me a year or two after the divorce that he never wanted to see us again."

Patricia and Henry Tippie bring home their son, Henry II, in 1957.

Henry went for nearly six years without speaking to or seeing his father. The timing was both poignant and ironic. During the years he wasn't communicating with Bob, Henry became a father to his own three children with Patricia: a son named Henry II, born in the summer of 1957; a daughter named Helen, born in 1958; and a daughter named Linda, born in 1961.

When Henry B. Tippie II was born in August 1957, his father beamed with pride. "I think that was his happiest day," Patricia said. "I'll never forget when I saw him, when he came in to see me after Henry II was born. He looked younger than I had ever seen him. He just looked so happy, he looked really different! I can't explain it, he just looked proud and happy."

Henry was definitely excited to be a father to all three of his children. But he's the first to admit that he was never a warm and fuzzy type of parent. He didn't shower his children with affection, and he never tried to reach out to them with words of endearment. It's not that his heart was ever filled with anything but the deepest love for his children, but Henry just didn't possess the words to express it. Coming from a family that was emotionally detached and incapable of showing physical affection, it wasn't in Henry's nature to be demonstrative.

Instead, Henry and Patricia early on carved out different roles for themselves in the family: Henry accepted the role of stoic provider, and Patricia embraced the role of loving nurturer for their growing family. Henry trusted Patricia to show enough love to the children for both of them, and he didn't really apologize for it either. "I am who I am," he would say. "What you see is what you get. And I don't really share a lot of things. I'm not out here flaunting myself. You almost have to dig it out sometimes. I am not a blabbermouth or jabber type person."

As a parent, Henry's primary goal was to give his children something he never had as a child: security. "I've always tried to provide a home and make sure we've got bread on the table and we're not going to be dispossessed," said Henry, who could never shake the haunting Depression-era image of a family sitting on the sidewalk in Belle Plaine after losing their home, or the struggles his own family endured to find enough food and money to survive on the farm. "There's no doubt that I always felt that my role should be to provide. I'm just from that generation."

Taking care of her family, Patricia soon realized just how much attention and love she gave her children to help them feel secure. Slowly, she began to fully understand the childhood that Henry had experienced, and the impact it had on him. Though she recognized that Bob and Amelia worked hard and took care of Henry's needs, "I don't think he

The Tippies became a family of four when daughter Helen was born in 1958.

had much interaction as a small boy," she said. "He went to bed at sundown, there was no radio when he was a child. And because he was well behaved, his parents took care of his needs and that was it." With no playmates or early friends to talk to, Henry rarely had a spontaneously joyful moment in his childhood unless it revolved around his beloved animals. Henry carried the quietness of his childhood with him his entire life, reflected in his reserved personality and measured responses.

Patricia pointed all of this out to Henry, but it didn't change him. And though he was never the parent who hugged a lot or gave out unbridled praise, Henry the father reached out to his children in his own way. In Delaware he bought his children little garden tools and, in the vacant lot adjacent to their home, tried to teach them how to plant a garden and grow some vegetables, just like he had done as a young boy in Belle Plaine. The results were mixed. "One or two years there was some corn, but the soil there wasn't any good," he said, laughing. "I tried to teach the children a little bit but I failed miserably."

On Saturday mornings, he would take one of the children with him to the office, alternating so that each had a turn, and the child would sit at his secretary's desk and draw or play with the phone while he checked the mail and reviewed some paperwork. And when they were a little bit older, Henry would take all three kids to see John Wayne movies. "John Wayne is from Iowa," Henry proudly told his children. "We have a lot of good Iowans." Once, when Helen wanted to ride on a train, Henry took her for a ride, just the two of them. And because he worked close by in Wilmington, "Tip always loved to come home for lunch," Patricia said. "And when the children were small, I thought that was really neat because they had lunch with their daddy. He traveled so much, as least they had that."

Patricia laughed about the time she had to leave town suddenly and visit her own ailing parents when the children were small. She naturally

The Tippie children: Henry II, Helen, and Linda, born in 1961.

left the kids with the babysitter and Henry. When they were under his charge, he created a military atmosphere. After making their own beds, they had to stand at attention as Henry inspected their work—it was Coe College, all over again! The results, however, were never quite military perfect. When Henry showed up at the airport with the kids to welcome Patricia home, their hair was disheveled, and no one had on a matching pair of socks. Patricia had a rare laugh at Henry's expense. "And I thought, *this* is taking care of them!"

When Patricia's father died about four years after the wedding, Henry II and Helen had already been born, and Patricia began to think about Henry's estranged father. "I thought, you know, the children have a grandfather who is alive and they ought to know him," she said. "I didn't know him at all because our wedding was the last time I had seen him."

Another year or two passed, and Patricia couldn't get the notion of a grandfather for her children out of her mind. "I always took the children every summer to stay at least a week with my mother-in-law, and Tip would come out for about a week. So Henry II must have been about five, Helen was four, and Linda was not quite one. Mother Tippie had gone to work at the florist shop, and I'm sitting there thinking, 'I'm going to call Henry's dad up and tell him I'm here with the children.' He had an electrical shop, and I said that I'd be there in half an hour. So I dress the kids all up in their little white shoes, and we're walking out the door and here comes Mother Tippie up the sidewalk! She had gotten off work early. And she said, 'Where are you going?' And I had already told the children, so Henry II is all excited and he said, 'We're going to meet Grandpa!' So she looked at me and didn't say anything and walked in the house. And I thought, 'Now what have I done?' Anyway, Henry's dad was down there waiting for us and took the children out for ice cream cones. And then he told me, 'When Henry comes out, I want to get together with him.'"

When Henry arrived in Belle Plaine and Patricia told him what had happened, Henry didn't hesitate. He went to see his father. "It was kind of awkward, but I decided, well, I need to go and see him. I went by there, and we got along just like nothing had ever happened. And we never did discuss anything about what happened. We got along good, and then I asked him if somewhere along the line he might be interested in coming to Delaware. And his answer was yes."

Bob kept his promise, and he soon came to Delaware to visit with his oldest son, his daughter-in-law, and his three grandchildren. For nearly two weeks in the summer of 1962, Henry shared some scenes from his life that his father had never seen before: they traveled to New York City, toured the New York Stock Exchange, visited Hell's Kitchen, and got wonderful seats to a Broadway play. He showed Bob around his office in Wilmington and introduced him to his colleagues. Both son and grandson accompanied Bob to a Major League Baseball game in Philadelphia, and he thoroughly enjoyed staying in Henry and Patricia's home just outside Wilmington. "He really enjoyed himself, and we had a great time," said Henry, relieved that the family division had been quietly resolved.

HENRY'S CHILDREN TALK ABOUT THEIR DAD

Henry and Patricia's three children all have distinct but different memories when it comes to their father and mother.

As a youngster, Henry II recalls pushing a plastic lawn mower behind his father while he cut the grass. Henry also taught his son to love baseball.

While living in Delaware, Henry II fondly remembers going to a Phillies baseball games with his dad. "But physical embracing, sitting in his lap," he recalled, "that didn't take place."

Helen, however, remembers sitting in her daddy's lap and watching *The Lawrence Welk Show* on television. Henry typically sat in the recliner in the family room after work. "And it was comfortable," she said. "He was a good dad. I don't think people know he has a sweet side. He is caring, and he doesn't show that sometimes, but you know it's there."

Even though Henry played the role of disciplinarian, Helen says that he hated to spank them. "You know, if we really did something bad, we would get spanked. And he really didn't like to do that, Mom told me later. But he said he had to, but he didn't like it. But he stuck to his word." His long absences didn't bother Helen; in her mind, everybody's father went to work and traveled in those days, but they all came back home. "I never felt like he wasn't there. We planted gardens together, and he would take us to the office and to the race track. If you needed him, he was there. There were times when he would cancel trips because he was needed at home."

Linda, the youngest, remembers Henry being the type of father that you almost have to tiptoe around. "He was not approachable at that time. He was maybe even a little intimidating, kind of bigger than life. I don't recall reading books together, jumping in his lap. It's just not his generation," she noted.

Henry's three children help him celebrate his 40th birthday in 1967.

Though Henry always tried to leave his work at the office, Linda remembers times when her father would quietly watch the business news on television, and he did not want to be disturbed. But even when surrounded by three children, Henry's thoughts often turned to work. Linda remembers picking up the *TV Guide* and finding figures and numbers scratched on the back. "I think he's always

The Tippie family in Delaware.

working, always figuring numbers," she says. "Except on Saturday evenings when Lawrence Welk would come on," she says. "We would all watch that show, and one time we all got to laughing so hard—and my mom was in on this too, she could be just as bad—we all almost got in trouble because we were disrupting the show."

Even though Henry could be withdrawn and reserved, Linda never doubted his feelings for her. "You could feel the concern from him, even though he was a hands-off type father. A lot of times, we would hear it through our mom, 'Your dad is proud of you.' It's not that he would come out and say those things a lot of time. I don't know if he was comfortable. So we knew how he felt, it was just kind of a given, but it wasn't always spoken."

A LOVE OF TRAVEL AND PATRICIA'S INFLUENCE

Despite the demands from his work and his obligations to his family, Henry found time to pursue his boyhood love of fishing. He loved to take the children fishing at Lake McBride, not far from Belle Plaine, when he visited his mom and dad back home in Iowa. And he frequently

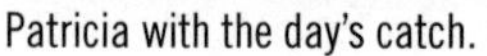
Patricia with the day's catch.

Henry on the dock for a fishing trip.

took fishing trips with Patricia to lakes in Minnesota and Canada or off the Florida coast, where he began to develop a taste for saltwater fishing.

And while living modestly in Delaware, the Tippies discovered and began to cultivate what would become a lifelong passion: traveling all over the world, a luxury that both Henry and Patricia soon enjoyed more than they ever dared to imagine. Patricia still remembers one of their first trips on a freighter cruise ship:

> We belonged to a club called the University Club when we lived in Delaware. They had special dinners each month and they had a Christmas dance, but we didn't go every weekend because the children were quite young. But one year, we decided to go on a freighter cruise, and Henry's mother and his brother John came to babysit. The freighter left New York and went to Baltimore. It got icy in Baltimore and it didn't leave for two days, and then we went down to South America. Our neighbors said that they couldn't figure out how we could afford to do this, and we told them, "Well, *you* went to the University Club every weekend and we only went to the really big things," so we told them that our trip was their liquor bill! Anyway, there were supposed to be 22 passengers on the trip, but just a few weeks before, another freighter had caught fire so a lot of people canceled the trip. There were only six of us, three women and three men, plus a doctor and a bartender. I was in my twenties then, and the other lady was in her forties, and the other in her sixties! And

> they didn't have a swimming pool, and I loved to swim, so they dropped this canvas into the cargo hold and filled it full of water for me. Tip liked that trip. He spent a lot of time with the captain and the first mate, and he was down in the engine room all the time. And we weren't really supposed to have a nice room but there were so few people on the ship that it didn't matter and they moved us up. We had a big room—it was two rooms combined—so we decided that we would have a cocktail party. We invited the officers and all the other passengers. The total bill was really cheap because drinks were like a quarter. It was really fun and that was the first trip we took on a ship.

From the outside looking in, it was clear to everyone that this young couple—as different as two people could possibly be, with this extroverted, welcoming, bubbly young woman married to a dry-witted, quiet, introverted, and slightly older businessman—were nonetheless perfectly matched. John Rollins Sr., who spent so much time with Henry for business purposes, was one of the first to see and appreciate the couple's unique bond.

"The beauty of Henry's life is that he's been married to a woman who is close to him and is with him no matter what he wanted to do," he said. "There would be a lot of spouses who would say, 'You've got all this money, let's do this or do that.' Patricia's not like that. She's really down to earth. She's just as thrifty as he is, maybe not quite."

Randall Rollins, who survived being fired by Henry to one day become cherished friends of Henry and Patricia's, once commented that Patricia "is unbelievable. I can't say enough about her. They are ideally suited for each other. I think they are very happy and satisfied with their place in life and with each other. They are not trying to put on any pretense. They are just nice people. The more you are around Pat, the more you'll like her. The kind of person you want to hug! She is so supportive of Henry and what he does."

A man not known for his effusive praise, Henry holds nothing back when he talks about his Patricia: "I want to say how fortunate could I be to have met her. She is an outstanding person, rarely ever complains about anything. She is an excellent homemaker. I think she's done an outstanding job raising the children, and she's always there. And if I was going to write any specifications, I couldn't come up with any specifications better than her. She's just 100 percent partner, best friend, confidante. I don't think they make them any better and I'm very proud of her."

Patricia is equally glowing about Henry, the man she has affectionately called "Tip" from the time they met. She is privy to a side of Henry that he keeps tucked away behind his formal business persona. "I see the soft side that nobody knows about. And I think it's good that we're opposite because everybody needs a softness in their life. He's taught me to think a lot, to be more organized than I used to be. I'm a dreamer and a romantic, and I would never have thought about making lists! I would probably be floundering through life if I was single."

In Patricia's defense, close friends don't see her that way at all. Rather than floundering, they see her as the ultimate source of strength that allowed Henry to succeed, the woman who showed him that love and joy could be a part of life, too.

"She is so kind. I have never heard her say an unkind word about anybody. And she just has a heart of gold," said Michele Rollins, John Rollins' third wife, who absolutely adored Patricia and her ability to bring out the best in Henry. "The depth and the quality Patricia has to look through veneers, to look at Henry as a person and to say, 'That's the man I love. I may not have wanted to wait on him when he came in my restaurant with his newspaper in his face, but I want to spend the rest of my life with him because under that's a great guy.' And her first act—'I won't wait on him'—was the beginning of their relationship. She was not intimidated by him. She set the ground rules. Pat Tippie, you're a hell of a woman."

CHAPTER THIRTEEN

JONAH SWALLOWS THE WHALE: ROLLINS BUYS ORKIN

IN THE SPRING AND SUMMER of 1964, as he continued to run Rollins Fleet Leasing to record profits and new levels of efficiency, Henry participated in crafting a business deal for Rollins that would make business history: Rollins, a $4 million company, purchased Orkin, an iconic American exterminating company worth $62.4 million.

It was the kind of deal that Henry had never studied about in textbooks at the University of Iowa, never read about in the *Journal of Accountancy*, and never heard about while watching evening business reports on television. This remarkable business deal became known as the country's first leveraged buyout, or LBO—described in basic terms as the acquisition of another company using a significant amount of borrowed money to meet the costs of acquisition. A detailed description of the deal would eventually be covered in a case study at the Harvard Business School. But as Henry and Wayne Rollins traveled back and forth between Wilmington, Delaware, and Atlanta, Georgia, from Memorial Day to Labor Day in 1964—constantly reviewing the mechanics of the deal on green legal pads broken down into 13 columns of numbers written in pencil—they didn't know they were about to make business history.

"From our standpoint, it was almost business as usual. We never thought about it being a leveraged buyout," said Henry, thinking back to all the broadcasting deals and leasing purchases that Rollins had executed up to that point, through lines of credit, assumed debts, and minimal cash outlays. "It wasn't anything new because we bought everything with very little or no money."

THE ORKIN DEAL

By the spring of 1964, the Orkin family had decided to sell the company founded in 1901 by Otto Orkin, a Latvian immigrant who had started the business by selling pesticide out of a little black satchel, going door-to-door in rural Pennsylvania. Over 60 years later, the Orkin family members who still owned the Atlanta-based national pest control company found themselves in an internal feud, such that selling the business became their best option. For nearly a year, a wealthy New York investor named Lewis B. Cullman had worked behind the scenes to craft an offer to buy the entire company from the family for $26 a share—for a total purchase price of $62.4 million. The Orkin family had tentatively accepted his offer, and Cullman continued to work to develop potential partners not only to finance the deal but also to manage and run the company after it was acquired.

The Orkin deal was complex, and many of the details were worked out long before Wayne Rollins heard in April that the company was for sale. According to Cullman's scenario, all of Orkin's assets would be sold to Kinro Corporation, a holding company created specifically to acquire Orkin; "Kinro," in fact, was simply a new word derived from the five letters in "Orkin." In order to finance the deal, Cullman had persuaded Prudential Insurance Company of America to invest $40 million in the purchase, and he was soon searching for a second partner to provide the remaining equity to finance the deal. To clear that hurdle, Cullman brought in George T. Weymouth, who was coincidentally a close personal friend of Wayne Rollins and president of Laird & Company, a small investment banking firm based in Wilmington. Weymouth was related to the DuPont family by marriage and attempted to convince several DuPonts to invest in the Orkin purchase. When the DuPont investors backed out, Weymouth mentioned the Orkin opportunity to Wayne Rollins.

Wayne's initial question was right to the point: "What kind of price are we talking about?" When Weymouth first floated the $62.4 million price tag, Wayne's immediate reaction was equally direct. "No. I'm not interested. I can already tell you that," he said, convinced that Orkin and the price were too big, and that he didn't have enough knowledge about the pest control industry to effectively evaluate the deal. But Weymouth finally prevailed upon Wayne to visit Atlanta and talk with Orkin executives before his no became final.

Wayne and John Sr. agreed to meet on Memorial Day with the leading Orkin executives, and afterward, he was convinced that he should continue to study the deal. Weymouth next arranged for Earl F. Geiger, the Orkin vice president and general sales manager, to meet with Wayne in Wilmington at the offices of Rollins Broadcasting. "I want to know all I can about Orkin," Wayne told Geiger, who then described pest control as "a remarkable business" with a minimal amount of accounts receivable and little inventory. Made up of both casual and habitual pest control users, Geiger allowed that changing the casual user to a regular customer would increase revenue and help Orkin continue to grow in revenue. "Orkin is really in its embryonic stage," Geiger concluded. "The market for pest and termite control is unsaturated, with plenty of room to grow, both by adding new customers and by offering more services to existing customers. We can build this company into a hundred-million-dollar business within the next 10 years. There's no reason we couldn't make it a billion-dollar company!"

Wayne was clearly impressed, but still cautious. "Let's make it a hundred million first," he said. Wayne agreed to take a closer look at Orkin, and for the next two months he and Henry traveled extensively between Wilmington and Atlanta. They discovered that Orkin's largest expenditure outside of labor was advertising, a need that Rollins Broadcasting and Rollins Outdoor Advertising could easily help meet. "That was part of why we had an interest in looking at it," according to Henry.

Wayne also retained a leading management consulting firm, McKinsey & Company, Inc., to conduct a comprehensive study of the pest control industry. McKinsey reported back that "the Orkin Exterminating Company has a strong position in a growing industry. Orkin's strengths make it unusually competitive." With 7,000 to 8,000 pest control companies in the $480 million U.S. industry, the average pest control company had sales of $50,000 to $75,000; Orkin had sales of $37.3 million. McKinsey pointed to the "strong motivation that Orkin has achieved at the branch level"; Orkin has some "unusually competent field managers. We were impressed with the ability and the imagination of several of the branch and district managers with whom we worked." And in a nod to Otto Orkin's tireless efforts to promote his company and create brand appeal, McKinsey noted that Orkin "is probably the best-known structural pest control company in the southeastern United States. Because the company has been established for many years, spends substantial amounts on advertising and has a large number of servicemen, trucks and offices, it would seem certain that Orkin is better known than any other competitor in its home marketing area. And in an industry where the quality of services is difficult to evaluate, such recognition is clearly a strong asset."

Second, McKinsey reported that after correcting some weak areas in management, field operations, and goal setting, "Orkin's prospects for growth appear to be excellent." One word of caution: "In all but three of the last 11 years, the Company has increased its sales by $2 million to $4 million. But while sales have been increasing, the company's percentage sales gains have been generally declining. . . . Orkin's growth throughout this period has probably been somewhat retarded by certain top-management policies. However, there is no indication to date, either in the absolute sales gains or in Orkin's prospects, that the Company's growth will stop."

As Wayne read the report, the fact that Orkin was inconsistently managed and financially underachieving was not a deterrent. As he had proven over and over in the broadcasting and outdoor advertising businesses, Wayne often looked to purchase underachieving properties that had excellent growth potential and could be improved. Henry completely agreed with that strategy.

After 11 years of working side by side with the Rollins brothers, Henry's role as "Dr. No," his financial expertise, and his honest, often blunt, business opinions—which Wayne once referred to as "Henry's firm positions"—had never been more appreciated than during the company's exploration of the Orkin purchase. Though the Rollins brothers had initially thought of Henry as solely a numbers guy when they hired him, his ability to structure complex business deals for all facets of the company, coupled with his successful management of Rollins Fleet Leasing since 1959, had dramatically increased Henry's stature in the eyes of the two brothers. Henry had long proven that he possessed more vision than the two brothers had perhaps predicted when they brought him on board as a controller in 1953. And his unique imprint on the organization had not gone unnoticed.

"Henry was always very serious, very self-controlled—or disciplined is a better word," recalled Randall. "And he was initially with an organization that really did not have any discipline. So it was almost like oil and water. There was always a lot of confrontation, because the things that Henry wanted to do were not popular. One thing that you can say for Henry, it didn't make any difference if it were popular or not. I don't think I've known anyone that was as set on doing things the way they should be done as Henry Tippie. Whether you liked it or not—and a lot of times, people didn't like what he had to say—Henry was so honest and convincing. I guess he wanted to do what was good for the welfare of the company."

Henry's talents came to the forefront during the Orkin negotiations. Though John Sr. was involved in the initial negotiations with Orkin, those closest to the deal recalled that Wayne and Henry led the final effort. "Henry really had a significant role in acquiring Orkin," noted Gary Rollins, Wayne's younger son, then a college student who would one day launch his own successful business career from the Orkin side of the company. "Dad and Henry and John were all involved, but from the mechanical side, the two architects were Dad and Henry." The complex deal brought out a trait that Gary always appreciated in Henry. "He is a great simplifier," Gary said. "He can cut through the smoke and hear a pretty complicated situation and say, 'Well, to me, we're talking about X and Y.' And my dad was the same way."

Together, Wayne and Henry spent the months of June, July, and August in Atlanta or in New York City, working out the multiple financial layers of the deal. "Wayne and I really constituted our team," said Henry. "Was I the one who made it all happen? The answer is no. I think

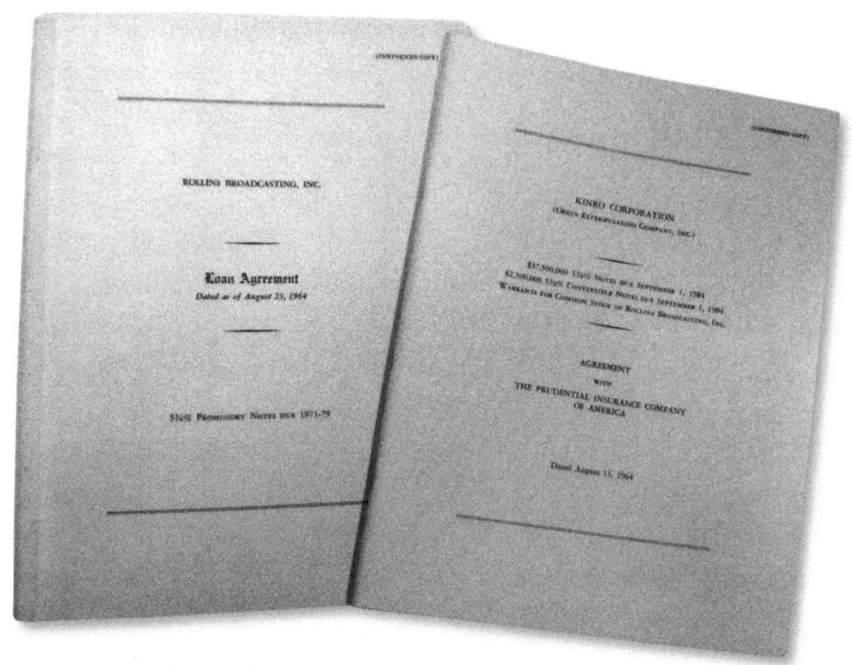

Henry helped craft the loan documents for the Orkin purchase.

I had a major role, but Wayne Rollins had the leading role. I don't want to overstate what I did, but I think I played a significant role. We had some assistance from a local lawyer in Wilmington, but in terms of having a big staff of people, we didn't have one.

"We were very calm about it," Henry continued. "Our deal consisted of a 13-column green accounting pad, which I fixed up in pencil, and each column was year 1, year 2, etc. We went out 15 or 20 years on it, and looked at different levels of growth: no growth, 5 percent, and then 10 percent. We looked at the interest expense and principal payments to see whether all of this would work. That's how we always approached everything."

The description of Henry, working with a pencil on a green legal pad to structure the first leveraged buyout in the country, was vintage Henry, remarkably similar to the 11-year-old who first tracked his gardening receipts and expenses, the 14-year-old who recorded every financial transaction he made raising hogs, and the college student who recorded every penny he spent. That side of Henry, as it played out in a complicated, multilayered business transaction, seemed to fascinate members of the Rollins family, including John Sr.'s son Jeff. "When you think about how much

Mr. Tippie had to have in his head, it's pretty remarkable," said Jeff. "Mr. Tippie was the numbers guy, and it really blows me away to think about the fact that when they were doing all that, they were doing it with pencils and columns on green sheets of paper."

On June 19, 1964, Wayne signed a "letter of intent" to buy Orkin. For the next three months, all parties remained focused on the details of financing this $62.4 million purchase. If the deal went through, it would be one of the biggest coups ever seen on Wall Street. After all, Rollins Broadcasting's revenues for the fiscal year 1964 were $9.1 million with net income of $894,000—compared to Orkin's revenues of $37.3 million with net profits of $3 million.

The deal was risky and unprecedented. There were many times, Henry later recalled, when he thought "the deal could have fallen apart. I think that Wayne's sense of humor, or on occasion a story of his, assisted in getting things back on track and allowed it to eventually move on down the pike to conclusion."

On Labor Day, September 1, 1964, Rollins bought Orkin for $62.4 million.

As finally agreed upon, the $62.4 million buyout was financed from several sources. Foremost was a $40 million loan from Prudential over 20 years at 5.75 percent interest, of which $2.5 million was convertible by Prudential into 19 percent of the equity of Kinro Corporation (the original company created solely as a vehicle for the transaction). Of the purchase price, $10 million was a capital contribution from Rollins, of which $4 million was borrowed from Chase Manhattan Bank and $11.5 million from Equitable Life Assurance Society of New York (the extra $5.5 million in loans was used to pay off Rollins indebtedness). Chase would be paid off first at 5.25 percent over a five-year period, during which time only the interest on the Equitable loan at 5.75 percent would be paid. The Equitable loan would then be paid off over the following nine years. The final parts of the deal were a $10 million subordinated note payable to the Orkin sellers over 15 years at 4.5 percent and $2.4 million paid to the sellers upon closing from Orkin's cash.

One of the first issues was how to leverage the debt. In most documented leveraged buyouts, the companies borrow against the assets of the purchaser. But Wayne wouldn't agree to borrow against the assets of his media company, and there were virtually no tangible assets to borrow against within Orkin; instead, Wayne argued successfully that Prudential should finance the deal based on Orkin's earning stream. With this move, Wayne demonstrated confidence in his predictions that Orkin would not only grow but grow dramatically.

Another significant negotiation issue involved Prudential's compensation. Executives at Prudential concluded early on that if they agreed to provide the $40 million loan, their company should receive some incentive beyond the interest return for taking on the risk. Prudential argued that the compensation could be provided by making $2.5 million of the senior debt convertible into common stock of the new company. Wayne, as it turned out, had anticipated Prudential's request; he knew that in similar situations, Prudential had obtained these so-called equity kickers. He understood that Prudential would request stock conversion privileges on part of the debt, but how much? Wayne insisted that the figure not go above 20 percent of the total common stock. He knew that if outside investors owned more than 20 percent of any subsidiary, the parent company would lose the ability to consolidate for federal income tax purposes. He was not about to concede on that point now, but the unresolved matter nearly brought the deal to a complete halt. Ultimately, Wayne prevailed.

Years later, when the Harvard Business School produced its case study of the transaction, the 20 percent equity kicker sought by Prudential was cited as one of the key factors that could have derailed the entire deal. "Negotiations leading up to this arrangement were time-consuming, and proved so difficult at one point that one of the Prudential officers sensed that the deal might not go through," wrote Harvard's John W. Aber Jr. in the case study. "Prudential had wanted more than 20 percent of the common stock. The [Rollins] group was insistent that the figure not go above 20 percent because, if it did, certain tax advantages would no longer apply. In the end, the arrangement described above was agreed upon."

Rollins began the complex transaction by acquiring Kinro Corporation for 55,000 shares of Rollins Common Stock. Then Kinro actually borrowed the $40 million from Prudential, with $2.5 million convertible by the insurance company into 19 percent of Kinro equity. As another equity kicker, Prudential was granted a warrant to purchase 115,000 shares of Rollins stock at $22 per share.*

The deal allowed Rollins to acquire Orkin with an outlay of only $10 million—and even that $10 million was borrowed from Chase and Equitable Life. As Henry pointed out, "No one had ever done that before."

Kinro, now a wholly owned subsidiary of Rollins, was liable for the remaining debt of $50 million—$40 million to Prudential and $10 million to Orkin. Under this structure, the debt was not carried on the Rollins books, thus freeing the company's assets for more acquisitions. What's more, Rollins did not guarantee the underlying loan, and there was no great risk. Even if something had happened, Rollins had sufficient earning power to service its own debts.

Under the agreement, the Orkin family would be paid 45 percent of Kinro-Orkin's net income annually after taxes and depreciation until the debt was retired, but no payments would be due until 1968 (four years later), when a lump sum would be paid for the preceding four years. The bottom line? This arrangement allowed Rollins to retain the use of $10 million of relatively cheap money.

For Prudential, it was a profit windfall. Ray Charles, who handled the financing package for the company, called it the best deal Prudential ever made. Ultimately, the company would reap not only the interest paid on the loan but a profit of $22.5 million when Rollins bought back all of Prudential's conversion options before the insurance company converted them. The equity kicker also paid off handsomely for Prudential when Rollins purchased the warrants a few years later.

And in the end, Rollins didn't even pay cash to their investment bankers; instead, 55,000 shares of Rollins stock were distributed to the Kinro organizers, George Weymouth, Lewis Cullman, and a few others. At the closing table, Wayne signed one check for $52.4 million—the largest

* In 1971 Orkin retired the first half of its convertible debt from the Orkin deal to Prudential Insurance Company for $11.25 million. Exactly one year and one day later, Rollins, Inc., retired the second half of Orkin's convertible debt for another $11.25 million, paying off the indebtedness without having it converted into Orkin stock ownership by Prudential. Reclaiming the stock had been a key goal of Wayne's when the company bought Orkin. And by paying off the leveraged buyout debt at an accelerated pace, the Orkin deal was even more profitable for Rollins and Prudential.

Henry stands beside O. Wayne Rollins as Wayne signs the check to purchase Orkin.

check he had ever signed in his life. The remaining $10 million needed to close the transaction came from the subordinated note payable to the sellers. The $62.4 million transaction was a done deal.

Rollins owned Orkin.

"It was quite an experience," Henry said. "What did I gain out of all of this? I gained tremendous experience. This was a huge acquisition, considered one of the first leveraged buyouts of a large operation by a small company where 100 percent of the money is borrowed. I gained a lot of experience with Prudential, Equitable, and the seller—they had several lawyers involved. There were a lot of ramifications. They had all kinds of loan documents and papers and so forth. Like I said, it was quite an experience. And we bet everything on making this thing go."

CHAPTER FOURTEEN

MOVING TO ATLANTA

BUSINESS MAGAZINES AND NEWSPAPERS AROUND the country had a field day when Rollins purchased the much larger Orkin. *Mighty Gulp for Rollins*, read one headline, followed by *Jonah Swallows the Whale* and *When the Minnow Swallows the Whale.*

The question on everyone's mind before the Orkin purchase was not whether Rollins' business executives understood the minute details of the exterminating business or whether they knew the difference between dry-wood and subterranean termites. The question, rather, was whether the Rollins team could transfer the business principles they had perfected in broadcasting, fleet leasing, and outdoor advertising businesses and impose them on a service company. Could they once more purchase an under-valued, family-owned business and upgrade it through the application of more aggressive management expense control and market research, just as they had done consistently in their other businesses?

Or as the *New York Herald Tribune* asked, "Can a small radio-TV chain buy a giant exterminating company and find financial happiness?"

The answer would be a resounding yes.

Within one year of owning the company, Rollins began to implement management and marketing enhancements that had proven successful in the company's other businesses. Backed by the preacquisition research from McKinsey & Company, Wayne and Henry were convinced that

Orkin was poised for tremendous growth, as long as someone applied the right business principles and leadership. And within five years of Rollins' ownership, their business instincts proved true: Orkin's revenues would double from $37.3 million in 1964 to over $75 million in 1969.

The Orkin acquisition so altered the course of business at Rollins Broadcasting that in January 1965, the company changed its name to Rollins, Inc., to reflect the new reality that Rollins had expanded and would be evolving even further. The company soon grew into one of the nation's leading multidimensional service providers, starting in broadcasting but eventually expanding into not only outdoor advertising and pest control but also oil and gas services, home security and protective systems, building maintenance, wallcoverings distribution, interior painting, and plantscaping and lawn care. And according to Henry, a factor directly linked to Orkin changed the mode of operation at Rollins more than any other single development: namely, cash.

"The Orkin purchase changed the MO of the company with the acquisition of a profitable, cash-generating business," said Henry. With little overhead and a business model based on repeat customers, Orkin's steady cash flow was a dream come true. And as everyone at Rollins knew, there was tremendous room for growth within the business. Almost as soon as Rollins took over Orkin, for instance, the company launched the Orkin Acceptance Corporation, a company-owned finance operation that allowed customers to finance the cost of termite treatments and, later, yearly pest control services. This step was just one of many made by the Rollins team that set in motion the growth foreshadowed in the McKinsey report. "Although Orkin's performance was positive, it was not well run, which provided great opportunities," said Henry. "And the money was multiplied in part because we paid no income taxes on the acquisition."

How was that possible? As it turns out, within weeks of closing the deal on Labor Day in 1964, Henry decided to seek some professional tax advice on how to handle various tax issues concerning the Orkin purchase. He arranged a meeting in Philadelphia with an expert attorney who had helped write IRS tax regulations; based on his advice to Henry, Rollins paid no income tax due to the acquisition, a result that saved the company millions of dollars. Next, Henry sought advice and approval from two experts at the SEC on how Orkin would handle its financial reporting. Again, Henry achieved an outcome that was favorable to Orkin, and the Rollins bottom line benefited. Said Henry, "These were major accomplishments since it provided substantially more cash from the acquisition."

A CHANGE IN ROLES FOR DR. NO

For the first time since it began in 1948, Rollins had more money than the company knew what to do with, and the company soon began an aggressive campaign of acquisitions and start-ups. The sudden availability of cash contributed to the notion that management had the magic touch and could make just about anything successful.

And as Henry had immediately discovered, the mammoth acquisition of Orkin resulted in tremendous fiduciary responsibilities for this 38-year-old accountant, who was now the company's executive vice president–finance and treasurer. In addition to running Rollins Fleet Leasing, Henry traveled with Wayne every other week to Atlanta to review financial operations at Orkin. "We were trying to make this thing go," he said.

Granted, walking into the Orkin headquarters on Piedmont Road in Atlanta was like walking into the Land of Oz for Henry and other Rollins executives, especially when compared to the spartan Rollins corporate headquarters located in the Moore Building in Rehoboth Beach where they first started out. In Atlanta the ultramodern headquarters—a two-story building made of concrete and steel, with its cantilevered, two-story lobby overlooking a signature Orkin diamond inlaid in terrazzo on the lobby floor—was nothing short of breathtaking for the three former farm boys who now ran the company.

But despite the beautiful setting, Henry realized by the spring of 1965 that he was being spread too thin, trying to work for companies in two cities. "There were too many things to be looking after, and I didn't have any staff. I was trying to look after everything that anybody has. And there were a lot of different entities that were growing beyond Wilmington," Henry said. "It was brought up that maybe I should get a staff, but I've never been too much of a staff guy. I'm more of the walking-around type."

The signature Orkin diamond in the lobby of the Orkin headquarters in Atlanta, Georgia.

On April 1, 1965, Henry left John Rollins Sr. and his leadership position at Rollins Fleet Leasing to work solely with Wayne Rollins and focus on Rollins, Inc., which now incorporated under one umbrella the broadcasting businesses, including radio, television, and outdoor advertising; Orkin and its network of branches nationwide; and any future expansions and acquisitions. As he exited the leasing business, Henry could not have been prouder of the company he had managed since 1959, which represented the first management opportunity Henry had experienced in his career.

"I ran that company on a day-to-day basis until the first day of April 1965," Henry reported, ticking off a list of accomplishments he considered his best management achievements. "When I quit running that company, it had over $1 million of cash in the bank. It had no liabilities with the exception of current payroll taxes and the equipment financing obligations. And it had in excess of $1 million net worth. And of course it had all the vehicles, which at that point were a few thousand. The last month I ran the company, which was March of 1965, it made

$110,000 before taxes in that month alone; it made $90,000 the month before that. And it made $95,000 the month after I left, which I think had to do, to some extent, with the momentum I had going in that place. It never did attain that $110,000 again for one month for a long, long time, to the best of my knowledge, so I was pretty proud of that. I had a good organization that I had put together and built. It had an incentive plan based upon how we did at the end of the year, and the company ran well."

With Rollins Fleet Leasing on solid ground, Henry also appreciated the fact that Rollins, Inc., was doing even better than expected after the Orkin purchase. In one year, Rollins' total revenue climbed from $9.1 million to $42.8 million, and net profits rose from just over $894,000 to $1.738 million. The company's stock, which was worth $12 a share in mid-June 1964, when Rollins signed the letter of intent to acquire Orkin, had shot up to around $50 a share at the closing in September, and had then climbed to approximately $156 a share by April 1965. "Not a bad run for a few months," Henry mused, giving new meaning to the word *understated.*

With this remarkable run in stock price, the unbelievable had happened. Henry B. Tippie—the young man who started life on a dairy farm in a house with no heat; who saved every toy and book he ever owned because he wondered if he'd ever have anything more; who tracked every penny he earned and spent since he was 11 years old; who joined the Air Force and took advantage of the G.I. Bill to earn a college degree in a blistering 24 months; who rode in a hog transfer truck overnight to Chicago in search of his first job; whose first salary was so low he couldn't afford to live for long in a single room for $1 a day at the YMCA; who once said his career goal was to make $15,000 a year when he joined the Rollins brothers—that same Henry B. Tippie had become a millionaire. "A millionaire on paper," he corrected. "When I first started out—it may have been Paul Caswell with me at Addison—somebody used to joke about being a millionaire by 40. But I never dreamed about that. But it did happen. I was 38."

Through he never shared the news directly with his parents, Henry heard through the grapevine that his father was aware of his financial fortune, courtesy of an article in the *Wall Street Journal* and a loudmouth at a bar in Belle Plaine. Said Henry,

> With all of this stock flying around, you have to make filings with the Securities and Exchange Commission. I bought some stock at that particular time in 1965, and those transactions (because they were considered insider trading) used to be published in a table in the *Wall Street Journal.* I heard later that somebody, I don't know who, in Belle Plaine had gotten the *Wall Street Journal* and they knew my dad. And they saw him downtown at a bar and they mentioned to him that I had become a millionaire, because all they had to do was take the market price of the stock and multiply it times the number of shares the paper said I owned. And so they mentioned to him, "Did you know your son was a millionaire?" That word got back to me and that was in the spring of 1965.

By early fall, the entire town of Belle Plaine likely knew of Henry's success. On September 5, 1965, on page 9D, the *Cedar Rapids Gazette* published a story with Henry's picture and the headline: *Belle Plaine Native Is Credited With a Hand in Firm's Success—Young VP-Treasurer of Rollins, Inc.* In the newspaper account, Henry made it clear that he had never forgotten his hometown, his early life on the farm, his education in a one-room schoolhouse, or his Belle Plaine High School classmates from the Class of '44.

Published in early September, the newspaper story about Henry's success was bittersweet to Henry and his entire family when, nearly three weeks later, they returned to Belle Plaine for his father's funeral. Robert W. Tippie, 65, died after a short illness on September 18, 1965. The family gathered for services at the Christ Methodist Church in Belle Plaine, and Bob was buried at the Oak Hill Cemetery, just outside Belle Plaine on a hill overlooking the railroad tracks. Bob's three sons, their wives, and his seven grandchildren were all present, along with his sister, who still lived in Des Moines. Henry's mother and Bob's former wife, Amelia, who Patricia found crying as though her heart was broken right before the funeral, nonetheless kept her distance as her sons buried their father not far from

Young VP-Treasurer of Rollins, Inc.

Belle Plaine Native Is Credited With a Hand in Firm's Success

By Robert J. Regan

NEW YORK (UPI) — For Henry B. Tipple, top echelon executive of widely diversified Rollins, Inc., there is no easy recipe for success without extra effort and "generous amounts of help and cooperation from others."

And for relaxation, says Tippie, there is nothing like fishing, whether at Lake Macbride — not far from his hometown of Belle Plaine, Iowa — the lakes in Minnesota and Canada, or off the Florida coast, where he is developing a taste for the salt water variety.

Tippie, recently elected executive vice-president-finance and treasurer of Rollins, which operates in industries that range from radio and television broadcasting through outdoor advertising to pest control and exterminating, is typical of the younger breed of top management people that came into prominence in the business world during the 1950s.

"Counted On"

Not given to garrulousness, Tippie is called by some of his co...

HENRY B. TIPPIE

uation. He served with the 20th air force in the South Pacific until December, 1946, when he was discharged with the rank of staff sergeant.

Iowa U. Grad

The war behind him, Tippie returned to complete his education and graduated from the University of Iowa in 1949 with a B. S. degree in commerce.

His early training in the business world was secured in certified public accounting firms in Des ... and Oma... was associated with private industrial firms in the Omaha and Des Moines areas between 1951 and 1953 before joining Rollins.

Rollins, which has radio stations in Newark, N. J., Santa Monica, Calif., and five other cities, and three television stations, had total revenues of $42.8 million in the fiscal year ended April 30, up sharply from $9.1 million the year before. Net profits rose to $1,738,766 from $894,254. The gains mostly reflect the 1964 acquisition of Orkin Exterminating Co.

Tippie predicted that the company's revenues for fiscal 1966 will go over $70 million. Rollins acquired Arwell, Inc., a Midwest pest and termite control company last May.

Rollins company stock, traded on the American Stock Exchange, closed Friday at 37. The year's range has been 51¾ to 29½.

Tippie lives in Wilmington, Del., which is company headquarters, but keeps contact with family and friends in and around Belle Plaine. He is married to the former Patri... Rush and h...

Local newspapers regularly reported on Henry's career.

the plot where Bob and Amelia had buried their first infant son nearly 40 years before. Bob's lifelong, complicated relationship with Henry had come full circle in a way, and Henry was grateful that they had reconciled and enjoyed each other's company during Bob's recent trips to Delaware. And Henry found some comfort in the fact that "at least he did have that awareness that I was having some degree of success. I never did tell him anything about it. That's not my nature to brag to my mother or him."

A CHANGE IN TEMPO

By now, Henry's nature and Rollins' business style were well known to everyone in the Rollins offices in both Wilmington and Atlanta. From the moment the Rollins team stepped into the executive suites at Orkin's Piedmont Road office, the new owners' orderly, detail-focused management style and emphasis on productivity were imminently clear. Overnight, it seemed, Rollins' top management established a new work ethic for the company: Wayne, Randall, Henry, and everyone around them worked six or seven days a week. "We are all created equal in the sense that we all have 24 hours in a day," Orkin employees soon heard Wayne Rollins preach. "It is what we do with this time that determines our success."

The new mood was apparent to everyone. "When Rollins came in, there was a change in tempo," said Glenn Martin, who had worked in Orkin's mailroom since 1960. "I felt things were more secure when the Rollins family got the company. You had more supervision, and they expected you to work more. The only one you really ever saw was Mr. Henry Tippie. He always wanted people working and not standing around. He was like a troubleshooter, always walking around. If you weren't busy, you weren't needed."

It's fair to say that Henry's management-by-walking-around style, his brusque manner, and his intolerance for inefficiencies did not make him initially very popular in Atlanta. At one point, he even rattled the nerves of the company's executive cook, Louise Copelin. Like the executive cook before her, Louise prepared soup and salads every day for the Rollins executives, and no one, including Wayne, ever suggested that she change. But as anyone from the Plantation Restaurant in Rehoboth could have told her, Henry did not like soups and salads. "And one day, Mr. Tippie came in and told me he was tired of eating soup and a salad," said Louise. "And if I couldn't make it, I could send out and get him a steak! And so from then on, I started cooking a little bit and if they didn't like it, I knew not to fix it again."

Though his Delaware reputation as "Dr. No" preceded him, that did nothing to prepare folks for Henry's sometimes mercurial personality as he worked his way through the Orkin operation, trying to pinpoint ways to make systems and people work more efficiently.

It was a daunting task, and at one point Gary Rollins admitted that the recently acquired Orkin organization reminded him of the Wild West. In addition to the lack of financial accountability in the branches when the Rollins family took over, there were few manuals and standardized procedures to help branch managers or district managers coordinate the pest control services then offered in 35 states. There was no concentrated effort to coordinate the inventory of thousands of vehicles and service trucks and drivers—a situation that drove Henry to distraction. After all, this was the same man who once traced a single missing Rollins lease car to the back of a body shop!

Randall, who had an office not far from Henry's in Atlanta, recalled Henry's wrath in the early days at Orkin, when Henry vented his frustrations in the executive suite. "'It's just a damn cesspool, just a cesspool!'" Randall recalled hearing Henry shout more than once. And Henry doesn't deny these outbursts. "I used to say that a lot over the years. It just wasn't very organized," admitted Henry. "And well, my mother said that my first words were swear words. That's just the way it was. I am who I am, and I've always said I have a limited vocabulary. But I could see what was going on down there pretty clearly."

Like the young man in high school who didn't give a hoot about being popular, Henry wasn't entering any popularity contests in Atlanta. And Henry is the first to admit that employees and coworkers always had to earn his trust. "I am *very* wary of people," Henry often said. Which helps explain why Henry, even as a young executive, would rarely drink in public. "People get loud and arrogant and say things they shouldn't," he said, adopting a rule to never drink at business parties, choosing instead to order his customary ginger ale, make the rounds, and observe from a sober, controlled vantage point. As many colleagues noted about Henry, "He would make an excellent poker player. He's got the face for it."

Even before she met him, Linda Graham had heard enough about Henry B. Tippie to know that "everyone was scared of him." She was the longtime secretary for Randall Rollins and would eventually serve as an officer for several Rollins companies. "He had a reputation for being a stickler for detail, and he didn't hesitate to tell you when you were wrong. And he didn't deviate from his high standards at all. So by the time I met him in 1965, I was probably at least in awe of him if not scared of him."

One of the first things that Linda learned about Henry is that he operated in what Gary Rollins once described as "the black and white." Said Linda, "To Henry, it was right or it was wrong—black and white. And I think that comes from an accounting background. Things either add up or they don't. He knew the rules, he abided by the rules, and he expected everyone else to abide by the rules. And if they didn't, he pointed them out."

Over the years, Linda said, Henry hasn't changed. "But the change is in the *perception* of Mr. Tippie," she explained. "When I first met him, he was intimidating. But the more you worked with him, the more he taught you. I found through the years that he's the best teacher that a person could want to have. He was very patient with me, even with the 1 + 1 = 2 sort of thing. He would be happy to take you and show you from A to Z—and you can't not like a person who takes that much time with you. And the more you got to know him, he became more understanding and therefore less intimidating. That made him more revered, perhaps, but less intimidating. But I don't know that he changed at all."

Starting in July 1967, the footsteps of Dr. No would be heard even more frequently inside the modern building on Piedmont Road. That summer, the entire Rollins family and 17 high-level executives, including Henry, moved the corporate headquarters of Rollins, Inc., from Wilmington to Atlanta. "There is nothing as good for a business as the footsteps of the owner in the hall," said Wayne.

And during the same year as the corporate move, to the surprise and delight of everyone in the new headquarters, the story of how Rollins purchased Orkin became a celebrated, much-reviewed case study at the Harvard Business School. For Henry it was further proof that the transaction was a significant business milestone. He loved retelling the story of the Orkin purchase and the case study, which he continued to do for each new generation of Rollins family members. And he often marveled at the fascinating story behind the Harvard case study, which was researched and presented for the very first time decades later in a corporate history called *Orkin: The Making of the World's Best Pest Control Company.*

THE STORY BEHIND THE HARVARD BUSINESS SCHOOL CASE STUDY

In 1967, then Harvard University business professor Charles M. Williams asked a young doctoral student named John W. Aber Jr. to be his research associate. The two-year appointment meant that Aber would develop case studies for Williams to use as teaching tools for a course called Management of Financial Institutions.

For his first case study, Williams asked Aber to review a business transaction that had fascinated the Harvard professor for several years—the 1964 purchase of Orkin by Rollins.

Williams, who taught hundreds if not thousands of case studies at Harvard before he retired and became a Harvard professor emeritus, remembered the Rollins-Orkin case study as "one of the more interesting ones to teach." And Aber, who became a professor of finance at Boston University School of Management before retiring as professor emeritus in 2012, still recalled that "a note of mystery was sounded when the deal was announced. It wasn't clear to anyone why Rollins would have anything to do with Orkin. It was a very famous transaction at the time."

For the case study, Aber focused primarily on the role of Prudential Insurance, which approved a loan of $40 million to finance the $62.4 million transaction. He met as many as four times with Prudential representatives from the company's Bond Department in order to discuss the case and develop the study. "They were on the forefront of leveraged buyouts," Aber recalled. "They were very innovative at the time. It was certainly something of a maverick deal when it was announced."

Williams, however, recalled that he "was not thinking in terms of a leveraged buyout" when he asked Aber to develop a case study. "We were thinking of looking at why someone would pay a sizeable price for what some would call a flimsy company," he said. "There was no security, really, with a pest control operation. You can't make people continue to buy your services. And it was a service company and a company that had virtually no assets. Given the extent of the debt incurred to make the purchase, we talked a great deal about the absence of solid assets and the reliance on cash flow. However, there was a lot of cash flow that could service the debt. I remember that there was a good bit of discussion, however, about how vulnerable the company would be to economic downturns. I don't remember, though, where we came out on that issue. But I think there was a feeling that the company was not as vulnerable as we at first believed."

Working in his research space on the third floor of Harvard's Sherman Hall, Aber organized his first case study into two parts: first, he described Prudential's role in putting together the financial package that was approved by the company Bond Department in late May 1964;

second, he described how Rollins executed the deal and used the loan to buy Orkin. The case study includes extensive charts and graphs to document the transaction, proposed loan terms, and debt payment schedules. Throughout the 31-page document, Rollins Broadcasting is referred to as the "Payne" Broadcasting Group, and Orkin is referenced as the "Pestmort" Company. The names of some individuals are changed, too. Wayne Rollins is known as "Harold Payne"; Otto Orkin becomes "Max Burgher."

"I'm not sure that the interested parties insisted on a disguise, but I preferred it. That was our requirement," said Williams, who claims that he invented the name "Pestmort." He laughed. "I was rather pleased with myself for coming up with that. It's better than 'Orkin.'"

But Aber recalls that in the real world of pest control, the "Orkin" name definitely worked. "Orkin had quite a brand franchise," he said. "When we studied it, it was just one of those instances where someone like Rollins comes out of the blue and takes over what was then a really successful business."

The case study was apparently a success, too. Aber noted that Williams "probably taught it 30 or 40 times. He used the case extensively in his courses—not only at Harvard but in a great deal of executive teaching in banks throughout the country and the world."

CHAPTER FIFTEEN

SUCCESS AT ROLLINS, THEN A MAJOR CAREER MOVE

COLLEAGUES AND FRIENDS AGREED THAT Henry rarely, if ever, changed his dogmatic professional demeanor and his detail-oriented approach to business. But in the years immediately after the Orkin purchase, the company he worked for underwent dramatic changes and expansion. The company basically pursued two different paths as it expanded the reach of its service business: Rollins actively acquired businesses like building maintenance and decorating services that would complement Orkin's pest control customer accounts, which Rollins viewed as the perfect opportunity for cross-marketing and growing the business as a whole; and Rollins expanded by purchasing additional pest control companies as a way to expand Orkin's national reach while developing additional locations that would support the Orkin brand.

To be specific: On January 1, 1968, Rollins diversified with the acquisition of Dwoskin, Inc., the country's largest wholesale distributor of wall-coverings and a leading source of drapery and upholstery fabrics. At the annual meeting of shareholders in Atlanta in 1969, Rollins introduced the first affordable wireless security system for burglar and fire protection; two years later, a new Rollins division called Rollins Protective Services (RPS) would begin marketing the systems to homes and businesses. And at the end of 1969, Rollins received FCC approval to begin operating its cable television system in Wilmington, while its building maintenance company, Rollins Services, continued to be the largest in the Southeast and Southwest. And at the end of fiscal year 1970, Orkin's continued growth through expansion and acquisitions had resulted in offices in 35 states, the District of Columbia, and Mexico, servicing more than one million residential and commercial accounts.

With every transaction and expansion, the company tapped Henry's expertise and relied on his ability to structure deals and stay focused during layers of negotiations. As Gary once noted, "Henry doesn't get off into the weeds, and that's important." And Henry had to agree: "I was very much involved. I was responsible for getting everything organized for the documentation and the closings. My role was on the financial side, putting all this stuff together for the whole works, reviewing taxation and legal implications. And I reported to Wayne."

Henry also suggested and helped establish the O. Wayne Rollins Foundation in 1967 and the Rollins Children's Trust in 1968, vehicles that became critical to both the family and the business for estate planning, for the transfer of wealth to future generations, and for all-important income tax purposes. As Henry explained to Wayne and other family members: "'You really should set this up because it controls your taxes.' At the time, you could take a 100 percent deduction for a contribution. Our stock was very high at the time, and I said, 'We can control your personal income tax by taking a few shares of your Rollins, Inc., stock and putting it over in the Foundation.' It was a wise move and, to some extent, my idea."

Despite the many changes, Henry also never lost his talent for being completely honest. As an illustration, Jim Hicks, who served as special assistant to Randall before moving to the corporate fleet department, recalled a story often told by Wayne about a transaction that involved Henry in late 1967. At the time, Wayne, Henry, and other Rollins executives, were seated around a large table with Dwoskin representatives and a group of lawyers, all negotiating to purchase Dwoskin. The meeting had gone on for quite some time, and Wayne finally called on everyone to give their concluding thoughts. According to the story, the Dwoskin representatives were overly optimistic about Dwoskin and its financial future, painting a picture that simply wasn't accurate. So when Wayne called on

Henry, he didn't waste any time. He put his hands on the table and said, "I think Rollins is making a very reasonable and very fair offer for buying Dwoskin, and the fact is that really Dwoskin is broke and financially insolvent." According to Jim Hicks, Wayne later said that Henry's declaration broke the meeting up, at least the tension in it. "Only Henry would say that in that way," Wayne noted. "And it achieved just what needed to be done." Rollins closed on the deal on January 1, 1968.

PROMOTIONS AND A TRIP TO THE NYSE

Six months after the Dwoskin deal closed, the company announced two important promotions in the July 1968 edition of *Rollins Today*, the corporate magazine written and published by Communications Director H. Tim Crow:

R. Randall Rollins, Wayne's oldest son, who had recovered from a few youthful missteps in Rollins Leasing to have an outstanding career in Rollins' media and outdoor advertising sectors, was elected senior executive vice president of the entire company, a promotion from his previous position as executive vice president–media communications and secretary.

And Henry B. Tippie, then executive vice president–finance and treasurer, was elected to the additional office of secretary.

R. Randall Rollins, Henry B. Tippie Elected to New Offices

O. Wayne Rollins, chairman of the board and president of Rollins, Inc., recently announced that R. Randall Rollins, left, has been elected Senior Executive Vice President of the Company. He was fomerly Executive Vice President–Media–Communications and Secretary. At the same time, it was announced that Henry B. Tippie, right, Executive Vice President–Finance and Treasurer, has been elected to the additional office of Secretary.

"Purely and simply, Mr. Tippie had a brilliant mind, from a financial standpoint," recalled Tim Crow, who eventually became a vice president of the company. "He completely understood numbers, what was right and what was wrong. Mr. Rollins was the same. They got along beautifully, and followed each other's advice. There were never any difficult times between them." In the same magazine issue with the promotion announcement, Tim highlighted Henry's career path in a special feature called "Do You Know Your Management?" that offered Henry's insights into the company's past and future:

> Mr. Tippie says of his early days with the Company, "We did whatever work was necessary to get the job done, to achieve the Company goals, many of which were most difficult due to the small size of Rollins and its limited resources at the time. Nothing was impossible; it just took a little longer."
>
> Mr. Tippie, of course, has had the satisfaction of watching and helping Rollins, Inc., grow into the respected Company it is today. He lists as particularly satisfying seeing the Company become publicly owned in 1960 and subsequently being listed on the American Stock Exchange in 1961, and he says, "I hope to see it move to the New York Stock Exchange at some future date."

Henry soon got his wish—and no doubt already knew at the time of the article that the date was imminent. On August 12, 1968, Henry joined Wayne, John, and Randall Rollins, along with Earl Geiger, Orkin's executive vice president, on the floor of the New York Stock Exchange as "ROL" appeared on the NYSE for the first time. Henry always treasured the oval trading floor admission buttons that the men wore throughout the day, pinned to their individual suit pockets. And he also saved the exchange tape that announced, for the first time:

■ADMITTED■TO■THE■LIST■AND■TO■DEALINGS■■■ROLLINS■INC■CO■

The five men, joined by then NYSE President Robert Haack, posed for a picture in front of the Exchange's Big Board, and everyone was smiling broadly. Henry, with his arms extended straight along his sides, stood

Rollins, Inc., lists on the New York Stock Exchange, August 12, 1968.

between Wayne Rollins and Earl Geiger, celebrating a moment he had long worked to make happen.

A PROFESSIONAL CONFLICT THAT COULD NOT BE RESOLVED

The happy scene reveals not one hint of the long-simmering tension between Henry and Earl. And though Henry for years declined to publicly identify Earl as someone he could not get along with, the animosity between the two was never any secret around Rollins headquarters.

For starters, the two men were a study in contrasts. Originally from New York, Geiger was flamboyant and charismatic, a sharp dresser and an eloquent speaker who came on the scene as an Orkin executive when Rollins bought the company. The Iowa-born Henry was reserved, modest in behavior and appearance, and someone who spoke in simple terms without exaggerating the truth or using words that embellished. Early on, Henry, who always believed that your word was your bond, felt that Earl shaded the truth and misrepresented situations to Wayne and other Rollins executives. And because Henry had been with Wayne and John and helped build the company for over 10 years before Earl appeared, Henry was loyal and fiercely protective—not only of the company but of his friendship with the two brothers.

When asked about the differences between the two men, Gary Rollins sketched this picture. "Earl was my boss when I started with Orkin, and Earl spent most of his time in the gray. And Henry was always black-and-white," Gary recalled. "Earl was articulate and smooth but not always truthful. That just got to Henry. And Henry kind of thought that maybe Dad was giving Earl more credit than he deserved."

Second, the two men definitely got off on the wrong foot. When the Orkin closing took place back in 1964, Wayne had a set of commemorative pens made to celebrate the transaction, and he gave them to Earl to distribute. Later, when Wayne asked Henry how he liked his pen, Henry was taken aback. "I never got one," he recalled. "So that irritated me." Earl also didn't invite Henry, one of the chief architects of the entire leveraged buyout, to the closing party. "The party took place after the closing, which had covered two days, and again Earl was given the responsibility to invite people to attend the party," said Henry. "And I was not invited. And I always felt, you know, I had a lot to do with this but I'm left out."

To add insult to injury, Earl was given a stock option after the acquisition, and Henry was not. "And that bothered me," said Henry. And though he never told anyone about the party and never said a word about the stock option, Henry did wrestle with how to put it all in perspective. He ultimately came up with a very Henry-like spin and professional approach.

The Orkin experience, Henry knew, was worth more than a pen or a party. "I had gotten so much experience out of this thing, and it really was quite a tremendous experience with things I had never been involved with before. So I figured I could use it at a later date."

And when it came to the stock option, Henry rationalized that "we had to pacify this fellow, he was promised one early on when the acquisition was taking place, this did not just come up later. I guess I felt I should have gotten a stock option, and you know, who has that responsibility? Well, it would be the Board of Directors, and Wayne's the president and CEO. And I am not holding that against him or anything, and I don't want it reflected like that. But I always felt I should have gotten one." Ever rational, Henry ultimately concluded, "But I made up for it many times later. Experience can be like money in the bank. The money just comes a little later."

As he continued to cross professional paths with Earl, various incidents contributed to Henry's distrust. For instance, after weeks of review, Wayne and Henry decided to move their corporate pension plan from Rollins Broadcasting over to cover Orkin, thereby replacing an Orkin plan that was expensive and only bought annuities. "We decided to get rid of that and put in our plan, and we went to Earl and talked about how we would not discuss this with anyone." But Earl did discuss it with others outside the company, and even suggested that they talk to Wayne and Henry because they had a better plan. "And needless to say we killed that from happening," said Henry. "But again, that was another thing that told me, 'Be careful.'"

The situation only got worse after the executives all moved to Atlanta. In the board room, Henry grew tired of Earl's presentations, filled with "lots of big words and all that sort of stuff. John Sr. and I used to look at each other during Board meetings sometimes, and I don't think John Sr. knew what he meant either. 'What the hell's he talking about?' And you know, I figured, well, I'm not in that league. He comes on like he's able to have total command of the English language and be an intellectual, and that loses me. And this fellow was good, at that. But now his results are another story."

The tension between the two escalated until the day Henry and Earl confronted one another. "We almost had a fistfight. And I remember Randall getting this fellow and myself over in a conference room trying to get things cooled down because it was a bad situation," said Henry. "Things were pretty hot. This guy was a two-timer, and I don't like that stuff. So it cooled down some, but nothing really changed. He had Wayne's ear and could do no wrong, and I would see these mistakes being made and nothing happening about it."

Randall clearly recalled the situation: "I tried, and I'm sure Dad tried, to resolve it. But they were just oil and water. Earl was a glory seeker and Henry wasn't. Henry didn't understand Earl, and Earl didn't take to that Iowa farm boy."

In extensive archival interviews conducted decades later by Wayne's biographers, one thing quickly becomes obvious in numerous interviews with Earl Geiger: Earl never once mentions Henry B. Tippie, the important role Henry played in the historical transaction, or Henry's work with the company after Rollins bought Orkin. Though interpreting this omission could go in any number of directions, it appears that the level of professional jealousy and animosity between the two men was definitely mutual. And over time, it did not improve.

PROFESSIONAL AND PERSONAL DISAPPOINTMENTS LEAD TO CHANGE

With Henry becoming increasingly frustrated with his professional life at Rollins, he was also increasingly disillusioned with living in Atlanta. After moving to Atlanta in 1967, Henry and Patricia bought a brand-new house on the north side of town, in an upper-class neighborhood with swimming pools and horse trails. She and Henry thought it would be an ideal environment for their three children, who were 10, 9, and 6 years old when they headed south.

As time passed, however, the Tippies said they felt out of place in this showy and wealthy neighborhood. Patricia never quite warmed to the neighbors, and she quickly discovered that their approach to raising their children differed from that of the people living around them. Said Patricia,

> I didn't really make good friends there. It was a different type neighborhood. It was a rich neighborhood and everybody was president of some company or something. The kids were the worst disciplined students in the school system. One kid, in particular, I mean, he was out shooting at all the gaslights in the neighborhood. I don't have anything against wealthy people, but sometimes I think it's not a real good environment for the kids. The kids in that neighborhood did not

Henry and his three children in the backyard of their Atlanta home.

have responsibility. My son cut the yards for everybody else that had sons the same age as he was! I just always felt that if you don't give children responsibilities, you don't let them feel good about themselves. At Christmastime, the grandparents could give every child $3,000 as a gift and for tax purposes, and the little kids would come and show the checks they got from Grandma. And when school started, their parents would take them to Saks and buy them beautiful little wardrobes. And you know, our kids never got any of that kind of stuff.

Henry agreed with Patricia. He never particularly liked their Atlanta surroundings either. After all, here's a couple who always tried to live modestly, to not spend their entire paychecks, and to invest wisely. From an early age, their children did chores around the house, and Henry and Patricia went so far as to try to shield them from ever knowing or living like they were wealthy. "The neighborhood we lived in, a lot of those

The Tippie family around the dinner table.

people were the kind that would like to impress you," said Henry. "And we're not that type. Here we are, sitting out here in this nice house, and our kids are being brought up a certain way. And across the street, here are some of these other kids being brought up in an entirely different manner. And that's a problem."

The fact that Henry and Patricia Tippie didn't seek to emulate the pretenses of their wealthy Atlanta neighborhood never surprised their friend Bill Windauer, who would years later comment that those very unassuming, modest traits are indicative of people from Iowa. "Henry grew up in a poor existence. They lived on a farm near Belle Plaine," Bill explained. "And it was Depression time, so he came from an environment where his family probably had to watch every penny and didn't have a lot. And because of that, he probably always remembered his past. And Iowans are funny people—they're not very pretentious. They are very low-key. They don't like a lot of recognition. They don't want to stand out in a crowd, because sometimes, for some people, it's embarrassing. Because they almost feel like they are trying to show off to their neighbors. You'll find that most people, no matter if you're lower income or higher income, they probably all live fairly much at a very similar level. He's always been very frugal and careful and everything. And even the way he dresses—he'll just have on a regular old trench coat, and a little hat that he tips the brim up. And if someone were to look at him, they probably wouldn't know him from anybody else. He doesn't stand out in that way. And I think people respect him for that, because he's not a fancy guy."

But even more disturbing to Henry and Patricia than their fancy surroundings was the school system in Atlanta. With public schools becoming newly integrated in Atlanta, the system involved a massive busing effort to move students across town and between neighborhoods. "The busing system became a zoo," said Henry, recalling that from 1967 to 1970, Henry II was bused to four schools, Helen to three, and Linda to two. "And that was just to get to school. As the kids started to participate in after-school activities, Patricia was in effect running a school bus!" Still, Henry remained adamant that his children would attend public schools, and he never deviated from choosing this path for his children. "I am a strong advocate of public schools. Yes, I could afford private schools, but the real world is out here in public schools."

Now faced with disappointments in both his professional and his personal life, Henry realized that he had to make an important decision about his future. Over and over, he analyzed his situation, mentally assessing the facts in front of him. First, he wasn't necessarily happy with the professional environment at Rollins, where he continued to clash with a leading executive who had Wayne's attention and respect. Second, he wasn't at all happy with a school environment that required busing for his children, and he no longer liked the affluent neighborhood where they lived. And third, it was hard for Henry to admit, but he had begun to wonder privately about his hand in Rollins' success. In less than a decade, Henry knew, the company had grown from a relatively unknown organization with modest revenues of $4.4 million, solely in broadcasting, to a well-known service company listed on the New York Stock Exchange with annual revenues of $119 million. But, he asked himself, "How much of this did I contribute to or did I not contribute? Maybe I didn't really have a big role in this. I don't know. And could I do this on my own? Could I build and manage a successful organization?"

With these three factors lined up like columns on a piece of paper in front of him, the 43-year-old Henry knew exactly what he had to do: "The time's come for me to move on." He quickly zeroed in on business opportunities in Texas, where the thrifty, ever-practical accountant knew there was no personal income tax. He was approached about and immediately explored the possibility of buying a company in Austin, Texas, that offered underperforming radio and television stations, a situation that matched Henry's penchant for "bootstrapping" and "working with something that's a problem in contrast to buying something that's well run." And when he had a clear idea of where he was headed, Henry announced his plans to Rollins.

"The only conversation I had with anyone was with Wayne," Henry said. "His reaction was kind of mixed. In addition to leaving my position with the company, I said, 'I plan to resign from the Board, too.' And his comment was, 'You don't need to resign from the Board.' But I said, 'I really think I should. I'm going to be in the broadcast business, and you're in the broadcast business and I see a conflict there.' So I resigned from the Board. I was also a trustee on the Rollins Children's Trust and the O. Wayne Rollins Foundation, which I helped start, and Wayne said he didn't want me to resign from those, so I did not."

Henry also told Wayne that he wasn't in any hurry to leave, that he wanted to give Wayne and Rollins, Inc., all the time necessary to make for a smooth transition. After 17 incredible years with the company, Henry was determined to leave in what he called "the right way."

"I'm a strong believer that if you're going to move or leave, you need to go out the front door, never the back door," he said. "And so I talked to Wayne about it. I wanted it done where there would be plenty of notice and ample time for people to reorganize. Not a two-week notice and 'It's been nice knowin' ya.' I didn't want to do it that way."

Word spread quickly through the company that Henry was leaving.

"It was a sad day for us," Linda Graham said. "We hated it, and I don't think he was happy to leave us—I never got that impression. But when you lose somebody like Mr. Tippie who had been there from the beginning, and who was a trusted advisor, it was *sad. Really sad.* You couldn't replace Henry Tippie, and we have never been able to."

Gary Rollins agreed. "I don't think you could ever replace Henry Tippie. I think my dad and my uncle certainly received far more attention through the various accomplishments than Henry, and I think he felt like it was time for him to go out and take the things he had learned, with his skills and his abilities, and build an organization himself. Not just be a part of an organization, but be the head of an organization. I guess Henry's smart enough to know that Texas doesn't have an income tax, and knowing him, it wasn't a random, emotional deal. There was quite a bit of thought behind it."

Henry showed his loyalty and his love for the family by actually staying longer than he originally intended, when the Rollins family suffered an unspeakable loss: On July 26, 1970, Rita Anne Rollins, Randall and Peggy's oldest daughter and Wayne and Grace's first grandchild, died in a freak accident just a month shy of her seventeenth birthday. "Of course that was a total blow to the family," Henry recalled, his typically quiet voice dropping even softer, remembering the event. "So I said, 'Well, I'm in no rush here, we'll just extend when I'm going to leave.' And I extended it for a couple of months. It was a terrible situation."

Henry left Rollins in November 1970, and he and Patricia moved with their family to Austin, Texas, in January 1971. And for a long time, Henry's absence from Rollins' headquarters, the missing sound of Dr. No's footsteps in the long marble hallways, was palpable.

"It was a loss for us. It was terrible," said Randall. "But we respected his decision. I think we understood all the reasons, no doubt. And another thing, we've always kept him on some of the boards. If we didn't think that Henry did the right thing, we wouldn't have done that. And by then, we all knew Henry. When Henry makes up his mind, I don't think there is anything you can do to change it. I don't mean that he is unreasonable, but he will just make up his mind. That's just the way he's going to be. And he knows what he's got to do."

Henry B. Tippie in Austin, Texas.

CHAPTER SIXTEEN

HENRY B. TIPPIE BECOMES HIS OWN BOSS

WHEN HENRY DECIDED TO LEAVE Atlanta for Texas in 1970, he first made a few trips to Dallas, looking for business opportunities. During a stop at an investment house, Henry learned about a broadcast organization in Austin called the Southwest Republic Corp., which was owned by a group of 20-plus shareholders; the company operated a NBC-affiliated television station, Channel 42, and an AM/FM radio station.

The opportunity caught Henry's attention for several reasons. He had been deeply involved in the broadcast business for the past 17 years, so he already had a lot of experience in the field. And the organization was losing money at both the television and radio stations, a situation that Henry considered the ultimate challenge *and* the ultimate opportunity. "I enjoy straightening out organizations," said Henry, who knew from his experience in broadcasting and the Orkin acquisition that turning around a lackluster business could result in greater financial rewards than assuming ownership of a well-run business.

On his way back to Georgia from Dallas, Henry arranged to stop in Austin and hear more about the opportunity. Henry liked what he heard and saw, and he returned to Atlanta to start the negotiations. In the middle of drawing up papers and agreeing on terms, Henry received an unusual call from a representative of the Austin broadcast shareholders: Would Henry be interested in buying not one but *two* companies, and taking them public? As it turned out, the sellers at Southwest Republic also had a second company, the Featherlite Corporation, which had been engaged in building materials and concrete products since 1947. Like the broadcasting company, Featherlite had 20-plus shareholders, but there were only five common shareholders in both companies. Was Henry interested?

"Well, of course I really didn't have that in mind," thought Henry. "I was more interested in just buying the broadcast property outright. So my comment was, 'I don't know, but send the information over and I'll take a look at it.'"

As he reviewed the financial information on Featherlite, Henry could see that it was a solid company, but he still saw room for improvement. He gradually realized that he could proceed with buying both companies and taking them public, with one caveat: Henry would be the one in charge. "I'm not going to have something out here where I'm being second-guessed on how to do this," he stated. He met with the two major shareholders of both companies, John Kingsbery and his father, E. G. Kingsbery, who agreed with Henry's plan. Following steps that were similar to those he had observed in working out the Rollins-Orkin purchase, Henry first created a holding company called Kingstip, Inc., which was incorporated in April 1971. He then merged Featherlite and the broadcast operation into the new company and began operations in September. The risk of owning two companies, Henry rationalized, was worth it.

"I think you have to take a certain amount of risk," he explained. "There's risk involved in achieving any success, and you have to be prepared to fail sometimes. A person who never had any failures has probably never achieved anything. The big thing is to have more successes than failures."

After the merger of the two companies, Henry owned 10 percent of Kingstip, Inc., and became the co-CEO with John Kingsbery. But there was never any question that Henry was the one in charge. As Henry allowed, "I'm the one who made all of the decisions. It was all foreign to them." As co-CEO, Henry assumed the role of operator of the company; though the father and son, E. G. and John Kingsbery, were full partners, their involvement was not as active as Henry's. "The son," Henry once said, "was brilliant. Highly articulate. Somebody that I always thought had forgotten more than I'll ever know. But let's just say that our work habits were different. I would start early in the morning whereas John generally started in the late morning or close to noon."

Arriving early and staying late, Henry soon learned that he had his work cut out for him. Henry already knew that Featherlite was financially sound; with 600 employees in operations throughout Texas in El Paso, Lubbock, Abilene, Midland, Ranger, Longview, and San Antonio, the construction materials division accounted for $13.2 million of revenues in fiscal year 1971, with $716,551 of net earnings. The new owner soon focused on ways to expand the company.

And though Featherlite was in good shape, the radio and television stations were another story. With around 75 employees and around $1.7 million in revenue, the stations were losing money, and their management teams were completely unprofessional, Henry soon discovered. "They were in bad shape," said Henry. Bottom line? "You've got to have more coming in than going out."

To raise money to expand Featherlite and to make improvements to the television and radio stations, Henry began working to take Kingstip public, a step he agreed to take when he bought the two companies.

Kingstip, Inc., lists on the American Stock Exchange on January 27, 1972.

Complications surfaced with some of the two companies' original 25 shareholders, and Henry felt he was trapped between Austin's unique blend of Old Guard money and politics when they sued in court to stop him from taking the new company public. "But I don't get scared," he said, noting that the shareholders accepted a last-minute offer from Henry that resolved the case before any legal verdict was issued. "When you get involved in stuff like that, I don't get scared. I move on down the road."

On Thursday, January 27, 1972, less than a year after incorporating Kingstip, Henry raised almost $1.5 million in new capital by taking Kingstip public on the American Stock Exchange, selling 100,000 shares of common stock for Kingstip and an additional 180,000 shares for selling stockholders. Total proceeds to both Kingstip and the stockholders of the original Featherlite and Southwest Republic companies were about $4 million.

Once again, a very happy Henry B. Tippie posed for a photograph, smiling broadly while holding the tape that represented the first moments Kingstip went public on the exchange. According to Henry, listing Kingstip on the American Stock Exchange made history in Austin. Though there were other public companies in town, Kingstip, Inc., was the first company *headquartered* in Austin and listed on a major stock exchange. The *Austin Statesman* announced the milestone the next day with a story and headline: *Kingstip Inc. Stock Brings $1.5 Million.*

Friday, Jan. 28, 1972 The Austin Statesman

Kingstip Inc. Stock Brings $1.5 Million

By CHRIS WHITCRAFT
Financial Writer

Austin-based Kingstip, Inc. owners of KHFI-TV and FM radio KTAP-AM, and the Featherlite Corp., construction aggregate materials company, raised almost $1.5 million in new capital Thursday through its first public sale of stock.

E. F. Hutton Co., Inc., at New York was manager of the underwriting group. It sold 100,000 shares of common stock for Kingstip, and an additional 180,000 shares for selling stockholders.

The stock priced at $14.50 a share sold out Thursday with the closing bid at $19 bid and $19.50 asked, John C. Aycock, Austin manager for Hutton reports.

Total proceeds to both company and selling [illegible] owning more than 10 per cent of the common stock on Sept. 30 1971 the Hutton preliminary prospectus dated Nov. 18 reports were John R. Kingsbery chairman with 28 per cent of the stock; E. G. Kingsbery chairman emeritus of Featherlite with 13 per cent; and Henry B. Tippie president with 10 per cent.

Other Kingstip officers include J. B. Bell Jr., secretary-treasurer; and Charles L. Bomar, Featherlite president.

Directors include Dan O'Laurie and Paul Turnbull. Both are geologists.

Kingstip was incorporated in April last year. It began operations in September by acquiring Featherlite, producer of construction materials since 1947, and The Southwest [illegible]

proceeds from sale of additional stock by the selling stockholders.

Combined revenues of the companies which make up Kingstip for year ended Sept. 30, 1971 were $14.9 million with net earnings of $[illegible]. This compares with prior year revenue at $12 million and net earnings of $[illegible].

The construction materials division accounted for $[illegible] million of revenues last year, and $718,551 of net earnings. The communications division accounted for $1.7 million of revenues and net earnings of $220,846.

Local advertisers accounted for 52 per cent of television revenue. National and regional advertisers account for 30 per cent. Payments from National Broadcasting Company (NBC) account for 10 per cent.

Kingstip has 675 employees of whom 75 are in communications and 600 in construction materials division.

The company owns plants in seven Texas cities and leases plants in three others plus in [illegible]

EXPANDING AND IMPROVING A NEW COMPANY

With money from the stock offering, Henry immediately began to expand the Featherlite operation. The operation in Ranger, Texas, specialized in lightweight aggregate, a type of coarse aggregate used in the production of lightweight concrete products such as concrete block, structural concrete, and pavement. The Longview, Texas, branch of the company functioned as the Standard Tool and Machine Company; in Longview, Henry took $300,000 from the stock sale to construct a new building, enlarge an existing building, and buy new equipment for this high-pressure vessel fabrication plant. In El Paso, the company produced prestressed concrete products, such as bridge beams; with nearly $700,000 from the public stock offering, Henry decided to move the El Paso plant to a better location and expand its operations with new buildings and new equipment. Henry then grew Featherlite's prestressed, precast product lines through the purchase of two companies in Austin. And after acquiring three more companies in Beaumont, Texas; Memphis, Tennessee; and Lexington, Kentucky, Henry built the Austin area's first concrete block plant in Round Rock. "There were none at the time," he reasoned. "All the products either came in from San Antonio or from Waco. We decided we needed to build a plant here, because if we didn't, somebody else would. It is in an excellent location and turned into a major operation."

Henry then took the balance of the proceeds from the stock sale and turned his attention to the communications side. Based on his experiences with Rollins, where underperforming stations were routinely repurposed and improved, Henry knew immediately what to do with Channel 42 and took steps to cut through the chaos of the company. He started first with the people. The management and the control room staff of the TV station "were a disaster," Henry said. "The manager had a tendency to drink, and the chief engineer, his concept of lunch was a hamburger and a bottle of beer." Henry soon hired new staff.

Next, Henry focused on the equipment and infrastructure. He figured out that almost all of the equipment was leased, which wasn't a sound choice financially. So he started a program to phase out the leased items in the station such that the station would eventually own its equipment. As he became more involved with the operation, Henry discovered that Channel 42 was a low-powered UHF station with 540,000 to 560,000 watts of power, even though a typical UHF station was allowed to operate on five million watts. Henry quickly applied to have the power changed to five million watts, which dramatically reduced the blackouts experienced at the station when the power was too low. By doing some basic research, Henry discovered that the opportunity to operate another television station—Channel 36—was available in Austin, so Henry applied for, and was granted, the license for air rights. Henry soon dropped Channel 42 and focused on Channel 36.

With the television station in a better position, Henry turned to the radio stations on the second floor. According to Henry, the scene at the FM station was even worse. Catering primarily to students at the nearby University of Texas at Austin, he concluded that it had a no-rules, anything-goes atmosphere, a direct assault on Henry's no-nonsense sensibilities: "It was on the second floor in the same building as the TV station and once you hit that floor, you could smell the incense. It was a psychedelic atmosphere with flowers and with music that nobody understood. It was Woodstock! It was a very, very bad situation, and the manager was scared to do anything about it." Henry might have overlooked the station's musical preferences if the station was being operated efficiently and profitably, but he soon discovered that the radio staff bartered advertising time in exchange for haircuts and other favors. Henry was livid.

One day, while investigating the control room, Henry found an unused automation machine that would basically broadcast formatted, preselected music without requiring staff input. One Friday evening, without any advance warning, Henry turned on the automation machine, switched the format to easy-listening, and fired all of the staff. "The people with all this incense and psychedelic business were let go," he said. For about a full week after he switched the station, Henry watched as students and outraged radio listeners called him "every four-letter word that you can conceivably imagine" in the local student newspaper, arguing that Henry was an out-of-towner and that this was *their* station. "It was terrible, terrible, terrible. We had all kinds of threats. We hired guards for the station. It was a really bad time."

But ultimately, Henry's vision of an easy-listening station paid off. "When we acquired the stations, they had a negative net worth initially," he said. "And as time went on, we were able to get the stations to make money, build up the net worth, overcome all the deficits, and get rid of all the liabilities and get them straightened out. The FM station soon developed a huge following."

Less than two years after taking the company public, Henry, as president and chief executive of Kingstip, wrote "To Our Shareholders" in the 1973 Kingstip Annual Report that the fiscal year ending September 30, 1973, was a record year:

> Revenues increased 34 percent to $23,712,447, compared to $17,713,971, while net earnings before extraordinary items increased 16 percent to $1,265,158, compared to $1,093,946. The net earnings were achieved even though depreciation and amortization expense increased 45 percent to $948,471, compared to $653,623. . . . It is expected that the substantial improvement and expansion of company facilities begun two years ago will be completed in early 1974 and will be an important factor in the future growth of the Company.

In just four years, Henry had increased the company's revenue to over $40 million. And as Henry celebrated each financial milestone with his new company, he was able to put his exit from Rollins into clearer perspective, recognizing that the differences he had with a former associate named Earl were a thing of the past. "In retrospect, it was a good decision for me" to strike out on his own, Henry admitted. "And I should have sent him a dozen roses for every year."

Others agreed. "In my view, Henry left Atlanta to go to Texas to see if he could apply what he knew to build his own company," said John Rollins Jr. "And he was very successful at that. You know, when you work for somebody else all the time, you're never quite sure whether you can do it yourself. And he proved that he could do it himself."

SOMETHING NEW IN AUSTIN

Because the Kingsbery family had what Henry called "some tensions" with Austin banks, Henry went outside Austin to Corpus Christi to find the major lenders he needed to help finance what would become Kingstip, Inc. But those tensions did not carry over to Henry, who quickly became known as the first man in Austin to list a company on a major stock exchange. Soon, banks were courting *him*.

For instance, shortly after Kingstip was listed on the American Stock Exchange, Henry recalled that the CEO of what was then Capital National Bank (later known as Texas Commerce, and subsequently merged into JP Morgan Chase) paid him a visit. Within no time, Henry offered Austin's bankers a taste of the sophisticated and innovative banking approaches that he had honed while working with the Rollins brothers. Recalled Henry, "His reason for coming to see me was to see how we could do business together. I told him, we really had no reason for anything from a banking standpoint at the present time, but if he wanted to establish a relationship, the way it would have to take place would be to set up a line of credit. And the second thing is, in conjunction with that, it would be done on the basis of negative covenants as contrasted to mortgages and asset pledges."

The banks in Austin had never before conducted business in this manner; the lines of credit they issued generally had to be supported by some type of collateral. But the CEO who approached Henry had recently moved to Austin from Dallas, and like Henry, he was somewhat familiar with doing business in this fashion. Capital National Bank shortly approved Henry's line of credit for $1 million and sent their loan officers to meet with Henry to finalize the conditions of the deal. Among this group was a young loan officer named Milam Johnson Jr. And with remarkable clarity, Milam remembered that first meeting with Henry, as well as the unorthodox banking methods Henry helped introduce to the Austin area while structuring that first $1 million line of credit:

> We had agreed to provide a substantial line of credit to the Featherlite Corporation. In fact, it was in excess of our bank's legal lending limit. And we were going to have to get another bank to participate with

us in the loan. So one of my associates, Clifton Lind, and I went over to see Henry, and the purpose of the visit was to discuss this line of credit and figure out how it was going to be collateralized. And after we kind of fumbled around a little bit in that conversation, Henry said, "Look, I really don't want to put up any collateral. What we need to do is operate under a loan agreement."

Well, we had really never done loan agreements in Austin, which meant that the loan was supported by an agreement that had certain financial covenants in it. And if the company had violated any of those covenants we would then have the ability to call our loan or accelerate the loan. So anyway, Henry realized that we weren't getting anywhere in this conversation—and we weren't familiar with loan agreements—so he says, "I'll tell you what," and he reaches and opens the drawer of his desk and he pulls out a loan agreement that he had already put together based on how he thought we should handle the deal.

So Clifton and I took that agreement back to the bank. We studied it for a day or two, and I remember very well one of the financial covenants had to do with the company's debt to net worth ratio. And Henry had proposed a 2 to 1 debt to worth ratio, which means the company had to stay within that ratio; their debt could not go up by more than two times their net worth. Well, at this particular time, the company's debt was less than their net worth, and we came to the conclusion that the ratio was just too liberal. It allowed them too much room to expand before we had the right to say anything. So we felt like that ratio ought to be 1.5 to 1.

Of course, we really wanted to do business with Henry and with Featherlite, so we went back to Henry to negotiate. He thought about it for just a little while and he came back to us and said, "Well, I want to do business with you. And just to show you what kind of guy I am, I will agree to a 1.9 to 1 debt to worth ratio." We realized that if we wanted to do business with Henry and do that deal, we would have to agree to that ratio.

The reason I remember it so well is that after we got the deal put together, we went to our corresponding bank in New York—which happened to be the Chemical Bank. They looked at the deal and when they got to that particular covenant, their one big question was, "How in the world did you come up with this 1.9 to 1 ratio?" And we said, "You won't really understand until you meet Henry!"

After Henry introduced this new banking method to executives at Capital National Bank, it became common practice for the Austin banks to operate under similar loan agreements. Years later, when Henry and Rollins Truck Leasing Corp. needed the backing of a major financial institution, Capital National Bank didn't hesitate and played a role in supporting the company's restructuring at a critical time. And Milam and Henry went on to establish a strong personal and professional friendship that included a 30-year banking relationship, with Henry playing an important role as mentor to Milam. "I give Henry credit for providing some of my education as a banker," Milam said. "Shortly after we met, I began to learn a lot about new ways of banking. And Henry is certainly the kind of guy who gives a banker a lot of confidence. He always underpromises and overperforms."

A CONCLUSION FOR KINGSTIP

Though at times it appeared as though Henry had a financial crystal ball, he could not foresee everything. Not long after Kingstip went public, the market collapsed, and its stock fell to under $2 a share. Henry, of course, bought more Kingstip stock in the open market, because "I figured it was terribly cheap."

In 1974, when business concerns began tugging at Henry to spend more time in Delaware, he decided to resign as CEO of Kingstip, but he continued as chairman of the board. Said Henry, "I figured I'd gotten all this put together and organized, but in terms of the day-to-day operation, I didn't spend a lot of time with it, especially on the construction and concrete side of the business. In the case of the communications operations, I was more active in that because I had been around that business for a long, long time."

At the same time that he stepped down as CEO, Henry also decided to separate Kingstip into two companies: Kingstip, Inc., would now be made up solely of Featherlite; and Kingstip Communications, Inc., would be the new company for the media concerns. Henry's rationale for doing so was simple: The two business lines that made up Kingstip were completely different, requiring different analysts and different areas of expertise. Henry figured that the two companies had more value apart rather than together. The spin-off took place in 1976. "I spun the communications company off as Kingstip Communications to the shareholders of Kingstip, Inc.," Henry explained. "In other words, it was for the same shareholders, but two independent companies rather than a subsidiary of one."

Subsequent to the spin-off, Henry sold Kingstip, Inc., and its Featherlite concrete businesses to Justin Industries, a building products operation located in cities where Featherlite did not already have a presence. It was a good match. The Kingstip shareholders received an attractive cash or stock settlement, and both Henry and John Kingsbery served as consultants to Justin Industries for several years.

Three years later Henry decided that he would like to be the sole owner of Kingstip Communications, Inc., and offered to buy out the Kingsberys and their interests in the company. But they said no. Henry then proposed that they buy him out; again, the answer was no. So Henry, by now eager to be in business without any partners, proposed a third alternative: "What if we sell to a third party?" The Kingsberys agreed. Henry reached out to a senior executive at LIN Broadcasting Corporation, a radio, television, direct marketing, and music company founded in 1961 and operating in cities around the country. The senior executive had once worked for Rollins, and he knew Henry. In 1979 LIN Broadcasting bought Kingstip Communications, Inc., with Henry continuing to advise the company as a consultant.

Less than a decade after moving to Austin in 1970, Henry had acquired, built, enhanced, and sold the "two companies that I had come to Austin about," he summarized, smiling. "And with a most profitable basis for all concerned."

Henry and John W. Rollins teamed up again in 1974 to save Rollins International.

CHAPTER SEVENTEEN

DR. NO RETURNS TO SAVE A ROLLINS COMPANY

IN THE FALL OF 1973, not long after Henry informed his Kingstip shareholders that the company had experienced a "record year," Henry received word that something he had privately feared had come to pass: John Rollins' company, now known as Rollins International, was in danger of failing.

Henry had been worried about John's company for a while, tracing his concerns backs to 1965, when he left what was then Rollins Fleet Leasing to work solely with Wayne and focus on Rollins, Inc. According to Henry, "The auto-lease operation at that time had become very successful. There's money in the bank, we didn't have a lot of debt, we're making money. But rather than stay focused, there were signs that John Sr. wanted to expand that operation into other activities. And I didn't think that some of them were going to work too well."

Two years later, when Rollins moved its headquarters from Wilmington to Atlanta, the remarkable loyal trio of the Dreamer, the Operator, and Dr. No were officially separated for the first time since they had teamed up in 1953. With his most trusted advisors elsewhere, John Sr. soon surrounded himself with what Henry described as "high rollers"—businessmen willing to gamble with John's money and his enthusiasm and encourage ventures that sounded attractive but might not be good investments. In the process, Henry felt that John Sr. lost his focus on automobile and truck leasing and spread the holding company's resources too thin on "all these other things that just didn't fit." The list of businesses John Sr. managed now ran from harness track racing to environmental services to apartment complexes, not to mention his recent investments on the island of Jamaica.

Sitting in his office in Wilmington, John Rollins Jr. recalled the perilous situation facing his father, starting with Henry and Wayne's leaving Delaware and what that meant to John Sr.:

> When Henry and Wayne went down to Atlanta, they weren't here every day with my dad, so he would make decisions up here about starting this company and starting that company and a lot of them turned out, by good luck, I guess, or hard work, to be excellent companies. But there were a lot of things that we entered into that we lost a lot of money on. For the most part, a lot of these were never run by my Uncle Wayne and Henry and it could be because of schedules, it could be the distance. And when you take two key players to Atlanta, the operator and the financial guy, and you have the sales guy up here in Delaware, it just gets harder to operate as a team. My father had no replacement for Henry. So he was inclined to listen to a lot of people who felt they had the background and experience that Henry had and help Dad out, but they didn't. I have never seen anybody in my life who has. I don't know what it is, it must be that Iowa farm boy stuff.

The picture at Rollins International was bleak by the end of 1973, and the explanations for this are varied. A recession that would last through March 1975 was in full swing, bringing with it high interest rates, high unemployment, an oil supply crisis, and gasoline shortages. While the automobile and truck leasing companies remained stable, other areas of the company suffered, including Matlack, the country's only coast-to-coast tank truck carrier, and other electrical, construction, and telecommunications ventures. "I can't even remember some of the things we were in, and these things were bleeding us," said John Jr. Too, Rollins had recently started a company division to deal with environmental waste, admittedly an important and progressive idea but one that was costing the company money instead of bringing in revenue. "Everybody wanted me to build those plants, but no one was giving me any business," John Sr. argued. But, countered John Jr., "Instead of building a pilot plant, my father the optimist built three plants from the get-go and we had to raise the money to do that, which meant we had to borrow money." The company was also building a controversial, 15-story Rollins headquarters just outside Wilmington (once called an "ungainly, high-rise temple" in the local press) at a time when interest rates were soaring and the real estate market had gone south; 10 floors of empty space in the building could not land a single tenant.

Last but not least, John Sr. was rumored to be on the verge of a second and, some allowed, expensive divorce; he would soon face federal tax evasion charges; he had invested $1 million in Dover Downs' race track facility while it was under construction in 1968, but the track was still not operational; John's housing and apartment development in Dover, Delaware, was under water and deeply in debt; and his dream of transforming Jamaica into a tourists' paradise was a constant drain on the financial coffers. In many cases, John had guaranteed loans personally, secured with company stock from both his and his brother Wayne's businesses. With disaster staring him in the face, John Sr. called on the one man he knew he could trust: Henry B. Tippie.

"My accountants keep telling me we're making money," John Sr. told Henry, according to John Sr.'s biography, *Hanging the Moon*. "But in the meantime, we've got no money and it's only getting worse." And though he hadn't yet admitted it to Henry, John Sr. knew exactly what was wrong. "To tell the honest truth," he said, "the financial organization was in a hell of a mess from the time Henry left until the time he came back. The worst mistake you can make in business is not having the proper financial control, I don't care how good you are at everything else. And I'll certainly take my part of the responsibility, because that was in an acquisition time. The choice of acquisitions left something to be desired, and we got into some businesses that we had no business being into."

HENRY GATHERS THE FACTS

Henry's approach to John Sr.'s financial meltdown was a classic example of how Henry approached any major business situation. He started, as always, by getting all the facts, a requirement fulfilled through a series of telephone calls and meetings from fall 1973 through March 1974.

Fall 1973

Based on the telephone call he received from John Sr., Henry agreed to come to Wilmington and "give him any thoughts that I might have." Walking around the virtually empty 15-story headquarters still under partial construction, Henry could see that things were "very, very bad now. You can't rent the space in the building. I mean it's a 15-story building and you've got about 10 floors of it with no one in them. There are birds flying through here, and there's office space all over Wilmington that was free back then."

Henry didn't like what he saw as he walked with John Sr. through the existing corporate headquarters either. "I pointed out different things to him, and we ran across one guy's expense account lying on the desk. And the guy had gone to Washington, D.C., and back on the train and had spent a day or two down there. I think he had a couple of thousand dollars in expenses. I mean it was totally outlandish."

Upon further review, Henry soon realized that while the company was showing profit, it was losing money from a cash standpoint while accumulating debt. How much debt? Henry wasn't sure. The balance sheet showed some things being capitalized and accounted for correctly, while other liabilities were not included. This accounting style reminded the ledger-trained, by-the-books Henry B. Tippie of so much smoke and mirrors, like some form of creative financing that he had never seen before. Henry had to wonder: "Was this thing salvageable or not?"

At one point during his Wilmington visit, Henry joined John's family for dinner, and one of John's younger sons recognized immediately that the situation was serious. "My first memories of Henry are around the dinner table, in the early '70s, when the business went down," recalled Jeff Rollins. "Dad said, 'Tomorrow night Henry Tippie is coming for dinner.

He's coming to help get the business together and you need to behave at dinner.' I was 7 or 8 years old. So it's a real struggle for me to think about when I was aware of Henry because he has just always been there. Dad just has so much trust in Henry's thought processes. And in Henry, there is no more loyal a friend."

Winter 1973

After his visit to Wilmington, Henry and John Sr. agreed that the company CFO and some of the financial and accounting staff should fly to Austin, meet with Henry, and get some basic tutorials in Accounting 101.

The meeting took place downtown in the Driskill Hotel, just around the corner from Henry's office in the Littlefield Building. It did not begin well. When Henry arrived after finishing a day's work at Kingstip, the Rollins financial team was already settled into a hotel suite with a rollaway bar filled with various amounts of expensive liquors and wines. "Well, this is interesting," Henry thought to himself as he surveyed the scene, with men in suits and expensive leather briefcases scattered about. "They wanted to know if I wanted something to drink, and I said, 'Well, not really.'" I figured their plan was to have me feel good and tell them how great they were. Now, remember, this was the first time I had met these people, and I thought to myself, 'This is part of the problem in Delaware.'"

What Henry saw in that Driskill Hotel room was this: a team of financial managers who were perfectly willing to spend a company's money on suites and alcohol instead of paying attention to a company's bottom line. The drinking particularly bothered him. "I might have had a soft drink or something but in terms of getting into the alcohol business, that wasn't about to happen. It indicated to me that the problems were at the top, because this was some of the top management." Henry noted immediately that the executives were focused on future projections instead of zeroing in on how to run the company on a day-to-day basis.

After a discussion about the company and what the acquisitions were, Henry had a pretty good sense of John Sr.'s staff, some of the problems, and how the staff tended to approach those problems. And by the end of the evening, Henry had concluded that John's finances were out of control. The company had reported revenues of $168 million in the previous fiscal year, but there were reams of deferred charges, capitalized items that should have been listed as expenses, and an inevitable "disaster in the making" when Henry finally figured out the extent of the company's debt: the company's ratio of debt to equity was an unsustainable 4 to 1. The people in charge were clearly well-educated individuals with MBAs and advanced degrees, but they practiced business based on theories instead of practical experience, an approach that made Henry chafe. As Henry once noted, "There's nothing complicated about businesses unless you make it complicated." From what he saw that night in the Driskill Hotel, Henry knew that all of the basic business procedures and the straightforward accounting principles that he had established before leaving the company in 1965 were long gone.

"We didn't accomplish much, but I gave John some of my thoughts based on what I had seen," said Henry. "And that's the end of that story. They went home. And I just kind of shook my head. Things continued to deteriorate up there in Wilmington, a few more phone calls took place, and things were getting into very, very bad shape."

January–February 1974

From his home in Jamaica, John Sr. once again reviewed the situation in front of him and the tremendous financial crisis looming before him. The list was daunting—and growing. Pressed to come up with money to pay off his debts, John Sr. had borrowed from his brother Wayne, so now his devoted brother's collateral and money were on the line, too, as John pledged stock in both companies as collateral for his personal loans. ("They would lend each other their last penny," Randall Rollins once said of Wayne and John Sr. "You couldn't break one without breaking the other.") A team of New York bankers had apparently tried to sell John's Jamaica property out from under him (nine banks were once listed as loaning money to the Jamaica project), and many of his financial friends had deserted him. By 1974 Rollins International was unable to meet either its operating expenses or its debt service requirements, and business and personal loans secured by John were nearing default with respect to both principal and interest. According to newspaper reports, analysts now viewed John Sr. as the cause of the company's "haywire acquisitions," as one analyst put it. In an effort to keep everything afloat, John Sr. had sold a large portion of his stock in Rollins International, which caused a panic about the company's value; the stock price then plummeted from around $45 a share to $4 a share. The *Delaware State News*, a newspaper in Dover, Delaware, had recently printed a humiliating cartoon of John W. Rollins Sr.—a former lieutenant governor who once ran for governor, a key figure in state and national Republican Party circles, and once a key GOP fund-raiser who had hosted President Nixon at his estate home. In the cartoon, a pathetic-looking John was sitting in the street with a cup in his hand, begging for coins.

"Enough!" John Sr. concluded. He picked up the phone and placed an urgent call to Henry. The tone of the call was one of frustration and desperation, recalled Henry, who later admitted "it was not a call that anybody would like to receive. He was asking for help." When the call was over, Henry immediately contacted Wayne to verify that Wayne knew John was making the call ("I did," said Wayne) and to confirm that the situation was serious ("It's quite serious").

Giving a somewhat startled Patricia a brief synopsis of the situation, Henry then flew to Jamaica to review everything with John in depth. With John's personal debt approaching $55 million, Henry knew his immediate goal was to prevent any bank from selling either Wayne's or John's collateral stock; his principal concern was that all of the banks would begin selling the collateral, which would further drive down the stock price in both companies and inhibit everyone's ability to repay the loans. For a time, Henry considered the possibility of declaring bankruptcy. "But that would have had so many dominoes coming out of it, we concluded that that was not a viable option," he said.

It wasn't long before both men agreed that they really had only one option: John Sr. needed Henry to bring discipline and financial principles back to a company that had lost both; to review what was broken in the company and get rid of inefficient procedures, people, and even lines of business that did not belong under the Rollins umbrella; and then salvage what was working and make it work better. Henry would work with all of John's personal and business lenders to reschedule the loan repayments and to obtain additional time to make the payments. In short, John Sr. needed "Dr. No." to save his company and rescue his personal financial situation, which was so inextricably linked to his business that separating the two was all but impossible. And it was going to be painful.

"I'll call all the shots?" Henry asked John Sr. in a tense moment, when all the cards were on the table and the depth of the crisis was clear. "Because I don't want to get involved with second-guessing or anything like that. You're going to give me full authority to do anything I have to do?"

"You'll call all the shots," John Sr. reassured Henry. "There will be no sacred cows. We've got to go through it from one end to the other."

After a day of intense discussions, Henry told John Sr. that he still needed to talk to Patricia before giving a final answer. On the way home, he stopped in Fort Pierce, Florida, where Wayne was staying at his ranch. "The reason I visited Wayne is that I wanted to get the inside story from both of them, and I knew from my past relationship that they were very close," said Henry. "I wasn't going to do anything until I was certain that they were both on board, and that everybody's on the same page of the hymn book so there's no questions. I wanted to make sure that Wayne was going to be supportive, and he was. Another reason it became important for Wayne is that in order to keep John afloat, some of Wayne's assets wound up being pledged for John."

With all the facts in hand, Henry continued his flight home to Austin, where Patricia helped Henry sort through the pros and cons of trying to rescue John's company. On the business front, Kingstip was running smoothly; Henry had recently stepped down as president of Kingstip but remained chairman of the board, so his new business in Austin would not suffer if he took on some added responsibilities. But when it came to family, the answer wasn't as clear. The children were now active teenagers, Henry would be away from home a lot, "and that's a major decision to be made as the head of the household with kids at that age." But Patricia was and always had been the primary caregiver, and the children had been settled in Austin for just over three years. And though the new Rollins assignment would mean he had to travel back and forth to Delaware, Henry and Patricia came up with a compromise: Henry would not commit to working full-time in Delaware, and he would not move to Delaware. "It would be as much time as I could spend, which would be a good deal, but it wouldn't be full-time," he said.

With Patricia, Henry also reviewed something that he felt as deeply as any stoic, midwestern farm boy from Iowa could ever feel: With all that the Rollins brothers had done for him and his career, how could he turn his back on them now?

"I had had the opportunity over the years, with the two Rollins brothers, to gain a considerable amount of experience in everything you could name: FCC stuff, legal procedures, going public, raising money, sales, marketing, managing a company, and listing companies on the stock exchange. I had all of this tremendous experience. I gained a lot of knowledge on a whole lot of fronts as to what to do and what not to do, and I had been able to utilize that experience successfully after I came to Texas. I certainly had done well, and I knew this would be an opportunity to try to balance the books by repayment. I looked at it from the standpoint of repayment for the opportunities they had given me along the way. They now have a crisis and a lot of bad things could take place. And apparently, everybody else had either figured that there's no way that things could be resurrected or straightened out, or they don't know how to. I always felt that at this time, if there was any shot to make anything happen, I'm probably as good a bet as there is—if not better. I was willing to put my ability, whatever it is, up on the line."

Henry called John Sr. and Wayne and gave them a simple answer: "Let's move forward. We are going to give it our best shot." There were a series of meetings in Atlanta and Wilmington, with Wayne, Randall, John Sr., John Jr., and Henry, but there was never any written agreement describing Henry's role or what was going to happen, no lengthy legal document to clarify timelines, expectations, or compensation. "From my standpoint, a handshake and their word is just as good as a whole bunch of papers," said Henry. "They already knew me. So I was a known quantity from their standpoint."

Indeed, the 20-plus years of history and professional trust among the three men provided the key ingredient that no one other than Henry could deliver to John Sr. and Wayne. "They knew his measure," Patrick Rollins, John Sr.'s son, once said about his father's and uncle's request for Henry to return to the fold. "They knew that he was going to give them the unvarnished truth. And Henry's loyalty is such that he has always been the rescue guy. No matter what it is, Henry has been willing to act."

Late February 1974

To make sure everyone else at Rollins International realized that Henry was the "rescue guy" and fully in charge, Henry and John Sr. revised the bylaws of the company to reflect Henry's authority. They named Henry vice chairman of the board and created a three-person Executive Committee made up of only Henry, John Sr., and John Jr. Henry became chairman of this Executive Committee, and this committee—not the full board—was empowered to make all decisions. "When we had the board meetings, I did most of the talking," Henry said. And he warned John Sr. that he was going to dramatically cut the company's board of directors, which had ballooned to over 15 or 20 members. "You have to unload half of this board of directors or I'm not coming," he pledged. "They are in the way and they have to be gone."

Next, the two men reordered the company's executive structure. John Sr. became chairman of the board and chief executive officer of the company. The existing president of the company retained his title, "but we put him in another office to get him off the premises and out of the company," said Henry. John Rollins Sr. wanted his son to be involved and thought he was the right person to carry out Henry's plans. In a glimpse of how brutal Henry was prepared to be, he briefly considered whether or not John Jr., then head of Rollins Truck Leasing, was up to the task and whether or not he "would follow the plan. And I didn't want to get on the trail of the son here and then find out that it's going to be a problem." Both Henry and John Sr. concluded, correctly, as it turned out, that John Jr. was an excellent person to be Henry's right-hand man, and they named him executive vice president (later president) and chief operating officer. "We cleared the decks," said John Jr., "so he and I could go to war."

And finally, Henry—who had years earlier sold all of his Rollins International stock when it hit a record high—bought more stock in the company, giving him "skin in the game" and an added incentive to turn Rollins International around.

Wednesday, March 6, 1974

Henry arrived in Wilmington, Delaware, and checked into the nearby Holiday Inn for an extended stay. He immediately got to work. Keeping his promise, John Sr. called a special board of directors' meeting and proceeded to dramatically reduce the number of people around the table. Gary Rollins, who was on the board at that time, remembers seeing it shrink before his very eyes as Henry quickly designated about eight board members who either resigned or were elevated to emeritus status with no voting privileges. As Gary recalled,

> The first board meeting I went to up there, every single chair was filled and there were people sitting around the edge of the room. I was just overwhelmed when I saw it, and one of the first courses of action that took place was Henry saying, "We've got to get all these people outta here. These people aren't making any contribution." So they shrank the board. Most of the people on the board were there because they were the president of a company that had been acquired, and these were not bad people, but they just were not contributing anything. And one of the first things that Henry said was, "We're going to have to be nimble. We're not going to have time to have a tremendous amount of discussion on these things that have to be done." The company was just bleeding to death.

Henry's loyalty to the family and his commitment to the onerous task in front of him impressed Gary, along with Henry's thrifty move to hunker down at the Holiday Inn. "Henry's like a celebrity up there at that Holiday Inn. I don't think you could have gotten more attention if you had been Wayne Newton or Mick Jagger. But gosh, for a guy to go up there and live in a Holiday Inn, week after week, away from your family, at a point in your life when you didn't need the money. I mean, it was more loyalty than anything else."

Randall Rollins agreed. "Things were pretty bad up there in Delaware, and Henry did the things that needed to be done," said Randall. "He spent a lot of time up there and did a lot of unpleasant things. He stayed out there in the Holiday Inn. Henry's a trooper and the kind of fellow you could call at three in the morning and say 'I need you' and Henry would be there. I can't express enough how dedicated he is. He is a friend's friend."

And Wayne Rollins, the older brother who first encouraged John to pick up the phone and call Henry, agreed with both of his sons. "Henry's a good friend. If I called him up today, and told him, 'Henry, I'd like for you to be here in the morning, I'd like to go over some things with you,' if he could at all, if it was possible at all, he'd be here," Wayne once said. "And I think probably the most valuable asset that I have is the number of people that I've built up a pretty close relationship over these years with. And I value that, that friendship and the fact that I can draw on their wisdom."

With the board significantly reduced, the new Executive Committee crafted a press release to make an important announcement: Dr. No was back.

Thursday, March 7, 1974

The two Wilmington, Delaware, newspapers, the *Morning News* and the *Evening Journal*, reported that Henry B. Tippie had returned to Rollins International: *Rollins exec returns; pictured as referee*, read the headline.

The Morning News, Thursday, March 7, 1974 •

Rollins exec returns; pictured as referee

By David L. Warsh

Henry B. Tippie, in a move apparently aimed at providing top managers, is returning to Rollins International Inc., the company he helped found 20 years ago.

He'll be vice chairman of both its board of directors and executive committee, the company said. He had been chief operating officer from 1958 until 1965.

The move comes after a year of sagging earnings and major write-offs for the diversified company which is controlled by John W. Rollins.

Although Tippie is expected to take an active role in management, he'll apparently continue to live in Austin, Tex., where he is chairman of Kingstip, Inc., a company that was formed in a consolidation of the Kingsbery family interests.

Rollins, Tippie and others incorporated the company together in 1954 as a new automobile leasing outfit. During the years of its explosive growth, Tippie maintained a vitally close but often stormy friendship with the broad-handed Rollins.

"Henry kept John out of trouble more times than you can count, just by saying 'no' and making it stick. Others would say 'no,' but John wouldn't listen. He always listened to Henry," recalled a student of the company's early years.

Tippie, an accountant, quit both the company and its board of directors in 1965, ostensibly to retire. He continued to advise both John Rollins and his brother, O. Wayne Rollins, president of Rollins, Inc. of Atlanta, and occasionally served as a source of last appeal from John's decisions, according to company insiders.

The new vice chairman lived in Delaware for 14 years before moving to Texas.

Rollins International, a corporate services company, has auto-leasing, anti-pollution and trucking operations.

THE RESCUE GUY GOES TO WORK

For the next two and a half years, nothing stood in Henry's way when it came to salvaging the business he once helped to build. Call it streamlining or downsizing or rightsizing, Henry's views on what and who would stay or go were brutal and swift. Besides poring over the books and financial reports, Henry and John Jr. together resorted to one of Henry's favorite tactics to find out what's going on in a company: they visited every office, from coast to coast, sometimes on the road for two weeks at a time, checking up on their operations from the bottom up.

In a management style referred to as "MBWA" or "management by walking around," Henry and John Jr. visited all the locations for the truck lease operation. Saving the manager's office for last, Henry would start at the truck terminals where they pumped fuel. Then he'd go through the maintenance area, talking with employees and constantly looking around. If he noted oil spilled all over the floor and old pieces junked over in a corner, he would say, "This isn't a well-run operation." By the time he got to the manager's office, he had a good picture of the operation.

"I do believe in walking around, talking to everyone in the business," Henry said. "I adopt the attitude that I'm not as smart as a lot of these people, and the only way I can understand what they're doing is to walk around, look at what they're doing, and talk to them. I feel very comfortable with that. And I think most of the time, people I get around at any level feel comfortable. That's important because I want to be a listener as well as a looker. I ask about how they're doing, how their family is doing, do they have any ideas about how to do things better. It's amazing—they'll let you know a lot of things, about problems and how we can solve them.

"And so I would go on these field trips and get out there and listen to what the people have to say at these locations," continued Henry. "And I found that to be interesting because they are complaining out in the field about how they can't get any answers, and of course the home office never has any problems. And you find out that your problems are at the home office. So that meant we had a lot of work to clean up and to get those people to understand that they're there to serve the field. You make your money out on the front line with the customer. You're not going to make it at the home office. The home office should be in a position to monitor what's going on and to provide the services and the facts out to the field so those people can do their jobs. It isn't the other way around."

Patrick Rollins worked in a truck leasing branch during the early 1970s, and still remembers the day Henry and John Jr. visited his branch office on one of their fact-finding missions. Though Patrick had hustled to get the branch clean and painted before the visit, there was still one closet filled with clutter. "And Henry went immediately to that closet in the back and said, 'What is all this business here?'" recalled Patrick. "Because he can walk through a place and he can tell you how the business is running by looking in the supply closets. If they're organized, the company is organized."

Henry soon realized that there was so much that had to be changed at Rollins International that he couldn't possibly keep it all in his head during these branch visits. So he started scrawling his ideas on the back of brown paper sacks when he didn't have his trusty legal pads. "It became obvious to me that a lot of things were bad news for the company, and they either needed to be shut down or we needed to have focus," said Henry. "So looking on from a long-range standpoint, we needed to be in the truck leasing and bulk trucking business. All these other things didn't fit.'"

John Sr. very quickly understood the extent of Henry's mission. By April 1974, John Sr. told the *Morning News*, "Hell, everything I've got—except my wife and family—is for sale, I suppose."

The liquidation program that Henry laid out and John Jr. implemented gradually eliminated the following businesses from the Rollins International umbrella: an electrical contracting firm, a telephone equipment and rental business, a stock registration and transfer company, Brandywine Raceway, and other unrelated operations. Henry then narrowed the company's focus to three main businesses: bulk storage and trucking under Matlack; the Rollins truck and automobile leasing companies under Rollins Truck Leasing; and hazardous waste disposal under an environmental services division, an area of the company that Henry later admitted he kept only because it had too much debt to get rid of right away.

"Henry would show up and hand me a list," John Jr. remembered, "and he would say, 'I want to know about this operation, I want to know about this.' And he would give me a list and he'd say, 'Next time we meet, I want the answers.' So I would go and get all that stuff for him and come back to the next meeting. And it was through that process that we got to know the details and the magnitude of the problems with some of these companies."

As businesses disappeared, so did people. As John Jr. soon learned, "Henry played no favorites." When Henry first came back to save Rollins, the company occupied five floors of office space. When he was finished clearing out what he calls the "deadwood" in people, bureaucracy, and duplications, the entire company could fit into less than three floors. The local papers once referred to Henry as "The Hatchet Man" because he had let so many people go.

"The joke around the office was that Henry would go from desk to desk and say, 'Thank you, we won't be needing your services anymore,'" said Jeff. "That was the lore, that's what everybody said, and he got the reputation of being the 'Hatchet Man.'"

One particular group of executives especially got Henry's goat. "Almost all of these fancy business school graduates were terminated," he said. "Unfortunately, they had not learned that you have to start down at the bottom of the company to find out what's going on, as contrasted to them coming in at the top of an operation. You need to get down in the guts of it to find out what's going on. There were people up there I really didn't figure we needed. And it became quite apparent early on that the president and CEO before John Jr. was not supportive whatsoever. I tried to get them to do the things I wanted done, and I would leave town for a few days and nothing would happen. He and some of the other people up there, who had come along after I left Delaware, felt that they could do me in, just like they had done others up here. But the thing they didn't understand, though, is that I had the authority. So it wasn't long until they found that out."

Ironically, John Jr., the man in charge of implementing Henry's plan, had an MBA from Northwestern University, near Chicago. But, Henry said, "I've always said I had to get him reprogrammed. Get him to where he forgot he ever had an MBA." But Henry never had anything but praise for John Jr. "He now has a Ph.D. in experience. He's a top operator. Because you can have the best plan in the world, but it's nothing if there's no one who can make it work."

Though the title of "Hatchet Man" would wear thin on Henry, he never forgot the time he fired a division treasurer. "One day John Sr. and I went out to McDonald's at noon to get a hamburger to eat, and on the way back we get on the elevator, and this treasurer's on there. And it's just past 1 in the afternoon, and the guy smells of beer all over the place. Of course that told me right there that this guy's history. He's the treasurer of the division, and he's apparently having a beer at noontime. Liquor during business hours is intolerable in a business operation. So he had to be relieved. Also, he had put together some numbers and when Continental Bank came out to check the numbers, there was a serious mistake in those. That's another reason he had to go out the door. That mistake was a $5 million error. 'Now that is embarrassing,' John Sr. said. 'Having to go back and tell them you need another five million!'"

Like everyone in the family, Patrick realized that "it was a quite a relief to have Henry there. But I don't like 'the Hatchet Man.' That denotes something negative, that there is an ulterior motive. Henry was doing what was right, what needed to be done. No matter what the consequence—personal, business, financial—Henry will do the right thing. And Dad would listen to Henry. He didn't listen to many, but he listened to Henry."

John Jr. agreed. "My dad lost more fortunes on things than he's made over time, and most of those times it has been when he didn't listen to Henry. There is no question Henry was instrumental in keeping the company alive."

Like low-hanging fruit, Henry took away extravagant business luxuries including chefs, Learjets, and big expense accounts. He asked corporate executives to make personal sacrifices, too. John Sr.'s estate-like home in Delaware was locked up for a while, and he relocated to Florida. John Jr. sold his home and most of his furniture. "That is pain, that is big pain," said Henry.

THE $22 MILLION PLAN AND ANOTHER YELLOW PAD

Henry's unerring adherence to the bottom line slowly began to pay off. And a large part of the success story involved the way Henry handled the company's exorbitant loans, acquired over time and during the height of John's financial crisis. Within months of Henry's arrival in Wilmington, he realized that various banking lenders wanted out of the agreements they had made with John and his companies; with so much of the Rollins' brothers personal stock tied up as collateral, Henry persuaded the banks to refrain from taking any action with respect to the collateral stock until mid-1975, while his overall plan involved attempting to consolidate the various loans when there were several loans from the same bank. Why? Because Henry wanted to prevent a bank from calling in all loans against John and his company if only one loan was in default. Plus, he argued, the banks would benefit from the company's turnaround and from having John be financially solvent.

Two banks immediately said no; they were not amenable to Henry's suggestions. Henry never forgot the banks that pulled out when times were tough. "To hell with them!" he said. "I have no time for fair-weather friends." But to his relief, most of the banks cooperated with Henry and worked out not only revised debt payment schedules but also loaned additional money. As Henry said, "The major bank involved was Continental in Chicago. So I put a plan together and, just to show you how serious it was, we met on Memorial Day of 1974 at the bank. All the top officers of the bank were there because that was the only day I could fit in to come to Chicago."

Henry presented two plans: the $22 million plan and the $30 million plan. Both plans included an existing loan of $12 million from Continental, "and they could be called upon to put up another $10 million or $20 million," said Henry. "And my point was, 'I don't know when I'm going to need it, but that's what you have to plan on. This company is in a lot of trouble. You need to choose one of those two plans and I think your decision is very simple. Because if you don't go along with one of the plans, I think you can kiss your $12 million good-bye because I don't think you'll ever see it.'" Continental decided on the $22 million plan—$12 million in existing loans and $10 million in new loans available when needed.

Ken Chalmers, then a senior banking officer at Continental who had direct dealings with Henry, recalled that "as long as Henry was with the company, I knew that things were going to be all right. Henry always arrived with John Jr., and he would sit down and pull out his yellow legal pad. And he would have his whole agenda organized and laid out, and he would just start going through all the points one by one. You know, he thought things through. I don't think Henry ever overreached. He could be very compelling. And you go through life and you have to make choices, and many of those choices are geared to your view of the character of a person. You either buy in or you don't buy in. Henry is the type of guy who makes you want to go with him."

Pausing, Ken, who advanced to executive vice president at Continental before retiring, was asked to consider the full impact of Henry's role on Rollins International, and on the future of the company. "He was certainly responsible for restoring John Sr. to viability. There was a lot at stake for John Sr., and for us, too. Henry pulled him out of the fire. So he was the man of the hour, and we all looked to Henry."

If there was ever any doubt about Henry's role in rescuing the Rollins operation and John Rollins Sr. from financial ruin, the 1976 Annual Report for Rollins International spelled it out in black-and-white. In the third quarter of fiscal year 1975, the company reversed over two years of net earnings losses and reported a meager profit after taxes of $358,000; by the fourth quarter, the company's profits after taxes had more than tripled to $1.9 million. The next year, Rollins reported profits in each quarter, ending the year with $195 million in revenue and $10.473 million in profit after taxes.

"Your Company has just completed its greatest year in history," John W. Rollins Sr. and John W. Rollins Jr. wrote in a letter to the shareholders on October 29, 1976. "The aforementioned fiscal year record results exceeded any previous year results of the Company by a wide margin. Pre-tax and after-tax earnings for the fourth quarter alone exceeded any previous entire fiscal year results. These results are a direct reflection of the redirection of the Company started 2½ years ago. Eighty-four percent of the Company's business is now oriented to the transportation field. All operations are now profitable. The environmental services division, consisting of three industrial hazardous waste treatment plants and environmental engineering services, has been developed into one of the better profit centers of the Company."

And in the last paragraph, the two Rollins executives saluted the man they had turned to in late 1973, when they were at risk of losing everything. "We particularly express our appreciation to Henry B. Tippie, who has, for the past 2½ years, served as chairman of the Executive Committee and vice chairman of the board. His planning, advice, and counseling have been invaluable in the restoration of the Company, not only to record profitability, but also to a solid foundation for the future."

Henry's ability to help save John Sr.'s company impressed legions of people, including the one person who mattered the most to Henry: Patricia. As she gradually heard others talk about his accomplishments in Delaware, she couldn't help but be in awe of the man she once first refused to wait on in the Plantation Restaurant. "It's like I'm finally realizing who I married," she said. "Little did I know at that time—I just thought he was a nice guy."

BACK TO TEXAS WITH TREMENDOUS SATISFACTION

With the crisis effectively over, Henry returned to Austin to focus on his own businesses and his family. He agreed to remain indefinitely in his two posts with Rollins International, which was renamed RLC and listed on the New York Stock Exchange in 1976, and renamed Rollins Truck Leasing Corp. at a later date. As long as John needed him, Henry would help ensure that the company stayed the course for a firm financial footing. There was no longer "a whole lot of talk regarding John Sr.'s personal stuff," said Henry, in one of his classic understatements. "As time went on, we got him extracted from his difficulties." In fact, John Sr. married for a third time in 1977 to the love of his life, Michele Metrinko Rollins, an ambitious lawyer and former Miss USA who was working for

RLC lists on the New York Stock Exchange in 1976. Henry stands between John W. Rollins Sr. and John W. Rollins Jr. (the other two men are not identified).

the Department of the Interior when they met. They soon welcomed four children to add to John's family of six.

And the good news continued. In 1980 the local newspaper reported that RLC had experienced a "peak year," with earnings that covered interest charges more than three times, while the ratio of debt to equity was down to about 2 to 1. To quote the newspaper article,

> *The man most financial analysts credit with putting RLC back on its feet is Henry B. Tippie, 52, a 27-year business associate of John W. Rollins, RLC's founder, and his brother, O. Wayne Rollins of Atlanta-based Rollins, Inc. When John Rollins realized that RLC was out of control, he immediately called on Tippie. Thus began the surgery that was to leave RLC lean and profitable.*

By 1984, newspaper headlines that had once predicted the company's demise now telegraphed its success: *RLC STOCK: State's Top Performer in 1983, Firm is 83rd on NYSE*, read the headline after Rollins reported a

93.8 percent increase in stock price from $6 a share in 1982 to $11.63 in 1983. By 1990, after a series of spin-offs involving the environmental services division (1982) and the bulk trucking company known as Matlack (1989), Rollins would be firmly established as a truck leasing company known as Rollins Truck Leasing Corporation—a move that reflected Henry's historical business preference to keep companies focused and easily understood by Wall Street analysts, and either spin off or get rid of unrelated enterprises. Henry continued to visit the company regularly, he retained his position as vice chairman of the board and the executive committee, and he had a say in every major corporate decision. "We didn't do anything unless Henry approved it," said Klaus M. Belohoubek, general counsel at Rollins Truck Leasing, who started with the company in 1989. "John Jr. would always ask if Henry had approved something before it went further."

Years later, Henry held in his hands the 1999 Annual Report for Rollins Truck Leasing Corp. He immediately turned to the page with an 11-year performance summary of the company. The report reflected the corporation's sustained success from 1989 through 1999, a period when the company's revenue doubled from $312 million to over $627 million,

Eleven-Year Performance Summary

	10-Year Compound Growth Rate	1999	1998	1997	1996	1995	1994	1993	1992	1991	1990	1989
Revenues	7.2%	627,397	610,157	556,704	513,779	482,612	450,903	408,788	380,384	341,882	331,173	312,025
Operating earnings	8.2%	148,095	136,689	119,481	103,408	111,273	103,226	89,085	76,013	69,846	70,233	67,334
Earnings before income taxes	12.9%	92,731	85,103	70,211	55,927	67,092	66,390	54,657	40,668	31,464	29,568	27,576
Net earnings	12.9%	56,473	52,023	42,794	34,116	41,336	39,828	30,416	24,639	18,967	18,033	16,798
Earnings per diluted share	13.6%	.97	.85	.68	.52	.61	.57	.44	.35	.30	.29	.27
Cash flows from operations	9.6%	267,212	245,230	221,575	202,369	198,521	173,655	166,531	140,875	130,678	120,255	106,427
Operating earnings margin	—	23.6%	22.4%	21.5%	20.1%	23.1%	22.9%	21.8%	20.0%	20.4%	21.2%	21.6%
Pre-tax margin	—	14.8%	14.0%	12.6%	10.9%	13.9%	14.7%	13.4%	10.7%	9.2%	8.9%	8.8%
Debt as a percent of total capitalization	—	71.5%	71.9%	69.9%	69.3%	67.6%	66.5%	66.4%	67.6%	69.8%	76.2%	77.9%
Pre-tax return on beginning shareholders' equity	—	31.7%	29.3%	24.6%	20.3%	26.7%	30.6%	28.6%	24.0%	23.5%	24.4%	25.8%
Number of employees	—	3,964	3,934	3,708	3,404	3,129	2,924	2,676	2,627	2,548	2,464	2,401
Number of branch locations	—	217	206	204	202	201	198	196	191	184	178	170
Number of vehicles maintained	—	38,968	36,873	33,915	31,403	28,145	26,326	24,726	23,543	20,957	20,527	18,789

The 1999 Annual Report, Rollins Truck Leasing Corp.: "A pretty fancy performance."

representing an outstanding 12.9 percent earnings growth rate. "When you get 12.9 percent in almost any business over 11 years, that's pretty fancy," he said, pointing specifically to the performance summary. "And when I look here at operating earnings margins, all of them are above 20 percent on every year. It's a pretty fancy performance. Every category in this chart is an impressive figure."

Loath to imply that he's taking sole credit for the turnaround, Henry quickly pointed out one of his time-honored business truths. "No *one* person ever makes things happen. If one person tries to tell you they are responsible, you might as well disregard it. It takes a lot of people to make things happen." He pointed again to the annual report. "This took a lot of people to make happen. There were an awful lot of people involved. You can have the greatest plan in the world, but if you don't have the people to execute it, it'll never work. I get a good feeling about having been involved with this, and a whole lot of other people should, too."

When asked what the numbers on the page ultimately represented to him, Henry allowed himself a moment of reflection before answering.

"Satisfaction," he finally replied. "Or let me say *tremendous* satisfaction. Everyone thought there was no way to survive. We were working against all the odds. Did I worry? Of course. But you know, did I think in terms of whether I could bring it off? I probably didn't think much about that. We were just going to give it our best shot."

CHAPTER EIGHTEEN

RAISING A FAMILY IN TEXAS

HENRY ALWAYS BELIEVED THAT "GOOD people can go haywire without a supportive partner." When Henry's professional life was stretched to the limit during the 1970s—as he worked in Texas to establish his own business and traveled frequently to Delaware to save Rollins International from collapse—he often thought to himself how fortunate he was to have Patricia in his corner.

"The right spouse can be a major factor in your success," Henry told a magazine writer when this particularly tumultuous time in his life was over. "I've been extremely fortunate, because I have a very supportive spouse. I consider Patricia my very best friend, and hopefully, she thinks likewise. We both came from next to nothing, and that common background makes all the difference. It's been a very supportive relationship."

And a traditional one. As Henry worked and focused on his career, Patricia was always in charge of the Austin household and the family's three children, creating a warm and nurturing home for not only the kids but for Henry, too. Patricia made sure that the man who never had birthday parties as a child celebrated each January 5 with balloons, presents, and lots of attention from children with homemade birthday cards—"Happy Birthday, HBT!" Though he didn't know to buy flowers or write cards for special occasions when they first married, Henry picked up on Patricia's cues and gradually remembered to do both for his wife "because he realizes

Henry and Waif the cat.

it is important to me," said Patricia. Henry was always drawn to animals, and the family dogs and cats over the years were as much for him as they were for the children—"he probably tells our cat Waif more than he tells me, because he knows that Waif can't repeat anything." Patricia admits she never loved to cook, but she coaxed Henry to expand his preference for Iowa meat and potatoes and try Italian and Mexican dishes, knowing he would still be drawn to lima beans and fried liver and onions served cafeteria-style at Luby's restaurants all over Texas.

From the outside looking in, Patricia gradually chipped away at the hard edges of her so-called numbers man, embracing her roles as wife and mother and never really wanting more. "She just quietly works her magic and moves around him, and makes happen what she needs to happen for her and for the children," said Michele Rollins, who immediately liked Patricia when they met in the late 1970s. "And it's to her credit and it's to his benefit. They have a wonderful relationship."

The Tippies established the parameters of their relationship from the moment they married and started a family in Delaware, continuing to embrace their separate roles as provider and homemaker when they moved to Georgia and then Texas. And neither Henry nor Patricia, it appears, ever wanted those roles to be any different.

"Some wives push and want to be everything and go everywhere," said Patricia. "I don't think Tip wanted me to have the role of a successful businessman's wife. He wanted me to be a mother and a wife. And we've always had our separate thing: I was the mother and he was the provider. I really am a homebody. He's gone to some things alone that probably I should have been with him, but I think the two of us feel more comfortable living the simple life."

A SIMPLE LIFE IN TEXAS

A simple life is definitely what the Tippies sought when they moved to Austin in late 1970. Still somewhat distressed from living in an Atlanta neighborhood where they felt socially out of place, they purposely avoided overly affluent neighborhoods when looking for their next home. Driving through the Austin city neighborhoods, Henry shook his head at the sight of grand mansions with three- or four-car garages. "I wonder how many of those homes are actually paid for," Henry would say, "and how many are just virtually there." Too, from his earliest days as an accountant in Iowa, Henry never forgot the lessons he learned by processing individual clients' tax returns. "That was fascinating," he recalled of his supposedly wealthy clients. "I would see their names in the newspaper, but I had done their tax returns, and I knew they had this show going on and some were having a hard time buying breakfast. But if I have a roof that doesn't leak and we have food on the table, I've always felt that we don't need to put on a display and Patricia feels the same way."

The Tippie family in Austin, Texas.

The Tippies stayed true to their beliefs about wealth and settled into a relatively modest four-bedroom ranch house with a small backyard, situated on a corner lot on the northwest side of Austin in an upper-middle-class neighborhood. While Henry focused on work, Patricia made sure the family got settled into their new lives. She immediately enrolled the three children in the local public schools, and the entire family was relieved to know that there would be no busing across town. Patricia found a Methodist church that she liked, and one of the Kingsbery wives invited her to join a garden club that helped Patricia make the friends she never quite found in Atlanta. The Tippies did not seek, nor would they ever accept, membership in a country club. "My mother used to say, 'Water seeks its own level,'" Patricia once said. "My friends have always been church people, Newcomers, and I just feel more comfortable with people who don't have a lot of wealth and don't like to socialize and have parties."

Like slipping into a comfortable pair of shoes instead of couture fashion pumps, the Tippies did not flaunt their wealth in Austin. If they made donations to deserving institutions in the Austin area, they kept it quiet. Years later, when their wealth and their philanthropic endeavors in other states became a matter of record in several local newspaper and magazine stories, almost all of their friends were genuinely shocked. They had no idea the unassuming couple with three children were exceedingly wealthy. "I like to fly under the radar," Henry once said. "I don't pat myself on the back, and I would have to say that Patricia and I did not change our lifestyle as our financial situation improved. So whatever gains we had, and they were certainly substantial, we just kept them and intended to live like we always lived, just like it didn't exist. I've watched others out here, frittering theirs away, and that was never going to be me."

In addition to their housing choice, Henry and Patricia raised their children in an environment that reflected modesty in possessions, from clothing to cars. "I bought each of them a nice pair of jeans, and if they wanted another pair, they had to earn the money for it," said Patricia. "The girls and Henry, all three earned money babysitting. And I think it's a good thing for them. Tip and I came from hardworking parents; neither of us had very much growing up. Everything we had, we earned on our own, and I think we feel that's the best way for our kids to do it."

Though they eventually dined in wonderful restaurants around the world, Henry always made sure that his family was equally comfortable at fast food restaurants and chain establishments, and Patricia's simple home-cooked meals were a given. And while Henry enjoyed buying himself a Rolex watch and expensive but tasteful jewelry and clothing for Patricia for special occasions, they never flaunted their purchases.

Henry with his mother, Amelia.

Henry also enjoyed giving presents to his mother. The devoted son regularly arranged for Amelia to fly out from Belle Plaine to Austin to see the grandchildren—trips that were routinely documented in the *Belle Plaine Union* in the social columns. But Amelia didn't make the trip as often as the Tippies would have liked, because her time was limited. Amelia's lifelong work ethic continued well into her 80s as she enjoyed working at the local flower shop, walking to work from her home each day.

THE PRICE OF SUCCESS

Henry's work ethic certainly mirrored the work patterns established by Amelia and Bob. And while the focus on work and career paid off handsomely in terms of financial security for Henry and Patricia and their three children, the Tippie family was the first to recognize that it may have come with a price.

Patricia feels that Henry, in his quest to be the ultimate provider, may have missed out with his children. "I don't think Tip had enough time for our children. But he tells me there are sacrifices. Especially when they were teenagers and he was back in Delaware. But he was always home when the bad things would happen, a car wreck, and he had to get involved when the girls started dating, because I needed him. If you're not around, though, you miss the band concerts and the baseball games and all of that. We didn't really think of it at the time. You think of these things when the children are older, that maybe you've missed some of it. And then you say, well, you have to make sacrifices. But when you're going through it, you just don't realize it."

Henry admitted, in a very raw and candid statement, that "I am not a person that anyone gets close to. And I'm not as close to my kids as I should be—and that has bothered me." And then he tried to put the situation into perspective, substituting emotions with facts. "This gets back to my era, in the country, you grew up different. There wasn't a lot of hugging." He believes, too, that he is simply a "product of the times," growing up as he did during the Depression, knowing he had to find a path off the farm that would lead to a better future. His generation of "head of the household" male providers focused on work and careers; there was no widespread recognition that fathers should participate in the everyday activities of children. "I'm trying to do things out here as I see it, and have integrity and honesty and try to do the right thing and that's not always easy," Henry concluded, without being defensive. "I know younger generations look at it differently, but I'm from the generation that needed to provide. And I think that I should do whatever I have to do and then Patricia's role is to be the homemaker. That doesn't mean she isn't a full partner, it's just that we have different roles, no different than in business. I think we are in full agreement on that. I think Patricia should receive a large part of that credit, for the way the children turned out."

Patricia always recognized that she knew Henry better than anyone else, that she is the only person he fully shares his heart with. So Patricia became Henry's voice, expressing the sentiments that he wasn't always able to put into words. "I don't think he's told them enough that he's proud of them," she explained. "I've always told the kids how Daddy felt and that he loves them. I'm probably closer to them than he is, and this could be because he is so busy. And I'm a mother. Maybe mothers are always closer to their children than fathers. But I think he sort of let the family be my department. And I think what they wanted was love."

It wasn't always easy for Patricia, and she recalled different challenges with each child. She missed having Henry around for father-son

Henry II, Helen, and Linda during Helen's high school graduation.

adventures or spontaneous talks with Henry II; she needed Henry's guidance when Helen was a rebellious teenager and ran away from home; and Patricia thought her heart would break the day Linda watched a neighbor swinging his little girl around by the arms in the backyard next door, and wondered out loud, "Why doesn't my daddy do that?"

Not surprisingly, perhaps, each of the three Tippie children expressed a different perspective on Henry's involvement, or lack of involvement, in their childhoods.

Henry II, for instance, always thought that his father was a "tremendous male figure" who set high standards for him. And Henry II clearly achieved. He was elected president of his senior class in high school, enjoyed making announcements over the radio, and developed an outgoing, unguarded personality. Of the three children, Henry II believes that he sought his father's approval the most. "I think maybe I wanted to do well because I wanted to please. If he's told me in recent years that he's proud of me, maybe I have gotten over wanting to hear that. It used to matter, though, and I was disappointed that it wasn't verbalized, but it was verbalized from other people."

As Henry II matured, he understood both of his parents much better. "As a child, you watch, you observe, and that becomes part of you. In my dad, I saw someone who works very hard, someone who is honest and has integrity, and someone who is committed to his wife. Someone who says,

'These are the rules in my house and you're not going to have long hair, and that's how it's going to be.' There are no gray areas, and I think more people should be like that. Your word is supposed to mean something. Mom and Dad were good parents. And I don't think he was a missing father. He traveled for work. I don't think you have to like it, but I think it's just part of doing business sometimes. I don't think it is a requirement to be a good parent to be at home every day."

Born just thirteen months after Henry II, Helen couldn't be more different from her brother. Patricia calls her the "free spirit" of the family who inherited Henry's hardheadedness and fierce independence; when Helen hit her teens, she already had a mind of her own and pursued choices her parents found hard to accept. "I'm not proud of those days," Helen said with a laugh, recalling that she ran away from home a few times and hung around Austin's fairly substantial fringe crowd. But she insists she wasn't rebelling against her parents. "I just felt like I could do what I wanted, that's all. And we would go to the park and play football and things like that. They just didn't like the people I was hanging out with. But it was not a big deal, they just had long hair and were kind of free."

Helen always knew where her parents stood. For instance, she remembered when she first started dating a guy who had really long hair and rode a motorcycle. "And you know how that must have hit! I wasn't allowed to go out with him until he had a car. And Dad never said I couldn't go out with him, but you knew he didn't like it. Mom would tell me later what he said. She was the one that would always kind of let us know. But you knew when he didn't like something. You just knew. But he would never say anything. I knew it wasn't going to change my mind. He would be polite and shake his hand and all, but you knew. So maybe he wanted us to find out for ourselves."

But unlike Henry II, Helen was spared the pain of not receiving approval from her dad simply because she never sought it. "I didn't think I needed approval for anything because I wasn't going to get it. They would say, 'You can't,' and I would say, 'I'll see you later.'" When she took off from home to hang out with her friends, she pushed Patricia beyond her limits as a parent. "There were times," said Linda, who had a front-row seat to the drama, "like the weekend my sister ran away from home and my mother refused to talk to her, that my dad would go and talk to her." In those trying times, Henry was forced to reach out to his daughter, using parenting skills he probably never knew he had to keep her close and not push her away. "He would meet me for lunch or come by where I was working at the clothes store and he would just ask me how I was doing. He wasn't talking me into anything," she says. During those talks, Henry never blew up at Helen and never tried to talk her into coming back home; he simply tried to give his daughter room to grow and the chance to learn from her mistakes.

In many respects, keeping Helen close was perhaps Henry's finest parenting hour, one that both Helen and Patricia later deeply appreciated. Helen would one day attribute the special way she and Henry sometimes relate to those heady, tumultuous days and how Henry handled them. "I think we had to have more talks," she explained, "because I got into trouble and we had to talk, he and I, more than the other two. But when it comes to the three of us, I won't say we wish we knew him better, because we all see him differently. But I wouldn't change anything. I like him the way he is. He doesn't talk much about himself, but why should you? He is a private person. There are just some things that people don't need to know. He doesn't do a lot of small talking."

For Linda, the youngest of the three Tippie children, Henry always seemed a little more distant. "He can be difficult to understand," she noted. "My mom has told us that there is a side of my father that only she knows—so we've heard that throughout the years—and you always kind of wonder, 'Well, what? And why not?'"

Listening to Linda talk about her father illustrates perfectly why it is often difficult to understand Henry. She says without hesitation that "our father has overcome a lot, and we are very proud of him. I wouldn't want to change a thing about him." But she wishes that she could be introduced to the warm side he rarely shows. "I mean," she says, "when do you let your guard down, and when do you stop being the tough guy?" While admonishing his "tough guy" persona, however, she admits she marvels at her father's strength of character, and how far he has come. "It's really amazing when you read about his background and his history and what he's done. I've come to realize that he grew up in a harder time. And as much as people think he's just a little square farm boy from Iowa, he's actually quite open to different things. I don't know where he got that character from. Maybe because if you're poor, it doesn't matter what culture or color you are. You all still have that same feeling. I think he is very open until he has all the facts. He's quite the fact gatherer. 'Let's not make our opinion until we gather all the facts.' And maybe that's because he was judged when he was younger. It's like that old cliché: 'Never judge a book by its cover.'"

A WALK ALONG THEIR FATHER'S PAST: A RANCH IN GEORGETOWN

In 1973 Henry took an ambitious step to connect with his children that also brought each of them closer to understanding him and how he grew up. With Henry II and Helen in high school, and Linda not far behind, Henry decided it was time for his children to be exposed to country life. So he bought a 500-acre ranch outside Austin in a rural area called Georgetown, a beautiful property that backed up to the South San Gabriel River.

With the Georgetown ranch, Henry met several goals. Ever since living in Delaware, Henry had been eager to get back to the land and own a farm. Henry was immediately attracted to the Georgetown spread, a gorgeous working ranch for raising a few cattle and growing hay. The property featured several ponds, groves of beautiful trees, and a natural, rolling habitat, along with a sprawling, one-story ranch house with three bedrooms for his family and another house closer to the road that would serve as living quarters for the ranch caretakers. Both Henry and Patricia loved it.

Georgetown ranch entrance.

Said Henry, "I'm mystified by those who get out in the business world and they don't want to be associated with being from a rural background. I don't know why. I am proud to be from a farm and be able to accomplish a few other things. But it kinda gets back to being a product of the land. I am a product of the land, and I'm proud of it."

Patricia called the Georgetown ranch "my little piece of heaven."

Said Patricia, "I called it my little piece of heaven. Georgetown was full of nature and trees. I've always loved being outdoors and working in the yard. One time I was sitting on the porch and the deer walked right up and I heard the wind coming up over the hill and I thought, 'This is heaven, God, and I don't care if I die right now!'"

Patricia and Henry soon filled the house with some of Henry's favorite possessions from his past: a piano from his grandmother, and furniture from Belle Plaine. In time, Henry even built a new climate-controlled facility at the ranch, just to house all of the memorabilia he had collected over the years, enormous piles of stuff that Patricia couldn't wait to get out of Austin. "He's very sentimental about the past and his childhood and where he lived," she said. "That's why he keeps everything under the sun."

Henry and Patricia also believed that the country life would benefit their children, who they thought needed an escape from teenage temptations and the reckless decision making the concerned parents were beginning to see among their peers in Austin. For the conservative Tippies, Austin's growing reputation for counterculturalism and its unofficial city slogan, "Keep Austin Weird," was pretty shocking, and they had already seen its impact on Helen. Frankly, if Henry couldn't tolerate this sort of free spirit culture in his first radio station, he certainly wasn't going to needlessly expose his children to it. "At that time, it was not good for young people in terms of being in the city," said Henry, and the ranch soon became a haven and a destination for the family every weekend.

"We would leave Austin on Friday evening and come back on Sunday evening," said Henry. "That way I had them out there. We did work out

Henry works with his children at the ranch.

Henry II, Helen, and Linda help bale hay.

there, picking up brush, picking up stones, baling hay. I really enjoyed that, but it was work from the kids' standpoint. But I know that at a much later date they look back upon that with a high degree of appreciation for having that kind of atmosphere. Some of their friends here in town wanted to come up and assist in making hay and spend the weekend. And so they would work out in the hay fields and after that they would have a guitar or something so they would have their own fun. It kept everybody busy and out of trouble. I think the big thing with young people is to have something they need to do, so they don't have time on their hands. And that's what that place provided."

Henry II learned to appreciate the Georgetown experiences for a lot of reasons. "We worked all weekend," he said, laughing. "We would leave on Friday and come back Sunday nights, and then I'd hear what everyone else had been up to. That way, I got to learn from everyone else's mistakes. In high school, students just seem to get into trouble. And though I probably didn't really appreciate that at the time, I learned to recognize that my parents were just really devoted and that the Lord was protecting us on the ranch."

According to Linda, the most important thing that Henry and Patricia passed on to their kids is honesty. She recalls her parents saying, "Just be honest with us and everything will be okay, because if you're dishonest, you can get into trouble." Linda learned this lesson the hard way one day when her parents returned unexpectedly from the ranch when she had just turned 16 years old.

"I remember one time, they said they were going out to the ranch, and I had just gotten my license and I took his Continental for a spin. I bet I wasn't gone 30 minutes and I got back in the driveway and they were home," she said. "I didn't know if I should just keep driving and never come home or what! So I pull in and I walked in the kitchen. They didn't yell. But we had the talk, 'Where have you been?' and 'I'm disappointed.' Which is worse than somebody going ballistic on you. I mean, my heart was in my throat. We talked about the dangers that could have happened, and again, they were not yelling, they would just chat with you and you would slink back to your room. You can't just look him in the eye and not tell the truth. You just feel terribly guilty, it's like he would know."

GROWING CHILDREN, SENTIMENTAL TIES

Though Henry always provided handsomely for his family, his generosity stopped far short of spoiling his children. "We have never helped our children financially," Patricia explained. And when it came time to send his kids to college, Henry was happy to do so, but his plan would reflect the way they had been brought up, without the trappings of affluence.

"We always lived average. I think we all feel good about that," said Henry. "And when they went to college, they were not provided automobiles to go to school. My program for going to college was this: I will pay for your tuition, your room and board, your books and supplies, but you're going to live in a dormitory. There will be no apartments, and no automobiles, and no charge cards. If you need some spending money, get a job. If you graduate, I will give you a brand-new car of my choice. And the bottom line is, I gave two automobiles, to Henry and Linda. And Helen got married."

Between Henry II's junior and senior year in college, Henry made time to take his son on a trip to the South Pacific, retracing the steps in his military career when he served in the 20th Air Force. Henry fondly remembers the vacation and many details of the trip: "We were gone three weeks. Patricia didn't go, it was just the two of us. We started in Guam and toured everything under the sun. Henry II celebrated his 20th birthday over there, and we had a luncheon with the governor of Guam and everyone sang 'Happy Birthday' to him. I recalled that I had spent my nineteenth birthday over there and, of course, no one was singing to me! We then went to the Philippines, then to Bangkok, and wound up in Hong Kong, where we headed for home. We had a great time."

As their children attended college, found jobs, married, and started their own families, Henry and Patricia returned to traveling. On a wall in their Austin home, they put up a world map that was soon decorated with colorful thumbtacks, marking all of the places they visited: the Great Lakes, Hawaii, Antarctica, Italy, South America, France, England, Bangkok, Hong Kong, and Russia. Helen likes to see her father enjoying his life. "I'm glad that he gets to do what he wants to do. He always worked when he was little. He had to get up early, deliver the milk, and then go

Henry and Patricia in Antarctica.

to school. We have it easy now. I'm sure it's been really hard for him. So I think everything he did was to change things for himself. And to help his mom out, she had it tough, and he would do anything for her. Everything has sort of come together for him. I mean, I think he's enjoying life; I think he's done a great job with all of us, both he and Mom together. I think they work well together."

There's never been any question that Patricia Bush Tippie is devoted to Henry B. Tippie. And there's never been any doubt that she fell in love with him the moment she danced with Henry on their first date in Delaware in 1955. Twenty-five years after that first dance, Patricia was in Georgetown, riding up to the ranch house in 1980 when she heard a song on the radio, sung by Anne Murray and called "Could I Have This Dance?" She sat in the car listening, knowing that the lyrics perfectly captured the way she felt about Henry on their first date and every night since:

I'll always remember the song they were playing,
The first time we danced and I knew.
As we swayed to the music and held to each other,
I fell in love with you.

Could I have this dance for the rest of my life?
Would you be my partner, then every night?
When we're together it feels so right,
Could I have this dance for the rest of my life?

I'll always remember that magic moment,
When I held you close to me.
As we moved together, I knew, forever,
You're all I'll ever need.

Henry and Patricia in Hawaii.

CHAPTER NINETEEN

TIPPIE COMMUNICATIONS

HENRY ESSENTIALLY RAN KINGSTIP, INC., by himself, but he still had business partners involved in that operation. So when he stepped away from Kingstip in 1979, Henry was truly on his own for the first time in his career. At the age of 52, he established Tippie Communications, Inc., in Austin. Over the next six years, from 1979 to 1985, Henry acquired four radio stations and built Tippie Communications into a highly profitable media company. In the process, he returned to the media business arena that he had first encountered with Rollins Broadcasting and then continued through Kingstip, when he transformed the college station into an easy-listening format station. And he proved beyond a shadow of a doubt that he could operate on his own and that his success did not depend on being in business with others.

It's important to recognize that each purchase Henry made under Tippie Communications further illustrated one of his favorite business maxims, one first honed during his days with the Rollins brothers: It's financially beneficial to buy a business that needs work rather than to buy one that's already successful. "Bootstrapping," Henry once explained, turned out to be one of his favorite approaches to buying and creating a business. "I buy one that has gone broke, reorganize it, and make a success out of it. I'd much rather work with something that's a problem, in contrast to buying something that's very well run. Why? Because, one, you have to pay a big

KVLY-FM's former location in a mobile home.

premium for a well-run organization, and two, can you really keep it running that well? Now if you find a company that's gone broke at a fire-sale price, you can't go down much further with it. Your investment is going to be less, the exposure less. But the rewards can really be far greater than buying something well run. I've developed a lot of companies over the years, and it's been a good road."

The first of the four stations Tippie Communications acquired was located in Edinburg, Texas. This FM station, known as KVLY, but originally known as KESI, covered the entire Rio Grande Valley in deep south Texas and featured an easy-listening format. When Henry bought it, the Edinburg station was based in a mobile home because the previous facility had recently been destroyed by a fire. In fact, the previous owner had originally operated the radio station as an AM/FM combination, but he decided to keep the AM bandwidth and sell the FM station because he didn't have enough insurance to rebuild both. Henry renovated the nearby Yazoo lawnmower sales and service building to serve as the new headquarters for the beleaguered FM station, which soon found a home in the single-story, white brick building with a red hip roof.

A FATHER-AND-SON BUSINESS TEAM

The purchase of KVLY represented a new chapter in Henry's life in more ways than one: Not only was he finally his own boss, but he was about to employ for the first time a member of his own family—his son, Henry II.

After graduating from Texas Tech with a degree in accounting, Henry II landed a job with Procter & Gamble in Memphis, Tennessee. He had been with the company for only a few months, working in sales, when his father flew out to Memphis for a visit in 1979. "He came to tell me that he had bought a radio station," Henry II said, "and asked me if I would like to come to work for him." The father reminded the son that he had enjoyed working with radio broadcasting in high school: "You have always liked that, and I want you to think about going into business with me."

Henry II took the weekend to make his decision. Though Henry II favors his father in looks and is all business like his dad, the son has always been more charismatic and extroverted than the father and early on considered a career as a politician or a minister. He realized that he could probably grow and learn more in a company with his own namesake than with Procter & Gamble, though he was initially skeptical of the daunting prospect of working with his dad. Said Henry II, "I thought he would be very demanding and have high standards. I knew that he was going to be a hard person to work for. And I thought a father-and-son thing would be difficult. But then I felt that there was probably not going to be any better teacher than him. The business was going to have our name on it, and he would be an excellent person to learn from."

Henry accepted his father's offer. Tippie Communications now included Henry in Austin, overseeing the daily sales reports and the overall finances, while Henry II initially kept the books for KVLY. It wasn't long before the situation tested the father-son relationship.

As Henry II remembered, "I was going to keep the books because it was a single operation. I had been writing the checks and keeping the ledger and Dad came down and said, 'Man, it's all wrong. We gotta start over. I thought you had an accounting degree.' So I said, 'Well, that was all

New KVLY headquarters.

Henry and Henry II pictured with staff members.

theory in college.' So we redid the books. He's an accountant, and we were not going to dinner till we got this fixed."

And while the moment could have been discouraging, Henry's follow-up that evening provided a lesson Henry II never forgot. "He said to me, 'You're going to make mistakes. And I'm willing to pay for that, because it's like taking a course. I just don't want to pay for the same mistakes and the same course twice.' So I could make mistakes as long as I learned from them and didn't repeat them. And he said to me, and he meant it, that hopefully I would not make any costly mistakes."

After hiring his son, Henry ran an ad in the local papers near Edinburg looking for a new announcer: "Radio Announcers Wanted." Tony Abrego saw the ad and knew this was his chance. Since he was five years old, this Edinburg native had dreamed of being a radio announcer, listening closely on his portable radio to all of the broadcasters and trying to mimic their style. He knew, without anyone telling him, that his Hispanic accent would work against him—"I had a pretty heavy accent, sort of like a Spanglish thing going on"—so he bought a black-and-white television set and made himself listen to newscaster Tom Brokaw in order to improve his pronunciation and speech. "At the time, I was working in a factory when I saw there was a little ad for a radio announcer in the paper, and I thought, 'That's not going to happen.' But I went and Mr. Tippie called me back and then he hired me. My first job in radio was as an announcer, on the air every day, six hours."

Tony worked for the station for 10 years. He described the Tippies' father-son working relationship as "at times intense because Mr. Tippie wanted to be sure of Henry's success in business. Mr. Tippie wanted to make sure that Henry understood the expectations to be met, when they would be met, and how they would get done."

Tony admits that he never had a particularly close relationship with Henry II. "My fondest business memories are directly from Mr. Tippie. I was a sponge around Mr. Tippie when he would come into town. If you called me ignorant in 1979, it would have been a compliment. Mr. Tippie gave me an opportunity to learn business, from the ground up. No one could have gotten the education I got, had he not stretched his most generous hand and supported my broadcasting career."

Along with business advice, Henry didn't hesitate to share some of his life's perspectives with Tony, too. When Tony bemoaned his hard times as "a Hispanic in deep south Texas," someone "raised here and there" and "only given low expectations," Henry was quick to admonish the man who was just a few years older than his own son: "You don't know hard times, Tony. When I graduated from college, I lived in a YMCA." Henry's stories would snap Tony back to the reality that people who started life with fewer advantages could still be a success. "Sometimes," he realized, "all an individual needs is a mentor of great character."

TIPPIE COMMUNICATIONS EXPANDS

By 1980 Henry was ready to expand Tippie Communications. In the next five years he purchased three more stations: an AM station in McAllen, Texas; an FM rock station in Corpus Christi, Texas; and an FM station in Colorado Springs, Colorado, with a predominantly female audience. Again, the conditions of each station had deteriorated to the point where Henry purchased each for a bargain and started rebuilding. And some of the stations came with their own Texas-style tall tales.

For example, Henry recalled that he purchased the rock station in Corpus Christi from an estate, amid rumors that the previous owner was the son of a judge and had died of a heart attack, though his business associates always allowed that the death may have been drug-related. Members of the Hell's Angels motorcycle gang showed up at the previous owner's funeral, and radio station employees later noted that it was quite a scene. Henry quickly moved to impose controls and systems on a radio station that had had none, and the station was profitable after one month.

The AM station in McAllen, Texas, provided another interesting story. Ranked third in its market, Henry bought the station for a good price, but the deal didn't close for nearly a month; during that time, the station was off the air for two and a half weeks, and the audience drifted away and didn't come back (Henry later wondered whether the previous owner had padded the ratings numbers in order to make a sale). Faced with a near fiasco, Henry ended up giving the station license to the local Bible institute in exchange for a tax deduction; the move pleased everyone, including Henry II, who was very involved with the religious organization. And even though the station had failed, Henry had what many often referred to as his "exit strategy"—a plan that would turn the venture into a financial gain. For Henry, that exit strategy included keeping the 26 acres around the transmitter site. When he sold the land some 16 years later, the once-rural site was at the end of a major thoroughfare coming out of McAllen, and much more valuable than if he had sold it when he donated the radio license. Recalled Henry: "I always felt it would be worth considerably more, and that has proven to be the case. I always said that land would be my bailout."

With the exception of the McAllen station, the three stations under Tippie Communications all became highly successful. In 1982 Henry established Tippie Services, Inc., in Austin to serve as an umbrella organization for his ranch activities and his radio stations. Between the four business locations, the Tippies employed more than 75 associates and adopted the motto, "Working to serve the community in which we live." And as Tippie Communications grew, Henry continued to promote his son, giving him more and more responsibilities. In 1988 the father-and-son team determined that Dick Delaney and Bill McCrae, the two men who had been in charge of the day-to-day

Henry II celebrates a station milestone.

operations of the stations, were not going to run the company anymore. "It would be me running it," Henry II recalled.

Henry II was, in theory, managing the entire company when he moved to Colorado Springs in 1988 to run the station there. In this new role, Henry II immediately recognized that "I had more flexibility than others did to do innovative things. For instance, in our business I thought that we needed to be up to speed with technology, and we became the first radio station to have a website." Now married with his own family, Henry II also had a renewed respect for how his parents raised him and his two sisters, discovering that he and his wife, Judie, wanted to raise their three children the same way. "We wanted to raise our children so that they had a work ethic, that we don't give them a lot of things," he said. "Our folks made sure we learned the value of money, of work, and the value of giving. That's just been a part of my DNA, my wife's DNA, and now it's a part of my children's DNA."

But there's no question that the working relationship was at times extremely difficult. Henry rarely, if ever, praised his son publicly or privately. And Henry II's biggest frustration with his father was always wondering, "Can I do enough to please you?" According to both men, they went through stages in their working relationship when both wondered whether they could continue. Patricia knew how much Henry expected of their son, and how tough he could be on him. "Linda heard Tip talking to Henry one day on the phone," Patricia recalled, "and she said, '*I* wouldn't work for him.'"

It all came to a head one weekend, during a series of contentious telephone calls between Texas and Colorado that began on a Friday night. Henry never commented publicly about the disagreement, except to say that it "worked out." But Henry II remembered it, word for word:

> **Friday night:** "If I'm really supposed to be running this, you really ought to let me do this," Henry II told his father. "But what you're really telling me is that I'm not running this company, you are."
> **Sunday afternoon:** Henry called to tell his son that he would miss dinner with the staff the next week: "I'm not coming." Said Henry II: "Look, if you're not going to let me do the things I want to do,

then I will go work for someone else and you're going to find out what you're losing."

Sunday night: "All right," said Henry to Henry II. "You run the company."

For the son, it was a watershed moment. "I don't know what he and Mom talked about that weekend, but he decided, 'All right,' and he let me run the company instead of him. But that was a swing weekend in our business relationship. That was a milestone, a marker, and it was good."

Until 1996 Henry and Henry II continued operating Tippie Communications and the three radio stations in Edinburg, Corpus Christie, and Colorado Springs. Though Henry II was in charge, Henry never dropped the "management by walking around" style he perfected as an executive at Rollins and Rollins Truck Leasing, and he regularly visited each station. Tony, the announcer, recalled that in Edinburg, the staff pulled out "white gloves when Mr. Tippie came to town. He wanted everything in order, everything tidy and clean, a good working environment. He would walk in quietly—no one knew when he arrived—and we would see him running his fingers over counters, shelves to see if there was dust there. He cared about his investments and his business."

Tony enjoyed recalling the day Henry came to town to take the top sales force out to lunch. "Mr. Tippie would drive up in his Cadillac and take everyone to McDonald's. And he'd remind us, 'Every dollar counts.'" And one of Tony's favorite stories involved the time Henry awarded him $500 for cutting costs at the station, a yearly bonus that he pledged to the staff if they could "trim the budget without trimming quality. As Mr. Tippie always said, 'Unnecessary expense saved is the easiest profit made.'" During the celebration at the station, Henry praised Tony, sharing the story of the long-term DJ's early efforts to learn English by buying a television and listening to news anchor Tom Brokaw. "Tony didn't know how to speak English and he went out and learned," Henry boomed to the crowd, Tony recalled. "And I thought the blood on Henry II's face would drop to the floor! We were getting more and more into political correctness at that time, and Henry II thought that would wreck me. But I thought, 'That's absolutely true!' Mr. Tippie was just complimenting me."

TIPPIE'S LAWS

Henry II often joked that he started to talk like his father after working for him for nearly 17 years. *There are no shortcuts in businesses. It's not how much you sell, it's how much you collect. Assume nothing.* With his father's voice in his head, Henry sat down in 1995 to write his quarterly "TipSheet" column in *The Tippie Communicator,* a quarterly newsletter for associates of Tippie Communications. "Remember any past mistakes just long enough so that we can all profit from them," Henry II wrote, a line that sounded just like something his father would say, an echo of the very words Henry had spoken to his son in 1979 when he started working for him.

Within a year of Henry's writing this particular "TipSheet" column, the father-and-son team decided it was time to sell the three radio stations. The reason why was very simple. In 1996 Congress changed the rules for ownership of radio stations, clearing the way for major conglomerates. This move caused the value of radio and television stations to increase dramatically.

Henry II and his father had already decided that they were not going to buy more stations—the prices were just too high after the new ruling. "So we knew that if we weren't going to be a buyer, we had to be a seller," Henry II recalled. "I remember saying to my dad, 'You always told me to run them as a good operator, so let me put on my hat and ask, What can we sell them for?' We were being offered very large sums of money to sell." And after years of disagreements, the Tippies did not once disagree about their last move. Said Henry II, "He was a majority owner, and I was a minority owner, and we were both in agreement."

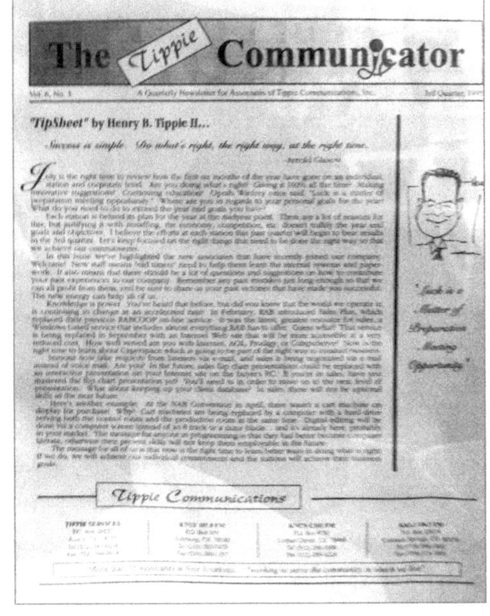
The Tippie Communicator

"TipSheet" by Henry B. Tippie II...

Tippie Communications

Henry II's "TipSheet" column in *The Tippie Communicator.*

Always known for his impeccable timing, Henry sold the stations to three different chains "for considerable monies" in the fall of 1996. For Henry, the sale of all assets in Tippie Communications meant stepping away from an industry that he had been involved with since 1953 . . . the industry that first introduced him to the Rollins brothers and brought him to Delaware where he met Patricia . . . the industry that made him a millionaire many times over and helped him launch his own enterprise in Texas . . . the industry that had allowed him to prove to himself that he could make it in business on his own. But make no mistake: for Henry, selling Tippie Communications and leaving the industry was a smart business transaction, not one wrapped up in nostalgia. "That was my exit out of the broadcast industry after 43½ years," he said, simply, after the sale. "It was a good business."

In honor of his father's accomplishments and their years working together, Henry II once put together a list of Henry's favorite sayings, "business basics that I had heard over and over from him." With Judie's help, Henry II named the list "Tippie's Laws." And over time, this list became an official and widely quoted summary of Henry B. Tippie's fundamental rules for business success:

Tippie's Laws

1. Assume nothing.
2. Say nothing, do nothing, be nothing.
3. When in doubt, ask.
4. Everybody sells by their attitude.
5. Do it 100 percent accurate and 100 percent complete.
6. Work smart.
7. Every day is a fresh start.
8. Time is money—don't waste it.
9. Do today's business today.
10. A premier product demands a premier price.
11. A sale is never complete until the money is in the bank.
12. Unnecessary expense saved is the easiest profit made.
13. Operate with a sense of urgency.
14. Think profit.

CHAPTER TWENTY

PRAIRIE HILL

ONE DAY, WHILE SITTING ON the cistern in his backyard on the farm near Belle Plaine, young Henry had a boyhood dream to own 160 acres of land. He figured that he would divide the land into "40 acres of corn, 40 acres of oats, another 40 for hay, and 40 for pasture for a few calves, hogs, and stuff. I could make a nice living on 160 acres."

Nearly four decades later, when he purchased 500 acres north of Austin on the outskirts of Georgetown in 1973, Henry exceeded his childhood dream to own 160 acres, and created a wonderful place where his children could experience life in the country. But the Georgetown property, with its rolling hay pastures, a few calves, and some cows, did not translate into the ranch enterprise that Henry now dared to dream about. A businessman and entrepreneur who had come a long way from his family's dairy farm in Iowa, Henry next wanted to operate a cattle ranch—not as a hobby or a leisure activity, but as a serious and successful operation. "I don't run hobby operations," Henry once said. "I run businesses."

In 1984 Henry started inquiring about potential ranch properties within driving distance of Austin. He ended up in Prairie Hill, a rural community less than two hours north of Austin and about 20 minutes off the I-35 exit at Waco. In this section of central Texas, the empty prairie stretches for miles without interruption, intersected only by country roads, fields where cattle graze, and clumps of mesquite and cedar trees that stand in stark silhouette against the horizon. Henry loved it. He knew he wanted to have a large operation, and he wanted to be able to expand and buy more land immediately adjacent to whatever property he purchased. Both opportunities existed around Prairie Hill in Limestone County, where small landowners and farmers still occupied a large portion of the area and properties frequently came up for sale. "My idea of expansion is this: I have no interest in land other than it has to adjoin to me. I don't want anything that is disjointed because there is a lot of time and expense involved in having to haul things around. If the land is adjacent and contiguous, you don't have to load cattle or equipment to move it around."

Henry started Tippie Ranch in Prairie Hill when he purchased 1,625 acres of prairie and ranch land in 1984. A later property addition included a sprawling one-story, tan brick home with two L-shaped wings that the Tippies soon called their own; the home, tucked into a dip of endless fields, sat at the end of a long, straight paved driveway lined on both sides by a white fence that eventually formed a white frame box around the house.

Patricia refurbished much of the home's interior, and even added a self-playing baby grand piano that featured Henry's favorite Big Band

The main house on Tippie Ranch in Prairie Hill, Texas, captured by Google Earth.

music in a corner of the massive, Texas-sized living room. From their front door, Patricia and Henry looked out over fields and a smattering of ponds that lay between their house and the main road, all connected by a twisty, shallow creek meandering through oak and cedar trees on the front side of the property. From their back patio, Patricia and Henry faced vast horizons and pasture fields, just steps away from grazing cows and Suzy, a pet donkey who helped to keep the coyotes away and enjoyed the crunchy feed the Tippies often held out in the palms of their hands for the animals.

Henry feeding livestock.

In this setting, Henry wore his cowboy hats and his favorite cowboy boots, ditching his business suits for comfortable jeans and flannel shirts. To get around his vast property, Henry kept a 1977 blue and white Chevy Blazer in his Prairie Hill garage that, over time, rolled over on 100,000 miles. And from his driver's seat, nothing gave Henry more pleasure than riding around describing his property, a process that could take four or five hours at least.

"You can tell where my place begins just by looking for my fence," said Henry, pointing to the side of the road where a distinctive fence separated the road from the expanse of cattle fields and pasture. The signature fence on Tippie Ranch is typically five to six strands of barbed wire, wrapped around cedar posts sticking up from the ground about every nine feet, with cedar-stick stays woven into the wire every three feet apart. This unpretentious, utilitarian fence stretches out endlessly over the landscape, where every vista seems to settle on land that belongs to Tippie Ranch. The mere sight of it will put a broad and satisfied smile on Henry's face, and he appears to even chuckle in delight as he gestures to the horizon on one side of the truck, and then sweeps his arm to point to the other side. "Tippie Ranch, as far as you can see in *that* direction," he declared, "and Tippie Ranch as far as you can see in *that* direction."

The signature fence on Tippie Ranch.

55 SQUARE MILES OF TIPPIE RANCH

Henry's claim to land "as far as you can see" would prove even truer the longer he owned his private slice of Texas. In over three decades, Henry patiently and carefully expanded his original 1,625-acre Prairie Hill ranch to include almost exactly 35,000 acres. That much territory, Henry loved to calculate, spans approximately 55 square miles, making Henry the largest private landowner in central Texas. Henry put his ranch together piecemeal through 150 different transactions that stretched north, south, and east of Prairie Hill, incorporating land that bordered other rural communities like Frosa to the southeast and Delia to the north on both sides of Highway 84 West. Not surprisingly, Henry always paid cash for the land. This strategy often gave him an advantage over potential buyers who had to secure loans before closing a deal, and it was a strategy that often swayed sellers who were desperate to sell.

As he acquired land, Henry kept a map in his Austin office that showed the outlines and plots of every transaction—a veritable patchwork quilt of land acquisitions where no two pieces were alike but each piece adjoined another along a common border. And Henry often noted that every transaction told a story.

"This land here—that was a tax sale and this one was from a divorce where the wife just wanted out, just one sad situation," said Henry, setting his finger on two plots of land between Highway 84 West and Country Road 359. "I've acquired land up here from tax sales, from divorces, from bankruptcies, from absentee ownership, from people that got into too much debt and wanted to try to get out, from people who have lost interest in agriculture, from older people who are just worn out—you name it. It's just unreal."

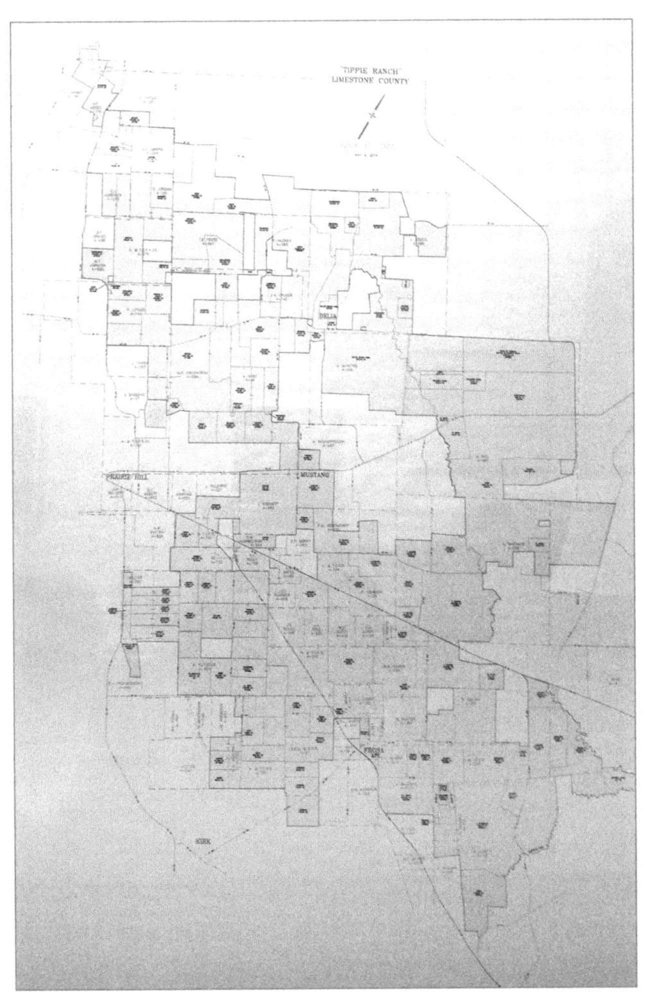

A map of the land parcels (shaded) that made up Tippie Ranch.

Henry took his time amassing the ranch properties. In addition to land, Tippie Ranch would one day include nearly 30 additional homes that he either rented out or provided as housing for his ranch staff; dozens of barns and storage facilities; hundreds of pieces of farm equipment, including 10 John Deere tractors and shredders; and over 6,000 head of cattle. “If anybody had told me back in 1984 that we’d be close to 35,000 acres, I would have laughed at them. Did I ever have any goals? Yes, but the thought was 5,000 acres. And I don’t ever rush to buy land. It takes patience. I don’t need it, I don’t have to have it.”

When buying land, Henry negotiated with the same eye for detail and frugal, bottom-line accounting tactics that he always used in acquiring or running his successful businesses or working with the Rollins family. Jack Mauldin, the former president of Groesbeck Title Company, which handled all of Henry’s acquisitions, recalled being constantly amazed at Henry’s attention to detail.

“I can remember one transaction in particular, it was about a million-dollar transaction,” said Mauldin. “The agreement was cut and dried—it was in writing. And it came right down to where there was a little fee that the seller was supposed to pay and the seller didn’t want to pay it. Well, the only other party in the transaction was the buyer, Mr. Tippie, and he said, ‘I’m not paying it. The agreement is this and you can pay it or I don’t buy your place.’ I thought it was so strange, on a million-dollar transaction, to worry about a $100 fee. I’m sitting there thinking, ‘You’re rich, why worry about this 100 bucks?’ And I asked him about it, and he said, ‘Well, Jack, I got here $100 at a time.’

“Another thing that’s really unique about Henry,” Mauldin continued, “is his tickler system or follow-up system. I’ll tell you about one transaction. There was a man who wanted to sell out lock, stock, and barrel—house, land, cows, tools, everything. It came time for closing and there had been a windstorm about a week before that damaged one of the barns. Well, if anything gets damaged during the contract period, the seller has to repair it because the time they went into contract they were at a certain condition and at closing they should be at the same condition or better. So we sat down at the table and Henry mentioned to the fellow, ‘When we signed the contract, there was a stack of lumber here at the barn and I noticed this morning when I came by on the way to closing that the stack was gone.' And the man said, 'Well, you know we had a windstorm and the barn was damaged so I used the lumber to fix the barn.' And Mr. Tippie reminded the man that that was his lumber, and his barn. The transaction still went off, but I'm just saying that he's a stickler for details."

From inside his 1977 Chevy Blazer, a rough-and-tumble version of the 2009 Ford 150 Platinum he later drove around his ranch, Henry is content to drive for hours, checking on his property, spot-checking his herd, stopping to speak with any one of the 10 ranch hands employed by Tippie Ranch.

"Mr. Tippie is very serious about what he does," said Charlie Williamson, a Beaumont, Texas–born rancher "about the same age as that Blazer," who grew up around horses and cattle and became the Tippie Ranch manager in 2014. "To work for a man like Mr. Tippie is one of the greatest honors you can ever have. You don't get many opportunities to work for a prestige place like this."

Tippie Ranch, as far as you can see.

Married with three children, Charlie had heard about the Tippie property for as long as he could remember. He manages Tippie Ranch with a crew of nine men: four are cowboys and the rest run the ranch shops, drive tractors, tend fields, and fix fences. This crew handles everything from "tractors to cattle to pastures to farming, and I mean daily. And you have to be proud of your team. They are caring for the cattle and this ranch as much as they care for their kids. Every morning, especially Monday, we start lists for the whole week. Mr. Tippie is big on lists, and I have patterned myself on that. I have lists. I have a list of what will be done, and I don't quit until I have it all checked off."

Charlie's lists frequently include starting on the east side of the ranch, making the rounds and "working" the cattle, which is another word for worming, castrating, ear marking, or giving vaccinations under a relatively new vaccination and medicine program promoted by auction houses like Superior Livestock. "It's a great plan for everybody," said Charlie. "Mr. Tippie has such a name for quality livestock—so all we try to do is better that every year."

When not working the cows, Charlie and his ranch team manage fields for growing crops like oats or hay and grass. If he sees that the grass in one pasture is "getting short, we need to move these cows and do what is best for the ranch." Charlie and the other ranch hands saddle up and ride their horses to herd the cattle to other areas, often with the use of specially trained dogs. "We can take two dogs on 100 head of cattle, and the dogs contain them—they are in front and we are in back. The biggest tools in a cowboy's life are a good horse and a good dog."

And Charlie is the first to admit that, in a very short time, he picked up a number of newer tools from Henry B. Tippie. "He's the best businessman I've ever seen or even heard about. You spend time with him and it wears off. It can be a challenge at times, because he doesn't slip any, and he doesn't expect you to. But dealing with men of his stature, I don't expect anything else. I wouldn't think as much of him if he weren't that way. But I respect that. He's expanded my horizons. We strive to make this a productive ranch. This is a business for Mr. Tippie, and that's the thing I like best about working here."

TIPPIE'S COWBOY LAWS

When it comes to ranching with 6,000 head of cattle, Henry has his own unique set of Tippie's Cowboy Laws, a few operating principles that reveal at once how much he knows about the ranching business and that he's a serious student of trends and developments.

Henry displays the American flag and the Tippie Ranch flag in Prairie Hill.

First, he said, "I like to be cattle short and grass long. There are a lot of places in south Texas and in west Texas that are much larger than Prairie Hill, but they can't run near the cattle that I do because they don't have the moisture. I have all these ponds and streams, and they aren't filled all the time but they fill up regularly enough, and my pastures don't run out of grass." Toward that goal, Henry uses what he calls a "high-intensity, low-frequency method" of pasture rotation, where the ranch hands keep cows in a small area and then move them out—a rotation that ensures the cows take the top of the grass, which has the most protein.

Second, he said, "I like to think that we're not a harem-scarem type operation. I run a cow-calf operation, and I know just about where every one of them came from." With 44 Farms and Black Angus bulls that they own, Tippie Ranch then breeds high-quality cows and heifers for calves, and then sells the calves at auction several times a year. "Almost all the calves are an Angus or a tiger stripe. It's a good hearty calf that probably has less health problems. The ranch has expanded so that we now precondition the calves with vaccinations, worming. We have a solid reputation for a healthy stock."

Henry always stayed actively involved in his ranch, traveling from Austin to Prairie Hill almost every other week, and never missing out when the cattle were weighed, sold, and shipped. "I like to run the scales when shipping cattle," he said. "We have an excellent reputation, and for a long time our calves have brought the top price in the sale for whatever our weight class is. And we know from feedback that the cattle do very well in the feedlots or in the pasture, and as a result we have many repeat buyers. You put up a Tippie lot and it will sell."

Russ de Cordova, a third-generation cattleman out of Groesbeck, vouches for the quality of Tippie Ranch products. He first started selling Tippie cattle through Superior Livestock's video satellite auction services in 1987, and they've been together ever since, with sales averaging twice a year. "When the 'Tippie Ranch' name comes up, we will never have to worry about getting the full market price, because they will bring top dollar," said Russ. "They literally top the market in almost every sale we have in the region that we are in, simply because he puts them up to sale."

Why are Tippie Ranch and Henry so successful? "Mr. Tippie educates himself very well, and he keeps up with the times," said Russ. "He wants to be the best there is, whatever business he is in. He asks me lots of questions, and he doesn't forget anything you say. Mr. Tippie is very conservative, and he utilizes his pastures very well. If he took a mind, he could probably run up to 6,500 cows—it's very good black land and productive grass—but he is conservative in that area. Typically, if he can make another dollar or two, he was all for it, but you have to produce."

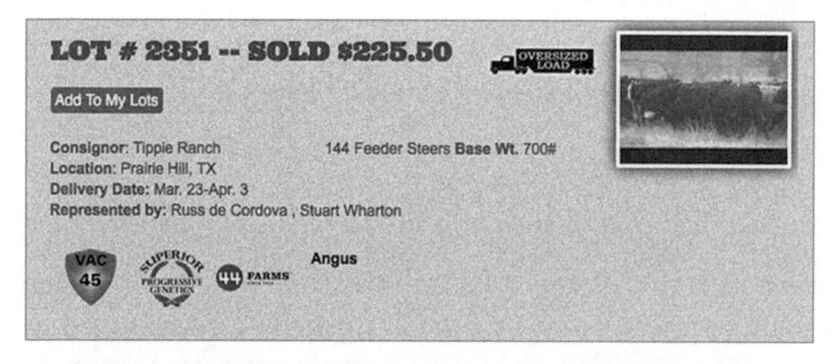

Superior Livestock's video satellite auction report shows Tippie Ranch livestock brought top dollar. For this lot of 144 head of steers, Tippie Ranch received $227,304 (700 lbs. x $225.50 = $1,578.50 per head x 144 head for $227,304).

Henry stands between cattleman Russ de Cordova of Superior Livestock (left) and Tippie Ranch manager Charlie Williamson (right).

"And with Mr. Tippie, if you don't mean it, you better not say it," Russ continued. "Just like he always says, 'Just the facts.' As long as you are totally honest, as long as you tell him like it is, there's not a better man to work for. I've had a very good relationship with Mr. Tippie and it's been an honor to know him. Coming from a dairy farm in Iowa and how he was raised, Mr. Tippie knows what a dollar is and what a penny is. He's proof that if you work hard and live your life and dedicate it to what you love, you can be successful."

Which brings up the third Tippie's Cowboy Law: Be a good steward of the land. Henry has won a smattering of environmental awards that recognize his efforts to leave his property a little better than he found it, a lesson he may have first learned from Wayne Rollins, who had extensive land holdings in Georgia and Florida. Though Henry prefers to keep the land in its natural beauty (he refuses to cut down any of the old oak trees), he sprays each year for mesquite brush, which can invade the land like a weed. "You've got to put something in the land to keep it productive. You can't just go out here and take, take, take—you have to worry about the weeds, thistle, and mesquite. If you don't stay after it, it will eventually take over. You have to put back in order to take." Though his land doesn't look landscaped, he often buys worn-out land, plows it, and works to improve it, including adding his signature fence line to what he calls "land with a gentle roll." It all points not only to a love of the land, but a love of business, too. "It is a business to me," said Henry. "I do enjoy being up here, but I enjoy business. My hobby is business."

If anything, the Tippie Ranch has provided another link to the Rollins family, who have owned and operated ranches in Georgia and Florida that include 30,000 acres of cattle ranches in Florida and another 5,000 acres for hunting. Henry and Randall have over the years discussed everything from the merits of drought-resistant jiggs Bermuda grass ("Randall is always trying to get me to plant jiggs") to breeding with Angus or black bulls ("The black grades better in the market, and it's easy to sell a black calf"). And like true businessmen, they are competitive. Said Linda Graham, "Mr. Tippie is so successful in his ranches. I say to Mr. Rollins, 'How does Mr. Tippie make money and we don't?'"

Gary Rollins laughed out loud when asked about the friendly competition between the Rollins brothers and Henry in the cattle business. "Usually you don't find people successful in business and cattle, but Henry has done it," he said. "He brought to the table his experience on the farm and common sense. I think Henry has had probably more time to work on it—Randall and I see it more like a hobby, but you don't dare mention that word to Henry. But I'm not trying to take anything away from his success. Henry has developed a reputation, and if the word gets out that you have healthy animals, you have more buyers."

On the subject of Henry and ranching, Randall just shakes his head and laughs, too. "It is very, very difficult to run a ranch," said Randall, "and Henry has done such a much better job at running a ranch than maybe we have! He has just stayed after that. Henry is a focuser. He just focuses like a laser, and he is focused on this ranch. He goes up and weighs the cattle when they ship them. I'm not involved enough to do that. I just don't spend the time with it that I should. That is the kind of excuse I give myself, because he is a hard competitor! Do I compete with Henry? Sure, we try to compete with him. It's just things like his cattle brought

X and ours brought Y—and why didn't ours bring X? And I mean it in a nice way."

Over the years, Henry and Patricia have generously shared Tippie Ranch with their friends—lining up special visits and coordinating chuck wagon barbecues for governors, university presidents and deans, college football coaches, corporate bankers, local ministers, and former Belle Plaine classmates and early Iowa business associates.

And through the eyes of those visitors, many see more than 55 square miles of Tippie-owned land and his successful ranching operation. They see a side of Henry that has nothing to do with business but has everything to do with the deep satisfaction of owning something he always dreamed of owning. As his friend and banking associate Ken Chalmers once said, "Henry can go out to the ranch and he can look as far as you can see, and that's *his* land. And my guess is that he says, 'That's my reward. This is what it's all about.'"

Michele Rollins, who admits to struggling at times to try to figure out the man who had such an impact on her husband John Sr. and his

Henry and Patricia on the ranch.

business fortunes, has decided that Prairie Hill might hold more than a few answers about Henry B. Tippie.

"There is a picture of Henry standing in the pasture with the cows," she said. "I had it enlarged because it was so spectacular—it was the man that nobody knew. And the truth is, how do you describe a cowboy? He's out there checking his cows, checking the fences, checking the calves. You have to be very content within the square framework of your mind. You have to be very content to be out there doing that. It's the loneliness of the cowboy."

Henry the cowboy, checking the herd in Prairie Hill.

CHAPTER TWENTY-ONE

THE HORATIO ALGER AWARD AND OTHER ROLLINS CONNECTIONS

HENRY AND PATRICIA ALWAYS CLAIMED they preferred to keep a low profile in Austin. And after 25 years in this Texas college town, it appeared that they had done just that.

By 1996, despite their growing philanthropic contributions to their two college alma maters and the town of Belle Plaine, the only real connections Henry and Patricia maintained in Austin were through their church community and the various clubs that Patricia had joined. Their three children were now grown and married, living elsewhere with a wonderful brood of nine grandchildren, so the Tippies were no longer involved with any of the local schools. Even Henry's business connections weren't widely known, despite the fact that he maintained an office suite in a northwest Austin office complex as headquarters for Tippie Services and once served as a director for the Texas Commerce Bank Norcross. Henry argued that "I just want to do my thing. And I don't want anyone to know what I'm doing."

How utterly successful Henry and Patricia had been in their 25-year quest for anonymity was revealed on Sunday, April 14, 1996, when the *Austin American-Statesman* landed on everyone's doorstep. The paper announced that two Austinites had been tapped to receive the prestigious Horatio Alger Award, a national honor given annually to men

D

Sunday, April 14, 1996

BUSINESS & PERSONAL FINANCE

Holistic finances
Understanding what's important in life and how you spend are good places to start when planning your financial future. Be your own adviser. D5

Jane Bryant Quinn
Congress may gut the Truth-in-Savings Act unless savers protest – and protest loudly – to their senators and representatives. D5

Austin American-Statesman

Austinites honored for generosity

■ Darrell Royal and Henry Tippie among 10 to receive Horatio Alger award

By Bruce Hight
American-Statesman Staff

David Kennedy/AA-S
Henry Tippie is a 1996 winner of the Horatio Alger award. Because of his commitment to help others achieve success, Tippie has been called a 'classic Horatio Alger story.'

This week the national Horatio Alger Association will honor two Austinites for their rise from modest backgrounds to high success and their use of that success to help others.

One of the two needs no introduction. Darrell Royal, the former University of Texas head football coach whose three national championships elevated him to the status of Sam Houston and Davy Crockett, at least in the eyes of UT alumni.

The other, Henry Tippie, is hardly known, although he has lived here for 25 years and once owned a local television station, which is now KXAN-TV Channel 36. He still owns three radio stations, two ranches and oil and gas interests, though none are in the Austin area.

But Tippie's first business success was achieved in his association with the companies founded or acquired in Delaware in the early 1950s by two brothers, John W. and O. Wayne Rollins.

Today Tippie is chairman of the executive committee and vice chairman of the board of Rollins Truck Leasing Corp. He is also chairman of the executive committee of Matlack Systems Inc. and Rollins Environmental Services Inc., and a director of Rollins Inc., which owns the Orkin exterminating business, and a director of R.P.C. Energy Services Inc.

Royal

Royal and Tippie — the two have never met — are among 10 people chosen to receive this year's Horatio Alger award at the foundation's 49th annual banquet Friday in Washington. Two others also are from Texas, Louise Herrington Ornelas, a cable company founder in Tyler, and Melvyn Klein, a Corpus Christi businessman.

The association this year will award more than $850,000 in scholarships to help high school seniors who have overcome adversity to attend college and to sponsor youth seminars on career opportunities or public or community service. It was named after author Horatio Alger Jr., who wrote more than 130 books about young people overcoming great obstacles to achieve success.

Royal, 71, who gave up his head coaching duties in 1976 and now is retired, has collected awards for a long time. But the Alger award, he said, is special.

"The big difference is that about every award I've received has been athletically related, like coach of the year," Royal said. But, he said, "There's a coach of the year every year. I was just overwhelmed when I got the call (for the Alger award). I didn't even know I was being considered."

The youngest of six children, Royal was only 4 months old when his mother died. Born in Okla-

See Path, D3

The story of Henry's Horatio Alger Award in the local newspaper, with Henry pictured in his Austin office.

and women from modest backgrounds who had achieved unqualified success and then given time, talent, and money to help others.

"One of the two needs no introduction," the reporter wrote about Darrell Royal, the former University of Texas head football coach who won three national championships. "The other, Henry Tippie, is hardly known, although he has lived here for 25 years and once owned a local television station, which is now KXAN-TV Channel 36. He still owns three radio stations, two ranches, and oil and gas interests, though none are in the Austin area.

"Tippie, 69, who has a comfortable but unpretentious office in Northwest Austin, said he has not been involved locally. But he has lavished affection, and money to match, upon his hometown in Belle Plaine, Iowa, his alma mater, The University of Iowa, and his wife's alma mater, Allegheny College in Meadville, Pennsylvania. Gary Fethke, dean of the College of Business Administration at the University of Iowa, said he did not have a dollar figure on how much Tippie has given the school but it was 'in the millions.' Fethke said that Tippie, for all his success and wealth, 'is an extremely understated' man, eager to help those who helped him: 'This is the classic Horatio Alger story.'"

The citizens of Austin were not the only people surprised when the award was announced. Recalled Henry, "I got the notice via Airborne Overnight that I had won the award, and I wasn't even aware that I had been nominated!"

The award, Henry had to admit, meant a great deal to him. After all, he had grown up reading his father's collection of books by Horatio Alger Jr., the author of more than 130 books about young people overcoming great obstacles to achieve success. And Henry now joined a circle that included two men he had admired as much as, if not more than, anyone else in his entire life: John W. Rollins Sr., 1963 Horatio Alger Award recipient, and O. Wayne Rollins, 1986 Horatio Alger Award recipient.

"It was a very happy evening," said Patricia, recalling the award ceremony and banquet in April 1996 in Washington, D.C. "Our whole family was there, and it was marvelous." Henry met fellow Austinite Darrell Royal for the first time and shook hands with two other award recipients from Texas—Louise Herrington Ornelas, a cable company founder, and Melvyn N. Klein, a businessman. A large contingent of Rollins family members, including Randall and his wife Peggy, Gary, John Jr., John Sr., and Michele, also joined the celebration. The only sad note in the entire evening, perhaps, was that Wayne Rollins was not there to see Henry receive the honor; the man who helped launch Henry's career had passed away in 1991. But Wayne was definitely represented that night when John Sr. joined Henry on stage at the black-tie awards ceremony and personally presented Henry with the 1996 Horatio Alger Award, just as he had done

Henry and Patricia, with their three children and their spouses, at the Horatio Alger award ceremony.

John W. Rollins Sr., a 1963 Horatio Alger Award recipient, presented the award to Henry in 1996.

for his brother Wayne in 1986. In a moving recorded tribute, John Sr. explained that Henry always kept a diary. "I asked if I could see this diary, and in this diary he had noted every nickel that he ever spent, all the way through college," John recalled, smiling broadly as he spoke. "If he had a Coca-Cola, he had that down. He had listed what he spent his money for, and he's been doing that ever since."

A brief but touching movie about Henry's life—with scenes depicting growing up in Belle Plaine, how he got his first Rollins job by not asking for directions to Rehoboth, his role in the Orkin acquisition, and his dream to one day own 160 acres—concluded with a quote from Henry that qualified for inclusion in Tippie's Laws, it is such a classic. "I think the word hope—H-O-P-E—is wonderful if you are talking about the weather," said Henry in his familiar deadpan delivery. "But in terms of things happening, you have to use the word *action*. You have to make it happen."

MAKING THINGS HAPPEN AT ROLLINS

There was never any question that Henry B. Tippie was part of the team that continued to make things happen for the Rollins companies. Though he officially left Rollins, Inc., in November 1970, a review of Henry's professional associations with companies run by both the Rollins brothers and other family members shows a continuous, seemingly unbreakable bond of professional influence, guidance, dedication, and friendship. Consider:

- After resigning from Rollins, Inc., and his position on the corporate board in 1970, Henry retained his position as a trustee for both the O. Wayne Rollins Foundation and the Rollins Children's Trust. In 1974 he was reappointed to the board of Rollins, Inc., eventually serving as the chairperson of the board's compensation, audit, diversity, and governance committees. Henry's financial insights and expertise played a major role in the Rollins board room, particularly when it came to recommendations for stock splits. "I recommended every stock split except the one in 1972 in Atlanta, when I'd gone off the board to start Kingstip," said Henry. "All the others, I made the recommendations that it's time to do two-for-one, or three-for-two. Where did I get that experience? Just from looking around, seeing what's going on. Then you have to ask yourself, 'What's the earnings going to look like afterward on a per-share basis? What are you going to do with the dividends? How many shares outstanding? What would it trade at?' I look at all those things and come up with my recommendations."

- After working with John Sr. and John Jr. to save and restructure Rollins International (later known as RLC and then Rollins Truck Leasing Corp.), Henry remained past 1976 as both chairman of the Executive Committee and vice chairman of the Rollins Truck Leasing board. He was a key factor in the company's decision to restructure in order to focus entirely on truck leasing operations, ultimately working to implement a spin-off of other business interests into two companies: Matlack Systems, Inc., for bulk waste hauling (1989), and Rollins Environmental Services, Inc. (1982). Henry served as a director for both of these new companies. In a reverse merger, Rollins Environmental was technically acquired by LaidLaw in 1997, and LaidLaw was then acquired by a company called Safety-Kleen.
- In 1984, in his role as director of Rollins, Inc., in Atlanta, Henry was instrumental in Rollins' decision to spin off two new Rollins companies: Rollins Communications, Inc. (ROC), and RPC Energy Services (RES). The three Rollins companies would reflect the company's three different lines of business: pest control and consumer services, media, and oil and gas services. The spin-offs, Wayne knew, would mirror the steps Henry had taken in 1976 when he separated Kingstip into two companies to reflect two very different sides of business—namely, media/communications and concrete

Wayne, John, and Henry—three farm boys—continued to work together and remained friends long after Henry left Rollins.

building materials. "Wayne and Randall saw the success in that," Henry noted, and the two Rollins men soon traveled to Austin to meet with Henry and discuss everything from specific stock ratios for each new company to what the new companies should be called. The trio determined that Rollins shareholders should receive 0.6 shares in each of the new companies for each share of Rollins, Inc., stock. The Rollins family would continue to hold the majority of stock in each company. The board approved the restructuring in December 1983, and on June 30, 1984, the spin-off occurred and three new companies were listed on the New York Stock Exchange: Rollins, Inc., continuing to trade as "ROL," would provide consumer services through pest control, lawn care, and home security businesses; RPC Energy Services, Inc., trading as "RES," would encompass all aspects of the oil and gas services businesses; and Rollins Communications, Inc., trading as "ROC," would include all cable television operations, three VHF television stations, one FM and five AM radio stations, and all of Rollins Outdoor Advertising activities. It didn't take long for analysts to appreciate the wisdom of the move. As Henry, Wayne, and Randall had anticipated, investment analysts welcomed the move and began recommending the stock of the three separate companies to investors. Henry served as a director on the boards of both new companies.

- By March 1985, the value of Rollins, Inc., stock had increased by more than 28 percent; Rollins Communications' stock was up 29 percent from its initial offering; and RPC Energy Services had increased 9.5 percent. By July 1986, the value of the communications company was so attractive that an Iowa-based communications corporation called Heritage Communications, Inc., offered to buy the media and outdoor advertising businesses for $608.1 million, the equivalent of $41 per share. As Henry pointed out to his fellow board members, the purchase price was 50 times the company's earnings of $12 million, a price that was simply too good for the company and the shareholders to turn down. On July 29, 1986, Rollins sold its communications company, just over 38 years after the two Rollins brothers had incorporated as Rollins Broadcasting in Rehoboth Beach, Delaware. Subsequently, Henry helped restructure RPC nearly 15 years later when the oil and gas services company spun off its boat-building enterprise into a new company called Marine Products Corp. Henry continued to serve as a director of both RPC and Marine Products.

- Working closely with John Rollins Sr., Henry also served as vice chairman of the board of one of John's key interests, Dover Downs Entertainment, Inc. Henry helped take the company public in 1996 and later directed the restructuring of the company when Dover Downs Entertainment split into two separate companies—Dover Motorsports, Inc., and Dover Downs Gaming & Entertainment, Inc.

- And in 1997, Henry played a role when Rollins, Inc., then a diversified services business anchored by Orkin, decided to sell off all of its non–pest control businesses and become a "single-focus" pest control company.

In summary, from 1970 through 2015, Henry operated and started his own companies in Texas and also served in various capacities for 11 companies, foundations, and trusts associated with the Rollins family. Under the Rollins umbrella, he helped orchestrate seven spin-offs and countless stock splits and dividend payments, working to ensure not only the financial security of the companies but orchestrating wealth for generations of stockholders to come, including the Rollins and Tippie families. But perhaps one of Henry's most important roles—and the one that's the most difficult to fully define—is how Henry personified a legacy of continuity and trust to the organization, a legacy that no one individual will ever equal or surpass.

"The things that Henry has done, you can't go out and get that," said Gary. "He understands the businesses that we are in and the history behind them and how we got into that, and you can't replace that. We have all this history together. Someone may come along and be brilliant, but if you don't have the foundation of trust and history with this person, it's not going to be the same. You simply cannot replace the trust we have with Henry. You are not going to find it again."

As secretary and vice president of Rollins Communications, and a fellow board member with Henry for two other Rollins companies, Linda Graham always appreciated Henry's unique role. And though she has watched that role become nuanced and infinitely layered over time, Linda manages to capture Henry's essence with a simplicity that even "Just the Facts" Henry can appreciate.

Flanked by John W. Rollins Sr. and John W. Rollins Jr., Henry is honored for his sustained professional and personal contributions to Rollins.

"Mr. Tippie's role was to *not let anything wrong happen*," Linda said. "And that's a wonderful role for someone in a family business—to be this overseer of not letting anything wrong happen. And when you think about how it started with John and Wayne—where John was the Dreamer and would go off on tangents, and Wayne was the Operator who would pull him back—they had Henry to help them both."

Over the years, John Rollins Sr. gave numerous talks about Henry. But perhaps his best and most heartfelt speech—one that mixed John's freestyle, bold humor with a deep sincerity that could bring those listening to tears—took place one evening at a company tribute in Henry's honor. For this occasion in Wilmington in 1993, John Sr. started with one of his favorite stories about Henry from when they first met in 1953, and then proceeded to illustrate how this man named Henry B. Tippie had changed the lives of every single person in the room that night:

> Back in those days, Rehoboth, Delaware, had no communication from the outside world; only a bus ran occasionally. And so if we had to go into a lot of discussion to tell a person how to get there, most of the time the people would become so discouraged they wouldn't come anyway. But Henry came in this Saturday morning, and he had this buffalo coat on that he's worn out from Iowa, and he had on about as much clothes as I had when I came up from Philadelphia, because we both had had the same kind of background. So on interviewing Henry, I said, "What's your ambition in life?" He said, "To make fifteen thousand dollars a year." And you know he's done a little bit better than that.
>
> But I think back over our times, and I think, just what is it that makes Henry Tippie different? I'll tell you what makes him different—he has integrity. And there's a shortage of that in the world today. He has above all tenacity. And he has the greatest follow-up system that drives you absolutely crazy!
>
> When we go through these crises, I tell him about how the world's going to be brighter, and he says, "Why don't you try doing this first?" And he gives me a list, and when he gives me a list I say, "Who the hell is he to give me a list?" and I throw it away. By the

time he makes it back, he says, "What items have you handled on that list yet?" So I pick the paper up and I think, hell, he's not gonna be back anymore today, I won't fool with this. And he comes back in 30 minutes. "How many have you handled?" And I said, "Well, I haven't exactly gotten to it." And he says, "Well, what time do you think you're gonna get to it?" So I tell him that I think that I'm gonna get to it sometime later in the day. He says, "Those people you were gonna let go, when are you going to do it?" I said, "Today." He says, "What time?" So he has a follow-up, and a sense of urgency that very few people in the world have. He follows up, and he plans. He's planned ahead, on what happens if this happens if the other happens.

Now most of us are half-assed; we make one part of the plan, and we dawdle by the roadside and don't tie it in with the second part. But not Henry B. Tippie. He's planning right now for all of our companies, what the hell we're going to be going to do in the next 10 years. But that's something that's a rarity in people. That you combine a person that has a sense of urgency, a person that follows through, and does today's business today, and absolutely NO procrastination. I have never in forty years ever seen Henry procrastinate on anything. And I know that a lot of times I procrastinate. I think the world's gonna be more beautiful tomorrow, and I won't have to face it but it's still there tomorrow. But over the years, we've worked and we've traveled together, and a lot of the things that we've had to do as far as leasing is concerned, Henry has never fallen back. He's never wavered in what he thought was right.

And he's got the hardest damn head I have ever seen in my life. You know that I think that I can kinda change him on some of these things, and I can make the greatest pitch in the world, but it doesn't change him any. If we had more people like Henry Tippie, the world would be a much nicer place to live in.

In 2000 Henry's legacy of continuous dedication to the Rollins family made him the logical and trusted choice for one last assignment from John W. Rollins Sr.

CHAPTER TWENTY-TWO

A FINAL FAVOR FOR THE DREAMER

ON TUESDAY MORNING, APRIL 4, 2000, Henry sat behind his desk in his Austin headquarters, going over some financial reports, when his executive assistant Terri Whetstone announced that he had a call from John W. Rollins Sr. "He was sharp and alert," Henry always remembered, noting that John Sr. had just returned to Wilmington from a trip to his estate in Montego Bay, Jamaica, where he had enjoyed some time with Michele, Randall, and Peggy Rollins. After catching up on business and a few personal matters, John mentioned that he was having lunch later that day with Tom Wintermantel, the financial vice president and treasurer of several of John's nonpublic entities. "Give Tom my best," said Henry.

Around noon, John Sr. walked down the hallway from his office on the 15th floor and motioned for Tom to join him. "Let's go downstairs and have lunch," he suggested to Tom, as they took the elevator to the corporate cafeteria on the second floor. "John didn't typically come down to the cafeteria for lunch," recalled Tom. "And as we're going through, cafeteria-style, he's talking to a lot of people, and for them, it was a big thing. That was the amazing thing about John Rollins. He treated the guy pushing the broom the same way he would have handled the president of the company. Everyone felt special near him." The conversation was casual that day—reviewing John's trip to Jamaica and his holdings there, the volatility of the stock market that morning, updating John Sr. with information from the business and his foundation. "He just hadn't seen me in a while and he wanted to catch up."

Late that afternoon, around four o'clock in Austin, Henry received another call from Tom in Wilmington, but this call was from a distraught, deeply saddened young man. John W. Rollins Sr., 82, had passed away. After having lunch with Tom and then taking care of some business and personal matters, John Sr. had retired to the sleeping quarters adjacent to his office for his customary afternoon nap. He simply never woke up. When he didn't respond to his buzzer around 5 p.m., the office staff immediately went to check on him. Someone called 911, someone else called Michele, and Tom immediately called Henry.

"To tell you the truth, I had a difficult time getting the news out, telling Henry what happened, that Mr. Rollins had died in his sleep," recalled Tom, who decades after the fact still becomes emotional describing the phone call. "Henry was quiet for a second, and he said something consoling. He was devastated by the news. He had just talked to Mr. Rollins that morning."

The passing of John Sr. meant more than the loss of a business colleague. For over 47 years, John Sr. had been an older brother, a friend, and a business peer to Henry. He represented the very beginning of Henry's successful business journey, and they had forged an unbreakable bond when Henry helped John Sr. and John Jr. save their company in the 1970s. The personal loss Henry felt was instant and deep. "I'm dumbfounded," Henry told a reporter later that evening, after news of John's death became public. "When the Lord created him, he threw away the mold because he's a one and only."

In spite of the tremendous personal loss Henry felt—"I didn't know how he was going to make it," said Patricia—Henry knew he had a final favor to do for his friend. In the years prior to John's death, Henry had agreed to be the sole executor of John Sr.'s estate. Reluctant at first to take on this assignment, Henry nonetheless understood John's reasoning. "Why me? I'm a non–family member, but with a large family, it would probably be better to have someone who could be objective—who could remove any emotions out of the decisions that had to be made. Also, I have

Rollins: 'He's a one and only'

FROM PAGE A1

He later opened a Ford automobile dealership in Lewes.

Rollins later became a multimillionaire from such enterprises as trucking, extermination, waste hauling and the Dover Downs entertainment complex.

He founded or co-founded seven companies taken public on the New York Stock Exchange. His interests included Rollins Inc., which owns the Orkin Exterminating Co., and RLC Corp., owner of Rollins Leasing Corp., the nation's third largest truck leasing and rental service company.

He owned a 6,200-acre former plantation in Jamaica, where he was currently building a third major hotel. One recent Delaware venture, the controversial Brandywine Town Center off Concord Pike, is nearing completion.

Rollins also was a philanthropist, giving millions to schools, churches, hospitals and museums. One of his pet projects was restoration of the Capitol Theater in Dover, to which he gave $1 million.

Rollins closely guarded the details of his wealth, which in 1988 was estimated at $220 million by Forbes magazine.

But in the political arena, the conservative Republican was proud of his connections.

He donated millions to political campaigns the last half-century, almost all to GOP candidates, and knew every president since John F. Kennedy. President Nixon's helicopter landed on the lawn of Rollins' 12-acre Greenville estate for a dinner party in 1971.

On the day the United States bombed Libya in 1986, Rollins ate lunch in the White House with President Reagan.

Among his friends were former President Bush and his son George W. Bush, the likely GOP presidential nominee. "We're very sorry to hear of his passing," former First Lady Barbara Bush said. "He was a wonderful man."

Howard Baker Jr., White House chief of staff for Reagan, said Rollins crammed more into one lifetime than most people could pack into several. "John Rollins was truly a unique American," Baker said. "I will miss him sorely."

Rollins is survived by his third wife, Michele, an attorney and former Miss USA, along with nine children and 11 grandchildren.

Friends and associates throughout Delaware said they would remember Rollins as an indefatigable businessman who personified the American rags-to-riches story. While passionate about work and politics, he also could poke fun at himself and others.

Henry B. Tippie, vice chairman of Rollins Leasing Corp., said Rollins was sharp and alert when they spoke Tuesday morning. Rollins had returned to Delaware on Monday from his estate in Montego Bay, Jamaica.

"I'm dumbfounded," Tippie said.

Tippie said Rollins constantly strategized about his next big deal.

"John lived business. Business to him was a hobby. He always had projects laid out for the next 10 years," said Tippie, who moved to Delaware from Iowa in 1953 to work for Rollins.

Tippie said Rollins often called him "Dr. No" for pointing out the downside to the plans he hatched.

"When the Lord created him, he threw away the mold because he's a one and only," Tippie said.

John Burris, Republican candidate for governor, said he might have been the last person to speak with Rollins, when they chatted for a half-hour late Tuesday afternoon about the campaign.

"He was really in rare form," Burris said. "We were talking about media and how he didn't think buying time in the Philadelphia market was a good move. We were going to get together to talk more about it."

Burris said Rollins was a font of energy. "There are just some people who you don't think have time to die," Burris said. "John just had so much on his agenda that you'd think he'd have lived another 80 years."

Sen. Joe Biden, a Democrat, said it was impossible not to like Rollins. As a New Castle County councilman, Biden fought Rollins' plans to land a helicopter atop the Rollins Building in Fairfax, where he ran his empire from a penthouse suite.

After being elected to the Senate in 1972, Biden said Rollins called him.

"He said, 'God damn it, kid, you won. If I'd have known you had a chance, I would have spent more money to defeat you.'"

Gov. Tom Carper, also a Democrat, praised Rollins' drive.

"If Horatio Alger could be personified by one Delawarean, it would be John," Carper said.

Befitting such praise, Rollins had been inducted in 1963 into the Horatio Alger Association for Distinguished Americans. He donated money to the group, helped set up its scholarship endowment that gives $2 million annually, and was serving as chairman emeritus and treasurer.

Priscilla B. Rakestraw, Republican national committeewoman for Delaware, said Rollins' impact on GOP politics in Delaware and the rest of the country is immeasurable.

"It's kind of like a pillar has been pulled out," she said, "and the other pillars will have to work all the harder."

She said Rollins was much more than a contributor. "He was consulted. People saw John as a person with a finger on trends. He didn't go to them with his hat in his hands. They came to him seeking help."

But Rollins' most endearing trait, Rakestraw said, was that he never put himself on a pedestal.

She pointed to the 1992 GOP national convention in Houston, where Delaware's delegation was assigned to a hotel in a somewhat seedy part of the city. Rakestraw assumed that the tycoon and his wife, Michele, would opt for a luxurious suite elsewhere. She was wrong.

"No matter where our hotel was located," Rakestraw said, "that's where John Rollins was going to stay."

Charles M. Cawley, president of MBNA Corp. and a top GOP contributor, described Rollins as one of the most impressive men he knew.

"His intellect and ability to make things happen were undiminished by age," Cawley said. "Some people are described as being larger than life but aren't. John Rollins was larger than life."

▶ Staff reporters Patrick Jackson and Tamara Chuang contributed to this article. Reach Cris Barrish at cbarrish@wilmingt.gannett.com. Reach Michele Darnell at mdarnell@wilmingt.gannett.com

THE SERVICES

Funeral arrangements for John W. Rollins Sr.:

Viewing — From 4 to 8 p.m. Friday at the Rollins Building lobby, 2200 Concord Pike, Fairfax.

Funeral — 11 a.m. Saturday at Aldersgate United Methodist Church, 2313 Concord Pike, Fairfax. Parking will be available in the church lot and at the Rollins Building.

Interment — Private

Contributions in Rollins' memory may be made to the Horatio Alger Association of Distinguished Americans, 99 Canal Center Plaza, Suite 320, Alexandria, Va. 22314.

The News Journal/FRED COMEGYS

Autographed photos of Rollins with Presidents Bush, Reagan and Nixon and invitations to White House dinners show Rollins' strong ties to the Republican Party.

When John W. Rollins Sr. died, the local newspaper quoted Henry's description of him as "a one and only."

the advantage, probably compared to others, that maybe I would have a lot of knowledge about his way of thinking and some general knowledge of what he was involved in. Sometimes we just kind of talked, and John said he could count on me."

The choice John Sr. made did not surprise a grieving Randall, who could see the wisdom in having Henry step into the executor's role. "Henry does what he needs to do, and he does not allow his feelings to direct those things," he said. "Henry had a very big job to do, a very unpleasant job, when John died. That was quite a responsibility to give to anyone, and John knew who to give it to."

Which is why, Tom recalled, Henry did not linger on sorrow or allow himself time to grieve when he first heard that John had died. Before the flag was even lowered to half-mast over Rollins headquarters on Concord Pike, Henry was making lists and thinking of everything that had to be done to protect John Sr.'s family. "As soon as I told him, after a few moments, then it was almost like, 'Okay. We have to handle this. Here is what I need you to do,'" said Tom. "And Henry went into damage control."

To say that John W. Rollins Sr.'s estate was complicated would be a dramatic understatement. On the personal side, there were three families and nine living children involved, all ranging in age from their late 50s to teenagers. On the business side, as Gary Rollins once described, "John's estate wasn't buttoned up." Though Rollins Truck Leasing posted record revenues and earnings in 1999, competition and deregulation issues would eventually force Matlack into bankruptcy. In addition, the evolution of Rollins Environmental Services, which Rollins had sold in 1997, continued to entangle Henry and John Jr. for years to come over accounting irregularities committed by the new owners. John Sr. was also the majority stockholder and founder of Dover Downs Entertainment, Inc., a business that combined casinos, NASCAR motor sports, and race tracks. In addition, John's private business concerns were extensive when he died. He was involved with several long-term and heavily leveraged construction projects in Delaware and Jamaica, including the controversial Brandywine Town Center on the site of the former Brandywine Raceway; Phase One of a new 260-room hotel and 18,000-square-foot ballroom in Dover for Dover Downs Entertainment; and a multimillion-dollar Ritz-Carlton Hotel complex nearing completion in Jamaica, where John Sr. owned over 6,500 acres and managed a 140-person security force, a well-drilling and water system operation, and a golf course leased to Wyndham Hotel.

As Michele had once noted about her husband, "John has on his plate five different projects, any one of which most 40-year-old men would consider a life's work." And it never dawned on him that he should finish anything on that plate or leave a buttoned-up estate, said his son Jeff. "We were on the plane one time, and I asked him, 'What the hell happens if something happens to you, Dad? Where is the succession plan?' He was tired and he said, 'Look. I'm not going to be here. It's not my problem—it's y'all's problem!'"

Through his various business ventures, John Sr. had substantial debt when he died, and Henry's first concern was how the banks would respond to John's death and his loans. "John Rollins had a lot of wealth, but it wasn't liquid wealth," noted Tom, who became financial vice president of John's estate and worked closely with Henry after John died. "He had a lot of loans, a lot of lines of credit at the banks, and the financial institutions all held stock in John's company as collateral. So we were concerned right from the get-go: We had to make sure we got the word out to the banks that we had a succession plan in place, nothing is going to change. We had to make sure the banks did not move to call in John's loans, just because John had passed away."

It wasn't easy. Banking relationships, long frayed by complicated deals and layers of both personal and professional entanglements within the Rollins family, threatened more than once to collapse. But once Tom and Henry reassured some of the key loan officers, the value of Henry's extensive historical knowledge of John's business dealings, coupled with Tom's day-to-day associations over the previous four years, quickly became apparent. Henry immediately recognized that the estate stood to benefit the most if he completed all construction projects and took every possible step to reduce John's debt. "My whole goal has been to try to get the estate so that Michele, the beneficiary, will benefit the best. That has been my whole goal and it has not always been easy," said Henry. "But I have looked at it in terms of what is in her best interest in the long run. I want to have a substantial estate that is debt-free."

It was a difficult concept to explain to the members of John's grieving family. In essence, Henry told everyone during a meeting the day after the funeral that it was going to take years to settle the estate, there was no real timeline, and there would not be significant individual distributions for some time. "With John Sr.'s sudden departure, I felt what I needed to do was to gather up everybody while they were still in town after the funeral, the next day before people began to leave," recalled Henry. "He had three families from his three marriages, and everybody lived all over the country. Tom made copies of the will, and I distributed a copy to everybody that would be affected, if not now then sometime down the road. And I let them know we would proceed to carry out his wishes.

There were terms about who would get what, but the executor would make the final decisions."

In her shock and grief, Michele remembered that she "wasn't quite prepared" for Henry's approach—for "the absolute emotionless way he attacked the decisions that had to be made."

Recalled Michele, "I was just so crushed when John died. I was looking for an empathetic supporter to make decisions, because John always acted as my partner. And that is a very different approach from Henry. But eventually I realized that it was good for me to see Henry's approach. We don't escape that in life, and we end up having to take our emotions out of a lot of things if we are going to succeed and move forward. So Henry became the person that everyone relied on for financial advice. Because you knew you were going to get the truth, an honest evaluation that had nothing to do with who you were or what you were. And that's invaluable. In today's world, no one wants to tell you the truth. So through the transition, with Henry as executor, he played that role on every level, to young kids, middle-aged kids, and certainly to the businesses."

John Sr.'s son Patrick took comfort in the fact that Henry was in charge. "I didn't know who the executor was going to be, and when they told me it was Henry, I was just relieved," said Patrick, who left the family corporation in 1986 and moved to Texas to start his own real estate business.

John Rollins Sr. and Henry at Prairie Hill. Before John died, Henry agreed to be the sole executor of his estate.

"Henry's loyalty is such that he has always been the rescue guy. No matter what it is, he has been willing to act. And Dad left a mess, with three wives, 10 kids, a penchant for not giving details—it was an ugly mess and he trusted Henry to figure it out. It took Henry about eight years to work it out. He had to put everything on a firm footing, because otherwise they couldn't get the value out of the businesses and have something left over. In some cases, my dad had borrowed more than the assets were worth if they were not completed or cleaned up. So Henry saved the businesses *again*—by putting them on firm footing."

The toughest decision Henry said he had to make after John Sr.'s death involved the sale of Rollins Truck Leasing Corp., which was often referred to as the "crown jewel of the company." John Sr. is considered one of the early pioneers of the auto and truck leasing industry, and Rollins was one of the most widely recognized names in the field—its signature black, white, and yellow-gold "Rollins Truck Rental/Leasing" logo proudly displayed on trucks and vehicles traveling throughout the country. After John Sr. died, Henry became chairman of the board of Rollins Truck Leasing. The company's 1999 annual report, which had been published just five months before John Sr.'s death, would be the last annual report to include the company's "holy trinity" of John Sr., John Jr., and Henry. Inside, a performance summary traced the company's growth from 1989 through 1999, showing that Rollins Truck Leasing had increased revenues of $312 million to over $627 million in 11 years, making it the nation's third-largest full-service truck leasing and rental company, servicing more than 53,000 vehicles from 270 facilities throughout the United States and Canada.

"I don't think I have seen a company run better," said Klaus Belohoubek, an acclaimed acquisitions lawyer who served as counsel for various Rollins family businesses since 1989 and general counsel for Rollins Truck Leasing at the time of the sale. "It was a very well regarded company, and there was a phenomenal interest in buying the company. The estate had a large amount of debt, and selling the company was necessary to help take care of the debts."

For Henry, a numbers man since he had tracked expenses and income as an 11-year-old farm boy, the financial statistics always told the story.

And Henry knew, within six months after John died, that selling the truck leasing business was the best decision for John Sr.'s estate and his heirs. "To get involved in selling it was not an easy decision, but on the other hand, when I got rid of all the emotions, it made sense to sell it," he said. "I think in retrospect everybody thinks it was a good move. I started that in the summer of 2000 and nobody ever knew anything about it outside of John Jr. Eventually, we had to bring in two other people, but we kept this extremely quiet until it was finalized in early 2001. This period covered almost six months of keeping this thing quiet—no meetings were held inside the building, etc. It was not an easy thing to bring off."

Patrick J. Bagley, then vice president–finance and treasurer of the trucking company, was one of the three people Henry involved with the sale. And Pat forever recalled the afternoon he thought he had jeopardized the entire thing.

"There were only a couple of people aware of this transaction and it was to be kept very quiet," Pat said. "I was working nights, weekends in preparation for it. There was one Sunday afternoon when I owed the investment bankers some information, and I had an elaborate spreadsheet. And when I finished it, I meant to send it to the investment bankers. Instead, one of the files went to one of Rollins' western regional offices by mistake. My life passed before my eyes! I called Henry that night after I had done that, and told him. I was shaking. Typical Henry stayed calm, started asking questions. 'Now what was it? Was something on there about the investment banker or about the sale? Chances are they are not even going to know about it, so don't worry about it.' And that was the end of it. And you know what? I don't think they noticed."

Was the sale of Rollins Truck Leasing difficult? "Yes," Pat allowed. "It was a difficult time. We were all grieving. Then the circumstances, with the need to raise cash for the estate, created this stress of selling our flagship company that had been viewed so favorably by so many. We were all part of a very successful enterprise. Having to sell it was a tough assignment. I think a lot of folks would not have been able to come to that conclusion as quickly as Henry did. You have to set aside emotion to get the job done. I am sure that was a very difficult time for him. I have not ever had a specific conversation with him about that, but my view is that it was a tough time for him to have to handle all that."

On January 16, 2001, the *New York Times* first broke the news about the deal that Henry and three others had worked for over six months to put together: Rollins Truck Leasing Corporation had agreed to be acquired by Penske Truck Leasing, a truck-rental company based in Reading, Pennsylvania, for about $2 billion in cash and assumed debt. "Penske will pay $13 for each Rollins share, 54 percent more than Rollins' closing price on Friday," the newspaper reported.

The news triggered an avalanche of emotions among employees and family members alike, but there was also a sense of pride and relief that the company John Sr. built had sold for such an outstanding price. "Henry pulled all the strings," admitted Klaus, who played a major role in structuring the sale of the company, which was finalized in February. "We hired investment bankers, but for the most part, it was done without anybody knowing about it. It is not unusual for the business world to keep it quiet, but it was unusual that so few people knew and that was Henry's preference. We got an inquiry from the SEC shortly after the deal closed, and they asked for a list of everyone involved in the transaction. And I told them the four—Pat Bagley, myself, Henry, and John Jr.—and they were surprised and did not believe it."

Employees inside Rollins were genuinely shocked, especially those like Tom Wintermantel who worked in close proximity to people involved in the sale and talked to them every day. "I had not heard even a whisper of it," Tom said. "But Henry is close to the vest, and his saying is always, 'On a need-to-know basis.'"

Henry was relieved when the sale was over. "I think everyone would agree that the timing was right," he said. And years later, with the benefit of hindsight, Henry said essentially the same thing. "The record shows we did all right."

Working closely with Tom, it took Henry until 2008 to completely close John Sr.'s estate. Tom called it an "enormous undertaking," pointing out that "we were extremely efficient in carrying out John Sr.'s last wishes while not only preserving, but increasing, the value of the estate's assets." The major remaining elements in the estate included:

- In March 2001, Matlack Systems, Inc., officially filed for Chapter 11 protection under the Federal Bankruptcy Code. The company was soon liquidated, and all assets sold. "I'd attribute that company's demise first and foremost to deregulation," said Klaus. "As an older trucking firm with legacy costs—such as unions, underfunded multi-employer pension plans, and environmental clean-up obligations—Matlack simply could not compete with lower-cost, nonunion start-ups."

- As planned, Rollins completed construction on the various hotel projects, as well as on major portions of the Brandywine Town Center, eliminating debt and stock obligations from the estate. By the end of January 2003, the Rollins estate had also transferred, sold, or merged all interests in the town center project to outside real estate holding companies, known collectively as Acadia.

- In 2005 Henry took the witness stand for four days inside a courtroom in Columbia, South Carolina. The extremely complicated and layered case over financial accounting irregularities involved what was once Rollins Environmental after it was acquired in a reverse merger by LaidLaw and then sold to a company named Safety-Kleen. The case involved so many multiple lawsuits filed on behalf of shareholders that Henry never could figure out if he was testifying for the plaintiffs or the defendants. "We finally got out of this all right, but it was an education," said Henry, who, despite some intensely negative press, was never indicted for any fraud or related actions. "But I have to say that it is an experience I'm glad I had. I had a chance to look at the justice system and how it works, and I don't like it." Ironically, Henry was the person who brought the accounting irregularities to the attention of the SEC, which triggered the lengthy lawsuits, according to Klaus. "And since no good deed goes unpunished, he is the one who got sued when Safety-Kleen went bankrupt," Klaus said. "But I think the fact that Henry brought the accounting irregularities to the attention of the SEC is important. It shows the character of Henry. He found something wrong and knew what to do with it."

After 2008, any lingering financial interests from the liquidated estate were handed in a marital trust comprising Henry, Michele, and Randall. "It has been a major undertaking," Henry concluded. "Tom did an outstanding job. And there has been a lot of support from Michele and from Randall, and from the entire family. We all have really good relations. It has been a strain, but you just do the best you can."

Randall once concluded that if John had asked anyone besides Henry to handle his estate, "it could have been a disaster. I think there would have been lawsuits and problems running out of their ears!" he said. "And what I think is so remarkable is that all those children respect Henry. They all trusted him. They were all positive. And Henry would not budge one speck. It doesn't matter how much something would upset another person, he doesn't let his emotions get into those things. He separates what he *should* do from what he *has* to do."

Perhaps no one knows this better than Michele Rollins. "John asked him to be executor, and Henry did it with all of the talent that he had," she said. "Everyone in this family grew up thinking that Henry walked on water, and that if you ever needed a financial person, he was who you wanted. There is no question: Henry was going to give us 1,000 percent."

Because John Sr. left the bulk of the Rollins Jamaican properties to Michele in a transaction outside of his estate, Henry was not involved as executor in the future developments there. But Michele did turn to Henry for some personal advice, and he visited Jamaica several times over the years to help her assess her options. His first advice was memorable, Michele recalled: "Henry hated Jamaica, because he thought John lost all of his money there. 'Jamaica will take you down. John wasn't able to get money out and you won't either.' And I thanked him for that advice, but Henry wasn't responsible for it. I think he wanted me to give it away, but both John and I knew that the journey in Jamaica is long."

Michele did follow one of Henry's basic business tenets when she first began to tackle Jamaica without John. "Henry gave me some advice. 'It's very easy: get the checkbook. Use the checkbook as a vehicle to see what's going out, to see where the charges are coming from.' He really reduced it to something simple."

But Michele has always argued that Henry is anything *but* simple. "If you really listen to Henry talk in his generational business tones and listen to his clichés that are so successful—'You have to have more coming in than going out'—that is very simple. But when you understand the plans and the projections that he makes so that more comes in, 'simple' would not be an accurate word. He reduces businesses to the simplest terms, which is the bottom line, but he is not simple and his approach is not simple."

Michele paused for a minute, sitting in her office outside Wilmington. Those who know her best concluded long ago that she and John Sr. were a perfect match—both ambitious, intelligent, wildly energetic, eternally optimistic. She can laugh now, thinking back to her rocky start with Henry, the man she once called an "all-time male chauvinist," who advised a 60-year-old John Sr. not to marry the 32-year-old Michele. "I didn't forgive Henry for a long time," she said, choosing her words carefully before breaking into a smile and shrugging her shoulders. "But the events of time have endeared me to Henry. We have that kind of relationship where I don't have to be with him to see the little smile on his face, the one that says, 'Oh there she goes again!' I am very fond of him. And I have grown fonder of him as I understand him better. It took me a while. It may be because I have grown, and I am more willing to have him say what *he* wants to say instead of what *I* want him to say. And that's been very valuable."

And in a closing thought, Michele drifted back to the years long before her husband passed away, thinking about the time when John Sr., O. Wayne, and Henry B. first came together as the Dreamer, the Operator, and Dr. No to build the Rollins empire. She wasn't a part of the picture then, but she has listened dutifully to every story from that era, and she has come to her own conclusions.

"You can never underestimate the job that Henry Tippie did," she said. "Imagine working with two absolutely wild entrepreneurs, whose ideas were flowing 90 miles per hour, with no thought to how the numbers came up, counting on Henry to make sure that the numbers added up. It's not easy! But that's what made them such a great team."

CHAPTER TWENTY-THREE

DOVER MOTORSPORTS AND DOVER DOWNS GAMING & ENTERTAINMENT

IN ADDITION TO HIS ROLE as executor of John W. Rollins Sr.'s estate, Henry found himself in a new business role. With John Sr.'s passing, Henry became the chairman of the board at Dover Downs Entertainment, Inc. This multifaceted entertainment company, incorporated by John Sr. in 1967, owned and operated NASCAR auto racing, harness racing, and a Las Vegas–style entertainment, casino, and hotel complex in the Dover area, while owning and operating a number of race tracks in other states: the Nashville Speedway in Tennessee, Memphis Motorsports Park near Memphis, and Gateway International Raceway near St. Louis, Missouri. Dover Downs also promoted the Toyota Grand Prix of Long Beach in California.

Henry first joined the board in 1996 as vice chairman after the company went public. But he kept a respectful distance from the operation, attending board meetings and staying informed while recognizing that this was John Sr.'s territory. It's safe to say that John Sr. considered Dover Downs to be a near-perfect cash cow business during his lifetime. "I've never been in a company where you get all your cash and there are no receivables and you have no inventory," John Sr. was known to say as he pursued the gaming business after the Delaware General Assembly authorized slot machines in 1994. "This is the perfect company!"

For over 10 years after going public, John Sr.'s words seemed very true. When Dover Downs Entertainment began trading on the New York Stock Exchange in 1996, it reported revenues of around $50 million. In just three years, those revenues had climbed dramatically, when motorsports and gaming reported revenues over $150 million in 1999. At the time of John Sr.'s death in 2000, the company had recently agreed to invest $285 million to make Dover Downs an entertainment "destination" for consumers, anchored by an expanded luxury hotel, an 18,000-square-foot multipurpose ballroom and concert hall, a gourmet restaurant, and an expanded 2,000-slot-machine casino, as well as an enclosed grandstand renovation and the addition of 13,000 new seats at the Dover Downs International Speedway. With the expansion completed, Dover offered 135,000 seats for NASCAR fans who flocked to Dover to watch race car drivers Dale Earnhardt Sr., Bobby Labonte, Jeff Gordon, and Dale Jarrett navigate the infamous high-banked turns at Dover's "Monster Mile" concrete race track. "It was like the Super Bowl here," admitted Tom Wintermantel, "and not everyone showing up was a NASCAR fan. This was simply the place to be and to be seen. We were selling out."

Dover Downs International Speedway once drew record numbers of NASCAR fans to every race.

When John Sr. died in April 2000, Henry became chairman of the Dover operation. "Right then—snap—he became a lot more involved," recalled Timothy R. Horne, senior vice president–finance, treasurer, and CFO of Dover Downs. "He is clearly involved, but he lets us run the business on a day-to-day basis. While he doesn't get into the weeds, we don't do any significant projects above $100,000 without his approval. He will have very specific questions, and we make sure we are ready before we talk to him. You want to anticipate the questions and have the answers, because you are going to get the questions. I think he is a really good chairman in that regard."

Tom Wintermantel, who joined the Dover Downs operations after John Sr.'s estate was settled, learned how to anticipate Henry's requests. Tom soon started putting together what he calls his "Henry Tippie Cheat Sheet," packed with numbers related to various questions Henry might ask. "I never want to wing a number off the top of my head around Henry," he said. "And every quarter, I always update my information. We'll be in a meeting and he'll say, 'Tom, I want to put together a schedule about . . .' And I'll say, 'Here you go, Henry!' and pass a sheet with information across the table. And he will chuckle a little bit, because it's gotten to a point where he kind of expects that now, too. And I have found that I like it when people I work with anticipate what I want. So you aren't always asking, 'Can you get that for me?' I have more confidence in someone if they supply it to me before I even ask for it, and I have Henry to thank for that."

DOVER DOWNS GAMING & ENTERTAINMENT

In many ways, Henry's association with Dover Downs appeared to be an odd fit. Gambling, casinos, and race tracks seemed like foreign worlds to this farm boy from Iowa who admittedly preferred the solitude of his ranch, small-town values, and the sounds of crooner Frank Sinatra or the "Gentleman of Swing," Tommy Dorsey. But take away the glitz of the casino floor and the interminable roar of the race track (Henry learned to wear earplugs), and Dover Downs is just one more business defined by Henry's overarching rule of success: Is more money coming in than going out?

"And I've made the statement a lot—I like what I do," said Henry, including his new interests in Dover. "Everything I'm involved with, I enjoy."

But being the head of the Delaware operations, Henry admitted, is a rather unique situation. Being chairman, he said, "came with the territory. John Sr. passes away, and I become the controlling shareholder. But I am not a micromanager. Micromanagers, in my opinion, should be fired. You destroy the incentives for the manager, and I won't try to micromanage here or anywhere else. But you can't be a controlling shareholder and vacate the responsibility. That doesn't work. I'm a major shareholder, and I'm also looking after my money." He smiled, and paused for a minute, before adding, "In that situation, I can assure you, I'm going to have some involvement."

In April 2002, two years after being named chairman, Henry took one of his most successful business strategies and incorporated it into the structure of Dover Downs. "We had to get focused," he said. In order to better define the operation for stockholders and analysts, Henry orchestrated a spin-off into two companies: going forward, Dover Downs Gaming & Entertainment, Inc., provided the structure for the casino, shopping, and hotel operations as well as live harness racing on its 0.625-mile outdoor track from November through mid-April, with simulcast harness and thoroughbred racing year-round; and Dover Motorsports, Inc., handled the motorsports business, which hosts NASCAR events on its one-mile track in Dover, as well as on three other permanent tracks and three temporary street race venues.

The main reason behind the spin-off, according to Pat Bagley, the former CFO for Rollins Truck Leasing who assumed the same position for Dover Motorsports after the spin-off, "was the evaluation of the motorsports business at that time. We were dragged down because there are two different businesses, motorsports and the casino operations. The casino business had a big run subsequent to that, but for a while the two different companies were being evaluated and the evaluations were way off. When you have that, there is a tendency for Wall Street to value one business lower and that creates a gap. If you split the two companies, the gap will go away."

Both companies were listed on the New York Stock Exchange on April 1, 2002—but it was no April Fool's event for Henry when he and other Dover Downs executives traveled to New York City that day for the listings. When the "DVD" for Dover Motorsports and the "DDE" for Dover Downs Gaming & Entertainment listed on the exchange, Henry celebrated a remarkable business milestone uniquely his own: since 1968, he had been involved in listing nine companies on the New York Stock Exchange, and two on the American Stock Exchange. Though apparently no records exist to confirm this accomplishment, "I'm not sure that anyone else has ever done that," Henry admitted.

For the next five years, the two new companies performed exceptionally well. Dover Downs Hotel and Conference Center, later renamed the Dover Downs Hotel and Casino, received the first of many consecutive AAA Four Diamond Awards. The casino increased the number of slot machines to 4,000 and began operating 24 hours a day (except Sunday mornings, Easter, and Christmas). A $56 million expansion program added an array of new services and features: a new main casino entrance; a 20,000-square-foot gaming floor with nearly 50 gaming tables for Blackjack, Three Card Poker, Baccarat, and High Card Flush, to name a few; a casino lounge with seating for 200; three branded restaurants;

Chairman Henry B. Tippie (center) and President and CEO Denis McGlynn (on Henry's left) in 2002, the day Dover Downs Gaming & Entertainment was listed on the New York Stock Exchange.

retail shops like Godiva Chocolatier, Swarovski Crystal, and a gourmet coffee café; and an expanded hotel with 500 rooms, the largest in Delaware. The Central Delaware Economic Development Council awarded its "Economic Development Leadership Act" to Dover Downs Gaming & Entertainment in 2008, noting specifically that the operation's 1,500 employees made it one of the largest employers in the state—as well as one of the largest tax-generating businesses. The palatial, sprawling entertainment complex—designed with architectural arches, columns, marble accents, chandeliers, and fountains to try to invoke a grand and wealthy era—seemed to be Dover's answer to Disney World. Indeed, this entertainment destination towered above the otherwise mundane shopping malls and fast food restaurants along Du Pont Highway, beckoning anyone who loved slot machines, gaming, horse races, NASCAR, musical concerts, and boxing.

As predicted, the stock of the two companies initially performed better apart than operating as one company. But by 2008, unpredictable shifts in the entertainment and racing industries and the economy began to create a downward spiral for the two companies. The recession in 2008 kept people away from the casino and the race track, and so far they have never fully returned. The revenue from slot machines alone dropped from $215 million in 2007 to $185 million in fiscal year 2014. In addition to the down economy, competition for casino customers ballooned. Adjacent states discovered the financial benefits of gaming and licensed their own casinos. From 2007 to 2014, the number of casinos within a four-hour drive of Dover jumped from 14 to 30. Out-of-state gamers, who had previously flocked to Dover, were nowhere to be found.

The neighboring states are "keeping their residents home instead of coming here," said Denis McGlynn, president and chief executive officer of Dover Downs Gaming & Entertainment. "There was a time when you could say that all casinos were cash cows, but those times are long gone."

Like salt in the proverbial wound—at exactly the same time competition intensified, Denis pointed out—Delaware lawmakers dramatically increased its tax on authorized slot machines, slicing off a significant percentage of the company's revenue every year. First implemented in 1994, the tax then ranged from 12.5 percent to just under 30 percent; the legislature has since raised the tax to 43.5 percent, with an additional 10 percent of slot winnings required to go to fund horse-racing purses. Denis notes that Dover Downs operates under the largest tax burden of any casino in the region, which has gutted the operation's bottom line. In 2014 alone, for instance, Dover Downs reported $91.3 million in adjusted pretax income—before payments to the state, the horsemen, and slot machine vendors, which totaled $92 million, Denis and Henry jointly reported in Dover Downs' 2014 Shareholders Letter in the Annual Report. "This left us with a $706,000 net loss for the year. The current revenue sharing model is simply not sustainable."

The solution? "What has to be done is politically challenging, but it's not illogical. It's very simple," said Denis. "We have to reset the gaming revenue distribution formula to reflect our current competition environment. We have to convince the legislature that this needs to be done. It's a politically heavy lift for them because they have to cut programs and raise taxes. But it has to be done. The current unbalanced and outdated gaming revenue-sharing formula under state law must be changed."

Despite recommendations from the Lottery and Gaming Study Commission to make changes, the Delaware legislature had by 2015 failed to fully pass those measures, which means that in the last few years, Denis and his management team at Dover Downs have tried different approaches to boost revenues. Gaming innovations such as online and virtual gaming with online apps for iPhones, iPads, and computers are now a part of the landscape, but nothing so far has overcome the heavy burden imposed by the revenue taxes. Moreover, refinancing debt and keeping the operation going has been challenging. In 2015 Denis announced that the casino would curtail unprofitable table games operations and eliminate more jobs—after freezing salaries and pension plans and cutting health care plans in several stages. "This further cutback is not a pleasant one to make, but unfortunately, in light of our positions, we must make it," said Denis. "The legislators have to realize that we are at the end of the phase where we can pick all of the low-hanging fruit. We are doing 100 percent of everything we can to survive."

The perfect storm of competition, increased taxes, and decreased revenue has been a disaster for Dover Downs' stock price, which has fallen from a high of $19.64 in 2006 to 72 cents in 2014, and then back up at the end of 2015 to 99 cents per share. Company executives, including Henry, a majority shareholder, have been scrambling to keep the stock price above $1, or face delisting from the NYSE.

DOVER MOTORSPORTS

The situation at Dover Motorsports, Inc., has also been difficult. And sitting in his executive office, as a race car driver took practice laps in the background, Denis outlines why.

Many in the sport's aging fan base did not return after the recession. The corporate sponsorships that once helped fill the luxurious owners' boxes and provide advertising revenue didn't come back either. Too, NASCAR has had a difficult time attracting new race fans to the sport in general. Nationally, NASCAR tracks across the country have battled sagging attendance since 2008, based on a myriad of factors: the loss and retirement of many key celebrity racers; safety regulations put into place by NASCAR that have changed not only the race cars' appearance but the way drivers can race; lack of diversity in drivers and fans; and the sport's repeated, but so far largely unsuccessful, attempts to attract young race fans. The increase in televised events across the board for NASCAR has been a double-edged sword: the contracts from cable and major television channels bring in revenue, but they also cut down on the number of fans who want to come out and sit in the sun for the race. And the downturn in attendance is a problem for television broadcasters: No one wants to see row after row of empty grandstand seats during a televised race.

At Dover Motorsports, executives have taken many steps to keep up with today's NASCAR reality. In 2011 they reduced the track seating capacity from 135,000 to 113,000 by widening seats. In 2015 they eliminated another 17,000 seats, dropping the track to 95,000 seats, with an eye toward going even lower. At a NASCAR race on Sunday, May 31, 2015, an estimated 65,000 fans turned out to watch Jimmie Johnson win Dover Motorsports' FedEx 400 with a green-white-checkered finish, the popular driver's 10th career victory at Dover International Speedway. Nearly a third of the seats were empty.

Though thousands of race car fans may be missing, members of the Rollins family are a constant at the track. In one way or another, the family has promoted NASCAR-sanctioned racing events for 47 consecutive years at Dover International Speedway, ever since John Sr. first got involved with building the track in 1968. This particular Sunday in May 2015 was no different. Jeff Rollins, John Sr.'s son, who is on Dover's board of directors, guided V.I.P. guests through a pit tour before the race: they rubbed elbows with famous race car drivers; followed the lead of Jeff's daughter and picked up lug nuts for souvenirs (she has a vast collection); took pictures of race cars undergoing last-minute inspections; and even listened as entire crew teams gathered under a big white tent in the infield for a prerace prayer. Before heading back up to the Chairman's Box, Jeff carefully positioned a few adventuresome guests behind protective new gates at the starting line, where the blurry blast of unbelievably close race cars traveling at speeds up to 150 mph—*vroom/vroom/vroom/vroom*—played out like a movie clip stuck on fast-forward.

From the enclosed Chairman's Box above the starting line, the race noise is muted and the intensity of being trackside is diminished. But the panoramic view of the track from a comfortable seat in the air-conditioned box, not to mention the catered buffet and bar amenities, are race day luxuries that Henry and Patricia often enjoy with Dover Downs executives and members of the Rollins family. As he has done for years at his Prairie Hill ranch, Henry frequently invites guests from all walks of his life to join him and Patricia for a night at the casinos or a day at the races. (Patricia on occasion enjoys playing the slot machines.) With the skill of a seasoned politician,

Henry mingles and greets his guests, always delighted to welcome local servicemen from Dover Air Force Base, presidents past and present from the University of Iowa and Kirkwood Community College, and friends from Belle Plaine and Prairie Hill.

At one point during the race in May 2015, Henry took a break from the Chairman's Box and stood for a moment on the outdoor balcony, facing away from the track and looking out below over the scattered vendors, a few musicians, and race fans milling about.

"It's been a challenge," Henry admitted, reviewing events since 2008 that have impacted the race car industry. Though both profits and earnings increased from 2012 to 2013 for Dover Motorsports, both categories dipped again in 2014 when admissions and event-related revenue dropped due to declining attendance and lower corporate spending at NASCAR event weekends. At one point Henry and the board considered putting the two companies back together, but outside shareholders protested and they dropped the idea. And with stock prices hovering at new record lows, the owners are reluctant to sell, and potential buyers are all but impossible to court.

For now, the board has embraced a few new ideas to try to offset declining revenue. In addition to the six major NASCAR events staged at the track every year, Dover Motorsports has expanded into the music venue business, hosting the Firefly Musical Festival on the track's adjacent property for three consecutive years. By 2015, Firefly was by all accounts phenomenally successful, featuring over 100 musical acts and such headline artists as rock star Paul McCartney and country star LeAnn Rimes, drawing over 90,000 fans to Dover. In June 2016, top artists ranging from Mumford & Sons, Kings of Leon, Florence & The Machine, and oldie but goodie Earth Wind & Fire promised to be "the most fan-driven lineup in Firefly's history."

"In its short existence, Firefly Musical Festival has become one of the most recognizable festivals in the world," Denis and Henry wrote to their shareholders in 2014. Could revenues from this event end up helping Dover Motorsports survive? "Only time will tell," said Henry.

Henry still believes that the business has a silver lining: namely, its four-star hotel with 500 rooms. "That's our savior in Delaware," he said.

"There's no place like it in the whole state." But, he admitted, "even with the big push to get younger people to come to the races, it's like the church business. If you don't get younger people in, you'll be out of business."

Neither Henry nor Denis will make any predictions about the future of the two companies, other than to say that some legislative changes must be implemented sooner rather than later for Dover Downs. And when it comes to his own future with Dover Motorsports and Dover Gaming, Henry, now 89 years old, said he has no plans to step down as chairman of either board.

It's no secret: Henry's continued involvement and leadership at an advanced age have "occasionally and delicately been questioned by shareholders who show up at the Annual Shareholders Meetings" in Dover, according to Pat Bagley, former company CFO and now a board member. "So there is obviously an uncomfortable feeling from the outside, wondering what is going to happen if something happens to Henry."

But, Pat concluded, "the people who do show up for the meetings see that Henry is holding the meeting and he is in charge. It is remarkable, because for all of the years I have known him, I don't see that much difference! Most people his age have gotten slower and less active, especially in business. But I don't think Henry got that memo. Or if he did, he purposely threw it away."

Henry, a reluctant but true mentor.

CHAPTER TWENTY-FOUR

A MENTOR TO THREE GENERATIONS

HENRY B. TIPPIE INSISTS THAT he doesn't give advice—"but I do make a lot of observations." And he believes that in his long journey from farm boy to successful business executive, entrepreneur, rancher, and philanthropist, he never tried to emulate anyone, nor did he have a mentor.

"I think I've done my own thing," he once explained. "I don't think trying to be somebody else works. You've got to be your own person. What works for one person won't work for another. I've seen a lot of people over the years try to copy somebody, and I think that's a mistake. Do it on the basis of what works for you. I have a certain personality, and what works for me will not necessarily work the same for someone else with a different personality."

This doesn't mean that Henry hasn't acknowledged the roles that O. Wayne and John Rollins played in his life. Henry often points to his years with the Rollins brothers as a key reason for his success, noting that working with them directly for 17 years exposed him to an extraordinarily diverse set of business situations that gave him a deep well of experiences and skills.

And the man who protests that he doesn't give advice has nonetheless evolved into a mentor for three generations of Rollins family members and countless other individuals who have come into contact with him over the years. Henry is the only non-Rollins family member invited to the family's two yearly hunting trips and retreats. At a recent family retreat, Randall and Gary Rollins called upon Henry to review milestones in their business history, including the complicated Orkin transaction, for younger Rollins family members. Henry is the only man still standing who was an eyewitness to those historical events.

No matter where Henry goes, it seems, personal acquaintances from every facet of his life speak with admiration about how much they have learned from Henry and his impact on their lives. With remarkable regularity, people repeat what they call "Tippie-isms" or "Henry-isms"—favorite, everyday observations and sayings dispensed by Henry that dip into the vast, commonsense wisdom he's gained by living a long, successful life. And a few even lapse into talking like Henry as they repeat these sayings, trying to match his uncharacteristically flat Iowa accent that delivers words with his own unique, nasal twang.

From friends, family, and business, civic, and philanthropic circles, these are stories about a reluctant but true mentor, beginning and interspersed with Henry's favorite observations:

I like to think that I start my day on a positive basis. I find that I feel better all day, irrespective of the fact that sometimes things may develop that are not necessarily pleasant. If you start the day thinking negatively, it will be a bad day.

"I consider Henry a very dear friend. He is one of the people I really idolize. He is so positive! You talk about a positive attitude—he's up there with Winston Churchill and Abraham Lincoln! Henry is what I encourage people to be, to know that you can do anything with your life if you are honest, set goals, work hard, look for opportunities, and give back and help others. Those are what I call the ingredients of success, and Henry Tippie epitomizes all of them."

—IOWA GOVERNOR TERRY BRANSTAD

"Henry has shown us that great things are possible when you greet the day with effort and recall each passing day with gratitude. He is what I consider to be a sage. You learn from him by just being around him."

—MICK STARCEVICH, PRESIDENT, KIRKWOOD COMMUNITY COLLEGE

As I get older, I have found that staying calm and not allowing myself to get all excited is an excellent approach. Also, I have always felt that irrespective of the circumstances, I will try to do the best I know how and move forward. I do not live in the past and spend time thinking about what could have been. I'm always moving forward.

"I learned technical things from him because he is a very technical accounting and business person, but he is broader than that. I also learned about perspective. There would be instances where I would feel like the world was ending in the next few minutes, because something happened or didn't happen, and I would make a call to Texas to Henry. And I would get, 'Now Patrick, let me just think about this with you for a minute.' We would talk about this, and he would have a solution or an idea and then we discovered that the world wasn't going to end in the next few minutes. So I learned it is perspective—rather than throwing resources at the problem or making a snap judgment—that would work."

—PATRICK J. BAGLEY, DOVER MOTORSPORTS

"He is a business laser-focused guy. However, there is a calming influence about him. He doesn't get too emotional one way or the other."

—TIMOTHY R. HORNE, DOVER DOWNS GAMING & ENTERTAINMENT

"Continental Bank failed in 1984, and the first inklings of what was to come happened in 1982. But since we had stood by Rollins, they made a judgment call that we were going to survive. They didn't panic. Henry sent word: 'We're not taking any of our money out. *In fact, we're going to put more money* in.*' And they left all their business with us. Everyone in our organization knew it was tremendous support. They stood up to be counted, and there were a lot who didn't!"*

—KEN CHALMERS, CONTINENTAL BANK

I am who I am. What you see is what you get.

"It is hard for some people to understand Henry. He is very direct and to the point, but you always know where he stands. He will do and tell you what is right, when it is unpleasant for him to do so, but he will always tell you. I do not have a better friend than Henry, and he is by far the best advisor I know. His judgment is very good to the point you can take his advice without question. If you have an agreement with Henry, you do not need to have it in writing. His word is all you need. But Henry will insist on putting it in writing, just to make sure there is no misunderstanding. It is just so valuable to have his wisdom at your fingertips. And he is loyal. He is just a loyal person, and there are not many of those. He is a rare person. You would have to look a long time to find someone equal. I am not very free with compliments, but in the case of Henry Tippie, it is very easy for me."

—R. RANDALL ROLLINS, ROLLINS, INC.

"Henry Tippie has really lived the American Dream. But he is so down-to-earth. Humble, honest, and unassuming. Those are Iowan traits. 'What you see is what you get.' And that's what I love about him. He understates things. He doesn't brag about all that he has accomplished. He'll say, 'I have a little ranch,' and it's one of the biggest ranches in Texas! He's a very unique individual, in a class by himself, but he is still an Iowan."

—IOWA GOVERNOR BRANSTAD

"I developed an immediate appreciation for his mind, and later for his personality. You know, Henry might seem kind of dry sometimes, but he's really as clever as he can be. He does have a warm side, but if you try to humanize him, you better take some other approach because he's unique. Unique in the most positive sort of way."

—JAMES B. WILLIAMS, RETIRED CHAIRMAN AND CEO OF SUNTRUST BANKS,
DIRECTOR OF ROLLINS, INC., SINCE 1978

"Think of Babe Ruth. When Babe Ruth stepped up to the plate, he either hit a home run or he struck out—there was nothing in between. So he led the league in home runs and he led the league in strikeouts. And Henry's really just the opposite. He's the guy that will go and get your single-base hits, and get men on base. And he doesn't strike for the fences, he keeps making sound decisions all the way along and that's really where the difference is."

—HANS KRAMER, FORMER SENIOR ATTORNEY, MORRIS, NICHOLS, ARSHT AND TUNNEL

Just the facts. Just stick to the facts.

"Henry will take the blue sky out of anything. His deal is 'just the facts.'"

—PATRICK ROLLINS

"I don't think I've ever met a person who has a better memory for names and numbers and facts. 'Just the facts. Just stick to the facts,' is what he always says.

—THOMAS G. WINTERMANTEL, DOVER MOTORSPORTS

"With Mr. Tippie, if you don't mean it, you better not say it. Just like he always says, 'Just the facts.' As long as you are totally honest, as long as you tell him like it is, there's not a better man to work for."

—RUSS DE CORDOVA, TEXAS CATTLEMAN

"More important than anything else is to find out the facts. And facts make people uncomfortable. Henry faces the facts as they are and makes the decision based on that for the long term. It makes him look unemotional, but he's just following the facts. People don't understand that he is one of the warmest, kindest people in the world, but what he does is just stay focused on the facts."

—JEFF ROLLINS

"He will always tell you what he thinks. 'Just the facts.' It will be straight, it will be honest, and it will be crushing at times. If you can't take the truth, don't ask him."

—MICHELE ROLLINS

You can wallow in misery or you can move on down the road. I do not live in the past and spend time thinking about what could have been. I'm always moving forward. Every day is a fresh start.

"Henry is never going to bellyache. He is not a Monday morning quarterback. And the thing I like the most, he places everything as an 'observation.' Not advice, but an observation because he has observed that if you do it this way, this happens. He is very, very smooth on how he directs folks. But if you said you are going to do something, he will check and make sure you do it. And basically, that's what I learned from Henry. Inspect what you expect. Go check. Every day, know where you are. He has mentored me in business and in a lot of the personal life things, like how he looked at schools for his children, how he basically situates himself close to his office. And in the last 10 years, my son Charlie, who is an investment advisor, would visit with Henry, and he would take us through how he evaluates companies, how he looks at investing. I've told him, 'Charlie, if you want to do well in the securities business, listen to Henry. If you take his advice and follow his conversations, you will do very well.' When you get him on his specialty, it's basically like seeing Michael Jordan play basketball; they switch into a gear that we don't have."

—PATRICK ROLLINS

"Henry sleeps well. He believes that right will win in the end. He does what he thinks he should do, and then hopes for the best. And if something goes wrong, he'll say, 'I did everything that I could do.' I think Henry is about that. He keeps moving."

—R. RANDALL ROLLINS

If you take one crumb, and then another crumb, soon you have a slice. Then soon you'll have two slices and pretty soon you'll have a loaf.

"He is cost-focused. He lives by the credo, 'a penny saved.' And he has that crumb analogy. 'If you take a crumb over here, the next thing you know it's a slice. And then you've got more slices and you've got a loaf.' And that's not a bad thing. He is also a 'keep it simple' guy. If it's too fancy, even if a financial mechanism, it's not worth doing. He keeps it simple and uses all the facts."

—TIM HORNE

"Working with people who have Henry's depth of experience is invaluable. They just give you insights that keep you from having to re-create the wheel and keep making mistakes over and over that others have made. Through the stories he tells, the experiences he relates, you can learn so much from him. The crumbs story—that is a favorite. We get that one about every year from Henry, and it is a good one."

—DENIS MCGLYNN, DOVER DOWNS GAMING & ENTERTAINMENT AND MOTORSPORTS

I've made so many mistakes in my life I've lost count. I look at it as furthering my education. I don't care who you are, you are going to make mistakes. And if you have a person who never makes a mistake, get rid of that person because they can't be doing much. If they repeat a mistake, that's another story. And if you don't know something, don't bluff. Just say, "I don't know," and we'll find it out.

"Dad came back to the radio station and I had totally messed up the ledger, and he's an accountant, and he said, 'We are not going to dinner till we get this fixed.' But he also told me, 'You are going to make mistakes and I'm willing to pay for that, and it's like taking a course and continuing your education. I just don't want to pay for the same course twice.'"

—HENRY B. TIPPIE II

"If I don't have the answer to one of his questions, I've learned from Henry to just say, 'I don't know. But I will find out and get back to you.' He wants the facts. But if you don't have them right at that moment, just say so."

—KATHY L. HALL, VICE PRESIDENT OF DEVELOPMENT, KIRKWOOD COMMUNITY COLLEGE

"Henry's delivery has never been, 'I've got all the answers and I'm smarter than you are.' He is, 'I'm thinking about this.' And I don't think Henry has regrets. I would probably have to say that."

—GARY W. ROLLINS, ROLLINS, INC.

The sun will go down tonight and it will come up tomorrow, and it will be another day.

"There is so much loyalty from Henry. And when I went through some personal issues, he was consoling. 'I know this is tough on you, Tom, but you will get through it. There will be brighter days ahead, the sun will come up tomorrow, and it will be another day.' It sounds corny when I say it out loud like this, but Henry is a very compassionate person. When you talk to him, you think you are the most important person around."

—TOM WINTERMANTEL

"He wants you to work hard, but when the day is over, it's over. He always said to me, 'Now Tim, the sun is going to go down tonight and it will come up tomorrow morning. So don't you worry about it. Tomorrow is another day.' And that's the way he looks at it. You will work hard and get after it again. That is a pretty good darn lesson. 'Don't get too worked up about everything and do your best.' I was talking to my son the other day, and he was stressed out, and I heard myself say, 'You've done everything you can do. What else can you do? So stop worrying about it.' And I probably heard a little bit of Mr. Tippie in that remark."

—TIM HORNE

"One of the great things about Henry, he's really good at giving you advice and you don't even know he's giving you advice—he calls them 'observations.' Usually I get a story from Henry, and embedded in that story is a nugget of advice. Oftentimes, it's 'Be patient, even though things might not look the way you might want them to look today, be patient, tomorrow's another day.' He takes the long view."

—FORMER UNIVERSITY OF IOWA PRESIDENT SALLY MASON

"Henry is a true gentleman and a good man. If my son could grow up with some of those attributes, I would figure that I was a successful father and person. Honestly, Henry is just a very special guy to us. We wouldn't want to disappoint Henry. He provides the standard for us to aspire to."

—PATRICK ROLLINS

Business at Iowa

THE UNIVERSITY OF IOWA ▪ HENRY B. TIPPIE COLLEGE OF BUSINESS

Henry B. Tippie

A Proud Name to Share

PART SEVEN: 1953–2015
Giving Back: "Repayment for Benefits Received"

CHAPTER TWENTY-FIVE

THE UNIVERSITY OF IOWA

ON DECEMBER 22, 1953, HENRY took out his Rehoboth Trust Company checkbook and wrote a check for $5 to the Chester F. Phillips Scholarship Fund at the University of Iowa. It was the end of Henry's first year with the Rollins brothers, and the almost 27-year-old accountant had come to a conclusion: he had an interesting job with a bright future, and it was time to give something back. Henry chose education in general because getting a college education had completely changed his life, providing a path to a business career that he could not have pursued without a college degree. And four years after graduating, he specifically wrote the check to the University of Iowa "because they let me in, then kindly graduated me." And from that day on, Henry gave back as a form of "repayment for benefits received."

"I'm a strong believer in education, because I feel my educational background ultimately led to a lot of opportunities," he said. "There's a high degree of probability that a lot of those good things would not have happened to me if I had not come to school at the University of Iowa. And without the G.I. Bill, my chances of going to college would've been next to zero. I've been able to do reasonably well with the education I received, and I look at giving back as a method of repayment."

Henry's $5 gift in 1953 began a tradition of giving back that would one day embrace educational institutions in Iowa and Pennsylvania, honoring not only the University of Iowa but also the Kirkwood Community College in both Belle Plaine and Cedar Rapids, Coe College in Cedar Rapids, and Allegheny College in Meadville, Pennsylvania, Patricia's alma mater. From 1953 to 2015, Henry's contributions to educational philanthropy increased dramatically as his financial circumstances improved, a 62-year legacy that included Henry's $30 million gift to the University of Iowa in the spring of 1999, recognized at the time as the largest single gift ever pledged by an individual to the university.

The story of how a completely unknown student became ingrained in the culture of a Big 10 university is a story that follows Henry to nearly every corner of the University of Iowa. In fact, if you walk across the campus—zigzag your way from Pat's Diner in the Tippie College of Business on East Jefferson Street to the Main Library on Madison Street, cross over the Iowa River toward the far pockets of campus along Park Road, meander back on Riverside Drive until you find your way past Kinnick Stadium on Evashevski Drive, enter the Hansen Football Performance Center, and climb the stairs to the Tippie Consensus All-Americans Room on the second floor—you will likely cross paths with business students, athletes, professors, a business college dean, a football coach, an athletic director,

Henry is a well-known figure throughout the University of Iowa, and he has a special relationship with its Big 10 football program.

numerous University of Iowa Foundation executives, a university president, and students from Belle Plaine who have all benefited in one way or another from Henry's support over the past six decades.

TIPPIE SCHOLARSHIPS, ALUMNI AWARDS, AND THE HENRY B. TIPPIE CHAIR

Henry's legacy of giving to the University of Iowa started with a single check in 1953, a giving ritual that Henry repeated every year for 13 years. But in 1967, some four years after the Orkin deal substantially increased the Tippies' net worth, Henry was ready to do more. He returned to his hometown of Belle Plaine and endowed a $500 yearly scholarship for Belle Plaine students who wanted to go to one of the three state universities, which included the University of Iowa. Beginning in 1967, the scholarship initially went to one boy and one girl each year from Belle Plaine who had "good moral character" but not necessarily the highest grade-point average. After all, Henry didn't claim the highest GPA in high school or college, and he knew what that felt like.

"I always feel the needy students sometimes might not have the best grades, because there may be a lot of other factors that preclude them," said Henry, no doubt recalling his own high school experience. "They may have a job that they have to do, and they may not have time to apply to studies. They may not have the environment, etc. Certainly the person would have to have ability, but there's a lot of ways you can judge a person as to whether they're going to be successful or not. Are they trying to take care of the family? What is their work ethic? Do they have integrity? If

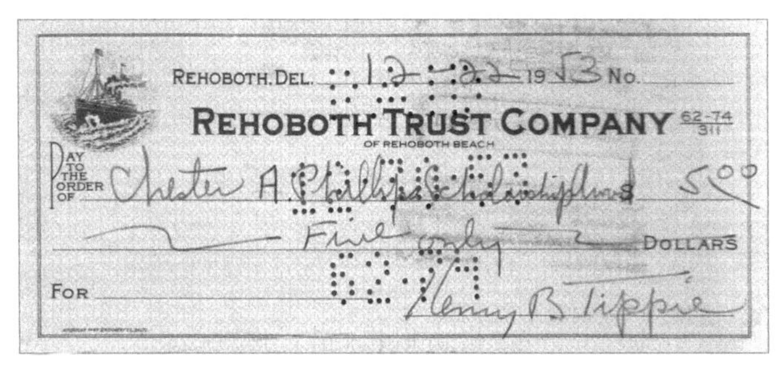

The first $5 gift Henry made to the University of Iowa.

they have the opportunity, are they the type of person who will do something with it?"

Future Belle Plaine Mayor Dave Fish was one of the first students to receive the scholarship in 1968, and he used the $500 to attend the University of Northern Iowa to study to be a teacher. "It pretty much paid my tuition for a year, and made the adjustment to college so easy, rather than trying to balance work and work study," recalled Dave. "The Tippie Award was a huge step forward for Belle Plaine, and Henry Tippie was a trend-setter for other groups or individuals to say, 'Maybe we need to do that.'"

Over the years, the Tippie Scholarship program has increased to over $12,000 annually for two Belle Plaine recipients and now goes only to students who plan to attend the University of Iowa. Henry keeps notebooks filled with personal letters from scholarship recipients over the years, including one from Zach Griffith, a 2015 University of Iowa economics and political science major from Belle Plaine. "As I approach my senior year at Iowa and begin to plan for graduate school, I cannot thank you enough for helping me achieve my lifelong goal of receiving higher education," Zach wrote to Henry in 2014. "I look forward to starting a career and one day helping young adults, like myself, pursue their dreams."

Henry's comprehensive files also contain a thank-you note from an 18-year-old Dave Fish in 1968. In 2012 Henry unexpectedly gave Mayor Fish a copy of that note, a gesture that reminded him of Henry's unique connection to his hometown.

"There could be other very successful Plainesmen, but they never ventured back to Belle Plaine and you don't know about them," said Mayor Fish during an interview in the Belle Plaine mayor's office in the summer of 2015. "But Henry's always ventured back. He's an icon to the city of Belle Plaine and an icon to our kids. 'Here's how you can live your life, and you too can be successful, and don't forget where you came from.' I encourage high school kids that the 'Tippie Scholarship is sitting there. Use it.' And I tell everyone outside of Belle Plaine that 'Henry Tippie is ours. The rest of you just borrowed him.'"

In 1981 Henry received the Distinguished Alumni Award for Service presented by the University of Iowa Alumni Association. He soon established the Henry B. Tippie Accounting Scholarship to be awarded to two accounting majors at the university, and in 1989 he received the University of Iowa Outstanding Accounting Alumnus Award. But in truth, Henry had only just begun to make his mark at the university. In 1984 the University's College of Business appointed a new dean named George Daly, who brought innovative ideas to the college that included a Board of Visitors, an advisory group of large and small business leaders and government leaders to help the college stay in touch with changing conditions and needs. Dean Daly invited Henry to be on the new Board of Visitors, and he remained a member for 13 years.

Henry also agreed to serve on the national committee for the Iowa Endowment 2000, a campaign conducted by the University of Iowa Foundation to raise $150 million in educational endowments by the year 2000 (the campaign exceeded its goal by more than 50 percent, raising $225 million in five years). On March 4, 1987—surrounded by then Dean Daly, then University of Iowa President James O. Freedman, and his mother, Amelia Tippie—Henry announced a leadership gift to the campaign that would fully endow a professorship and create the Henry B. Tippie Chair in Business Administration, later called the Henry B. Tippie Chair in Accounting. "As a native Iowan, I wanted to show my appreciation to the University and its College of Business Administration because the education I received has helped me achieve whatever success I've enjoyed in my career and in my life," Henry told the *Belle Plaine Union*, which featured a front-page story and photograph of Henry standing beside his

Henry and Patricia after the Medallion Ceremony, in honor of their gift to establish the Henry B. Tippie Chair in Business Administration, later called the Henry B. Tippie Chair in Accounting.

mother, Dean Daly, and President Freedman, who all looked delighted. The story noted that endowed faculty chairs typically required a $1 million level of support, which Henry had made possible.

Daniel W. Collins, professor of accounting and head of the business college's Department of Accounting, was the first accounting professor to receive the Henry B. Tippie Chair, a position he still held in 2015. And, as he pointed out, he was also a fellow Iowa farm boy and a graduate of the University of Iowa, receiving his undergraduate degree in accounting in 1968 and his Ph.D. in accounting in 1973. "Your support has allowed me to continue my active research agenda, which has led to publications in leading accounting research journals and to research workshop presentations at several schools both in the U.S. and abroad," Professor Collins wrote to Henry. "I continue to enjoy working with doctoral students. Their success after leaving the University of Iowa continues to spread the Tippie legacy far and wide."

THE HENRY FUND

In 1994, while continuing to serve on the Board of Visitors and working with new business college dean Gary C. Fethke, Henry Tippie and Henry Royer, then chairman and president of Merchants National Bank of Cedar Rapids, decided to create the Henry Fund. This endowed equity portfolio is managed each year by 12 MBA students who must apply to get into the competitive, two-semester program. Through the Henry Fund, the students use real cash to invest in the stock market, an opportunity to blend academics with real-world portfolio management experience. "Before this, the students were experimenting with the market, but it was all done on paper," said Henry. "I think when you've got your money in the pot out there, then you've got the real world. And I thought there should be a fund with cash, and the other Henry thought the same thing."

Henry established how the fund should be operated, and his terms were nonnegotiable: the fund would embrace a long-term, "buy and hold" investment approach through carefully researched and selected stocks ("I specified that I didn't want to see any hotshot-type stuff like commodities, etc. It needed to be with established companies."); no IPOs, no puts, no calls, no overseas companies, no hedge funds, no mutual funds, no bonds. "They could hold some short-term money, maybe some cash, but not much."

The Henry Fund was one of the first student-managed collegiate investment funds in the country when it started in 1994, established with an initial investment of $50,000 in the spring of 1994. By 2015, over 250 students (who call themselves "Henry Funders") had participated in managing the Henry Fund, which is highlighted and continuously tracked on a sophisticated, electronic display that hundreds of business students pass by every day on the way to classes. And according to Todd Houge, Ph.D., a student in the first Henry Fund class who now teaches the Henry Fund course, the Henry Fund has grown to over $5 million in assets since 1994 and is now divided into three different account areas: the original account set up by Henry Royer and Henry Tippie, where a portion of the dividend income supports annual scholarships to MBA students; a University of Iowa Foundation account managed by the Henry Fund since 2007; and a third account started with a $1 million donation from Henry and Patricia Tippie in 2011 and another $1 million donation in 2015, where dividends are used to fund scholarships for University of Iowa football players who are business majors.

"My role in the Henry Fund is not to give lectures but rather to serve as advisor to the fund. I'm the quality control manager," said Professor

Henry and MBA students who manage the Henry Fund. Professor Todd Houge, a student in the first Henry Fund in 1994, now teaches the class (pictured to the left of Henry).

Houge, who has been in his position for over 13 years to guide group discussions, written analyses, and detailed valuation models. "This is not your average case study. This is a case where there are no right answers. Students must learn to support their opinions with data and move beyond the facts, explaining in a convincing manner where they're going and why each stock selection is worthy."

When the Henry Fund started, there were fewer than 20 student-managed investment funds in the entire country, Professor Houge said. "Now they are pretty common, with at least 300 programs like this for undergraduate or MBA students, but we are definitely one of the larger funds. And the charter that we have is the same charter that was written by Henry and a professor over 20 years ago. We've made small changes over time, but it is essentially exactly the same investment charter. There are a lot of rules that prevent us from doing crazy things. For instance, they can't invest in IPOs—only stocks benchmarked to the S&P 500. We can't day-trade—our process doesn't allow us to get in and out of securities quickly. We have to have two-thirds of students vote in favor of an idea. On the other side, we have a new group of students every year, but they inherit the portfolio that the previous team left them. We have the ability to continually bring the portfolio back to center."

Todd Nelson, a CPA at Ernst & Young for seven years, applied to the MBA program specifically because of the Henry Fund. Before graduating in 2006, he landed an internship with Goldman Sachs in New York City, where he now serves as vice president–investment banking. "My Henry Fund experience lent credibility to my candidacy during a competitive interview process and reinforced Iowa's top-tier reputation," said Todd, who serves on the Henry Fund's Advisory Board.

Professor Houge sends monthly performance reports to Henry. "Henry loves the Henry Fund," he said. "He is very involved, and he keeps a very close eye on what we are doing, but he does not micromanage what we are doing. He is interested and passionate but very hands-off."

Henry admits that he is particularly proud of the Henry Fund's overall performance. "It's phenomenal what they've accomplished with a different set of students every year," he said. Since the fund's inception in April 1994 through July 2014, the Henry Fund reported a yearly total return average of 12.82 percent compared to the fund's S&P 500 benchmark average of 11.3 percent. "If we were a mutual fund, we would be a multimillion-dollar company, to the extent that this track record could be repeated," said Professor Houge. "We have had this performance in every year. We did not just get 'lucky' once."

The success of the Henry Fund mirrors not only the students' and Professor Houge's hard work but also Henry's investment philosophies and his own success in the stock market. In fact, over the years, his investment prowess has rivaled his reputation as a successful businessman and rancher, said Jim Martindale, Henry's former, but now retired, stockbroker who first met Henry by knocking on his office door when he started his career in Austin, Texas.

"Henry's got a very simple philosophy of investing, and he doesn't do anything strange," said Jim. "He won't do derivatives or commodities. He typically won't do a lot of new issues, no options. It's all about finding good companies that are financially stable, that are growing their earnings, and then just buy 'em and hold 'em. And just let them grow. And he has been very successful at doing that. You know, he'll sell a company on occasion, maybe one that gets into some kind of trouble, but typically he does his research, he picks good companies, and he just keeps them forever. I remember when the market crashed in 1987, it was down 40 percent in two days, and then again in 2001 when the market tanked after 9/11, and he was in there buying. He always realizes when you want to be buying. He's always stepping in there, big-time, with both feet. I always joke with him and call him 'Warren Buffett West.'"

THE HENRY B. TIPPIE COLLEGE OF BUSINESS

While creating the Henry Fund, Henry and Patricia contributed several gifts from 1993 to 1994 to help complete the business school's new administration building, the largest academic building on campus, with 171,000 square feet and some of the most advanced integrated technology of any teaching facility at the university. Inside the $35 million facility known as the John Pappajohn Business Administration Building, they established the 175-seat Henry B. Tippie Auditorium, the Patricia

Bush Tippie Student Lounge, and a small indoor student cafe lovingly called Pat's Diner.

By 1996 business school officials began to approach Henry about a remarkable opportunity: Would Henry be interested in participating in the naming of the College of Business? It was a long courtship, appropriate for the size of the gift the school requested. According to then Dean Gary Fethke, "It wasn't a letter in the mail one day. It took some time." As the process continued, Henry and Patricia continued to give to the school and, in 1997, endowed six research professorships in the business school. Within the year, university officials again approached Henry about a gift that would put his name on the school he had so consistently supported. And in April 1999 Henry agreed to meet in the president's office and discuss the topic with Dean Fethke; Michael New, then head of the University of Iowa Foundation; and then University President Mary Sue Coleman.

Dean Fethke recalled the specifics of that meeting: "Henry met us, and he let us mill around. I mean, this was an awkward thing. You're talking about someone giving millions of dollars, and that's more than anyone else in that room will ever make in their life, together. So we're talking around this event, trying to convince him how excited we are about it, and he just let us talk, probably for about twenty minutes or so. And then he said, 'Are you through?' And we said, 'Yes.' And he looked around and he went, '1, 2, 3,' he counted us, and he said, 'Three against one, that's about right.' So then he paused, and he brings out this letter. All the while we were sitting there talking, he had already developed this specific proposal. And he had it in his pocket! He was just hearing us out, waiting for us to pause. And then he pulls out the letter and puts it in front of us. He had written this all out, and had thought it through very carefully. He said, 'There are details in here that you will want to consider.'"

Unbeknownst to the surprised university officials, Henry had a history of pulling out letters in the middle of negotiations. Sly Henry, it turns out, relishes the rare moment of surprise if he's the one who orchestrates it. In 1972, for instance, when bankers in Austin met with him to discuss the merits of an unusual loan agreement, Henry reached into a drawer of his office desk and produced a letter that detailed the entire agreement.

In Iowa City, the letter Henry produced from his suit pocket carefully outlined the specifics of his $30 million pledge to the university. Never a "bricks and mortar kind of guy," Henry stipulated that his gift was not for additional buildings but for educational programs, professor salaries and endowed chairs, and research fellowships and student scholarship endowments that would allow the business school to compete on a national level to both retain and recruit "the very best and most talented" professors and students. "And of course we were flabbergasted," said Dean Fethke. "So we went away and pondered, but not for too long, and we pretty much agreed at that time to the details on the proposal that he made."

Ever the savvy, controlling businessman, the agreement was also "reasonably beneficial to his advantage," Dean Fethke noted. "Henry wanted to make sure he was getting a good deal. He's looking at this as a business proposition, so he's taking into consideration the payment period and all kinds of events that can occur that will give him the maximum flexibility in paying this off. He's complex, but down-to-earth and accessible. He's a very sharp observer. He's a prototypical Iowan, and an American original."

At the time, Henry's pledge was recognized as the largest gift ever made by an individual to the University of Iowa, and the fifth-largest gift by an individual to a U.S. business school. In Henry's honor, the university renamed its College of Business Administration as the Henry B. Tippie College of Business, the first time in the history of the university that an academic division was named in honor of an individual. "Henry B. Tippie—A Proud Name to Share," the business school noted that spring in a magazine cover story about Henry, described as the man whose "name is now part of our culture." Local newspaper headlines on February 19, 1999, the day after the announcement to the full board, mirrored an entire community's surprise at the extraordinary accomplishments of this former Iowa farm boy: *Once-poor Henry Tippie of Belle Plaine gives $30 million to the business school.*

At the ceremony on April 9, 1999, when the business college officially became the Henry B. Tippie College of Business, the staff presented Henry with two significant gifts: a painting and a book. The painting was of a farm boy on a hilltop, sitting on a cistern and lost in a daydream. The portrait no doubt recalled for Henry his father's cautionary words that his daydreaming son would not amount to anything, a memory the University of Iowa now firmly put to rest with a celebration of Henry's life of accomplishments. Sharon Scheib, then director of communication and external relations, next presented Henry with an inscribed copy of *The Greatest Generation*, written by NBC anchorman Tom Brokaw to celebrate Americans who were born in the 1920s and came of age during the Great Depression, fought in World War II, and went on to build America though honesty, integrity, and hard work—attributes often used to describe Henry. "I think what has motivated Henry to give back is his gratitude for what he got here at the university, and the fact that he was a poor kid," said Sharon. "He certainly did not have any wealth when he was growing up, but education made that possible for him. And now he's trying to pass that on."

Members of the Rollins family, sitting in the audience during the ceremony, were shocked to hear the amount of Henry's donation to the university. "He never told anyone!" recalled Michele, who said the announcement came as such a "surprise because Henry is so tight! This is a man who kept a record of the three pennies he spent for lunch, and he was always so careful. John would tell stories about how Pat didn't have a television set, and they would buy it for her when Henry was on the road. So yes, it was shocking—and it was wonderful!"

The event was truly significant for Henry, Patricia, and their family members, but, at the same time, simply a part of Henry's strategy to provide "repayment for benefits received." He was humble when interviewed by a writer for the business school's magazine, who asked about what motivated his generous gift.

"So why did I choose the College of Business at the University of Iowa? The number-one reason is because they let me in, then kindly graduated me," said Henry, repeating a favorite phrase. "The number-two reason is because it's a great honor to be asked to continue assisting the growth of this college."

But then he dug a little deeper, reflecting on the success he had experienced since graduating from the University of Iowa in 1949. "I feel like my whole life has been, to some extent, accidental. If someone had told me 50 years ago that I would be capable of giving this kind of support, I would have thought they were having a pipe dream," Henry concluded. "I look at the college now and think what it was like when I was a student here, and there's no comparison. It's like night and day. It's come a long way in 50 years, and I've been able to see that progress and have a small role in it. I find that gratifying. If I had to do it over, I would choose Iowa again."

The impact of Henry's "repayment" was almost impossible for university officials to describe. "When you commit that amount of funding to an entity like the college, it says that somebody has that kind of confidence in the college, it gives the college confidence, it gives a depth of resources that it didn't have before," said former University of Iowa Foundation President New. "And it allows them to look at the future in a very different way. It allows them to start thinking about being in a different league than they might have been thinking about otherwise. It really kind of permeates the college, and it makes the college a better place, there's no question about it. And you know, in the business school world, to be a named college brings stature with it. And this is a very good thing, and people can say, 'Wow, there's something of importance going on there, they have someone's name attached to that.' So many of the major business schools are named in this fashion. So this puts them in a higher league than I think we would have been before."

Henry and student Lindsey Morris, who received her BBA in accounting and her master of accountancy from the Henry B. Tippie College of Business.

President Coleman focused on what she called Henry's modest beginnings and why he was a "fabulous role model. Because he doesn't come from a family that had great wealth. He was the one who created the wealth. And to have his name on the college is very meaningful—meaningful to students, that they are able to come and see what he was able to accomplish and that he's a very good person. He's a very centered person. He has remembered where he's come from. He's remembered all these people who helped him and he's invested back. And it's harder for me to imagine a better message for students. I'm grateful that he did it, but I'm also grateful for who he is."

As he had done for years on the streets and in the restaurants of Belle Plaine, Henry began to show up unannounced at the college that now carried his name. Students and faculty could spot him walking through the beautiful rotunda area that featured his oil portrait; see him settle into a chair in the auditorium named after him; or stop for a cup of coffee at Pat's Diner, where he once slipped $200 to the cashier and said, "Here. Use this on student lunches until it runs out." He often walked the hallways with his hat on, former Dean Fethke once said, "with the same unassuming gait that he did 50-plus years ago when he was a student." But unlike the once completely unknown business student from the class of 1949, Henry soon became something of a celebrity in the halls of the College of Business that bore his name.

"It is priceless to have Henry Tippie walking our halls," said Sarah Fisher Gardial, Ph.D., who was named dean of the Henry B. Tippie College of Business in the spring of 2012. "There are a lot of colleges that are named for people who aren't alive, but we have a donor who walks the halls and talks to our students. He once stepped out of my office and went over and started talking to one or two students in the hall, and pretty soon, they were flocking to him. He is an incredible role model. He shows that you can come from a rural, humble upbringing and have the kind of success that he has had. Money can't buy the impact he has on our students."

Make no mistake: Henry enjoys every minute of these student interactions. "I relate to the students. They think I'm up here [he gestures with his hand at eye level], but I'm down in the trenches, someplace with them. They know I'm not some Phi Beta Kappa," he said. "They have all these 'selfies' now and they love to get their pictures with me. They go on these blogs and Internet, and that spreads all over the place. I don't have any problem with it. A year or so ago, I'm walking up and down the halls, and one of the students says, 'That's Henry Tippie out there.' The professor is teaching a course on management science, and he's calling me. He wanted me to come and talk to the class. And I did. And really, they treat me like a rock star!"

CONTINUED SUPPORT, AN HONORARY DOCTORATE

In addition to his generous gifts to the College of Business, Henry soon became an influential presence in other areas of the university. At the University of Iowa Foundation, Henry served for years on the Foundation Board as well as on the Investment Advisory Committee. The foundation's Bill Windauer, who played an instrumental role in convincing Henry to name the business school, once noted that Henry "can provide so much quality advice that would otherwise cost a fortune. To have him on our board, along with others like him who can guide us on investing policies, it can only make us better. And he does it totally voluntarily. We send him our annual reports, and he checks things down to the penny. And after a while I could predict questions that he would have: *Why didn't we make as much money invested this year as we did last year?* or *Where did these expenses go? What was this $10 charge?* He writes all that stuff down in that little notebook pad in his pocket, and I would always try to have the answers ready. Because as an accountant, he looks at things differently than maybe I would, or other people. And he was very careful about that because it was his money that he gave to us to use in the best way we could."

People often recall one particular story featuring a thrifty Henry. When Michael New assumed the position of president of the Foundation, Henry wrote Michael a letter of congratulations in February 1999, and included a penny he found on the campus grounds. "He picked up that penny," Bill Windauer remembered, "and when he got back to Texas, he taped it on the letter and wrote, 'I don't know what this signifies other than there must be plenty of funds floating around for money to be laying on the street. Please credit my account accordingly. I am a strong believer in compounding!' Because even a penny makes money, if you invest it, and I think he was trying to send a message that if you watch your money carefully, it will help make more money for you."

Gifts far more valuable than a single penny continued to find their way from the Tippies to the University of Iowa. The university recognized these steadfast, generous contributions in 2002 when they awarded Henry the Hancher-Finkbine Medallion, given annually to seven individuals (but only one alumnus) for distinction in leadership, learning, and loyalty. In December 2005, recognizing the importance of excellent leadership for the school named in his honor, Henry made a $5 million gift commitment to the University of Iowa Foundation to endow the deanship of the Henry B. Tippie College of Business—a move designed to further enhance the growing reputation of the school and its ability to attract top talent.

Despite his reputation as a major benefactor and a financial expert, Lynette L. Marshall admitted that she was nonetheless "disarmed" when she met Henry for the first time at a board meeting in 2006 after she was named president and CEO of the University of Iowa Foundation. "You are taken by his down-home personality and the fact that he grew up poor on a farm," she said. "And you are struck by how remarkably smart he is and the discernment in his remarks. What I've always cherished is his constant support of leaders on this campus. There are so many 'Henry-isms' that come to mind. . . . *Every day is a new day; if something goes wrong there is always tomorrow, so press on.* . . . He certainly has had his own fair share of challenges in life, and he lives that way."

Foundation President Marshall, an experienced fund-raising professional from the University of Illinois before coming to Iowa, said it is not unusual for wealthy donors to give to many areas of the university, just as Henry and Patricia have done. But it is unusual, she noted, for donors to make such substantial gifts while they still have the opportunity to interact with students and faculty, putting a welcome face to the name behind the generosity. "It's really fun to see Henry and Patricia come to campus and walk around on their own, to see them interact with students," she said. "And then, once the students realize it's Henry Tippie, 'Oh my gosh. Henry Tippie. Here he is among us!' It's the star power. We've all heard the story about Henry walking down the hall, and a faculty member comes out and recognizes him and asks if he can introduce him to his class. The Tippies are so supportive of the college, and it creates this sort of pride and commitment and desire to have the opportunity to meet

Henry and Patricia with scholarship recipients and students during an annual spring luncheon.

them. There is a spirit and enthusiasm and appreciation that the student body has because they know the impact he has. And I think that Henry appreciates the joy that comes from his gifts, a joy that continues on year after year."

In a coincidence they both enjoy, Foundation President Marshall shares a farming background with Henry: She grew up on a fifth-generation family hog farm, graduated with a degree in agriculture from the University of Illinois, and still proudly reports that she was once National Pork Queen. "If you can't be proud of that in Iowa, where can you be proud of it?" she said with a wonderful, confident laugh. And it all adds up to one thing: This polished, articulate foundation president understands the agrarian experience of people like Henry who come from rural, agricultural backgrounds and succeed in business and philanthropy; and Henry, with his penchant for speaking in the vernacular and trading on his humble beginnings, feels appreciated for exactly who he is and not just for what he has given and may still give in the future. "There are a lot of studies on why alumni give back to a university, and the number-one reason is usually that it will make a difference in the life of the institution and shows a belief in an institution's leader," she said. "In Mr. Tippie's case, he wanted to allow the business school to excel, to expand, and then, once you have invested that way, you allow your name to be associated with the brand of that institution, to help it move forward. But fundamentally, it comes out of a sense of gratitude for what the school gave to him once he got off the farm and came to college on the G.I. Bill, and believing in the vision of the institution. And there are only a handful of people who can make the transformative gifts that Mr. Tippie has made."

When Sally Mason was appointed president of the University of Iowa in 2008, Henry Tippie was near the top of a list of people she wanted to meet. President Mason and Henry quickly became professional acquaintances and personal friends, with President Mason and her husband, Ken, visiting the Tippies at the ranch. She soon determined that Henry was a "straight shooter and a genuine person," she said. "If there's something going on that he needs to know about, I just tell him. He is not someone who will rush into anything, without giving it a lot of thought and fully analyzing the ramifications that could come from a big decision. And you can ask him anything, and maybe he will answer and maybe he won't. That's Henry."

Henry with President Sally Mason, receiving his honorary Doctorate of Humane Letters from the University of Iowa in 2009.

Just a year after she arrived, President Mason was part of an event for Henry that she considered very special. On December 19, 2009, at Carver-Hawkeye Arena, the University of Iowa recognized Henry's remarkable level of contributions and loyalty to the university by bestowing on him an Honorary Doctorate of Humane Letters. Months of preparation and letter writing, spearheaded by faculty and supported by President Mason, had been kept a secret from Henry—something that's generally anathema to Henry B. Tippie. And even though his executive assistant Terri Whetstone admitted that Henry was really surprised when he found out about the honor, for once he was not upset that he had been kept in the dark.

During the impressive ceremony, Henry proudly wore the distinctive doctoral hood against a formal black robe adorned with Iowa gold embellishments. In his prepared speech, he succinctly reviewed his undergraduate experience some 60 years back, his successful career, and why he chose to give back to the University of Iowa. "I believe my Iowa education has been instrumental in helping me become who I am today," he said, echoing a lifetime of familiar statements. "I have been fortunate enough to make some repayment to the university. I feel very strongly about the disadvantaged having an opportunity to further their education. In today's world, there are many bright young people who have a very difficult time gathering the resources needed to attend a university, college, or a community college. Being able to help others achieve that education is one of the most rewarding things I have been able to do."

After giving a nod to Patricia, "who I have been lucky enough to share the last 53-plus years with," Henry's heartfelt, humble speech took a decidedly atypical, nostalgic turn. "I am extremely proud to be recognized for this high honor at this university," said Henry. "Without question, it is a highlight of my life. When President Mason called me about this award, I told her that this was a topper. For me, this is a long way from the farm and a one-room schoolhouse. I guess a few more people know my name than they did then. I will always be student No. 30748, and I will always be grateful to this university."

A BENEFACTOR GIVES—AND RECEIVES

From 2010 to 2015, the Tippies continued their legacy of giving to the university, supporting not only the Tippie College of Business and the Foundation but branching out into some new areas, too—namely, athletics. Football season-ticket holders for more than 50 years, the Tippies traveled to Florida on January 5, 2010, to watch and cheer from the university's V.I.P. Box as the Iowa Hawkeyes beat the Georgia Tech Yellow Jackets 24-14 in the Orange Bowl, the first major bowl win for the Hawkeyes since 1959. Now *this* was a birthday party! The victory was a very special present for Henry, who celebrated his 83rd birthday during the halftime festivities when Athletic Director Gary Barta and President Mason surprised him with a cake and a round of "Happy Birthday"!

Still basking in the glow of the Orange Bowl victory, Athletic Director Barta and Head Football Coach Kirk Ferentz visited the Tippies' Prairie Hill ranch in May 2010, hoping to interest these loyal Hawkeyes in their vision for a new practice facility. The two men already knew of the Tippies' dedication to providing scholarships, and decided to see if the couple would consider a gift that would go toward both scholarships and a new facility.

Head Hawkeye football coach since 1998, Coach Ferentz admitted he was initially skeptical about interacting with donors on the collegiate level. "But being here for the past 17 years, one of the biggest blessings I've experienced is the interaction with our donors, people like Henry and Pat," he said. "They allow our program to thrive. I've had the opportunity to interact with people who are simply inspirational, and Henry and Pat are at the top of that list."

"And being at the ranch was just unbelievable. You have no idea what to expect," Kirk continued. "I mean, Henry owns a country down there, and every parcel of land has a story behind it. And the hospitality from both Pat and Henry was so warm and genuine. It was just so enjoyable."

Henry and Patricia soon parlayed their love of Iowa collegiate sports into major gifts to the football program. The Henry B. and Patricia B. Tippie Athletic Fund, established in 2010–2011, contributed substantially to help create the new football practice facility and established scholarships for football players who are also students in the Tippie College of Business. And their devotion to Hawkeye athletics has always gone beyond football. Members of the I-Club for more than three decades, Patricia and Henry routinely attend football and basketball games in Iowa City or share their season tickets with acquaintances and Henry's former high school friends from Belle Plaine. And they are often seen on the sidelines for games and rowing events in Texas near Austin and Waco, whenever a Hawkeye team competes nearby. When the softball team played in the Gettermann Classic in Waco in 2013, the Tippies drove over from the ranch to watch the game. Henry and Patricia posed for pictures afterward with the team, proudly wearing the Iowa sweatshirts the athletes presented to them and keeping the softball signed by the young women as a gift.

For all their efforts, Henry and Patricia received the Hawk of the Year award in 2013, the University of Iowa's annual award that pays tribute to exceptional loyalty, enthusiasm, and generosity to the school's athletic programs. Athletic Director Barta noted that the department's most prestigious award does not reflect "one moment in time but an accumulation, to honor those who have been a part of the program for a long time." To

Henry B. Tippie, grand marshal of the 2013 Homecoming Parade.

celebrate, Henry served as the grand marshal of the university's Homecoming Parade. Perched on the back of a tomato-red Chevy Corvette, Henry rode through the streets of downtown Iowa City, smiling and giving a thumbs-up to the homecoming crowds that waved back from the sidewalks. Just imagine, for a moment, what this former student from Belle Plaine must have been thinking, riding on the back of a convertible, watching people wave to him, 64 years later. It's a story even Hollywood couldn't make up.

As exciting as that moment turned out to be, Coach Ferentz treasures even more an afternoon with the Tippies in April 2015. The new $55 million Hansen Football Performance Center had recently opened on the edge of campus, just beyond Kinnick Stadium, and Henry and Patricia were touring the facility for the first time. Inside the sprawling, state-of-the art training center that Coach Ferentz calls "one of the best in college football," the Tippies stopped to admire the new Tippie Consensus All Americans Room—a unique, second-floor dining and meeting area named in honor of the Tippies that salutes the program's long history of football All-Americans. Instead of scattering all over campus for meals, team members gather around football training tables in this room for breakfast and dinner together every day.

After the tour, Coach Ferentz invited the Tippies to meet with members of the football team on the new indoor practice field, right before the team started their afternoon drills. Anticipating their visit, Coach Ferentz had earlier reviewed Henry's background with the team, telling his players:

> Here's a guy who grew up on a farm and ended up serving in World War II. . . . He went to the University of Iowa on the G.I. Bill, stuck his neck out and took a shot as an accountant in Delaware with a small company that grew into a great company. . . . The Tippie College of Business is *this* Henry B. Tippie, and so is the Tippie All-Americans Room upstairs. . . . I think it's a great story.

"They were all eyes and all ears, suited up in their football uniforms but just before practice," Coach Ferentz recalled. "Henry, being Henry, just talked to them, and he was pertinent and to the point. Pat and Henry

University of Iowa Head Football Coach Kirk Ferentz and Henry huddle with football team players before indoor practice drills.

were both there together, and Henry assured them that the team had their full support. It was the first time he had ever addressed the team, and it was very special."

At one point, Henry, wearing his favorite WWII Veterans baseball cap and surrounded by white, gold, and black uniforms, gave the team a thumbs-up. And before he left, the team members all gathered in a huddle, some watching in awe as Henry stood side by side with their coach and raised his right hand in a team high-five salute. "Go, Hawks! One, two, three, WIN!"

"It was," concluded Coach Ferentz, "a unique moment for all of us."

FEELING THE LOVE

In ways both big and small, officials throughout the University of Iowa enjoy creating unique moments to celebrate Henry and Patricia. Some, like the huddle with the football team, are rather spontaneous. But others take a lot of planning to make sure that Henry and Patricia feel the love of the entire university community.

For instance, Barbara Thomas, executive director of communications for the Tippie College of Business, put together a Quiz Bowl Contest, using questions and trivia about Henry's life to recognize his 80th birthday, complete with a visit from Henry Tippie II. And for his 85th birthday, Barbara pulled out all the stops when she helped coordinate a Flash Mob Dance in the vaulted central gallery area of the Henry B. Tippie College of Business. The dance, choreographed by Marisha Johnson, a business and dance major and Henry B. Tippie Scholarship recipient from Woodbury, featured two rows of V.I.P. university representatives, as well as Henry's two daughters, Linda and Helen, who came to surprise their father. As each dancer took to the floor, Henry laughed in surprise, swaying to the music and pretending to direct the musical numbers unfolding before his very eyes. As the dance concluded, "Henryfetti"—dime-sized paper coins featuring photographs

During his 85th birthday celebration in 2012, Henry laughed as University of Iowa Foundation's Lynette Marshall joined the Flash Mob Dance, followed by Professor Daniel W. Collins, who holds the Tippie Chair in Accounting.

Henry posed with students, including Flash Mob Dance choreographer Marisha Johnson (far right, first row).

of Henry—floated down throughout the vaulted space like so much personalized parade confetti.

"When you put on the Chattanooga Choo Choo, I almost joined you," said a joyous, laughing, and totally delighted Henry. "I may be 85 years old, but I can still move." During the party, Henry posed for picture after picture with students and admiring guests. And before the event ended, a reflective Henry took the microphone and, while still wearing his black top hat sprinkled with pieces of Henryfetti, saluted the crowd with a special message: "You honor *me*. But I want you to know I am honored by what *you* do. You're the people making this place hum, not me. I feel proud of what I see here. You are the future."

When asked later if the business college does as much for all donors, Barbara had to chuckle. "Oh no. It's *HENRY!* His name is on the door!" she said, while acknowledging that the college tries to make every donor feel appreciated. "And a big part of my job is to make sure that Henry and Patricia are involved and feel the love. They are grounded and sweet and down to earth. There is great respect for what they have done for us, and we love them greatly. It's always a joy to work with him, and it amazes me that he knows his calendar in his head. I remember at one point in time, we were thinking about his 80th birthday, but we wanted to celebrate when the students were on campus, which was after January 5th. And he stopped and said, 'I could do January 26th, but let me check . . .,' and he pulled out the little calendar that he carries in his pocket. 'Yes, I could.' I was just amazed that six to nine months in advance, he knew what date might work."

"And for the students to meet the man whose name is on the college, he is a rock star," Barbara added. "It's kind of surprising, because you won't even know he's here, and there can be a buzz in the building and then you'll *know* that Henry B. Tippie has arrived. He is always extremely gracious. He will pose for a million pictures and selfies with students, but he will always ask, 'Where are you from? What are you studying?' It's amazing for them. He has a quiet persona and he likes to have time just to be in the hallways, too. He will just walk right up to a student and say, 'I'm Henry Tippie.' I'm always impressed with how much he appreciates student interaction."

Henry's two daughters, Helen (left) and Linda (right), surprised their father and danced alongside University President Sally Mason (center).

At the University of Iowa Foundation, Tiffani K. Shaw, CPA, executive vice president and COO, finds that her accounting background helps her understand what she calls "Henry's complex, 60-year giving history." Not long after she arrived at the Foundation in 1997, Henry first expressed an interest in a detailed annual donor report. "That's where my relationship with Henry started to grow. He wanted a more thorough report, which as an accountant I can appreciate."

The annual Henry and Patricia Donor Fund Activity Report is a comprehensive record of every Tippie donation ever made to the University of Iowa and the University of Iowa Foundation. It tracks the balances of every Tippie account; how the funds were expended during the year of the report; market investment returns both historical and yearly; and the historical gift value, which charts the growth of donations over time. Chock-full of numbers, the report also includes names, pictures, and personal letters that Tiffani thoughtfully solicits and includes from every student, faculty member, and program leader who has benefited throughout the year from the Tippies' philanthropic efforts, as well as pictures from annual faculty and student scholarship luncheons where Henry and Patricia have a chance to connect the faces with the names of those who hold a professorship, fellowship, chair, or scholarship that bears their name. "When you see this book, and all these notes from every faculty member and every student, this is something that Henry probably never anticipated when he made his first gift," she said. Henry receives two donor reports each year: the June 30 report is the more comprehensive one, with pictures, letters, and reports; a separate financial report goes out at the end of every calendar year with just numbers.

Tiffani noted, respectfully, that Henry prefers not to publicly discuss specific dollar amounts of his gifts and approves information before it is released by the Foundation. But the sheer depth of the Tippies' donations can be told in these simple facts from the Tippie College of Business: during any given school year, 47 or more students on campus receive academic support from Tippie scholarships; 12 professors hold Tippie Chairs and Tippie Faculty Research professorships; and at least 20 faculty members are Tippie Faculty Research Fellows, whose work is briefly described every year in the Donor Report. "When donors give during their lifetimes, it gives us an opportunity to thank them and show them the impact of their gifts," said Tiffani. "I hope this Donor Report is a small part of that. But really, I can't do Henry justice with words."

In the fall of 2014, Henry and Patricia announced an ambitious giving challenge campaign that would become a part of Tiffani's 2015 Donor Fund Activity Report. To inspire more high-impact gifts from a new generation of donors—and to help the Tippie College of Business reach its *For Iowa. Forever More* campaign goal of $125 million—the Tippies pledged up to $15 million to the college if their gift was matched by individual gifts of $1 million or more from alumni and donors by the end of December 2016. Along with the challenge, the college established the Tippie Society, an elite donor recognition category that acknowledges gifts of more than $1 million since the start of the campaign. The purpose of the Tippie Society is to recognize those donors who follow the Tippies' example of generous giving to the college and to encourage the next generation of donors to engage with the college.

And last but not least, Henry and Patricia stipulated that part of their generous $15 million donation be designated to establish the Amelia Tippie Chair in Finance at the Tippie College of Business, in honor of Henry's mother, who passed away in 1993 when she was 94 years old. "She always encouraged me to get off the farm, and I couldn't think of a better thing to honor that," said Henry. "And Patricia is the one who came up with the idea." The announcement of the Amelia Tippie Chair in Finance came just after the Tippie College of Business announced the establishment of another endowed professorship with significant ties to Henry: in 2015, in tribute to the remarkable history between the Rollins and Tippie families, the O. Wayne Rollins Foundation provided $2 million to establish the Tippie-Rollins Chair of Excellence.

Like many Tippie moments, the story of how the Tippies agreed to provide the challenge gift for the *For Iowa. Forever More* campaign is priceless. To sow the seeds for such a bequest, Dean Gardial and Barbara Thomas met with Henry in his Austin office in August 2014 to explore the concept of matching funds. "Henry," Dean Gardial said boldly to begin the meeting, "we think if you would put up $15 million in matching funds, we could go out and bring in the people who will then bring their own gifts to the table. With your help, we will incentivize the people who are not giving. We need something to fuel the campaign, because it is languishing."

For nearly an hour, Henry grilled the college executives with questions. *How would it be set up? When would the match be required? How would other donors get recognition?* "Henry's mind is just so analytical," said Dean Gardial. "We surprised him, and he didn't know that was coming, and he had no preparation, and I was later told that he doesn't like surprises, so that wasn't ideal. And for an hour, he just grilled us. And then he said, 'Let me get back to you in a week. I need to think about this. Let's go to lunch.' And we said, of course, that's fine. We hadn't expected him to give us an answer right then."

Over lunch at Henry's favorite Chinese restaurant not far from his Austin office, the conversation was 100 percent social. Patricia joined them. "No one said a word about why we were there, and the purpose of the proposal," said Dean Gardial. At the end of the meal, the waiter dropped four fortune cookies in the middle of the table, and Henry ended up taking the very last one. According to Dean Gardial, Henry opened his fortune cookie, and "at first he smiles. And then he started laughing. And then he *really* laughed. And none of us could imagine what it was. And then he read his fortune to us: 'Giving Makes You Smile.' And we almost fell off our chairs! It was like Divine Providence! And when we walked out of the restaurant, he stuck the fortune in his pocket."

Back in Iowa City the very next day, Dean Gardial received a phone call from Henry. "All right, I'm going to do it," the dean heard Henry say, "and here's what it's going to look like." Henry then proceeded to outline the conditions of the challenge gift, which Dean Gardial accepted. Within no time, the Tippies' challenge grant had "a positive impact on our fundraising picture. It has been a real game changer," she said. "And Henry has fulfilled his desire to bring the next generation of donors forward."

Dean Gardial and Barbara sent Henry a special commemorative gift to mark the challenge gift commitment: a perfect replica of the fortuitous fortune cookie, made out of crystal and engraved with Henry's perfectly timed fortune: *Giving Makes You Smile.* The crystal cookie sits in a prominent spot on Henry's desk at home in Austin.

A VERY SPECIAL PHILS DAY

In 2013 a newspaper story about Henry featured this headline: *Tippie's Presence at the U of I More than Just His Name.* The headline was a perfect reflection of Henry's brand of stewardship—the kind that includes not only giving money but taking time to go to football and softball games; to speak to students in the hallways of the college that bears his name; to attend faculty and student luncheons every year to hear about business research and activities funded by the Tippies; to pay anonymously for student lunches and pose for pictures at Pat's Diner; to eat breakfast and share observations with Henry Funders; and to write letters back to appreciative scholarship students who send him thank-you notes throughout the year.

And on May 1, 2014, in keeping with his "more than just his name" persona, Henry was the keynote speaker at "PHILs Day"—an annual event that aims to educate students and the University of Iowa community about the benefits of philanthropy (PHILs) in hopes of creating future philanthropists and fund-raisers. In one of his most impassioned speeches ever, Henry started out by joking about the time he was a student at the university, taking an undergraduate communications course. "I had to give a speech twice, because I was told I didn't move my mouth enough." Reassuring the standing-room-only crowd in Iowa Memorial Union that this wouldn't happen again, Henry then shared stories of his student life, his career, and his belief in philanthropy. The jokes and laughter continued: *I was admitted on probation—that ought to tell you something right there . . . ! I did not belong to any organizations because I wasn't invited to join any. . . . They found one picture of me from the yearbook; on the front the picture had that I was "self-supporting" and on the back they had my academic record. It's a good thing it was on the back! . . . At my age, when I wake up every morning, it's a GREAT day!*

But the captive audience heard more that day than Henry's humor, as the 87-year-old soon delivered not only business and philanthropy wisdom but a dose of grandfatherly mathematical advice, too. "I am the recipient of someone giving me a chance to go here," he said, challenging the standing-room-only crowd to take a simple $5 bill (the amount he first gave in

1953), multiply that by 30,000 students for $1.5 million, take a return of 4.5 percent, multiply that times 10 years, probably factor in some growth, and realize that you would then have nearly $20 million in a student fund if everyone participated. "I feel very strongly about repaying for benefits received. And the $5 is what I call my bread crumb theory of business: it's a little here, a little there. And after a while, you've got a slice. Keep at it, you get two slices. Then you've got a half a loaf, and then after a while you have a full loaf. That's my $5 theory. Now think about that."

As everyone listened intently, Henry delivered his final pitch. "Now I fully realize that not everyone is going to be able to build buildings with their name on them. That's fine. It's all the other smaller items that add up, like the bread crumbs, that you need to think about when you leave here. Don't forget the university. Just think what it's done for you. It's given you a foundation to expand your life. You are the future. You are the future PHILs. The time to become engaged is NOW. I recommend that you bring PHIL into your life and build beyond what you have done right now. And, I would say, the best is yet to come."

The crowd in the Iowa Memorial Union auditorium gave Henry a standing ovation at the end of the speech. The applause was loud and sustained. A student named Ashley P. cheered because "when Henry described the importance of giving through his crumb theory, it seemed so much more important that I ever envisioned, and he spoke about giving with so much passion and pride that it was hard not to be touched." A student named Samuel J. clapped because "I realized how you can come from nothing and truly become whatever you want to be." And a student named Jonathan M. said he suddenly realized that "I was only going to give back if I was able to give a large sum of money, but now I know that even a smaller sum helps."

Looking slightly amused, Henry motioned several times for the students to sit down, but the crowd continued to stand and applaud. President Mason noted that Henry "had that look on his face," even laughing at one point, as she approached the podium to bring the highly successful PHILs Day event to a close.

In many ways, Henry represents both ends of the philanthropy spectrum at the University of Iowa: he's the person who can talk about the value of giving $5 and still hope to make a difference (because he has), and the person who can be courted by university officials to give millions (because he's done that, too).

But Henry, according to President Mason, before she retired in the summer of 2015, "remains very coy" about any future donations that he plans to make to the university. "He won't tell us what it is, but he's not coy about telling us that there will be one. Since I am getting ready to retire, I just decided to ask him outright, if he would share it with me. He got that look on his face and said, 'No, I'm not ready yet.' So I'm not sure what his plan is, but I am sure he has one. He has said with a wry smile that he intends to be very generous to the university, and I understand that, and I understand that he won't tell you till he's good and ready. Does it change the way anyone approaches him? Not really. Henry is Henry."

President Mason was asked to describe what she means when she references "that look on Henry's face." Well, she said, "Henry's features soften. He gets a wry smile or grin on his face, and his eyes twinkle. That's the look. When I see Henry reacting in that way, I know he is completely comfortable, enjoying himself. And this is good. It's a *very* good thing."

"That look on Henry's face."

CHAPTER TWENTY-SIX

KIRKWOOD, COE COLLEGE, AND IOWA GOLD STAR MILITARY MUSEUM

THOUGH THE UNIVERSITY OF IOWA is only an hour from Belle Plaine, Henry determined early on in his career that he wanted to support educational opportunities that were closer to his hometown and closer to his experiences growing up as an Iowa farm boy. And by taking steps to address the educational needs of students who gravitated to community colleges and vocational educations instead of a university setting and a four-year degree, the Tippies expanded their growing educational legacy to students from all walks of life.

Henry's ties to Kirkwood Community College, Iowa's largest community college, can actually be traced back to Belle Plaine. In 1967, when Dr. Norman Nielsen was superintendent of the Belle Plaine community school district, Henry announced that he and Patricia would like to offer a four-year college scholarship to two high school students from Belle Plaine. Dr. Nielsen helped put the scholarship plan in motion, and the tradition was still going strong in 2015.

When Dr. Nielsen was appointed president of KCC in the late 1970s, the supportive relationship of the Tippies followed him to the school's 885-acre main campus outside Cedar Rapids. The Tippies became increasingly interested and involved in the college's mission to reach out to potential students in the college's seven targeted counties, which included Belle Plaine's Benton County at the far western edge of Kirkwood's boundary. Henry understood the college's growing efforts to provide on-site classes to everyone in the service area, requiring no more than a 20-minute drive. But one of the areas where that goal proved to be most challenging turned out to be his hometown of Belle Plaine.

According to KCC officials, Henry took the lead to create a collaborative approach to address this situation. Through discussions and negotiations, he and other community leaders, including the Mansfield Trust officers, formulated a plan to build a new public library in downtown Belle Plaine and then donate the existing Carnegie Library building to serve as a Kirkwood educational center. In 1992 Henry and Patricia supported the effort with a capital gift and established Kirkwood's Tippie-Mansfield Center in Belle Plaine in the former library building at 1214 Ninth Avenue. The center offers an array of college-credit and adult basic education programs to area residents, who no longer have to go outside the county for their courses.

The result, noted KCC officials, was not only a new Kirkwood extension program but also a richer learning experience for the wider community. "I felt it was an excellent idea for providing opportunities for individuals of the Belle Plaine community who desired additional education," said Henry. "It has all the high-tech equipment in there. And when they are having a class in Cedar Rapids on the main campus, it can be beamed to the outreach facility. So it's brought something to Belle Plaine that probably otherwise a certain group of students wouldn't have the advantage of."

Henry could certainly see himself in those "certain group of students" who, like him, grew up in this whistle-stop farming town and might not be as prepared as the rest of the world for four years of college. His thinking proved the perfect match for KCC and the windows of opportunity that the community college offers for primarily underserved students. "Kirkwood does an outstanding job of providing services and programs for individuals who might not otherwise have the opportunity to receive an advanced education," he said.

It didn't hurt that the Tippies and the Nielsens became "very good friends," said Dr. Nielsen, who retired as KCC's president in 2004. "Not only because of his support of the college, but he's just a genuine human being and one of the most caring and charitable people that I have ever met. And I think he likes what Kirkwood does, the students we serve. He likes agriculture."

The Tippies' generosity to KCC has, over the years, gone from strength to strength. Consider:

- In 1995, in a step that mirrored the Tippies' scholarship program for Belle Plaine students attending the University of Iowa, the Tippies established an endowed scholarship fund for students from Belle Plaine who enrolled and studied at the Tippie-Mansfield Center.

- With a nod to Henry's successful foray into the beef business in Prairie Hill, Texas, the Tippies made a capital gift in 1997 that established the Tippie Beef Education Center on KCC's main campus. This 8,600-square-foot facility offers a heated concrete arena with portable seating for up to 300 during judging contests, exhibitions, or training; two classrooms for students and professors; and enough stalls and six adjacent yards for up to 300 head of cattle. The new

The Tippie Beef Education Center on KCC's main campus.

facility opened in January 1998, when falling snow created a white blanket over the adjoining fields and cattle yards and helped highlight the new two-tone gray building. A newspaper headline, *No Beefs with New Building*, announced the opening of the new cattle production and educational building, which soon attracted the attention of local beef and veterinary associations interested in using the facility. At the dedication of the beef center on June 25, 1998, Henry noted that "it is my hope that the Tippie Beef Education Center will assist students in meeting the challenges of beef production and the technological changes required in our changing business environment."

- In 2001 the Tippies established the Henry B. and Patricia B. Tippie Beef Education Endowed Scholarships. At the time, the Tippies' gift of $300,000 was the single largest endowment donation in KCC's 35-year history. Kirkwood President Nielsen noted, "There have been some challenging financial times for many of our rural students. Henry and Patricia Tippie know that. It's a testimony to their boundless optimism and belief in rural Iowa as well as Kirkwood that they put in place a support system for generations of young beef production professionals. For this, we are extremely grateful." The first scholarship funds from the endowment became available for students in the 2001–2002 academic year. The Tippies' support of the Kirkwood beef production program was a cornerstone in the school's efforts to put its agriculture science programs in the forefront of agriculture education in America, and it would soon be ranked as the second-largest community college in terms of total ag science degrees.

- The Tippies established the Henry and Patricia Tippie Endowed Faculty Chair program in 2004 to honor their friend and former KCC President Nielsen, who had retired. The program provides direct support to college professors in research, curriculum development, travel, and other efforts aimed at improving the learning experience for students and the entire college community.

- In 2012 the Tippies announced a $1 million gift to start the Henry B. and Patricia B. Tippie Business Education Endowed Scholarship, with the first awards made to Kirkwood students in business programs in the fall of 2014. In honor of this gift, the college named a key meeting facility the Henry B. Tippie Business Event Room. The room is incorporated into the Hotel at Kirkwood Center facilities, which is the only teaching hotel and meeting space of its kind at a two-year college anywhere in the country, according to Kirkwood officials.

"Henry has never forgotten his Iowa roots," noted Kirkwood President Mick Starcevich. "He has never forgotten that personal success must include the stewardship of the world around you."

Driving around the main Kirkwood campus, it's easy to see why visitors frequently note that it looks like a four-year college. Its rolling, bucolic landscape is home to more than 27 buildings and adjacent to a 400-acre working farm, where the Tippie Beef Education Center and its mix of cattle, students, and teachers stand as a physical reminder of the Tippies' generosity. Though the Tippies do not like to divulge financial

Henry and Patricia in front of the Henry B. Tippie Business Event Room at KCC.

summaries of their total philanthropic efforts, President Starcevich notes that they are without a doubt Kirkwood's biggest financial donor, a distinction he traces back to their association with Norm Nielsen.

And Dr. Nielsen always understood one defining characteristic about Henry's philanthropic educational efforts. "Henry doesn't just give to charitable organizations," he said. "He sees everything as an investment. And so the difference with Henry may be that it's not just charitable causes, but it's causes that have a purpose, that are going to serve a need. And so whether it's Belle Plaine's library, whether it's a scholarship program at Kirkwood, whether it's the College of Business at Iowa that's going to serve thousands of students over the years, he sees all these as investments in people. And these are things that are going to help people and eventually yield dividends to a better lifestyle, to a better society. Even though they're charitable, I really believe he contributes or invests in things he believes are going to make a difference."

Kathy L. Hall, Kirkwood's vice president for development, believes that the measure of Henry's heartfelt support for education has always gone beyond his generous financial contributions, something she pointed out in a letter in 2009 to support the University of Iowa's nomination of Henry for an honorary doctorate. As anecdotal proof, Hall described a chaotic, stressful day in the summer of 2008, during the devastating floods in eastern Iowa. Kirkwood had undertaken a massive animal rescue effort in several buildings, including the Tippie Beef Center. One morning after the flood, rescue volunteers, college staff, and local veterinarians were hard at work when they happened to notice a gentleman walk in, asking to see the set-up. He noted that he had "heard of the big job" they were doing, and he wanted to see for himself how the thousand-plus animals in Kirkwood's care were faring. "It was Henry Tippie," Kathy wrote. "If one staff member hadn't recognized him and thanked him for his interest, he could well have come and gone with no fanfare at all."

Three years later, on the evening of October 19, 2011, Henry could not escape some carefully planned fanfare. More than 200 people on Kirkwood's campus that night honored Henry with a standing ovation as he accepted the Samuel J. Kirkwood Society Legacy Award from the Kirkwood Foundation, the highest honor given by the foundation and one that recognized Henry's long record of generous donations of endowed scholarships and capital improvement gifts to promote Kirkwood's mission.

Kirkwood President Starcevich saluted Henry's "many decades of industry, energy, and services to his home state." Henry, dressed in a charcoal gray pinstriped suit with an American flag pin in his lapel, was absolutely beaming. A newspaper reporter later wrote that he was "measured and thoughtful" in his acceptance speech, noting that he was grateful for the opportunity he had to go to college on the G.I. Bill and musing on his unlikely path from his boyhood on a Belle Plaine farm to the height of business success.

"I'm glad I grew up on an Iowa farm," he said. "That's how I understand that in education, it's just like farming. You have to put back into the farm, into the land. That's why we've always tried to give back to this state and its people, to look out for the next generation coming along."

COE COLLEGE, CAMP DODGE, AND THE IOWA GOLD STAR MILITARY MUSEUM

Over the years, Henry has expanded his educational philanthropic reach to include the first two places where he lived on his journey out of Belle Plaine: Coe College and Camp Dodge, home of the Iowa Gold Star Military Museum.

In 2012 Henry officially recognized Coe College, the liberal arts college in Cedar Rapids where Henry studied briefly in preparation for service as an air cadet. Henry and his fellow Air Corps enlistees lived in the lower level of Eby Fieldhouse while studying at the college from June 1944 through early 1945. A grateful Henry returned to Coe College some 67 years later and gave $1 million in May 2012 to

Henry and Coe College President James Phifer in 2012.

establish an endowed chair called the Henry B. Tippie Professorship in Business and Economics.

"Just as he has been generous in support of education elsewhere, Mr. Tippie has stepped forward with an important gift to Coe College, one that will touch the lives of students for generations to come," stated then Coe College President James Phifer.

Henry also created a President's Special Assistance Fund with numerous contributions over the years to Coe College. This fund gives the college president flexibility to offer loans of up to $1,000 to students in dire financial need. These interest-free loans do not require repayment for five years, offering respite to students who find themselves in difficult situations.

In 2013 Henry traveled back to Camp Dodge, the military base outside Des Moines where he and all newly enlisted servicemen from Iowa first went to be processed during World War II. Henry never forgot that he arrived at Camp Dodge just hours before D-Day in 1944, staying in the camp for a short while before he was transferred to Coe College. Over 70 years later, Camp Dodge serves as the headquarters for the Iowa National Guard and is now home to the Iowa Gold Star Military Museum, a conceptually sophisticated and comprehensive military museum that combines history, artifacts, equipment, and poignant narratives that honor and depict the military experiences of Iowa citizens and Iowa veterans. A proud veteran, Henry contributed financially to the museum after being approached by Robert M. Holliday, an attorney and fellow veteran who serves as chairman of the board at the Iowa Gold Star Military Museum.

"Mr. Tippie is a patriot from the word *go*," said Robert, walking through the various displays and exhibitions at the museum, graciously providing expert descriptions of everything from the Civil War Room, the Korean War Display, and the rare World War I German machine gun to the uniform of a World War II paratrooper and a replica of a nuclear attack submarine. And there, on a wall lined with portrait photographs for a relatively new exhibit of notable Iowa veterans, Robert points proudly to a photograph of Henry B. Tippie, posing in a dark suit and wearing his

World War II veteran's cap while holding a vintage photograph of himself as a young staff sergeant with the 20th Air Force. The exhibit pays tribute to Henry's 27-month military career, right where it all began on the grounds of Camp Dodge.

Henry pictured in the *Notable Iowa Veterans* exhibit at the Iowa Gold Star Military Museum near Des Moines, Iowa.

Patricia at the 2005 dedication of the Patricia Bush Tippie Alumni Center.

CHAPTER TWENTY-SEVEN

ALLEGHENY COLLEGE

IN THE SPRING OF 1956, a beautiful college coed named Patricia Sue Bush—who everyone said bore a striking resemblance to movie actress Deborah Kerr in that year's phenomenal movie *The King and I*—was on the verge of graduating from Allegheny College and marrying the love of her life, Henry B. Tippie. There was only one problem. She was about to fail a course because her final paper was incomprehensible, and her professor told her she couldn't graduate. With her wedding scheduled in less than two weeks, the situation was simply unacceptable to this future bride. "If you allow me to pass this course and graduate," a wily Patricia proposed to a very surprised and no doubt bemused professor, "I promise you that I will never use my accounting degree." Patricia passed the course, graduated, married an accountant, and kept her promise.

Flash-forward nearly 59 years to February 6, 2015, to a very special ceremony at Allegheny College designed to recognize individuals of distinction and national stature who are graduates of liberal arts colleges. This time, a very surprised Patricia Bush Tippie stands before friends and fellow trustees as Allegheny College President James H. Mullen Jr. presents the college's inaugural President's Medallion to Patricia—a member of Allegheny's Class of 1956, a longtime member of the College's Alumni Council, and a College Trustee since 1992. The award celebrates liberal arts graduates, Dr. Mullen told the group, who are "transcendent in their fields, who have made a profound difference as citizens and who stand as worthy role models for the current generation of students and for those who will follow. It is with particular pride that Allegheny awards the inaugural President's Medallion to Patricia Bush Tippie, whose extraordinary vision for the College has done so much to enrich the life of every Allegheny student and alumnus. The example of her life and her generosity of spirit is a powerful lesson for all who aspire to use their liberal arts education to do good."

Patricia was deeply moved, and fought back tears when she accepted the award. "This was the first time in my life that I have been surprised, so at first I was shocked and overwhelmed," she said. "Then I realized that all of my trustee friends were responsible for me receiving this high honor and I felt humbled, honored, and loved. It was an unforgettable evening."

"Unforgettable" truly describes Patricia's relationship with Allegheny College, an academically rigorous liberal arts school with nearly 2,000 students in the northwestern corner of Pennsylvania. From its 79-acre campus in Meadville, tucked between forests like a perfectly placed pocket on the front of a jacket, this once stumbling, almost-didn't-graduate coed has become one of the college's most ardent and beloved supporters. "Patricia represents the best of Allegheny and the liberal arts tradition in America," said Dr. Mullen.

After graduating in 1956, Patricia didn't think too often about her alma mater in the early years of her marriage, when she was busy raising her children and creating a home. It was Henry who eventually encouraged Patricia to maintain the connection, suggesting that she give annual donations the same way he had started to give to the University of Iowa. "I probably wouldn't have stayed connected if it wasn't for Tip," she said. "He insisted that we give. And he decided to focus on education because it changed his life. He's always called it, 'repaying for benefits received.'"

Patricia's stance on education soon became just as strong as Henry's. Over the years, Patricia joined the Allegheny Alumni Council, and the family's gifts to the school began to increase as the Tippies prospered financially. In 1992, college officials approached Henry and asked him to be a trustee. Patricia laughs, recalling Henry's response. "Tip told them they asked the wrong person!" she said. But when she received the invitation to be a trustee, Patricia initially said no. "Are you sure? Do you know that I almost didn't graduate?" she remembers asking college officials. Henry encouraged her not to turn down the offer, to think about it for a week or so before giving a final answer. "This will be a good thing for you," he advised. "If something happens to me, what will you do? If you had Allegheny in your life, you would be busy and you wouldn't go to Georgetown and lock the gate."

Patricia accepted the offer and became a trustee for Allegheny College in 1992. It was initially quite intimidating, and she claims she never spoke during trustee meetings for the first two years. "I had never been with judges and doctors and people making decisions for a college," she admitted. "But I gradually learned to speak up. And I think the experience helped me grow intellectually and gain self-confidence. It really broadened my world, and I've made some lifelong friends."

One of those friends is Dr. James C. Bulman, an internationally known Shakespeare scholar and professor of English at Allegheny who was appointed interim dean of his department in the spring of 1993. He met Patricia at his first trustees meeting that spring, when she was just finishing her first year on the board, "and I had been dean all of a month. She and I hit it off from the beginning. Patricia was relatively new, and I was finding out things about the college that I never knew existed, so neither one of us were comfortable talking!" he recalled. "But I have seen her become increasingly knowledgeable and articulate. It's very clear that she defines her thoughts and opinions, and in a way, being on the board has continued her liberal arts education."

The board asked Dr. Bulman to take over as president for five months during a 1996 search for a new president, and during this time his relationship with Patricia continued. "I could talk with her about issues and know that she would be supportive. But more than anything, Patricia just loved the school."

Following their earlier decision to provide scholarships for students from Belle Plaine, Henry and Patricia soon established a scholarship program for students from Patricia's hometown of New Castle to go to Allegheny. "That scholarship attracted students who wouldn't have come to Allegheny," said Dr. Richard Cook, who was named president of the college in 1996.

When Dr. Cook met the Tippies for the first time, Patricia's warmth put him at ease right away. "I enjoyed getting her wisdom and guidance on college decisions," he said. "She is balanced, wise. She has a tendency to hold back, she is not the first one to speak. But there was always a time in a meeting when someone would turn to Pat—or you could see she was ready to speak and have a thoughtful comment, almost always brief, insightful, and well thought out. She certainly stood on her own two feet and had opinions about her college."

But Dr. Cook admits to being intimidated by the prospect of meeting Henry, based on stories of "his tremendous business success and my concern about making sure I measured up. But I think it was the first time we went out to dinner, the three of us, and he was warm and gracious and a very interesting conversationalist. Any apprehension I had was quickly put to rest. He could do the opposite if he chose to, but he is so gracious, and he has nothing to prove to anyone."

The Tippies shared with Dr. Cook some ideas for their next philanthropic effort at Allegheny—an endowed professorship. "They both wanted to attract and keep the very best talent at Allegheny, recognizing that some professors could go to any number of other places. They wanted to reward and keep them here," said Dr. Cook, who enjoyed the process. "The fun part about watching them together is that Henry knows it is her college, but they are a team. She turns to him, and he turns to her."

The Tippies ultimately agreed to endow the Henry B. and Patricia Bush Tippie Chair to recognize a distinguished faculty member, an honor that provided salary enhancements, money for creative independent research, and money for academic assistance. Delighting everyone involved, Dr. Bulman, arguably one of Allegheny's most outstanding and widely recognized professors, was named the first recipient in 1997, and he has held the endowed position ever since. He is proud to point out that unlike some endowed positions, the money from the Tippies goes not only to the professor but to the students as well, allowing for learning experiences and educational trips that "resonate with the goals of a liberal arts college. Patricia wanted a part of this chair to be for students in order to be a part of that tradition."

With money from the endowed position, Dr. Bulman enjoys traveling with students both stateside and abroad, often exploring theater and

Shakespeare through live performances that "can be wonderfully transformative. When I spend Tippie funds for students, the vast majority have never traveled out of the country before, but they come here because they are hungry with intellectual curiosity," said Dr. Bulman. "It is exciting to teach students like this."

From 1997 to 2004 Henry and Patricia contributed to many other projects at Allegheny, including improved science facilities and the Wise Sport and Fitness Center. And beginning in 2004, the Tippies zeroed in on a project that would become not only a cornerstone of the college but a lasting reflection of Patricia's legacy: an alumni center for Allegheny College.

Immediately, Dr. Cook and his staff came up with the idea to restore the college's Sarah Cochran Hall, a grand 1908 building at the center of campus that offered a mix of architectural styles, ranging from Roman-style arched windows and columns to a great English-style entry hall and a dining room done in Italian villa style.

"It was a gracious, wonderful building, and pleasing to the eye with its massive oak beams. But over the years it had been modified and neglected, and it was virtually ramshackle," said Dr. Cook. Originally used as a student residence and dining hall, it had been converted to a warren of rooms for a mixed bag of activities, including a student center, a bookstore, a mailroom, and rooms for the English Department upstairs. Important architectural features had over the years been covered in Sheetrock or discarded instead of being properly restored, and the "building was heavily trafficked but it looked awful and it was dangerous. Many people thought it should be torn down."

Sitting with Henry and Patricia in his office, Dr. Cook presented his vision to not only restore Cochran Hall but to use this "old jewel" as the centerpiece of a new alumni center. By now, he knew that Henry preferred to invest in people and wasn't usually drawn to brick-and-mortar projects. But Dr. Cook also recognized that the restoration project appealed tremendously to Patricia, and he decided to take a chance.

"I got through my pitch, and there was a pause. Patricia looked a bit skeptical, but she looked to Henry. 'What do you think?' I gulped, and he said, 'Well, you know, it doesn't look good. It's a terrible building. Maybe

The Tippies with then Allegheny College President
Dr. Richard Cook in front of the new Alumni Center.

it should be torn down.' I think he was testing the idea a little. 'But,' he said, 'if that's what Patricia wants, that's what we will do.' I could tell his major interest all along was something for Patricia to be proud of. He was asking all of the right questions about stability, feasibility, financial. He wanted to be sure. And when he said that, she looked at him and said, 'That's what I want.' They work as a team, with ideas back and forth, respecting each other's opinion and Henry giving way to her preferences. We had so much joy and fun working together."

For this special project, Henry and Patricia did more than write a check. For over a year, Patricia flew back and forth between Pennsylvania and Texas, working with designers, craftspeople, and architects on nearly every phase of the historically sensitive restoration project, consulting on everything from colors and decorations to furniture and light fixtures. Much of the work on the first floor and the western exterior replicated the building's original appearance, and the redesign of the east side created a beautiful columned entrance facing the campus. Dr. Cook remembers walking through the building one day, only to look over and find Patricia on her hands and knees in a newly restored room, inspecting the texture of new carpets.

When the historic building reopened in the heart of the campus on North Main Street in 2005, it represented the most extensive restoration of a historic structure on campus, reclaiming its rightful place alongside venerable campus buildings like Bentley, Reis, and Montgomery. Inside, the Patricia Bush Tippie Alumni Center offers an elegant "home away from home" for Allegheny alumni, friends, and family, one of the finest alumni centers to be found on any small college campus. Inspired by the Tippies' generosity, other alumni families named Parent, Hoag, and Tillotson stepped forward with significant gifts to restore the building's original library and its oak-paneled dining room, and helped create a new gallery space in what was once an original kitchen.

The building's dedication ceremonies brought together a mix of trustees, faculty, friends, and family members who were close to Patricia and Henry, including Michele Rollins. "Patricia is so accomplished," said Michele, "and it was wonderful to watch Henry take a backseat, graciously and proudly. Our dealings are always in business, and he is always out in front, and I had not seen that side of him before. It was just magical."

The Tippies soon provided funds for a permanent endowment to maintain Cochran Hall, appropriately combined with funds left by Sarah Cochran for the same purpose. And during commencement ceremonies on May 14, 2011, Allegheny College conferred honorary Doctorates of Humane Letters upon Patricia Bush Tippie and Henry B. Tippie, honoring their longtime support of higher education in general and Allegheny College specifically. By now, after serving nearly 20 years as a trustee, Patricia had elected to become a Trustee Emerita of the school. As one of the first women to serve on the male-dominated Board of Trustees, Patricia and others on the board had a "double hill to climb because they were women and I think sometimes they were overlooked," said Dr. Cook, now retired as president. "Pat, in conjunction with other women who served on the board, helped change that culture. While I was there, we added more women to the board and we ended up with a first woman chair of the board. Pat definitely had a role in leading the way for making those changes."

As a Trustee Emerita, Patricia has continued to be involved as a board member and in other roles, too. In 2014 she agreed to be cochair of

Henry and Patricia received honorary Doctorates of Humane Letters from Allegheny College in 2011.

the college's comprehensive capital campaign, with a $200 million goal and the aim of doubling the college's endowment. In 2015 Patricia and Henry began work to develop another professorship endowment in her mother's name and to provide additional funds for student internships. Dr. Mullen, who became Allegheny's president after Dr. Cook retired in 2008, noted that no matter what effort Patricia gets involved with, "she works so hard that she raises your game through her passion. She cares so deeply. That has not waned, that has only intensified. She is a quiet, effective, engaged, and passionate leader."

Some of Dr. Mullen's favorite recollections about Patricia are based on her visits with students. Many times, he has watched Patricia walk into a room filled with students and faculty, and sit down at a table. "Everyone goes to her table. The room gravitates to her. Students know and appreciate her love of the campus, and she invites you to share who you are with her. She draws out their stories, and she listens to them. She makes them feel that they are the most important people in the world at that moment. And that's just her way."

When Patricia received the college's inaugural President's Medallion in February 2015, the college also gave Patricia a Birthday Book to celebrate her upcoming 80th birthday on March 17. Inside were letters from trustees, college friends, and students who had received scholarships from the Tippies, all wishing her a happy birthday and sharing some personal messages of thanks:

> *Pat Tippie is one of only several people who epitomize Allegheny College to me. Intelligent, a sense of presence with an extra dose of generosity . . . Your generosity to me as an undergraduate student was a lifelong help. I have benefited from a small college because of you! . . . Congratulations on being the first ever recipient of this new and prestigious Allegheny College award. There could be no better choice to receive this inaugural recognition. . . . Thank you for your love, loyalty, and dedication to Allegheny. The college is certainly better because of you.*

Patricia keeps both the Birthday Book and her award in her home office in Austin, a quiet room with pictures of family and friends, memories from travels with Henry, and scenes from the two ranches on bookshelves and on the wall over her computer. The woman who nearly didn't graduate from Allegheny College recognizes the impact she has had on the college, but Patricia thinks more about the impact that philanthropy has had on her.

"You get back more than you give, and then you just give some more. And it seems to me my money increases when I give it away," she said earnestly. "I just wish people would try it and see what happens. Most people, when they talk about giving and getting back more than they gave, they are talking about having warm feelings and things like that. But I'm talking about the good old checkbook. I give little amounts, compared to Henry. But I honestly feel that Tip and I are blessed with our income because we give, and because we're supposed to keep giving."

Patricia received the inaugural President's Medallion from Allegheny College President James H. Mullen Jr.

Henry and the road named for him in Belle Plaine.

CHAPTER TWENTY-EIGHT

BELLE PLAINE

HENRY B. TIPPIE HASN'T LIVED IN Belle Plaine for any extended time in over 70 years, not since he left in June 1944 to join the Air Force. But those who know him best readily admit that Henry's heart will always be in Belle Plaine. When it comes to his Iowa hometown, Henry "doesn't want to see Belle Plaine dry up and blow away," said his daughter Linda. "He is sentimental without even knowing it."

Over the years, as Henry and his family traveled back to Belle Plaine to visit his mother and other close friends, Henry witnessed the economic and demographic changes that brought severe decline to many rural communities throughout the country, including rural Iowa. As the transfer of goods by railroad dramatically declined, Belle Plaine's once-bustling railroad depot dwindled from freight to just passenger trains before it eventually closed. Long-standing businesses associated with rail freight disappeared, too, like the brickyards and Funks Bros. (where Henry once worked to save money for a car). The small town struggled to survive the construction of a major highway that bypassed the town to the north, taking traffic and potential shoppers with it. The town's population, once 3,887 in 1920, declined to just under 2,500, and the small shops and business owners along 12th Street, once packed with people and cars on Saturdays during Henry's childhood, could no longer compete with the emerging shopping malls and big box stores in places like Cedar Rapids and nearby Waterloo. A brief building spurt in

the late 1970s brought affordable apartments, a Bevins Motor dealership, a new S&W Home and Auto on 13th Street, and a new Chelsea Bank on the site of the former railroad roundhouse. But the major farm crisis in the 1980s caused even more businesses along the town's main street to shut down. In what many considered a last gasp, Belle Plaine was selected to take part in the state's Main Street Iowa program in the mid-1980s, a small town revitalization effort that held out the promise of funding and other resources for small towns. Area residents and merchants rededicated themselves to keeping Belle Plaine safe, clean, and attractive as it rebranded itself as a historic downtown district along America's former historic Lincoln Highway. The dedication of numerous city officials, not to mention several bond issues, eventually resulted in a new aquatics center, new schools, and an attractive main street makeover. The historic King Theater, where Henry and his brothers watched their first silver-screen movies, still stands.

Throughout this survival roller coaster, Henry insisted that "economic development is a necessity for a small town to survive. You need educational facilities, transportation, and a workforce." And from 1967 to 2015, Henry worked consistently to create opportunities, programs, and buildings in Belle Plaine that would enhance his beloved hometown and help it survive. Like walking through the campus at the University of Iowa, a drive through Belle Plaine in 2015 traces Henry's lifetime of giving back to nearly every corner of this small town: from the local high school to the airport, from the library to the Kirkwood Community College center, and from the Veterans' Memorial in front of City Hall to the Belle Plaine Area Museum and the Henry B. Tippie Annex.

Jim Magdefrau, a columnist for the *Belle Plaine Union*, noted that Henry and his family once "delivered milk in the early morning hours to half of Belle Plaine. Now, through his entrepreneurial work and philanthropy, he's still delivering to Belle Plaine."

SCHOLARSHIPS

Henry began his career as an educational philanthropist in his hometown in 1967, when he first started a scholarship program for two high school students in Belle Plaine. The Tippie Scholarship Program at Belle Plaine High School, which gave out its first two awards in 1968, has over the years expanded to include scholarships for two graduates who choose to attend the University of Iowa, as well as an endowed scholarship program starting in 1996 for Belle Plaine High School students who attend Kirkwood Community College. In July 1985, when the theme of the Fourth of July Parade in Belle Plaine was "A Salute to Youth," no one argued when Henry was tapped as the parade's grand marshal. "Tippie has been saluting the young of Belle Plaine since 1968 with generous scholarships to graduating seniors," the local paper reported.

By 2015, hundreds of high school students had benefited from the Tippies' scholarship programs in Belle Plaine—including those like David Fish and Carrie Jo Sayre, who not only used Tippie scholarships to help pay for college but then returned to Belle Plaine to give back to their hometowns. Dave is a longtime teacher, coach, and now mayor of Belle Plaine. And Carrie, who graduated in 2012 with her Ph.R. degree in pharmacy from the University of Iowa, returned to her hometown in 2012 to be the pharmacist at the just-opened Cornerstone Apothecary on 12th Street, part of the town's revitalization efforts.

"It was so nice of you and Pat to stop by the pharmacy a while back when you were in town!" Carrie wrote to Henry in September 2014. "Also, I want to thank you for your generosity toward Belle Plaine and the University of Iowa. You were truly instrumental in my education, and I appreciate it so much."

THE MANSFIELD/TIPPIE AIRPORT AND INDUSTRIAL PARK

In 1985 the Tippie brothers joined forces to try to convince the town that building an airport in Belle Plaine was a necessity. Ernest Tippie, then an executive with Iowa Electric Light and Power Company in Cedar Rapids, noted that "an airport was important to a community to attract industry." Henry agreed, saying that "an airport is a must. In this day and age, if you're going to have any organizations in your city, they also want to know how close you are to the nearest airport."

The development of an airport became a frequent topic in city council meetings. And according to Mitch Malcolm, Belle Plaine historian and head of the Belle Plaine Area Museum, an economic study suggested that a modern airport would make Belle Plaine more attractive to businesses, while a study done by the Iowa Department of Transportation supported the proposal for an airport between Cedar Rapids and Grinnell. With generous donations from local citizens and endowments from both the Mansfield Trust and Henry Tippie, along with state and federal funding, Belle Plaine opened the Mansfield/Tippie Airport in 1992, a hard-surface, 4,000-foot runway on the south side of town, with an additional hangar added in 1994 and an automatic fueling system added in 1999.

The airport brought together two of Belle Plaine's prominent benefactors: Henry Tippie and Wesley Mansfield, who operated the King Tower Restaurant in Tama and served as a director of the Citizens State Bank in Belle Plaine. He created the Wesley and Irene Mansfield Charitable Trust in 1985 as a vehicle for giving to charitable organizations throughout Iowa, and both Belle Plaine and Kirkwood Community College have benefited over time from the couple's generosity.

"The airport had been talked about for a long time around there," recalled Henry. "With the Mansfield Trust, a grant from the state of Iowa, and myself, we provided the funding to develop it. It is an excellent airport. I have flown in there on several occasions, and I think that had a lot to do with the economic development."

For a time, the nearby 31-acre industrial park, part of 127 acres purchased for the airport development, attracted important new business operations to Belle Plaine, including BENCO Manufacturing, a division of Magna Corporation out of Toronto, Canada, one of the biggest auto parts manufacturers in all of North America. With five plants in Iowa, BENCO employed nearly 350 people in Belle Plaine before it closed its operations in 2010 after an economic downtown impacted the automotive industry.

Henry, however, continued to believe in the importance of the airport for the future of Belle Plaine. "I hope this airport will serve as a magnet in economic development not only in Belle Plaine but also in the surrounding community," he once said. "My being able to participate in the development of the airport and other local activities is but a small repayment to this community and to this state."

BELLE PLAINE GETS A NEW LIBRARY AND A KIRKWOOD COMMUNITY COLLEGE CENTER

While working to improve the economic landscape around Belle Plaine, Henry always focused on trying to improve educational opportunities. In Henry's eyes, the two went hand in hand. "When businesses have an interest in locating to a small community, they want

Henry Tippie has long history of helping Belle Plaine

Henry B. Tippie, Austin, Texas, and a former Belle Plaine resident, offered matching funds of $200,000 for a new library, if the local part was raised by Dec. 31, 1989.

In January of 1990, library officials announced that the challenge put forth in November of 1989 was met by the people of Belle Plaine. That prompted Tippie to send a check of matching funds for the new library.

Tippie was born January 5, 1927 on a farm east of Belle Plaine. He is the son of Amelia Tippie, Belle Plaine, and the late Robert W. Tippie. He has two brothers, Ernest A. Tippie and Robert J. Tippie.

In 1956 he married Patricia S. Bush, and they had three children, Henry B. Tippie II, Helen Louise Tippie Smith and Linda Lee Tippie Forrest. He has eight grandchildren.

His education started in the rural one-room Buckeye School east of Belle Plaine. He later attended Belle Plaine schools and graduated from Belle Plaine High School in 1944.

There are plenty of places to sit and read in the new Belle Plaine Community Library, including this reading lounge area near the periodical and adult fiction sections of the library.

Henry's history of helping Belle Plaine was documented in the newspaper when the new library opened.

to know what is available to them in terms of ongoing education," he said. After his scholarship programs were firmly established, Henry's approach to educational improvement was twofold. First, he helped fund the construction of a new library in town in 1991 to replace the former Hart Memorial Library on Ninth Street, a 2,000-square-foot building that first opened in 1931, when Henry was a young boy. Second, in 1993, he helped turn the former library into a new outreach center for Belle Plaine residents who wanted to stay close to home and attend Kirkwood Community College.

"I remember when the Hart Memorial Library was built," said Henry. "I was very small, but I remember it because of the milk route. At that time it was a very nice facility, but in today's atmosphere, it was out of date and not in keeping with what you need today if you're going to have a first-class library in the city."

When longtime high school friends Mike and Bette Bevins visited Henry and Patricia in 1988, they happened to mention the town's hopes for a new library. The existing building was too small, and it wasn't easily accessible by handicapped and senior citizens. Though she didn't ask for any support, Bette's description piqued Henry's interest, and he made a few calls about various properties that he thought might be suitable for the location of a new library. Said Henry, "You need to have a library that is accessible, and I felt in the case of Belle Plaine it ought to be on Main Street." He got in touch with another lifelong friend and classmate, Genevieve "Genny" Conklin, who happened to be the librarian, and she helped Henry decide on the location for the new library, on the northeast corner of 12th Street and 9th Avenue. She beams, "I was *so* proud."

Only then did Henry write a letter to Bette to let her know he was interested in helping out with a new library. First, he wanted to help purchase the land, on an anonymous basis. Then, after the land was purchased, Henry offered to provide matching funds for every dollar the library could raise, up to $200,000, stipulating that the town needed to raise a minimum of $100,000.

Bette never forgot the day she got Henry's letter, describing his contribution. Said her husband, Mike, "One day in the mail she received a letter from Henry stating that he would give a matching contribution of

$200,000 if the community would match it. He did, and the rest is history. It's probably the most memorable letter my wife has ever received."

In addition to Henry's matching grant, the library project received a donation of $100,000 from the Mansfield Trust and a $120,704 grant through the Library Services and Construction Act. When the modern Belle Plaine Community Library opened in August 1990, Henry declared it to be "probably one of the finest for a community that size." Henry was particularly thrilled that Iowa Governor Terry Branstad, who had a special fondness for small-town ribbon-cutting ceremonies and rural Iowa, accepted an invitation to the new library dedication and met Henry for the very first time. From that moment on, Governor Branstad was a true fan of Henry's, and they became lifelong friends. "He is one of the people I really idolize," Branstad said. "He is what I encourage people to be and do. He shows that you can do anything with your life if you are honest and you set goals and you work hard. Great things can happen."

Henry and Patricia mingled and posed for pictures with everyone at the opening that summer, delighted and perfectly comfortable being a part of Belle Plaine's latest educational and building initiative. "If you talked to him, you'd think he's just another fellow who grew up on a

Henry, Patricia, and Iowa Governor Branstad at the dedication of the Belle Plaine Community Library.

farm in Iowa," said Claude Conklin. "When he comes back to town, he's just the same old Henry. You wouldn't know he had any more money than anybody else in town. They've got a nice home, and it's not a big mansion or anything like that. Henry is just as common as he was the day he left."

With the old library now empty, both Henry and the Mansfield Trust soon contributed funds to develop a Kirkwood Community College outreach center in the former library building, which had been purchased by the city. Renovations soon provided two classrooms on the ground floor, rooms that were equipped to provide sophisticated online and virtual classes to local students who no longer had to travel to the main campus in Cedar Rapids for classes. A lower-level renovation created a classroom and open learning lab for adult students who wanted to finish high school. The unique 1930s exterior of the historic brick building was still intact when the full-service Kirkwood Tippie-Mansfield Learning Center opened in 1994.

"The building will continue to assist in education, but in a different form," said Henry. "The new learning center, the new library, and the airport add an extra dimension to what Belle Plaine has to offer to potential new businesses."

Some 11 years later, Henry and Patricia created the Tippie Education Center next to the first Kirkwood Tippie-Mansfield building, providing much-needed classroom space for college credit, lifelong learning, and community program opportunities in Belle Plaine.

"I have never met anyone who has had such an impact on a community, as Henry and Patricia Tippie have had on Belle Plaine," wrote Jeff Orvis, a local columnist, after the dedication of the Tippie Education Center on May 12, 2005. "But if you had never met this couple, you would probably never be able to guess that their bank account was any larger than most other people you might meet in town. It seems like whenever the Tippies come to town, they draw a crowd. But to be perfectly frank, Henry and Patricia Tippie are nice people to be around and they still have a lot of friends around here."

One of those childhood friends agreed. "He has never forgotten where he came from," said Bette Bevins. "He's just an all-around nice,

nice person. He's not the type of person who throws money around. He's not only given us monetary support, but direction."

James R. Daily, Belle Plaine's mayor from 2003 to 2011, believes that Belle Plaine "probably wouldn't even be here, if not for Henry Tippie and the Mansfield Trust. Keeping a small town alive in rural Iowa is tough." Daily often worries, however, that until the area attracts more jobs, the considerable efforts made by Henry to keep the town alive may not be enough to sustain the community and make it a place where people want to live. And with both regret and awe, he reluctantly admits that there may not be any more Henry B. Tippies in Belle Plaine's future. "I don't think anyone ever grew up here who had the success that Henry had," said Daily. "He had more determination and go-get-it-ness than anyone I've ever met."

A PARTY TO REMEMBER

Henry's determination and "go-get-it-ness" did not rule out having a little fun in his hometown. And that's exactly what Henry and Patricia had in mind as their 50th wedding anniversary approached in June 2006 and they decided to sponsor what Belle Plaine locals called "a party to remember." Billed as a grand high school reunion for the classes of 1931

Henry introduces the Glenn Miller Orchestra to Belle Plaine.

to 1961, a crowd of 800 Belle Plaine High School graduates and friends made their way to two billowy white tents set up near the Mansfield/ Tippie Municipal Airport on the evening of June 24, 2006, just hours after a torrential rain threatened, but didn't wash out, the event.

Dodging a few rain puddles, revelers from as far away as California and Florida found their places at tables set up just for the event, which featured the world-famous 19-piece Glenn Miller Orchestra, courtesy of the Tippies. For one entire evening, the sounds of Henry's favorite Big Band tunes—"Moonlight Serenade," "At Last," "Stardust," "Speak Low," "Rhapsody in Blue," "Juke Box Saturday Night," and, of course, "It's a Blue World"—drifted out over the town of Belle Plaine. Musical director Larry O'Brien led the orchestra while vocalists Julia Rich and Matt Johns sang the lyrics of a bygone era. Henry and Patricia enjoyed the evening's first dance, celebrating their upcoming wedding anniversary on June 27 and a lifetime of affection for Henry's hometown and high school friends. And then everyone joined them on the dance floor and proceeded to jitterbug, waltz, slow dance, and fox-trot as the early evening's cloud-filled skies gave way to a clear canopy of stars and moonlight.

Henry and Patricia dance in Belle Plaine to celebrate their upcoming 50th wedding anniversary and Henry's high school class reunion.

"Magnificent, too marvelous for words and beyond all expectations!" an exuberant Henry wrote after the event, taking time to thank Kirkwood Community College officials, as well as representatives from Belle Plaine and the airport for helping the Tippies make the evening such a success. "My only regret was that I was unable to spend much time with anybody other than to shake hands and say hello, with maybe a brief word or two before somebody else wanted to do the same. I hope everyone understands. It was particularly joyous in some instances to see people I had not seen since long-ago school days as well as meet others for the first time."

For a former student who was never part of the so-called in crowd during high school, it must have been particularly poignant and, without a doubt, enormously satisfying to return to Belle Plaine and sponsor a high school reunion for 800 people, an event that was so spectacular, people talked about it for years. *Remember that night when Henry Tippie brought the Glenn Miller Orchestra to town?* "It was always interesting to me," Henry once said, "several years ago when I began to enjoy some success, one person mentioned to me—and I will never forget this as long as I live—his exact words were, 'We always knew you'd make it.' And all I did with that comment was smile."

A COMPREHENSIVE GIFT TO BELLE PLAINE: THE HENRY B. TIPPIE ANNEX

Many claim that Henry has "made it his mission" to revitalize his hometown. And over the years, as Belle Plaine's favorite son worked to keep the town alive, he didn't just write checks: he kept showing up, continuing to give a surprising amount of time and attention, expressing an unmistakable love for the community where he grew up, even after his 94-year-old mother passed away in 1993.

With no fanfare, Henry continued to stop by and eat lunch at the Lincoln Café, where he once delivered bottled milk from Tippie Dairy. He continued to faithfully help plan, and never failed to attend, class reunions for the Belle Plaine High School Class of 1944. In July 1985, Henry and Patricia, along with his brother Ernest and his wife, Margaret, served as grand marshals of the Belle Plaine Fourth of July Parade and afterward received a key to the city; three days later, Henry was one of only 30 former students of the Buckeye School who got together for a few hours to trade cherished memories of the one-room schoolhouse that closed in 1955. "It was evident that Tippie still possessed a certain country charm . . . characteristic of an Iowa farm boy," a reporter at the event wrote for the Benton newspaper. In 1998 he and Patricia donated bronze plaques engraved with the names of every area veteran of World War I and World

War II, plaques that were soon installed on the north exterior wall of City Hall and dedicated in a touching commemorative ceremony.

Every few years or so, Henry and Patricia are the guests of honor for "Henry B. Tippie Day" celebrations in Belle Plaine, staged because "almost everyone in Belle Plaine has benefited in one way or another from the generosity of Henry B. Tippie," Isabelle Severson wrote in a "Letter to the Editor" in the *Belle Plaine Union* on June 9, 2004, right before the upcoming dinner in the Tippies' honor. And when then Belle Plaine Mayor Daily approached Henry in 2006 about a proposal to rename a section of 13th Street in his honor—the stretch that runs right in front of the house where Henry grew up along what was once the historic Lincoln Highway—the man behind the soon-to-be designated Henry B. Tippie Boulevard responded that he would be honored. "Overwhelmed and delighted," he said, accepting the first green-and-white Tippie Boulevard street sign during the memorable night the Tippies brought the Glenn Miller Orchestra to town.

But what many consider Henry's finest salute to his hometown is the Henry B. Tippie Annex, a two-story, 5,352-square-foot attachment to the Belle Plaine Area Museum that holds Henry's remarkable collection of

Donation made by Belle Plaine native

Veterans are honored with plaques at Belle Plaine City Hall

Henry Tippie, Austin, Texas, speaks to the Memorial Day crowd. Plaques containing the names of World War I and World War II veterans were donated by Mr. and Mrs. Tippie and are located on the north side of the Belle Plaine City Hall. More pictures are on page 3.

Ribbon-cutting ceremony in 2012 for the Henry B. Tippie Annex. Left to right: Belle Plaine Mayor Dave Fish, Beverly Winkie of the Belle Plaine Historical Society, former Belle Plaine Superintendent and Kirkwood President Norman Nielsen, Iowa Governor Terry Branstad, University of Iowa President Sally Mason, and Henry and Patricia Tippie.

memorabilia, celebrating not only his life's story but also the bygone era of family dairy farming, one-room schoolhouses, movie tickets that cost only 15 cents, and going to college on the G.I. Bill.

From the moment they enter, visitors are greeted by all things Tippie, including a life-size cutout of Henry with a caption that welcomes his guests and pays tribute to his hometown. "Thank you Belle Plaine. I've had an interesting life." Visitors then freely explore every aspect of Henry's story from 1927 to the present, through a series of beautifully arranged historical displays that pull together personal narratives and artifacts representing Henry's 89-year history: stories from ancestors to business associates to University of Iowa scholarship recipients; artifacts collected by Henry, as small as a milk delivery ticket stub to as large as the cast-iron Buckeye school bell; newspaper clippings that document Henry's RBIs during a high school baseball game and announce his involvement in the first leveraged buyout in American business history; report cards show-

Henry with Robert Bodnar, who created the Tippie Museum exhibits, including a replica of Henry's home office.

ing Henry as a struggling, disinterested student and the robe he wore to receive an honorary doctorate; the original Horatio Alger books he read as a child, and the treasured medal he received as an adult from the Horatio Alger Association; pictures taken of a boy on his family's 46-acre Iowa dairy farm, and pictures taken of Henry as an adult on his 35,000-acre ranch in Texas.

One of the most remarkable things about Henry's museum, said Robert Bodnar, a museum exhibition designer from Omaha, Nebraska, who designed the exhibit, is that it combines both a great story *and* a remarkable collection. "Usually, if you have a great story, you lead with that. Or a great collection, you let the collection lead. With this, you have both. And that's the whole crux of Henry. He loves his history. He loves this town. And it's really an understatement that he's had an interesting life. Henry's had nine lives. He's really had nine lives. And it was all there, organized in boxes in his warehouse. He never threw anything away, and these collections have a story to tell."

Robert enjoyed working with both Henry and Patricia, who has embraced the museum project and made it her own. Before and after the Annex opened in 2012, Patricia and Robert have worked together to regularly update the material and expand it into additional spaces. And while Henry is the sentimental collector who can't throw anything away, it's been Patricia's enthusiasm and Robert's vision that have made it come alive. "I'm going to do this for the rest of my life," Patricia once said, referring to the museum and the couple's plans to keep it reflective of Henry's life and meaningful to the town where he grew up.

Mitch Malcolm, president of the Belle Plaine Historical Society, said the reaction from visitors to Henry's collection is pretty remarkable.

"When it opened, everyone was just awestruck," said Mitch. "Because everyone knows how successful he is and what he has done, but you forget how far-reaching his philanthropy is. He has given back tremendously, and that's what this room helps educate people about. When we get students who come through, they look at his report cards and see that he wasn't an A student, that he struggled. And yet he worked hard and he made it. That's a good life lesson for kids, and they come through and they hear that. The games, the books, the band uniform—the students resonate with that. And I think it's also good for people to see that Henry earned his money, that there was a lot of hard work and the differences that he made for companies and that he has given back. I don't think that this should be missed. His money was earned, he is a successful businessman, but he is just a guy from Belle Plaine. And he hasn't forgotten that."

University of Iowa dignitaries and the Iowa governor celebrated the opening of the Tippie Annex. Left to right: Athletic Director Gary Barta, Foundation President Lynette Marshall, Ken Mason, President Sally Mason, Governor Terry Branstad, Henry B. Tippie, and Head Football Coach Kirk Ferentz.

In many ways, Mitch believes, Henry's story of being from a small town where the railroads and the Lincoln Highway came through is the "story of the United States and how it grew. It's a great story to tell. And now the museum gives everyone a nice snapshot of someone's life from beginning with nothing to a conclusion with a wonderful success story. It gives everyone an idea of what is possible. It's unique, yes, but it is the American Dream because people think that it *could* and *should* happen to them, too. A lot of people in this small town can relate to Henry's story."

At the front door of Henry's museum annex, the staff keeps a guest book. Bob Upah—a volunteer who works at the museum's front desk and whose daughter Emily was a Tippie Scholar at the University of Iowa—enjoys pausing occasionally to read the comments:

> *This is an incredible collection. Thank you so much for giving Belle Plaine this gift.* —Sue Riherd of Belle Plaine.
>
> *A great example of a man who applied himself and left an example for others to follow.* —Dale Dvorak of Kirkland, Washington.
>
> *Common roots with every Iowa farm family—good to have this story told where it began.* —Nancy Beyer of Marengo, Iowa.
>
> *It has been rewarding being a part of the journey with Mr. and Mrs. Tippie.* —Mike Miklus, the Tippies' pilot, of St. Georges, Delaware.
>
> *A treasure for the whole community.* —Steve and Nancy Junge of Johnston, Iowa.

When Foundation President Marshall first saw the Henry B. Tippie Annex and his expansive collection, she immediately noted how clearly Henry expresses his appreciation for the education he received at the university. But she was also struck by the collection's recurring theme, focusing on his appreciation for Belle Plaine and how he grew up. "He credits his mother with saying, 'Get off this farm, leave this farm, and make something of your life,'" she said. "You could do that and be bitter and dismissive, but Henry cherishes this relationship. He has this wonderful sense of appreciation for those roots and for Belle Plaine. And this museum, above all, is a clear testament to that."

EPILOGUE

A FARM BOY ON DETOUR PUTS EVERYTHING IN PLACE

WHEN HENRY B. TIPPIE DRIVES through the streets of Belle Plaine, this Iowa native son doesn't see just the airport or the library or the community college center he helped build, or the museum annex that bears his name and pays tribute to every chapter in his life's story. In addition to seeing everything in the present, Henry has a unique ability to see everything from the past, too.

"To this day, I still associate certain houses in Belle Plaine, as well as businesses on Main Street, with names that I knew as a small kid when we were in the milk business," he said on a drive through his hometown in the summer of 2015. As Henry winds his way past his former high school building on the north side of town, he points out the Victorian home where his grandmother and two bachelor uncles lived, the one-story house Amelia B. Tippie called home until she passed away, the hill where he used to go sledding in winter. Heading down 7th Avenue, he crosses the old Lincoln Highway that's now Henry B. Tippie Boulevard. "One block over, that's the old Lincoln Café, still in operation, and we delivered milk there, too," he said, before turning left on 12th Street toward the Belle Plaine Area Museum and the Henry B. Tippie Annex. He stops in front of the Annex at the corner of 12th Street and 9th Avenue.

"This Annex is located where the E. A. Tappen grain elevator was located," he recalled, his mind's eye traveling back over nearly nine decades. "The adjoining museum to the right is located on what used to be a Stokes Implement and McCormick Deering franchise. I well remember when he used to get thrashing machines, tractors, and other farm implements shipped in here by rail and unloaded immediately behind the building on a railroad spur, which ran back of the elevator and on east. Next to the Tappen elevator was the O. A. Rucker Gas Station and bulk distribution for Sinclair Oil Company. Gas came in on the railroad right back of the station in tank cars. Continuing on, you then had Kenny Frezell Produce, followed by the railroad freight depot. In fact, I picked up a boar hog a couple of times at the freight depot."

He points to his left. "Here, immediately across the street on the corner, instead of the library was the old Opera House. Next to that was the Ewing General Store, followed by Malcolm Brothers Chevrolet, Buick, and Oldsmobile auto dealership. When you walk on down to the Legion Hall, where we had the luncheon after the Tippie Annex dedication, you will be going by an attorney's office, which occupies where a creamery used to be. When I was young, there were still a few horse-and-buggies tied up in front of the creamery. Across the street, headed east, used to be not only a junkyard but also where you could sell wool from your sheep."

He pauses. "I could go up and down all the streets and certainly point out how things used to be. But, of course, today a lot of this has totally disappeared. Time marches on."

FAMILY AND PERSPECTIVE

Walking inside the Tippie Annex, Henry finds Patricia talking with Robert Bodnar, reviewing the final placement of additional materials about Henry's life and work, including a collection of beautifully framed newspaper articles and pictures. The collection adorns a small room that's been converted into additional museum space since the Annex opened three years ago, and it includes a newspaper article that is absolutely one of Henry's favorites. When a reporter from the *Iowa City Press-Citizen* newspaper interviewed Henry in 2014, Henry described himself as "just a farm boy on a detour"—and the description became the headline. "I think that really sums it up," said Henry. "My whole life, I'm just a farm boy on a detour. I think about all these things that have happened"—he gestures to articles and artifacts that surround him, reflecting everything from his work at Rollins to creating Tippie Communications to his donations to the University of Iowa and Belle Plaine—"and that still sums it up pretty well."

When designing the museum exhibit, Robert once noted that Henry seemed to have nine lives. But Henry prefers to say that his detour away from the farm now finds him living seven different lives, each one devoted to a category he finds important: family, country, board room, educator, financial, observer, and common sense.

He admits that his family life continues to change. Six great-grandchildren, representing a fourth generation of Tippies, recently joined Henry and Patricia's legacy of three adult children and nine adult grandchildren. The gift of living a long life has helped Henry put his perceived shortcomings as a father into perspective, and he thinks it has helped his children understand him, too.

The extended Tippie family.

"I don't know if they understand me or not," Henry admitted about his children, "but I think it's always interesting. I think they probably look at Patricia and me differently today than when they were in high school. And the reason is, they now have children that have been in the teen category, and now they are grown. So I think they have warmed up to the fact that maybe we weren't so dumb after all."

Linda now understands and appreciates the drive and the motivation behind all her father's hard work. "I think he wanted security. I don't know if making money was his goal," Linda said. "I don't think he anticipated it getting this big. He wanted what he never had growing up, and he wanted it for his kids and his grandkids." She often found it both puzzling and amusing to watch Henry when his grandchildren were growing up. Once, she recalled, "when the kids were running around in his house and being loud, I would say, 'Stop it and be quiet!' And he said, 'They're only young once.' So you get these comments just out of left field, and it's like, 'What? You never let us do that.'"

Helen pointed out that her father continued his entire life to have a special relationship with animals, often volunteering to watch her pets while her family was on vacation. "I think he is reserved, and I have always thought of him as getting along better with animals than with people. He's got something there that just clicks. He'll come out and the animals that don't get along with other people get along with him just fine."

Henry with a fawn he found on the ranch.

Helen once noted that she likes to watch her father from afar at family gatherings like weddings and reunions. There, she can see him laughing and witness his lighter side escaping. She knows his days started out much darker, and she is satisfied, knowing that her father made a better life for himself. "He has a strong mind.

Yes, getting off the farm sounds good, but how? A lot of what drives him has been, 'I'm going to do it for me.' And a lot of people say it's luck, but it isn't. It's luck he met Mom, though." One of her favorite memories of her father occurred when she dropped out of college and decided to get married. "Dad told me one time, if I ever got married, he didn't care who I married, just be happy. I don't know what he told anybody else, but he told me he just wanted us all to be happy."

Henry II still remembers that after he married Judie, she ran up to Henry and gave him a hug. "And he didn't know what to do. And it is interesting, over the years, when she visits, he expects that now, and he hugs her, but the rest of us still don't do that." But Henry II admits that he has, over the years, taken important steps to get to know the man behind the headlines, particularly after he attended an event honoring his father at the University of Iowa. At that event, Henry II realized, "Everyone there knew my father better than I did. And I told him, 'That's not right.' So I invited him to come and just talk with me, and that went very well. We talked about everything."

Both Henry and Patricia are extremely proud of their children and their three successful marriages and families. Patricia even admitted that she once sat down with her nine grandchildren and advised them to appreciate their family's marriage history and "to choose a partner wisely"—the same advice that Henry often relates to business students at the Tippie College of Business.

And when it comes to her own marriage, Patricia noted that she would change almost nothing at all, though she wishes Henry played card games with her, and she always wanted a swimming pool, but she knows he's terrified of swimming. So she teases him: "My second husband is going to play bridge! And if your second wife gets a swimming pool or wears my jewelry, I'm going to come back and drown you!"

Joking aside, a few years ago, when considering whether to buy a new house or fix up their existing Austin home, Patricia was amazed to discover that the man she married is now "very sentimental about *us*! I knew he saved everything, but attached to our house? I would think nothing of selling this house and moving, but Tip wanted to stay. He kept saying to me, 'What about all the memories?' He just wants to keep everything the way it is, but I was ready to move forward." So they compromised. The Tippies stayed put in the home where they have lived since 1970, which made Henry happy ("I'm superstitious—that's why I don't want to move out of this house"). But Patricia finally got the beautiful, spacious home she wanted when an extensive renovation project added a second story to their house and included a first-floor renovation with a new master suite, two home offices, additional bedrooms, and an updated kitchen and den. New landscaping and a screened-in porch gave Patricia the outdoor space that she loves, even in their urban setting. The renovations required the Tippies to move out and rent a house nearby for nearly a year, but their cat wouldn't budge. Gary Rollins loved to tell the story that it was Henry's job to stop by the house every day to feed the cat on his way to work.

A TRUSTED PRESENCE IN THE BOARD ROOM: AN "ARTIST AT BUSINESS"

Five of the companies that Henry helped list on the NYSE during his extensive business career continued to operate successfully in 2016. And Henry remains an important and trusted presence in the board rooms for each of them: chairman of the board for Dover Motorsports, Inc.; chairman of the board for Dover Downs Gaming & Entertainment, Inc.; and the presiding director on the boards of Rollins, Inc.; RPC, Inc.; and Marine Products Corporation.

Henry B. Tippie, "an artist at business," 2016.

Richard R. Hubbell, who has been with Rollins in various capacities since 1970 and now serves as CEO and President of RPC and Marine Products, fully appreciates that the Rollins family of businesses "respect experience. They respect age. They honor it." And when it comes to sitting beside Henry B. Tippie in the board room, Richard doesn't mince words: "The guy is amazing. He is very knowledgeable, particularly on the accounting side. And because of his time and interests in Texas, he is knowledgeable about oil fields and oil wells. He brought back an expertise as a customer. We usually just see it from the service company's point of view, but he had the view of a customer, which is a little different. There is such value in everything he brings to the table."

Linda Graham, an officer and fellow board member at RPC and Marine Products, gives this description of Henry as a board member: "He sits back, he squints his eyes, you would think maybe he is asleep, and the minute something is said about which he has a point, he is right *there.* Right *there.* He sits one person down from Rick Hubbell, and he has his head focused on the operations being discussed. The minute something should be said that wasn't—he speaks up. But other than that, it is silence. And silence is golden when it comes to Mr. Tippie."

Gary Rollins has always admired how thoroughly Henry prepares for board meetings and issues. "If we have some issue on bylaws coming up, Henry has read 18 annual reports for insights. He is a student of business and corporate governance," Gary noted. "And he has a lot of the characteristics and beliefs that Dad had. He notes that it's healthy to have a certain amount of cynicism; to be cautious; to do it now and don't put it off; to run the next lap; and to remember that you can't spend yourself rich. Henry just picked up where Dad left off. He's like the Pony Express!"

Henry's long history with Rollins puts him in a unique position to not only be knowledgeable but also trusted, said Larry L. Prince, formerly head of Genuine Parts Company and a director for Rollins since 2009. "Because Henry is who he is, and due to his experience around here, they trust him so much. And when he reports on committee meetings, he is also always considerate. He is listening, and he always asks if his colleagues on the board have anything additional to add. Seldom do we, because he is so thorough. It's all smoothly done by Henry, and he makes it look like it is not that difficult. It's just his manner. I don't think I would ever be worried about a decision that Henry would make because it would be totally honest and ethical. I think he has a special gift for business. It is simply innate. He has developed it over a long period of time with experience and really hard work. But I think he has something that is a gift. He loves businesses. He is what you call 'an artist at business.' He's as good as I've ever seen."

And Randall Rollins, who survived what he called a "rough, bumpy start" with Henry to now call him "a wonderful friend and associate," admits that "I just can hardly visualize life without Henry Tippie. And I hope I never have to."

As much as Henry admired O. Wayne Rollins, he believes that both Randall and Gary are every bit as astute as their father, if not more so, and that they have evolved into outstanding businessmen. One of Henry's key goals is to make it to Wall Street with Randall and Gary in August 2018 to celebrate the 50th anniversary of Rollins, Inc., on the New York Stock Exchange. Randall and Henry were both present for the initial listing on August 12, 1968, and Gary, Randall, and Henry returned in 2008 for the listing's 40th anniversary. Having two original company executives present after 50 years would be a major accomplishment, Henry noted. "I don't know if that has ever happened before."

Henry B. Tippie, R. Randall Rollins, and Gary W. Rollins in 2008 on the 40th anniversary of Rollins, Inc., on the New York Stock Exchange.

At Dover Motorsports and Dover Gaming & Entertainment, Henry continues to guide the companies through difficult times. And in the fall of 2015, for an event that actually had nothing to do with business, he took over the ballroom at the Dover complex and once again sponsored an evening with the Glenn Miller Orchestra. A sold-out crowd of over 1,200 listened intently as Henry took the microphone to describe the bygone era of "live remotes" before announcing, "Live, from the beautiful Dover Downs Ballroom, the world-famous Glenn Miller Orchestra with director Nick Hilscher. The dance floor is open!" When the band played "A Stairway to the Stars," Henry listened for a moment to one of his favorite songs and then turned to Patricia. "It's about time to get out there," he said. And they proceeded to dance throughout the night, back in the state where they first met.

Over the years, Tom Wintermantel, who first got to know Henry while working to settle John Rollins Sr.'s estate, has grown to appreciate another side of his board chairman in Dover. Said Tom, "People see Henry and a lot of times they just see numbers. But I see him when he comes here for board meetings, walking around the casino, talking to waitresses, asking how their families are. 'How is your daughter?' 'What about your husband?' When he's here for board meeting week, he goes to eat at these restaurants and talks as an ordinary person. He's a very caring, compassionate person."

Henry has always insisted that he has no business regrets. Even an unsuccessful and brief venture into a family business of specialty food items in the late 1990s reminded Henry that he should always trust his instincts, and "all my life I've said I didn't want anything to do with the food business." And the considerable ups and downs of being in the oil business in Texas, which Henry continues to pursue in various capacities, remind him that there are "no rewards without some risks. You have to be prepared to fail sometimes, particularly when you get involved in things that are beyond your control."

But, Henry admits, if he could change anything about his business career, he would love to have O. Wayne Rollins and John Rollins Sr. witness what Wayne's sons have accomplished and to see what Henry has done, too; at age 89, Henry has lived longer than both Wayne and John, and he has been a director for their various companies for more years than either of them served. "I think it would be hard for them to believe what Randall and Gary have been able to carry on and develop. It's way beyond their expectations," he said. "And it would be my opinion that the two brothers would be astounded at the resources I've accumulated and what I've done. I remember when John came up and saw the University of Iowa naming at the Tippie College of Business, which was just the year before he passed away, and he thought it was going to be $1 million and then he found out it was $30 million! So it had started to bubble up that maybe I was a little more successful than people thought. I think it's unfortunate that the two Rollins brothers are not around."

Do you miss them? Henry was asked. "Yes," said the former accountant, whose life changed forever that January day when he put on his winter coat and made his way to Rehoboth Beach without asking the Rollins brothers for directions.

THE UNIVERSITY OF IOWA—"NOT THROWING IT AWAY LIKE CHICKEN FEED"

At the University of Iowa, the Henry B. Tippie College of Business continues to climb in prestige and in national rankings, thanks in no small part to benefactors like the Tippies. *U.S. News & World Report* now ranks the school the 22nd-best public business school in the country. Over 2,000 students are enrolled throughout the Tippie College of Business, which offers undergraduate degrees in six different areas and graduate programs that include a master of accountancy and Ph.D. degrees, as well as several MBA programs (despite Henry's history of disdain for employees with MBAs, he now fully supports the college's MBA programs). Over 20 percent of the college's students study abroad; 25 percent pursue double majors; 80 percent graduate with academic distinction; 83 percent graduate in four years or less; and 94 percent are employed or enrolled in graduate school within six months of graduation, a statistic Henry is particularly proud of. And last but not least, about 50 of these students are Tippie scholars every year.

In one hallway of the college, not far from the dean's office, portraits of the professors and research fellows supported by Henry and

Patricia line an entire wall, another tangible reminder of the reach of their donations beyond student scholarships. The Tippies' contributions have allowed the college to not only attract but also retain top faculty, said Professor Collins, director of the Ph.D. program in accounting and holder of the Henry B. Tippie Research Chair in Accounting. "The reputation of a college depends on how the faculty is perceived from the outside," he once said. "Without his support, I know in my case, I probably wouldn't still be here."

The challenge to keep outstanding faculty was well known to Jack Evans, the former Iowa Board of Regents president pro tem from Cedar Rapids. A friend to both Henry and former Tippie College of Business Dean Curt Hunter, Jack recalled Dean Hunter frequently stating that "his biggest challenge, and the one that kept him up at night, was losing a good faculty member because Princeton or whatever university with more money would make a better offer," Evans said. "It became critical during my tenure to have endowment income to stay competitive, because that money is not going to come from the state. And that is one of the many things that Henry has provided—the support to keep Tippie College of Business at the forefront of leading business schools, with the ability to attract and keep excellent faculty."

Henry and Dean Sarah Fisher Gardial (front row, third from left), pictured with Tippie professors and faculty chairs in the Henry B. Tippie College of Business.

Despite having until the end of 2016, Henry and Patricia paid off their $15 million *For Iowa. Forever More* commitment in full in 2015, following the same pattern they established in 1999, when they pledged the original $30 million to name the business college and paid it off two years later. And throughout 2015, Henry continued to review his intentions for future gifts, but did not reveal the scope of those donations.

Foundation President Marshall said she talks openly with Henry about the role of philanthropy in a university setting. "We used to call it the 'margin of excellence, the icing on the cake,'" she said, "But it's not that way anymore. In some ways, we are starting to rely on philanthropy for university essentials like for research and salary assistance."

New exterior signage for Tippie College of Business.

And she has also talked specifically with Henry about his role as one of the major philanthropists in the history of the university. "My job is to raise money for the University of Iowa. I talk about 'more' with Henry all the time, in ways that share the vision of the university and share what we hope to achieve and accomplish. A lot of us who are products of modest homes and who are fortunate that we went to great institutions of public education feel very deeply about making sure that others are able to access that as well. And I know how important that is to Henry. He knows what my job is." Henry, however, has not given the university a figure that represents any future giving amounts. "He just says, 'That's for me to know and you to find out, Lynette.' But he knows that we care deeply about wanting him to feel good about his experience."

When asked, "What do you enjoy more: Making money or giving it away?" Henry doesn't hesitate. "I enjoy both equally. You've got to make it to give it away," he said. "I think we have reached the stage in life where the kids have all they need as far as we are concerned, and we are going to give it all away. One the other hand, I'm not just going out here, throwing it away like chicken feed. Hopefully, I'll be able to grow it bigger. And both Patricia and I both intend to give it away in ways that mean a lot to everyone involved."

The Tippie College of Business is already planning to celebrate Henry's 90th birthday in January 2017; like Henry and his future philanthropic plans, school officials are keeping the details of that milestone celebration a secret. Until then, Henry intends to be a presence at the school that bears his name. He continues to attend annual student and faculty luncheons to hear from the people who receive his scholarships and hold positions funded by the Tippies. Though he has never had any official input into the college's curriculum, Henry says he has "been on a kick for them to teach a course on common sense. There is an absence of common sense in the world. And I finally got someone to listen at the university." At a recent faculty luncheon, Henry was thrilled when a Tippie faculty research fellow announced a study on the "absence of common sense."

And in the spring of 2015, Henry returned to campus to share investment strategies during a breakfast meeting with 24 students involved in the Henry Fund. For nearly two hours, Henry sat around a table with the students and reviewed his personal investment approach, how he finds ideas for new companies, and what characteristics he looks for in investments. Occasionally he passed around the relatively old-fashioned Value Line surveys on individual companies instead of looking up company and stock values online through a student's iPhone or an iPad. Professor Houge had to laugh. "Henry is not a technologically savvy person, but even I was surprised that those surveys still exist in print."

Professor Houge is quick to point out, however, that much like these printed financial surveys, Henry doesn't change. "He's a very humble guy. He doesn't seek attention. But in this one square block at the University of Iowa, there are a thousand people who know him. The students know him, and they recognize that he has been tremendous in giving back to the university. They are proud of who he is."

AN OFFER HE COULDN'T REFUSE: HENRY SELLS TIPPIE RANCH

Henry has often admitted that it's hard for him to give up anything. "I don't want to say that I am sentimental, but I probably have a little bit of an attitude of sentimentality," said the man who built a warehouse to house his lifetime collection of memorabilia and then built a museum to showcase much of its contents. "It's hard for me to give up anything."

But in 2015 a group that wanted to purchase Tippie Ranch in Prairie Hill approached Henry unexpectedly. In his heart, Henry never wanted to sell Tippie Ranch, a 35,000-acre spread that he had "built up from zero" through 150 different transactions since he purchased his first 1,625-acre parcel of prairie and ranch land in 1984. But when Henry put all emotion aside, he knew it was time.

"From one standpoint, if I was 15 years younger, I wouldn't talk to anybody," said Henry in the summer of 2015 as the private sale was being finalized. "But I'm going to be 89 years old, and I've lived longer than my two senior associates at Rollins, Wayne and John Sr., and they both went almost instantly, and so that's been bothering me a little bit. And I have no one in my family who knows anything about ranching

In 2015 Henry sold Tippie Ranch in a single cash transaction. He then separately sold over 6,000 head of cattle, heavy farming equipment, and a wide assortment of tools that were advertised in complete dispersal sales brochures like the one above.

and agriculture. And if something did happen quickly, I didn't want Patricia to have these burdens. She doesn't need that. So when I back off, get rid of all the emotions, and look at it from a clinical standpoint, it's the right thing to do. And the price had to get to where you can't say no, and it did."

The buyer, whom Henry prefers not to disclose, represents one of the biggest cattle operations in the United States. The new owner will keep the ranch land "intact and bring in their own operation and take it to a higher level," said Henry. "That gives me a good feeling."

Henry sold all of the land in a single, relatively simple cash transaction, he said. Working with ranch manager Charlie Williamson and cattle auctioneer Russ de Cordova, Henry then separately sold over 6,000 head of cattle and dozens of pieces of heavy farming equipment (tractors, trailers, trucks, haymaking equipment), along with an assortment of tools "too numerous to count" in sales advertised as complete dispersals. "Thirty years of hand-picked, high-quality cows and heifers are offered in this rare opportunity to expand your herd," read one Groesbeck Auction and Livestock advertisement about the sale of Tippie

Ranch cattle in September. Henry attended every sale and every auction, personally overseeing the final chapter of his Tippie Ranch.

"He worked so hard to build this," said Russ de Cordova. "I'm not saying this in a negative way, but for someone to build what Mr. Tippie's built and no one in the family to have an interest in it—that's something. But I guess not everyone can be a cowboy."

The Tippies spent several days cleaning out and packing up the ranch house they loved so much. They moved some furniture and mementos to their Georgetown ranch and gave away other items to their children or nearby friends. They arranged for Suzy, the donkey, and eight calves to make the move to Georgetown, too. One afternoon, they stopped and said good-bye to a few folks at the Prairie Hill community center and the fire department. The local Masonic lodge sent Henry a card signed by all of its members, thanking the Tippies for their support over the years. And both the local sheriff and the territory's Texas Ranger stopped by the ranch unannounced to say "how much we were appreciated," said Henry.

And in a final farewell to both a life and a place they loved, Patricia and Henry climbed into their pickup truck and rode around Tippie Ranch for hours, quietly recalling stories of acquiring land and running a ranch for the past 31 years. Patricia said it was very emotional. This beautiful ranch, where she nurtured her love for animals, gardening, and bird-watching, would soon be a memory. The place where they enjoyed entertaining family and friends, hosting chuck wagon barbecues for people from every corner of their lives, would be no longer. And one of Henry's most successful business ventures would be gone, too.

But Patricia, like Henry, knew it was time to sell. "It was something he created and he was so proud of it, but I felt like maybe it was a miracle and it was supposed to happen," she said of the sale. "It was traumatic and sad, and at one point I just lay down on the bed and cried, but then, with tears in my eyes, you slowly get over it. But I'm so thankful, because he said his first thought was that I didn't have to take care of it if something happened to him."

The possibility that something might happen hit Henry particularly hard during the sale of Tippie Ranch, when he received a call while

Henry and Patricia owned, operated, and loved Tippie Ranch for 31 years.

driving to the final bull sale in October: his lifelong friend, Edward B. Jobe, had passed away unexpectedly. Henry and Ed, who lived together in Des Moines when "we were starting out and just starving to death," had remained wonderful friends throughout their successful careers. Ed spent over 50 years in the insurance industry, including his role as CEO of American Re Corporation and American Re-Insurance Company. When Ed retired in 1995, Henry gave a speech in Ed's honor at the "tuxedo retirement affair" at the Metropolitan Museum of Art in New York. Laughing, Henry claims that "I liked to have took the place down" when he recalled how he and Ed lived next to "a lady of the evening" in Des Moines. "Most people there that night only knew Ed from the East Coast, but that's how we started out," said Henry, unusually wistful and nostalgic. "And Ed was two years younger than me when he died."

Ed's sudden passing, said both Henry and Patricia, reinforced that it was time to sell the ranch and put that part of their lives in order. But it did remind Henry of one personal regret. Much like he wishes the Rollins brothers had lived to see his tremendous business success, Henry wishes his father had lived to see Prairie Hill. Amelia visited often, and Henry recognizes that his mother was extremely proud of him. "But I guess I regret my dad didn't live long enough to see a lot of my accomplishments. He didn't see anything, really," he said. "The Prairie Hill operation, I mean that would have been something for him. He was from the country, and that would have meant a lot to him."

As she had done for the previous five years at Tippie Services in Austin, Trudi Jewell assisted with the paperwork and tax filings with the sale of the ranch, bringing her accounting skills to the table for one last review of ranch operations. "Mr. Tippie is not a micromanager. He is a really good boss like that," she said. "He's sharp. He loves it when I make a mistake! He gets this wonderful look on his face because nothing gets by him."

And Terri Whetstone, Henry's executive assistant for the past 18 years, admitted that she will miss hearing Henry talk about Prairie Hill, allowing that she was one of the few people who knew that Henry was in negotiations to sell. She laughs. "I have been a fly on the wall, on the inside and over the years exposed to so many interesting business transactions that a 'normal' person would never have the opportunity to be exposed to. It is fascinating to me and I really do love it."

Did selling Tippie Ranch in Prairie Hill represent the end of an era? "I've had a lot of ends of an era," said Henry. "I'm always moving forward. I just keep moving on down the road."

HENRY B. TIPPIE IN YOUR CORNER

The sale of Tippie Ranch will no doubt be incorporated one day into the Henry B. Tippie Annex exhibits. With Patricia's keen interest in continuing to update Henry's story in the Belle Plaine museum, she will certainly revisit the building's layout to see where she can add special memories and artifacts from Prairie Hill to the collection.

One item once associated with Prairie Hill is already safely installed and a part of Henry's story—the Buckeye school bell from the one-room schoolhouse. "It took me a long time to get that bell but I got it many years ago," said Henry, pointing to the restored treasure now mounted in a section devoted to Henry's life as a young student. "It's a huge bell that was in the bell tower, and I had it for a while at Prairie Hill." Henry returned the Buckeye bell from Texas to Iowa in 2012 and had it restored in Iowa City. "I'm thinking that bell must be one hundred and fifty years old. It had a big rope on it, and I can well remember that bell being rung."

Walking around the museum, Henry still misses a few collectibles he knows he has in his Texas warehouse, objects he wants to include in the museum but can't quite put his hands on. There is that collection of dinosaur stamps, and that grade school paper he wrote on Belle Plaine's last living Civil War veteran. "I'll find them," he said. "One day."

And occasionally, Henry comes across something to include in his collection that totally takes him by surprise. In late 2015, Henry was notified that he had received the Iowa Society of CPAs' Public Service Award, a fitting tribute to the Iowa CPA who proudly holds certificate No. 276. And in March 2015, he received a letter from Marie L. Stratford, president of the local Belle Plaine School Board. "Just woke up thinking about you and all that you have done for our town," Marie wrote, and then, for several pages, described the ongoing efforts and meetings by local officials to transfer, sell, or dispose of unused buildings and playing fields that once belonged to the area's public schools. "Then your part came into play," she wrote to Henry, with a bit of suspense starting to build. "Your mentoring of people who care about our town and our future, stepping up and saying, 'I want to help.' Seconds after talking to the guy from the state—so excited I could barely breathe—I got a call from a woman in town who said, 'I will give you the money for the land, I don't want it to go for housing, I want the kids to be able to play here, find out who I write the check to." She offered $35,000. . . . When I met with her and her husband to say, 'It's a go,' she said, 'We have seen Mr. Tippie do this and we thought we could do it, too.'"

Holding a copy of that letter, Henry was more than pleased. "I was dumbfounded when I read this. This was out of the blue! I haven't had a letter from Marie for a long time. I just can't get over this: *We have seen Mr. Tippie do this.* I was honored with this statement. Honored." And he throws his head back and chuckles, quietly.

When people try to capture Henry's impact on Belle Plaine, Kirkwood Community College, Allegheny College, or the University of Iowa, few can be as succinct as saying, "We have seen Mr. Tippie do this." Because it's difficult to capture the full extent and lasting impact of Henry's philanthropic endeavors and what he will always call "repayment for benefits received."

"What Henry has done for the university, what he's done for his family, what he does for his hometown community in Iowa—he's a person who is truly a philanthropist," said David Dierks, vice president, University of Iowa Foundation. "He gives altruistically but he also gives in the sense that this is just the first phase. He likes to stay connected to whatever he does. I often find it amazing that he has found the time to keep all of his connections going, because as he got older in life, they increased almost exponentially. Yet he gives us the impression that he cares as much about what goes on here at the university as I bet he does with every organization he works with—wherever he lived, whoever he saw, whatever he was involved with. And that's a true art that can make you feel truly special, and yet he does that with everyone. But that's typical Henry."

Perhaps Governor Branstad best captured Henry's importance to his home state in one brief but perfect statement at the Tippie Annex dedication ceremony. "Every community in Iowa," said the state's governor, "would love to have a Henry B. Tippie in their corner."

ENDING WHERE IT ALL BEGAN

After leaving the Henry B. Tippie Annex, Henry proceeds to drive one block north until he turns right onto Henry B. Tippie Boulevard, heading east out of town toward the Oak Hill Cemetery. Driving through these peaceful cemetery grounds to a slight crest on the hill,

Henry points out his family's cemetery plot. There, under an oak tree, two footstones already mark the spots where he and Patricia will one day be buried. Driving back to the main road, Henry turns left and makes his way to his home place that still stands at the intersection where old Lincoln Highway once curved away from town. He stops the car and points to the original site of the wayfarer's camp established by members of his family, motioning to the spot where he heard his first radio broadcast and then, in the distance farther still, to the empty site where the one-room schoolhouse once stood. Opening the car door, he soon stands on the side of the road and looks toward the fields in back of the house. It's late afternoon, it's quiet, and there's not another soul in sight.

"The cistern was there," he said, pointing to a slight knoll behind the house. "I used to sit out there, and think about what my life was going to be."

He pauses, glances over the fields he used to farm, and then continues. "There are a lot of people I felt were smarter than me, but they had blinders on," he said. "Blinders have a purpose in agriculture—we put blinders on the horse or mule to keep them looking straight ahead, otherwise they might wander all over the place and not stay on track. Well, you need to keep your eyes and ears open in all directions to pick up and learn. Then, as things develop on down the line, you're more prepared to take advantage of opportunities."

This farm boy from Iowa—who took advantage of opportunities in accounting, broadcasting, transportation, history-making leveraged buyouts, oil fields, ranching, investing, and philanthropy—then shakes his head for just a moment, half in disbelief, half in wonder, as he lingers near the side of a road named after him in Belle Plaine, the rural town in America's heartland where his life began and where, one day, it will end. He's not sad. He's got that look on his face, the one that means he's completely comfortable, enjoying himself, and content.

"I certainly never dreamed," said Henry B. Tippie, "that my life would turn out the way it has. Incredible."

— THE END —

APPENDIX

Henry B. Tippie

Educational Support

1967 Established endowed scholarships for Belle Plaine High School at the University of Iowa

1982 Established University of Iowa Accounting Scholarships

1989 Established Business Chair at University of Iowa School of Business

1990 Major contributor to Belle Plaine Community Library

1991 Endowed Patricia Bush Tippie Scholarships at Allegheny College for students of New Castle, PA, High School

1992 Major contributor Mansfield/Tippie Airport in Belle Plaine, Iowa

1993 Major contributor Tippie-Mansfield Center for Kirkwood Community College in Belle Plaine, Iowa

1993 Contributor of 175-seat Henry B. Tippie Auditorium, Patricia B. Tippie Undergraduate Student Lounge, and Pat's Diner for new University of Iowa Business School Building

1994 Participated with Henry Royer in the establishment of the Henry Fund (a student-managed investment fund at the Henry B. Tippie College of Business)

1996 Endowed scholarships at Belle Plaine High School for Kirkwood Community College

1997 Endowed six Research Professorships in Business Administration at the University of Iowa

1997 Established Professorship at Allegheny College

1998 Major contributor for the establishment of Tippie Beef Education Center at Kirkwood Community College in Cedar Rapids, Iowa

1999 University of Iowa Business School renamed Henry B. Tippie College of Business

2001 Endowed the Tippie Beef Education Scholarships at Kirkwood Community College in Cedar Rapids, Iowa

2001 Established the Patricia Bush Tippie Alumni Center, Allegheny College

2001 Participated with Marvin Pomerantz and John Pappajohn in the establishment of 100 Horatio Alger Iowa scholarships at the University of Iowa

2003 Established President's Special Assistance Fund at Coe College

2004 Major contributor to the Belle Plaine Museum

Educational Support (cont.)

2007 Established the Henry B. Tippie College of Business Dean Endowment Fund

2011 Established scholarships at the University of Iowa Department of Athletics along with major funding of the new football administrative offices

2012 Established Henry B. Tippie Annex to the Belle Plaine Museum

2012 Established Professorship in Business and Economics—Coe College

2012 Established Professorship at Allegheny College

2013 Established The Henry B. Tippie & Patricia B. Tippie Business Scholarships Endowment at Kirkwood Community College

2015 Endowed Chair in the Arts—Allegheny College

2015 Endowed Chair in Economics—Allegheny College

2015 Endowed Fund for Scholarships and Internships—Allegheny College

2015 Endowed four Chairs—The Henry B. Tippie College of Business, the University of Iowa

2015 Endowed Matching Fund for Chairs, Professorships, Research, Grants, and Scholarships at The Henry B. Tippie College of Business at the University of Iowa

2017 Endowed Tippie Business Education Center at Kirkwood Community College

Honors and Awards

1981 Recipient, University of Iowa Distinguished Alumni Service Award

1989 Recipient, University of Iowa Outstanding Accounting Alumnus

1996 Recipient, Horatio Alger Award

2002 Recipient, University of Iowa Hancher-Finkbine Medallion

2004 Inducted into the Junior Achievement of Eastern Iowa Hall of Fame

2009 Honorary Doctorate of Humane Letters—University of Iowa

2011 Honorary Doctorate of Humane Letters—Allegheny College

2011 Recipient, Kirkwood Community College Legacy Award

2013 Recipient, University of Iowa Hawk of the Year Award

2016 Recipient, Iowa Society of CPAs' Public Service Award

2016 Recipient, University of Iowa Football Players Appreciation Award

2016 Recipient, University of Iowa Hawkeye Distinguished Veteran Award

HENRY B. TIPPIE

Austin, Texas

Current Associations, June 2016:

Chairman of the Board of Directors
Dover Downs Gaming & Entertainment, Inc. (NYSE*)
(Hotel, harness racing, and casino entertainment with slot machines)

Chairman of the Board of Directors
Dover Motorsports, Inc. (NYSE*)
(NASCAR motorsports)

Director
Rollins, Inc. (NYSE*)
(Pest control—Orkin Exterminating Co.)

Director
RPC, Inc. (NYSE*)
(Oil field services)

Director
Marine Products Corp. (NYSE*)
(Manufacturer of Chaparral boats)

Chairman of the Board and President
Tippie Services, Inc.
(Management services)

Trustee
O. Wayne Rollins Foundation
Henry B. Tippie Foundation
Rollins Children's Trust

Director Emeritus
The University of Iowa Foundation

* *Listed on the New York Stock Exchange*

NOTES ON SOURCES AND PHOTOGRAPHY

The majority of the information for this book came from extensive personal interviews conducted in Iowa, Delaware, Georgia, and Texas by Margaret O. Kirk and May K. Cobb. Information was also obtained from three previous biographies and corporate histories written by Kirk for the Rollins family: *O. Wayne Rollins, An Authorized Biography; ORKIN: The Making of the World's Best Pest Control Company;* and *The Art of Change: The Story of Rollins, Inc.* Some details about the life and career of John W. Rollins Sr. came from *Hanging the Moon: The Rollins Rise to Riches* by Drury Pifer. Kirk obtained information about the history of Belle Plaine, Iowa, from multiple sources, including: *Belle Plaine, Iowa: Centennial History Book; Iowa Heritage;* the newspaper archives at the Belle Plaine Public Library; and extensive historical documents provided through the Belle Plaine Area Museum, the Henry B. Tippie Annex, and Mitch Malcolm, president of the Belle Plaine Historical Board. In Chapter 18, the lyrics to "Could I Have This Dance?" were sung by Anne Murray and written by Wayland Holyfield and Bob House, Universal Polygram International Publishing, Inc.

The majority of photographs and images used in this book are from the personal collections of Henry B. and Patricia B. Tippie, and on display in the Henry B. Tippie Annex. Photography of events at the University of Iowa and the dedication ceremony for the Tippie Annex are credited to Impact Photo/Joe Photo, and Ed, Molly, and Dan Kempf. Photographs of University of Iowa Football scenes are credited to Max Allen, Director of Football New Media, University of Iowa Football. All photographs at Allegheny College are by Bill Owen for Allegheny College. Photographs of Kirkwood Community College are courtesy of the college and Impact Photo/Joe Photo. Kirkwood Community College is credited with the panoramic image of the Tippie Annex. Photography for Dover Motorsports and Dover Downs Gaming & Entertainment is credited to iStockphoto.com (roulette wheel) and Johnathan Ferrey/Getty Images (race crowd).

INDEX

Numbers in *italics* indicate images.

———